GANESH

Studies of an Asian God

Robert L. Brown, Editor

State University of New York Press

Published by
State University of New York Press, Albany

Printed in the United States of America

For information, address State University of New York Press,
State University Plaza, Albany, N.Y., 12246

Production by Marilyn Semerad
Marketing by Dana E. Yanulavich

Library of Congress Cataloging-in-Publication Data

Ganesh: studies of an Asian god / edited by Robert L. Brown.
p. cm. —(SUNY series in tantric studies)
Includes index.
ISBN 0-7914-0656-3. —ISBN 0-7914-0657-1 (pbk.)
1. Gaṇeśa (Hindu deity) 2. Asia—Religion. I. Brown, Robert L.,
1944 Oct. 6– II. Series.
BL1225.G34G37 1991
294.5′2113—dc20 90-46163
CIP

Contents

Foreword

A. K. Narain

It all started in 1953. A. D. H. Bivar, then at the Christ Church, Oxford, showed me a coin of Hermaeus when I was working on my dissertation on the Indo-Greeks at London. It was unusual. On the reverse of the coin the deity that should have been Zeus appeared to have an elephant's face; the trunk was clear. Both of us became curious, and we checked various private and public collections for other specimens. We did not find any and accepted it as a unique piece. But we were reluctant to publish it then, firstly because we wanted to wait for more specimens to be found, and secondly because we could not convince ourselves of reasons for Hermaeus to issue such a coin. The coin was acquired by the British Museum, and the matter rested there.

But I did not forget about it. When P. Bernard sent me photographs of some coins of Agathocles found in his excavations at Ai Khanum in Afghanistan bearing the queer depictions of two Indian deities, now identified as Vasudeva and Saṅkarṣaṇa, I remembered again the Hermaeus coin. I went through the relevant literature, and I thought of giving the coin's image the benefit of the doubt. I thought if such an early king as Agathocles among the Greeks of Bactria and India could experiment with the depiction of Indian divinities, and Heliodorus, an emissary of Antialcidas of Taxila to Vidiśā, was bold enough to declare himself a Bhagavat, why could not the last of the Indo-Greek kings, Hermaeus, think of paying respects to the local elephant-deity of the mountains nearby the city of Kapiśa. But I was afraid to provoke Gaṇeśa as well as his votaries and the scholarship on him. Nevertheless, since this unique coin of the British Museum was not known to many, I felt justified in bringing it to the notice of those who were not numismatists and who would not visit the British Museum collection of coins.

In 1973 I read a paper at the Paris conference of the International Congress of Orientalists that for the first time dealt with this coin publicly. To reduce the shock, I also discussed the coins of Agathocles showing Vasudeva and Saṅkarṣaṇa as identified and published independently by both Jean Filliozat and myself. The response was mixed as expected, and some Sanskritists plainly refused to accept the identification of the image as a therianthropomorphic figure with an elephant head. I published a brief note on the coin and continued discussing it in the States, finally organizing a panel at the Washington, D.C., session of the Association of Asian Studies in 1984 to deal with Gaṇeśa afresh in the wider perspective of various academic disciplines and cultural areas. We decided later to publish the papers presented at the conference, supplementing the panel papers with additional articles. But all this could not have happened if Bob Brown had not taken upon himself the task of editing the manuscripts and seeing the book through the press. I also take this opportunity to thank the publishers for their patience and production. I only hope our Gaṇeśa receives it kindly.

Acknowledgments

The road to completion of this book has not, as is perhaps appropriate for one devoted to Gaṇeśa, the creator of obstacles, always been smooth. Nevertheless, it would have been impossible without a number of people's interest, advice, and help. A. K. Narain organized the initial panel on Gaṇeśa from which a number of these papers came. His long interest in the god, and his sense that Gaṇeśa should be studied outside as well as inside India and from a variety of scholarly perspectives, were the book's first inspiration. The contributors, often scattered around the globe and working under trying circumstances, responded to my questions and requests with enthusiasm. Robin Messick, a graduate student at UCLA in Indian art history, was involved in the project throughout, assisting me in editing and contributing the drawings to the article by Tiwari and Giri. Others who read portions of the manuscript, and gave me their helpful critiques, include Peter Brown, Amy Catlin, Kathy Harper, and Nazir Jairazbhoy. I want to thank them all.

Note on Transliteration

There has been an attempt to make spelling and diacritical marks for words not normally spelled in roman script consistent in the volume. Nevertheless, particular word forms and transliterations have been used when the author requested. Non-standardized transcriptions occur particularly when the word comes either from vernacular or geographical usages or from texts with idiosyncratic spellings (the later being particularly true for Sanskrit in the Tibetan texts). In all cases, however, the final decision for transliteration forms was that of the editor.

Introduction

Robert L. Brown

I. Various Gaṇeśas

Gaṇeśa is often said to be the most worshiped god in India.[1] As the lord of beginnings, he is worshiped by devotees of other Hindu deities — of Śiva, Viṣṇu, the Goddess — either as the initiator of the path to these deities or as the direct road to mundane goals and success. He is also worshiped by some as the primary god (*iṣṭadevatā*). His cult has its own texts, such as the *Gaṇeśa Purāṇa* and the *Śrī Gaṇapati Atharvaśīrṣa*, where he is presented as the all-encompassing cosmic deity. Thus, he functions on multiple levels in the hierarchy of Indic gods, from the level of the subsidiary gods to that of the supreme deities, and his worship crosses boundaries among the various sects.

His popularity in India, however, is more than a matter of the sheer number of worshipers in his role as initiator of activities. He is favored with a singular affection. Part of this popular appeal has to do with the way he looks. He has an elephant head and a human body. Usually his body is depicted as short and squat with an enormous belly. Its girth suggests an elephant, but it also can be seen as the body of a chubby child. Gaṇeśa is considered the child of Pārvatī, and usually also of Śiva. When Gaṇeśa is depicted as a child in texts and art, he is shown as participating in cozy domestic scenes with his parents and his brother Skanda.[2] The Indian delight in children and the importance given to the family, seen as well in the popular child manifestations of other Indic gods,[3] afford an attraction to the baby Gaṇeśa. The elephant head seems actually to add to the adorableness of the little Gaṇeśa. From the earliest artistic depictions there has been a tendency to anthropomorphize the head by moving the eyes to the front and flattening the face while the eyes become human, sometimes complete with eyebrows. This allows for a direct human-to-human reaction, along with the accompanying emotions.[4]

Thus, Gaṇeśa's popularity is multifaceted and widespread. He functions in many contexts other than the three I have mentioned—that of lord of beginnings, cosmic deity, and child of Pārvatī and Śiva. This book is about these multiple contexts, these various Gaṇeśas, and the underlying reasons he could take the forms and perform the functions he did. Wendy O'Flaherty writes that

> Gaṇeśa has everything that is fascinating to anyone who is interested in religion or India or both: charm, mystery, popularity, sexual problems, moral ambivalence, political importance, the works. One can start from Gaṇeśa and work from there in an unbroken line to almost any aspect of Indian culture.[5]

Certainly this versatile god reflects in his many contexts a broad range of Indian cultural characteristics. While Gaṇeśa's multiplicity is due to his taking separate and distinct roles, the essays in this book reveal themes that knit together disparate aspects of Gaṇeśa's character. It is foolhardy to say that Gaṇeśa is unique among Indic gods, but it emerges from these essays that Gaṇeśa's popularity stems from hopes and desires he uniquely fulfills, from unique powers and premises attributed to him.

Most interestingly, Gaṇeśa is not only an Indian god. He appears in China by the sixth century, and perhaps as early in Southeast Asia. By the seventh and eighth centuries, Indian texts dealing with Gaṇeśa are being translated by Buddhist monks in China. Likewise, Indian Gaṇeśa texts are translated into Tibetan and introduced into Tibet by monks in the tenth and eleventh centuries. While based on Indian texts and art, Gaṇeśa develops unique forms outside of India, such as the dual Gaṇeśa found in China and popular in Japan. The pan-Asian Gaṇeśa has never been so thoroughly studied as in this book. As we shall see, it was Gaṇeśa in his Tantric guise that became most influential outside of India. This side of Gaṇeśa, little explored in India itself, becomes an important window on an obscure aspect of Indian culture.

II. Gaṇeśa in Indian Myth

The mythic Gaṇeśa's character and life are developed predominantly in the Purāṇas, a group of texts that date beginning from around A.D. 300 and in which, over the next one thousand years, modern theistic Hinduism took its form. In the Purāṇas, Gaṇeśa is associated with Śiva and his family: Śiva's wife Pārvatī and his son Skanda. His origin within this familial context is given great stress, particularly in an attempt to explain his having an elephant's head. These Purāṇic origin myths, supplemented by numerous others in regional texts and oral traditions, provide a wide variety of explanations for his form. Many of them have him violently losing his human head after birth, the elephant head being placed on his body as a substitute. In a number of the stories, it is Gaṇeśa's own father, Śiva, who cuts off his son's head. Śiva in these cases usually does not recognize his son because Pārvatī has created him unilaterally[6] and Śiva has never seen him before. Pārvatī's motivation for creating Gaṇeśa without Śiva's participation stems from her longing for a child and Śiva's unwillingness, as an ascetic (who must retain his seed) and an eternally living god (who does not need the *śrāddha* ceremonies upon death), to produce a son. She wants a child due to her loneliness and maternal yearnings, but she also, in these myths, creates Gaṇeśa to guard the door to her inner chamber or bath. It is here, at the access to Pārvatī's sexuality, that Gaṇeśa's attempt to keep Śiva from entering results in the physical confrontation that leads to Gaṇeśa's defeat and death by beheading.

The replacement of the head by that of an elephant takes a number of scenarios in the myths, but often involves Pārvatī's disconsolation and sometimes her threats, and Śiva's consequent surprise at what he has done and his attempt at rectification. The search for a replacement head is something of a scramble, due to the immediacy of the problem, with the head of the first creature that can be found, an elephant, being used. In a reconciliatory gesture, Śiva makes the restored and now elephant-headed Gaṇeśa part of his own family and entourage by appointing him as leader of his army of *gaṇa*s. (Thus Gaṇeśa is frequently called Gaṇapati, "leader of the *gaṇa*s.")

Even this very abbreviated condensation of a small portion of the Gaṇeśa origin myths shows how rich these stories are in characterizing the god. In the Indian context, Gaṇeśa is the liminal god of transitions: he is placed at the doorway of temples to keep out the unworthy, in a position analogous to his role as Pārvatī's doorkeeper, and he can set up, as he did for his father, obstacles to the successful completion of goals. His parents' ambivalent relationship, founded on the opposing concerns of asceticism and sexuality, places Gaṇeśa in between. He is created by Pārvatī as a result of Śiva's asceticism and refusal to have children, but is annihilated due to Śiva's sexual interest in Pārvatī, only to be restored, transformed, as a bond between the two. He is here fulfilling his transitional role as a means to integrate opposing elements. The Oedipal themes of Gaṇeśa's attraction or attachment to his mother, his attempt to keep his father from access to his mother, and his confrontation with his father in which part of his body is cut off, invite psychoanalytical probings of psychosexual development.[7]

While the reason Gaṇeśa needs a head is supplied in these myths, the question why it is an elephant's head is not answered. Why not another human head, or the head of an animal other than that of an elephant? The failure of the myths to explain the choice may be best explained in historical terms: the form of Gaṇeśa as an elephant-headed human existed prior to the development of these Purāṇic myths. They thus were dealing with an already existing but etiologically unexplained god. Certainly, Gaṇeśa appears late in Indic literature (say, around the fifth century A.D.). He does not appear, for example, in either the *Rāmāyaṇa* or the *Mahābhārata* (except, for the latter, in a clearly late interpolation).

Much of Gaṇeśa's character is regionally defined, most particularly in the popular mind. This is perhaps best brought out in Lawrence Cohen's essay ("The Wives of Gaṇeśa"), where Gaṇeśa's bachelor and celibate nature (as *brahmacārin*)—the aspect that has been traditionally stressed in the scholarship—is shown to be predominantly a South Indian characterization. It is true that Gaṇeśa is not a womanizer as is his father, Śiva, or as is Viṣṇu in his *avatāra* as Kṛṣṇa, yet in other characterizations he is married and is even said to have children. With the possibility of such regional qualifications in mind, we can finish our composite sketch of Gaṇeśa's mythic character.

Gaṇeśa's cleverness is often contrasted to the slower wit of his more athletic brother, Skanda, as in the frequently told tale (a version is given in Cohen's essay) of the contest between the brothers in which, for a prize that varies depending on the story, Gaṇeśa and Skanda must go around the world. Skanda dashes off, but Gaṇeśa merely circumambulates his parents, arguing that in doing so he is gaining as much merit as one would by circling the earth. His parents, flattered by his devotion and impressed by his cleverness, award him the prize. Gaṇeśa's association with mental agility and learning is probably one reason he is assigned the role as scribe for Vyāsa's dictation of the *Mahābhārata* in the eighth-century interpolation to this text.

Gaṇeśa may have to be brainy to compete with Skanda's brawn. At least Gaṇeśa's body puts him at a certain disadvantage and makes him sometimes a comic figure. Lee Siegel writes that "the elephant-headed god is a dispenser of magic, of surprise and laughter."[8] His rotund form is maintained by his insatiable appetite for the sweet cakes that are a major devotional offering of his worshipers and that he usually holds in his artistic depictions. In another frequently repeated myth, Gaṇeśa has gorged himself on the cakes until his belly bulges. It is night, and mounted on his rat vehicle, he begins his ride home. The rat becomes frightened by a snake that crosses the road and shies, causing Gaṇeśa to fall, breaking open his distended stomach and spilling the cakes over the ground. This scene is humorous, with the bloated Gaṇeśa tottering on the tiny rat, and his fall causes the moon to laugh. In anger, Gaṇeśa breaks off one of his tusks and throws it at the moon. This act caused the moon to disappear, and while Gaṇeśa restores it, it continues even until today to wax and wane. Gaṇeśa's comic nature is also associated with his role as leader of the playful and naughty dwarf-like *gaṇa*s. Further, Gaṇeśa is described as dancing, although the imagery for this form of Gaṇeśa comes predominantly from art rather than from texts. The fat, short-legged god dancing, in clear imitation of the beautiful and manly Śiva, is again humorous.

III. Gaṇeśa in Indian Art and Ritual

This description of the mythic nature of Gaṇeśa—a child, devoted to his parents (particularly his mother); clever, comic, greedy; the defender of doorways and integrator of opposites—could be much expanded, but in its broad outlines it is a characterization that applies to Gaṇeśa in art and ritual. It is not, however, that in the art of India Gaṇeśa simply illustrates the Purāṇic myths. His images are predominantly iconic in nature, with few of the popular stories ever represented in art. For example, the crucial episodes of Gaṇeśa losing his head or having it replaced by an elephant's head have never to my knowledge been depicted in art. In later Indian painting we have some narrative scenes depicted, but it is not until the twentieth century and under the influence of Western realism that there is an attempt to show Gaṇeśa in the Purāṇic panoramas, usually done in papier-mâché, that have become popular in India.

One characterization of Gaṇeśa that is avoided in the myths is his demonic nature. Paul Courtright says that

> the Purāṇic texts are uncomfortably aware of the discrepancy between the malevolent, obstacle-creating powers of Vināyaka and the positive, obstacle-removing actions of Gaṇeśa, and they attempt to disguise Gaṇeśa's demon background through the clever use of false etymologies for the name "Vināyaka."[9]

Actually, there are a variety of possible "true" etymologies, or interpretations, for the name,[10] but the Vināyaka form of Gaṇeśa is indeed seen as having a malevolent side, which in some contexts, such as that of Tantric

Buddhism, predominates. Unlike the myths, the earliest artistic depictions of Gaṇeśa appear to partake in this, the dark side of Gaṇeśa. Even after the Purāṇic Gaṇeśa is well defined, in art Gaṇeśa remained predominantly important for his dual role as creator and remover of obstacles, thus having both a negative and a positive aspect.[11] He is usually, therefore, presented as an icon, to be propitiated, and his narrative and mythic character is not particularly developed in art.

Gaṇeśa's earliest artistic depictions are controversial in their dating. Alice Getty, writing in 1936, argued that the earliest images of Gaṇeśa date only to the fifth century, the date at which she suggests the Gaṇeśa cult also began.[12] Since this is also the approximate date at which he appears to have entered the Purāṇic tradition, we have an apparent dovetailing of mythic, artistic, and ritual evidence for his late appearance in Indian religion. Scholars, including Getty, have nevertheless consistently noted surprise at his sudden fully developed appearance at this date, and wondered what his sources might be. Both A. K. Narain and M. K. Dhavalikar argue in their essays that the ultimate source is to be found in elephant worship in the northwestern areas of the subcontinent. Narain ("Gaṇeśa: A Protohistory of the Idea and the Icon") has argued this thesis in detail elsewhere, suggesting that Gaṇeśa (or more precisely, a deity with an elephant's head and a human body) first appeared on an Indo-Greek coin of the first century B.C.[13] But Narain and Dhavalikar ("Gaṇeśa: Myth and Reality") disagree as to the significance and date of the earliest representations of Gaṇeśa in India itself. Narain accepts Getty's fifth-century date, while Dhavalikar (and myself as well in my essay "Gaṇeśa in Southeast Asian Art: Indian Connections and Indigenous Developments") feels some images can be dated much earlier, back to the second century A.D.

The question of when the earliest Gaṇeśa appears is of critical importance, and justifies here a short exploration of some additional artistic evidence. We might ask: When does the elephant-headed therianthropomorphic image become Gaṇeśa? Narain is very careful to separate the various textual and artistic strands that eventually coalesce to produce Gaṇeśa. He feels, for example, that the *vināyaka*s who occur in such early texts as the *Mānava Gṛhyasūtra,* characterized as malignant demons who must be propitiated, are quite distinct from Gaṇeśa, although they are eventually going to participate in defining him. Likewise some early artistic depictions of an elephant-headed therianthropomorphic figure, such as Narain's own first-century B.C. coin image, is, while "an incipient Gaṇeśa," not yet Gaṇeśa. The images that Dhavalikar and I believe are earlier than the fifth century, most of which come from Mathurā, are small, independent images. They do carry some of the attributes that we will see become standard for Gaṇeśa, primarily the bowl of sweet cakes, and some of them have the serpent cord that is also to become a common decoration[14] (see Brown, figs. 5, 6, and 8). But none come from a context in which we can judge their use. There is, however, a relief image carved in a cave at Udayagiri (Madhya Pradesh) that can be dated to ca. 400[15] and can be assessed in the context of the cave's overall iconography.

The Gaṇeśa image in Cave 6 at Udayagiri (see Brown, fig. 7) is located on the viewer's left as he or she enters the shallow porch that precedes the small inner chamber with a Śiva *liṅga*. Opposite the Gaṇeśa, on the viewer's right, are two sets of very worn seven mothers (*saptamātṛkās*). Other deities—two Viṣṇus, two door guardians, and two images of the goddess Durgā as slayer of the Buffalo Demon (Mahiṣāsuramardinī)—are on the back wall of the porch. It is difficult to know how these various images were worshiped; the cave curiously combines both Vaiṣṇavite and Śaivite deities, and its very small size would appear to argue against any extensive movement through space by devotees, such as circumambulation that we find used in worship in later Hindu temples.[16] Nevertheless, Gaṇeśa is clearly spatially paired with the mothers, as worshipers would have passed these deities first as they progressed toward the inner and most sacred area of the cave. The *mātṛkās* and Gaṇeśa are in fact going to be associated in art and ritual from this time onward as Gaṇeśa becomes regularly placed at the end of the standardized set of seven mothers. The *mātṛkās*' role in Hinduism is, of course, complex,[17] but I wish to stress two points. One is that the mothers and Gaṇeśa were undergoing very similar processes of change from predominantly malevolent to benevolent deities as they both were being adopted into Hinduism at this time.[18] The second point is that both Gaṇeśa and the mothers were deities that had to be propitiated in order not to cause trouble, a notion that, even if put into a positive sense of removing, rather than causing, problems, made them deities to propitiate before worshiping other gods; thus their placement in the cave before other deities. In addition, both Gaṇeśa and the mothers were deities to whom one worshiped for this-worldly success and objectives. Again, their placement at the outer edge of the sacred space is appropriate in the hierarchy of Indic sacred architecture where the mundane tends to be relegated to the outer or the lower sections, the most sacred to the inner or upper areas.

While this is not the place to argue fully these ideas, they are substantiated in a surprising context, the Buddhist caves at Aurangabad. At Aurangabad, in Cave 7, the veranda shrines, those first encountered by the worshiper, are on the left dedicated to a very unusual set of six females flanked by a bodhisattva and a Buddha, in clear imitation of the Hindu *sap-*

tamātṛkās.[19] The shrine opposite has images of the Buddhist god of wealth and the goddess of children (Jambhala and Hāritī).[20] Jambhala in particular can fulfill some of the functions of Gaṇeśa.[21] But also at Aurangabad is the recently discovered cave located between Caves 5 and 6 that contains as its major icon an image of Gaṇeśa.[22] He is at the center rear of the cave, with the seven mothers with Śiva on his right and Durgā and two Buddha images on his left.[23] Thus we have here again the association of the *saptamātṛkā*s and Durgā with Gaṇeśa, as at Udayagiri, but in a Buddhist context. One likely interpretation of this unique cave is that its images functioned, as did these same images at Udayagiri, as removers of obstacles to further worship, but for the site as a whole, as well as a focus for the fulfillment of specifically mundane desires. The Gaṇeśa Cave and Cave 7 date to the second half of the sixth century.[24]

Returning now to the topic of the earliest artistic images of Gaṇeśa and the question of when we can call the elephant-headed images truly Gaṇeśa, we can say that as early as ca. 400 A.D. images of Gaṇeśa functioned in a defined and sophisticated role within temple worship that involved his functions as remover of obstacles, as initiator for further worship, and probably as locus of worldly desires. This is indeed our "real" Gaṇeśa.

In art, Gaṇeśa, like other Indic deities, is frequently given multiple arms and carries attributes. The attributes vary, but perhaps most frequently one sees the axe, noose, sweet cake(s), elephant goad, and tusk. The latter is Gaṇeśa's own tusk, and the images often show him with one tusk broken off or missing. We have seen how the broken tusk is explained in one myth by Gaṇeśa's throwing it at the laughing moon. Other myths have Śiva or other deities cutting off the tusk. The cut tusk can be explicated as mutilation or castration, in terms similar to the beheading,[25] but, as with the elephant head, these explanations rely on myths probably created to explain an already existing attribute. The earliest Gaṇeśa images, which tend to be two armed, do not hold a tusk; nor do they appear to have a broken tusk (see Brown, figs. 5, 6, 7, and 8). They hold the sweet cakes, usually placed in a bowl, in their left hands, but the attribute in their right hands varies considerably.[26] By the sixth century, however, there are examples that hold a radish or turnip, and I have suggested in my essay that the tusk may be a misunderstanding of the radish. The radish would have been an appropriate attribute as it was an offering, as were the sweet cakes, to Vināyaka, according to such early texts as the *Yājñavalkyasmṛti*.[27] Being a tuber, the radish is, like onions and garlic, a food that grows underground and is shunned by Brahmins. It is an apt food for the demonic and later Tantric Vināyaka.

Gaṇeśa's low class origins and clientele have been frequently noted. Alfred Foucher presents him as a "jungle genius" who attempts to rise to respectability with his adoption into Śaivite Hinduism and the Purāṇic myths.[28] He nevertheless retains his primitive heritage. Manu in his *Laws* says Śiva is to be worshiped by the Brahmins, Gaṇeśa by the *śūdras*.[29] There is the notion of Gaṇeśa being the god for Everyman. This is why Bal Gangadhar Tilak chose Gaṇeśa and his annual festival, around which he hoped "to bridge the gap between the Brahmins and the non-Brahmins and find an appropriate context in which to build a new grassroots unity between them"[30] in his nationalistic strivings against the British in the late nineteenth century in Maharashtra. Tilak, and Gaṇeśa worship, were wildly successful. In art, Gaṇeśa images for use by the common people in household shrines are very prevalent, and these tribal or folk images—made in bronze, mud, and plaster—are found throughout India. Even textiles are a popular medium for Gaṇeśa imagery. For example, the embroidered cotton hangings from Gujarat show Gaṇeśa functioning in the household much as he does in the temple. These hangings are designed and sewn by household women; each hanging is usually highly individual.[31] The hanging is worshiped by a bride and groom before their wedding, and then it is installed in the shrine of their new home. Here, Gaṇeśa, worshiped before the marriage is undertaken, is seen as a deity controlling transitions and new states and is then brought into the house to promote auspiciousness and insure future success of the undertaking.

IV. Gaṇeśa Outside India

It is difficult even to speak of Gaṇeśa in Tibet, China, Japan, and Southeast Asia without referring to the essays in this book. There has been very little written on the Asian Gaṇeśa, and Getty's book *Gaṇeśa: A Monograph on the Elephant-faced God*, published over fifty years ago, has remained the major reference for the extra-Indian Gaṇeśa. It continues to be a very useful anthology of visual and textual references, despite its early date, but many of Getty's facts, and much of her interpretation, must now be modified. For example, she says in reference to Gaṇeśa images in Thailand (Siam): "Not until the Ayuthian period [1350 – 1767 A.D.] in central Siam is a Siamese representation of Gaṇeśa to be found which is worthy of study."[32] All of the images from Thailand that I discuss in my essay are, in fact, from before the Ayuthian period.

Gaṇeśa had in Southeast Asia, unlike elsewhere in Asia, a significant Hindu presence. His earliest images and inscriptions date to approximately the sixth or seventh century, and there is evidence in Cambodia that from this time he had his own temples and perhaps was worshiped, again as early as the seventh century, as the focus of a cult and as an *iṣṭadevatā* (primary god), even earlier than extant evidence shows for the practice in India itself. Also in Cambodia there appears to be a highly unusual form of Gaṇeśa, one with a human head. Indeed, Gaṇeśa was very popular in many areas of Southeast Asia, and continues to be today, and developed interesting local variations, most of which remain to be fully explored. Nevertheless, his Purāṇic forms and nature are rarely encountered in Southeast Asia, either in art or in literature.

Many areas of Southeast Asia shared with Tibet, China, and Japan an interest in the Tantric Gaṇeśa. This is the Vināyaka or demonic Gaṇeśa discussed above. In China he becomes an almost entirely negative force, not causing or removing obstacles, but frequently being the obstacle itself. The Chinese Tantric texts are frequently those brought from India and translated by Indian and Chinese monks in the seventh and eighth centuries. These texts are very explicit in their discussion of the way in which Vināyaka is to be worshiped and in the goals that are thus achieved. They share with the Tibetan Gaṇeśa texts, many of which are translations of Indian texts of the same date, the mundane goals and Tantric ritual used to get them. These can be startlingly explicit:

> make a drawing [of Gaṇapati] on cotton with mixed together secretions from an elephant's temples (S. *Gajamada*), blood, and maddening semen. Prostrate, worship, praise, and make prayers to it. Recite the proper *mantra* and admonish him. You will become equal to a Noble One. You must not show this image to everyone. Offer your prayers with radishes and *mantras*.

or

> Make a copper Gaṇapati the size of a thumb. Put it in your left hand. Take some milk from the king's woman and pierce it with the elephant's trunk. Think "She truly loves me" and recite the *vidya* of the name. Then she will certainly come.[33]

It is important to note that these are Buddhist texts, written and translated by many of the well-known Buddhist teachers of the time. The author of the lines above, from *The Practice Method of the Secret Commitment of Gaṇapati*, was Canakīrti, and the text was translated into Tibetan by Vairocana and Chos kyi Grags pa. Canakīrti is probably Candrakīrti-pāda, an eighth-century Indian Tantric author, while the Indian Vairocana and his Tibetan colleague, Chos kyi Grags pa, were eleventh-century monks; Vairocana studied at both Nālandā and Vikramaśīla, among the most famous of Indian monasteries. Obviously, the Tantric Gaṇeśa was a deity of importance for the most renowned monks and was worshiped at the most famous monasteries in India from as early as the seventh and eighth centuries.

These texts tell how Gaṇeśa, usually in the form of an image, is to be worshiped, but they are more manuals than histories, so that we know little about the social or historical dimensions of the Tibetan and Chinese cult from them. In Japan a form of Gaṇeśa, that of two Gaṇeśas embracing, became popular as part of Shingon (Tantric) Buddhism. Usually shown as standing and embracing frontally, the two Gaṇeśas are male and female and are thought of as sexually linked. This form of Gaṇeśa was introduced to Japan as early as the eighth century, apparently from China, where it was also known, but we have little information about it. In Japan, from the seventeenth century on, there are texts that supply actual social and historical evidence of the cult.

The dual Gaṇeśa very much interested Getty, and she discusses the icon, its possible sources, meanings, and uses, at length.[34] But early in her study she wrote that

> very little is known of Gaṇeśa in the Tantras and not until more Tantric texts are accessible for study will it be possible to determine the exact position of Gaṇeśa in relation to the other gods who were worshipped in the mysteries, or to find the key to the puzzling Tantric aspect of the Elephant-faced god.[35]

In his interpretation of the dual Gaṇeśa, James Sanford ("Literary Aspects of Japan's Dual Gaṇeśa Cult") has the advantage of having access to texts unknown to Getty. While the puzzle of Gaṇeśa's Tantric form has not been solved in this book, his Tantric occurrence in Tibet, China, and Japan has been greatly clarified by extensive use of new textual sources.

V. Shared Themes of Gaṇeśa in the Essays

In outlining Gaṇeśa's character and roles, I have dealt with the god in art, texts, myth, religion, and ritual—in other words, Gaṇeśa as seen from a cultural viewpoint that is intrinsically multidisciplinary. I have had the opportunity to mention in the discussion several of the book's essays, and my brief overview has been based in large part on these essays. Do the essays in this book present a new view of Gaṇeśa?

One hopes, by looking at Gaṇeśa interdisciplinarily and crossculturally, to approach him in new ways and through new evidence, and many contributors have used previously unanalyzed texts and images in their essays. For example, Phyllis Granoff ("Gaṇeśa as Metaphor: The *Mudgala Purāṇa*") examines an extremely complex Purāṇa and finds it rich in suggesting the philosophical sophistication that Gaṇeśa worship sometimes took. In her discussion, Granoff attempts to understand the text using the conceptual framework of its ancient authors rather than that of the contemporary scholar. The use of texts that until now were little known by scholars is also stressed, as we have seen, in the essays on Gaṇeśa in Tibet, China, and Japan. These texts, which date beginning from the seventh and eighth centuries, are interesting because they enable us to see a predominantly Tantric Gaṇeśa in contrast to the mythic Gaṇeśa of the Purāṇas. Although these are written in Tibetan, Chinese, and Japanese, they are often translations from Indic texts that are now lost, and thus help us to understand Gaṇeśa in India as well as East Asia. Two authors, James Sanford and Christopher Wilkinson ("The Tantric Gaṇeśa: Texts Preserved in the Tibetan Canon"), have incorporated extensive translations of texts in their articles, which will be a valuable resource for other scholars working on Gaṇeśa.

As with previously unanalyzed texts, previously undiscussed visual evidence of Gaṇeśa is a strength of several articles. Maruti Nandan Tiwari and Kamal Giri ("Images of Gaṇeśa in Jainism") discuss, for the first time since Getty's book, Gaṇeśa images in Jainism. Their conclusion is that Gaṇeśa images were adopted by the Jains only very late, perhaps not until the ninth century A.D., and always in his positive role as remover of obstacles. In my paper, I focus on visual evidence that analyzes Gaṇeśa in Southeast Asia in an attempt to determine what was adopted from Indian conceptions of the god and what was the Southeast Asian contribution.

While both texts and images are standard categories of evidence used in past studies of the deity, Amy Catlin ("'Vātāpi Gaṇapatim': Sculptural, Poetic, and Musical Texts in a Hymn to Gaṇeśa") uses a type of evidence that is rarely seen in discussions of Gaṇeśa: music. She shows us how music, like art and literary texts, is used in India to express a South Indian Brahmin's understanding of the god. This understanding relies on an interplay among all three types of "texts" and is constantly reinterpreted in performance, in a process analogous, perhaps, to that in which Gaṇeśa is reinterpreted through history, for different communities, and in different geographical regions; there is no one Gaṇeśa. Her essay exemplifies the fruitfulness, perhaps even the necessity, of an interdisciplinary approach to Gaṇeśa.

New evidence, new translations, new approaches are all strengths of the essays in this book, but do they form a new conception of Gaṇeśa? Is there, in fact, any coherence to the picture of Gaṇeśa that we get from the various approaches, cultures, and time periods that are dealt with in these essays? Five themes seem to define Gaṇeśa in these essays: Gaṇeśa's practical role, Tantric nature, dual positive/negative character, adaptability, and transformative power. These do not, of course, define a completely new conception of Gaṇeśa, but they do amplify, and frequently modify significantly, our understanding of the god.

Here and Now

Gaṇeśa worship is unapologetically concerned with success. The goals of the worshiper are practical and this-worldly, and there is stress put on the mechanics of ritual that will produce the desired results. Thus, extensive ritual manuals were produced to guide the worshiper (some of which are explored in detail for the first time by several of this book's authors). The practical, materialistic orientation of Gaṇeśa reflects his historically original nature, as Vināyaka, and it is as a means to mundane success that he became popular outside of India. Gaṇeśa's second role in India, as a member of Śiva's family, is to my mind a product of the mythmaking of the Purāṇas and, from artistic evidence, begins only from around the sixth century A.D., when Gaṇeśa begins to associate himself with Śiva, as at Bādāmi Cave 1 and Elephanta. It is likely that the late adoption of a mythic role for Gaṇeśa is a reason why he does not appear in the epics, such as the *Mahābhārata,* where he would have been classified as one of the *vināyaka*s, who, like the *yakṣa*s, are mentioned as much by class as by name. One thing is clear: his mythic role never became popular outside of India.

It is possible to see the absence of his Purāṇic identity in East Asia as in part due to this role being Hindu and thus never spreading outside India with Buddhism. Nevertheless, even in Southeast Asia, which had a strong Hindu face, the mythic Gaṇeśa never became popular.

The analysis of Gaṇeśa's role in Buddhism is a particularly helpful aspect of this book, especially as it is rarely developed in other studies of Gaṇeśa. Most generally, Gaṇeśa in the Hindu context is perceived as a positive force, while in the Buddhist he is negative. One need only read through Cohen's paper to sense with what affection Gaṇeśa is regarded by contemporary Hindus in India. And while his informants saw Gaṇeśa associated with a variety of goddesses in ambiguous relationships of both son to mother and husband to wife, they clearly felt these relationships were fruitful and sustaining. Cohen suggests, in fact, that this duality of relationship is "central and perhaps essential to the social construction and psychosexual maintenance of Indian masculinity." Granoff shows us perhaps the ultimate reflection of Gaṇeśa's positive image in the *Mudgala*

Purāṇa, where forms of Gaṇeśa are used as a frame on which to order sophisticated commentary on understanding reality and the process of creation.

Tantrism

On the other hand, the depiction of Gaṇeśa in Buddhism is usually that of a demon whose malevolent nature is to be propitiated either to avoid harm or to direct the harm toward an enemy. Lewis Lancaster's paper ("Gaṇeśa in China: Methods of Transforming the Demonic"), for example, shows us that Gaṇeśa was consistently considered a negative deity in China. This is, according to Lancaster, the Tantric Gaṇeśa. Based on the papers by Wilkinson, Lancaster, and Sanford on Gaṇeśa in Tibet, China, and Japan, the Buddhist Gaṇeśa is Tantric in nature. Undoubtedly, it is mainly in this guise that he entered Buddhism. Nevertheless, the Tantric character of the Buddhist Gaṇeśa—that of a malevolent spirit who demands propitiation in the form of offerings and ritual in order to avoid harm—is shared by the deity's earliest form as a *vināyaka*. The view that what we call "Tantric" is a later label for a constellation of early Indian religious practices that stretch back perhaps to the Indus Valley civilization is given a strong boost by this analysis of Gaṇeśa's nature.[36]

Positive/Negative

We might, therefore, see Gaṇeśa as almost two separate deities, the negative Gaṇeśa, who takes both an earlier form as a *vināyaka* and a later Tantric form, which is the predominant type of Gaṇeśa adopted into Buddhism, and the positive Hindu Gaṇeśa, a creation of the mythmakers who are producing Purāṇic Hinduism. It can be argued, however, that Gaṇeśa's positive/negative personality can also be seen as two sides to the same deity, rather than as aspects of two "separate" deities. But it is important to realize that Gaṇeśa does not so much have a split personality, such as we might find with Śiva, whose benign or horrific and ascetic or lover forms are difficult to integrate, as he has a modus operandi that has negative and positive aspects. Gaṇeśa participates in a worldview in which goals are achieved by overcoming obstacles. As lord of obstacles, Gaṇeśa

controls their existence, through either creating them himself or allowing those already there to exist (which is negative) or by not creating them or removing those already there (which is positive). My point is that this in itself is not a matter of Gaṇeśa's character as much as the nature of his praxis. One must consider his intentions, and perhaps the worshiper's expectations, to judge Gaṇeśa as either negative or positive. If we do this, I

think there is again a clear split between the Purānic Gaṇeśa, who is expected to aid the worshiper in his tasks (for example, the Gaṇeśa whose image honors the shrines of businesses throughout India), and the Gaṇeśa who is expected to be dangerous, difficult, and deceptive (for example, the Gaṇeśa with whom Tankai fought most of his life, as outlined in Sanford's essay). While goals can be achieved through both, and their basic method of removing obstacles is the same, one is predominantly positive, the other negative.

Gaṇeśa is called "Vināyaka" in the seventh- and eighth-century Chinese texts (most of which were originally written by Indian monks) used by Lancaster in his essay, where Gaṇeśa's negative nature transforms him into a demon who must be controlled and is thus the object of the worshiper's spells and rituals in an attempt to drive him away.[37] Gaṇeśa in this case is not worshiped to control obstacles, but is himself the obstacle that must be removed. This appears to be the original nature of the deity, and Dhavalikar suggests in his paper that Gaṇeśa was "first the obstacle-creator (*vighna-kartā*) and later became the obstacle-averter (*vighna-hartā*)." He does not specify exactly when this transformation came about, but implies that it is around the sixth century and is responsible for his admission into the "hierarchy of major divinities." It is not, however, that Gaṇeśa gave up one role for the other, but that the earlier obstacle-creator role continued on, defining particularly his Tantric and Buddhist forms as a demon.

Adaptability

In fact, Gaṇeśa's character, whether Purāṇic deity or Tantric demon, was never narrowly defined. His diversity of form, variability of nature, and ambiguity of relationships are stressed in some way in all the essays and are features I have termed, in the context of this book's crosscultural and interdisciplinary focus, "adaptability." I mean by this Gaṇeśa's mutability, which allowed him to adapt to a variety of contexts. Within India itself, Cohen shows how important regional differences are in the perception of Gaṇeśa, and then how, even within regions, each individual's own perception of the god often varies dramatically. Indeed, the various viewpoints are often in conflict within the same individual, producing an ambiguous picture of Gaṇeśa, but one that I would argue adds to his adaptability within a variety of contexts. Even in the Purāṇas themselves, as Ludo Rocher ("Gaṇeśa's Rise to Prominence in Sanskrit Literature") points out, the portrait of Gaṇeśa is inconsistent and multiform. And the one aspect of Gaṇeśa that we might think is by definition immutable, his elephant head, is in fact done away with in some Southeast Asian sculpture where he takes a fully human form.

Transformative Power

Gaṇeśa's constantly shifting character, incorporating sometimes opposing traits, fits, of course, with his combined negative/positive nature. The incorporation of conflicting characteristics is an example of his transformative power, a capability that most fundamentally, in my opinion, defines the special nature of the god and goes far to explain his popularity. Gaṇeśa transforms either by synthesizing disparate elements or by mediating among them; in either case, he acts as a linkage through which relationships can be reordered and changed. The god's abilities to mediate, synthesize, and transform are discussed in almost every paper in this book. Sanford shows how the embracing dual Gaṇeśas in Japan are interpreted as combining opposites. Granoff argues that Gaṇeśa in the *Mudgala Purāṇa* is above all a visual symbol for synthesis: "Gaṇeśa, in having both elephant head and human body, stands as a perfect symbol for the concept that reality is always a combination of seemingly disparate building blocks or constituents." Cohen speaks of Gaṇeśa as mediator between the material and divine worlds and as facilitator of the new relationship formed during weddings. Wilkinson translates texts that give Gaṇeśa the power to transform non-Buddhist things into things Buddhist. Gaṇeśa's liminal roles as door guardian and as lord of beginnings have already been mentioned. All of these examples, and many more that could be added, show Gaṇeśa being used as the means to bridge transitions and make changes, a capability that gives him a powerful and unique position among Indic deities and makes him attractive outside normally restrictive religious and cultural boundaries.

Gaṇeśa is not easily defined. He contains within himself a variety of personalities and characteristics. Yet, like the seemingly ludicrous amalgam of elephant head and human body, their compresence somehow manages to appear natural. The essays in this book add significantly to our understanding of Gaṇeśa's multiform personality, of the human processes that have produced it, and of the human needs that underlie its integration.

NOTES

1. Stella Kramrisch, *Manifestations of Shiva* (Philadelphia: Philadelphia Museum of Art, 1981), 74.

2. For paintings of the family see Kramrisch, *Manifestations of Shiva,* nos. P-39, P-40, P-41.

3. One thinks most immediately of the baby Kṛṣṇa.

4. The phenomenon is of course well known with children's stuffed animals, such as the worldwidely adored teddy bear, as well as animated cartoon animal characters like Mickey Mouse.

5. Wendy O'Flaherty, "Preface," in *Gaṇeśa: Lord of Obstacles, Lord of Beginnings*, by Paul B. Courtright (New York: Oxford University Press, 1985), vii.

6. Śiva as well creates children himself, most particularly Skanda, when he spills his semen into the mouth of Agni, who in turn, unable to hold its heat, discharges it into the Ganges River, which in turn throws the embryo onto the bank, where the child is finally raised by the six Kṛttikās. Śiva and Pārvatī are seen as never having children through intercourse. See the various discussions of this motif in Wendy Doniger O'Flaherty, *Śiva: The Erotic Ascetic* (Oxford: Oxford University Press, 1973).

7. See particularly Courtright, *Gaṇeśa*.

8. Lee Siegel, *Laughing Matters: Comic Tradition in India* (Chicago: University of Chicago Press, 1987), 13.

9. Courtright, *Gaṇeśa*, 134.

10. Narain explores these in detail in his essay. He suggests that the word comes from *vi* > *ni* (= *nayati*), "to lead or take away," which agrees with Courtright, yet Narain interprets this as meaning to take or lead away obstacles, while Courtright says it means to "lead people astray and place obstacles in their paths." Compare Courtright, *Gaṇeśa*, 131–32.

11. Gaṇeśa has two other popular names that explicitly state these: Vighnakartā ("producing obstacles") and Vighnahartā ("removing obstacles").

12. Alice Getty, *Gaṇeśa: A Monograph on the Elephant-faced God* (Oxford: Clarendon Press, 1936), 25 and 10 (respectively).

13. A. K. Narain, "Iconographic Origins of Gaṇeśa and the Evidence of the Indo-Greek Coinage," in *Orientalia Iosephi Tucci Memoriae Dicata*, Serie Orientale Roma 56, no. 3 (Rome: Instituto Italiano per il Medio ed Estremo Oriente, 1988), 1007–19.

14. The snake belt is explained in the myth given above as the snake that caused Gaṇeśa to fall off his rat being used by the god to tie up his split stomach.

15. The dating is made in connection with an inscription; see discussion in my essay, infra.

16. There is, however, the question of whether there was a built structure attached at one point to the front of the cave that is now lost.

17. See Katherine Anne Harper, *The Iconography of the Saptamatrikas: Seven Hindu Goddesses of Spiritual Transformation* (Lewiston, NY: Mellen Press, 1989).

18. Harper, *Iconography of the Saptamatrikas*.

19. The identification of these standing female figures is problematical. They may represent on some level the six *pāramitās*. There are other interpretations; R. S. Gupte, for example, identifies them as the "Śaktis of the Dhyani Buddhas." See R. S. Gupte, "An Interesting Panel from the Aurangabad Caves," *Marathwada University Journal* 3, no. 2 (1963):59–63.

20. For illustrations see Carmel Berkson, *The Caves of Aurangabad: Early Buddhist Tantric Art in India* (New York: Mapin International, 1986), 115, 116, 118, 119, 120, 121.

21. Jambhala (or his Hindu equivalent, Kubera) and Gaṇeśa are sometimes placed together with a female figure, possibly Śrī-Lakśmī. See, for example, Getty, *Gaṇeśa*, 33.

22. The cave had been completely hidden by a fall of the escarpment above it.

23. For illustration see Berkson, *The Caves at Aurangabad*, 226, 227, 228.

24. It might be mentioned that a small Gaṇeśa occurs on the doorframe at Cave 3 at Aurangabad, which dates to the second half of the fifth century.

25. See, for example, Courtright, *Gaṇeśa*, 74–90, 117, etc.

26. For example, the Gaṇeśa that Getty illustrates as the "earliest" image and that has thus been subsequently cited by many scholars, holds what is probably a citron (*matūluṅga*), based on comparison to other early images, such as Brown, fig. 6. It definitely is not a tusk. (See Getty, *Gaṇeśa*, Pl. 2a.)

27. See references in Brown, infra.

28. Foucher, "Introduction," in Getty, *Gaṇeśa*, xv–xxiii.

29. Monier Monier-Williams, *Brahmanism and Hinduism* (London: J. Murray, 1887), 221n; quoted in Getty, *Gaṇeśa*, 2.

30. Courtright, *Gaṇeśa*, 233.

31. See, for example, J. LeRoy Davidson, *Art of the Indian Subcontinent from Los Angeles Collections* (Los Angeles: Ritchie Press, 1968), fig. 199.

32. Getty, *Gaṇeśa*, 47.

33. Quoted from Wilkinson, infra.

34. Getty, *Gaṇeśa*, 78–87.

35. Getty, *Gaṇeśa*, 9.

36. See Thomas McEvilley, "An Archaeology of Yoga," *RES* 1 (Spring 1981):42–77.

37. Any question whether Gaṇeśa's origins can be found with the *vināyakas* is, I think, answered by his later association with them in these Tantric texts, a fact that is not apparent when only his Purāṇic form is discussed. Nevertheless, see Narain's discussion, infra, for a different point of view.

1

Gaṇeśa: A Protohistory of the Idea and the Icon

A. K. Narain

I. Introduction[1]

Gaṇeśa is an everyday household god of modern Hinduism. He is one of the five deities of the *pañcāyatana* of the Smārta tradition. He is the patron deity of a cult, a *sampradāya*, known as Gāṇapatya, the members of which consider him above all other deities of the Hindu pantheon. Gaṇeśa is probably the most ubiquitous of Indian gods, and his popularity is not limited to the sectarian boundaries of Brahmanical Hinduism. He has a place in Buddhist and Jain worship, too. And he crosses even the territorial boundaries of India. His presence has been noted in what are now Pakistan, Nepal, and Sri Lanka, in Afghanistan, central Asia, Tibet, and Mongolia, in China and Japan, in Burma, Thailand, Cambodia, Laos, Vietnam, and Indonesia, and as far as Borneo in the Pacific.[2]

The historical identity and iconography of this god, in his classic form as an elephant-faced deity, is generally recognized from the fourth to fifth century A.D. By about the tenth century A.D. his independent cult had come very much into existence. During the centuries that followed two Upapurāṇas, namely the *Gaṇeśa Purāṇa* and the *Mudgala Purāṇa*, as well as a Gītā, namely, the *Gaṇeśa Gītā*, were written.[3] Finally, the most important work for the Gāṇapatyas, the *Śrī Gaṇapati Atharvaśīrṣa Upaniṣad* or *Gaṇapati Upaniṣad*, was composed during the sixteenth or seventeenth century.[4] Thus, starting from the fifth century A.D., Gaṇeśa's history is fairly clear for about fifteen hundred years.

But what is inscrutable is the somewhat dramatic appearance of Gaṇeśa on the historical scene.[5] His antecedents are not clear. His wide acceptance and popularity, which transcend sectarian and territorial limits, are indeed amazing. On the one hand there is the pious belief of the orthodox devotees in Gaṇeśa's Vedic origins and in the Purāṇic explanations contained in his confusing, but nonetheless interesting, mythology. On the other, there are doubts about the existence of the idea and the icon of *this* deity before the fourth to fifth century A.D.[6] Various attempts have been made to look into the antecedents of Gaṇeśa and how they coalesce in due course to bring forth the standard Gaṇeśa.[7] But the frustration is evident when, in the latest monograph on the subject, Courtright wants to stress the point that there is no need "to create a theory about Gaṇeśa's origins" and that "there may not be any compelling evidence for Gaṇeśa prior to his emergence into the Brahmanic fold simply because he was never there."[8] The point is well taken, and, in my opinion, indeed there is no convincing evidence for the existence of this divinity prior to the fifth century. We also cannot agree more with him that there is no need to create a theory for theory's sake. But the fait accompli in history is the result of a process through time and space. Surely this process and its dynamics need to be examined. Could it be that so far Gaṇeśa has been subjected to too narrow a focus restricted to the *orthodox* Brahmanic or Sanskritic tradition and limited to the geocultural boundaries of India only? A broader perspective is indeed required to distinguish the separate elements that made so great a creative achievement possible. Such a perspective is, in fact, demanded by the emergence of the classic form of the elephant-faced deity, Gaṇeśa, and his hieratic acceptance into the orthodox Brahmanic fold, as well as his popularity outside of it.

Mythology is not history. Though at times it is supposed to hide kernels of historical truth, the Purāṇic myths of Gaṇeśa are little more than grandparents' stories. One can conclude from them that Gaṇeśa was a member of the family of Śiva and that his hieratic legitimation was linked to a god who himself perhaps did not originally belong to the Vedic orthodoxy.[9] Going beyond this, delving deeply into the myths and interpreting their ritual meaning or psychoanalyzing the sexual symbolism involved, is neither my inclination nor my intention, and I prefer to leave these approaches to others.[10] Moreover, all the myths are actually brain children of the mythographers and therefore not of much real use for my purposes. I propose to go to the time prior to the making of these Purāṇic myths and find the historical background and factors that led to the very fact of creation of Gaṇeśa and inter alia his myths. Points of myths become relevant to us only to the extent they reflect or camouflage those factors to explain or justify the fait accompli. We would also agree with Foucher not to be "as short-sighted as a bookworm" to believe that this divinity could have suddenly been conceived ex nihilo. We therefore make a fresh survey of the ethnographical, linguistic, archaeological, numismatic, and art-historical data to see if there are meaningful clues to explain the processes of syncretism and synthesis that went into the making of the melting pot of Indian culture, a veritable example of which, indeed, is our Gaṇeśa. Our exercise here, in brief, is to investigate the protohistory of the idea and the icon of Gaṇeśa.

II. A Survey of the Names and Their Etyma

The names by which Gaṇeśa became popularly known in the sources from the fifth century A.D. are many.[11] The names Gaṇeśa and Gaṇapati literally mean the same thing—the lord or leader of a *gaṇa* (= a host or a group). This may be a group of kindred gods or demigods, humans or animals, a body of followers or attendants.[12] Specifically, apart from its political connotation in ancient India in the sense of nonmonarchical states, the word *gaṇa* meant the followers of the teachers of various cults.[13] Much later, it also meant the troops or classes of inferior deities, especially those of demigods or spirits considered first as Śiva's attendants and only much later as under the special superintendence of Gaṇeśa.[14]

Of the two names, Gaṇapati is the oldest known; it occurs in the *Ṛgveda*.[15] But it is used there not as a personal name but as an attribute of Bṛhaspati or Brahmaṇaspati, who is known in the *RV* as a "lord" of a group of gods, or of *mantras*, as well as the god of rain;[16] he is also called a "Jyeṣṭharāja."[17] The *Ṛgveda* provides some idea of the form and attributes of Bṛhaspati.[18] There is nothing there, however, to do with the elephant-faced Gaṇeśa. In fact it is significant to note from the story of the birth of Vighneśvara in the *Liṅga Purāṇa* that Bṛhaspati and Gaṇeśa were clearly different from each other.[19] Indra is known as another Gaṇapati, in the sense of both a "lord"[20] and a "leader."[21] But Indra had not yet acquired an elephant (Airāvata) as his vehicle in the *Ṛgveda;* that is a later acquisition. Thus the elephant as a connection between Indra and Gaṇeśa is not provided in the *Ṛgveda*. Coomaraswamy and Courtright refer to the same text of the *Aitareya Brāhmaṇa* of the *Ṛgveda*[22] for Brahmā and Rudra respectively as other Gaṇapatis, but I am unable to confirm their references. However, Rudra as a Gaṇapati is referred to in the *Taittirīya* and *Maitrāyaṇīya Saṁhitas* of the *Kṛṣṇa Yajurveda*.[23] Nonetheless, it is doubtful if Gaṇapati was used as a personal name in the early Vedic literature.[24] In the long and formidable list of as many as eighty-five names of gods and folk deities in the *Pāpamocana Sūkta* of *Atharvaveda*, Gaṇapati and Gaṇeśa are conspicuous by their absence, although the names of many Vedic gods—including Brahmaṇaspati—and even non-Vedic ones are there.[25] The occurrence of Gaṇapati as a personal name in the *Baudhāyana Dharmasūtra*[26] as well as in the *Bodhāyana Gṛhyasūtra,*[27] is considered by Hazra[28] as of doubtful authenticity.

The second name, Gaṇeśa, is not found at all in the Vedic literature whether early or late. Nor is it found in the *Mahābhārata.*[29] Its variants, Gaṇeśana and Gaṇeśvara, however, do occur there, but they are used for Śiva and not for our Gaṇeśa.[30] In one place Gaṇeśvara is used as an epithet of the *vināyakas,* and it is said that these "gaṇeśvara-vināyakas" control all the world.[31] Also, Gaṇeśvara occurs in the *Harivaṁsa* as the name of a demon causing diseases.[32] Its occurrence in the *Bodhāyana Gṛhyaśeṣasūtra,* in the section on Vināyaka,[33] is hardly a reference to Gaṇeśa. Some scholars have referred to a synonym, Gaṇanāyaka, in a text of *Mānava Dharmaśāstra,*[34] but the passage under reference is considered a modern forgery.[35]

The next popular name by which the elephant-faced god Gaṇeśa became known is Vināyaka. This word could literally mean a leader or guide (from *vi* > *naya*)[36] for regulating, controlling, or implementing order and discipline (in a group or system).[37] But this has been derived also from *vi* > *ni* (= *nayati*)—to lead or take away, to drive away, dispel, expel (a disease)—to illustrate the meaning "remover (of obstacles), name of Gaṇeśa."[38] However, in the eighth century A.D., a commentator of *Yājñavalkyasmṛti,* Viśvarūpa, provides an ingenious derivative meaning of the word as "one who was appointed (*viniyukta*) as the head of a diverse (*vi* = *vividha*) group or class of men."[39] So also, if the *upasarga vi* indicates the quality of distinction (*viśiṣṭa*), it means "without" or "deprived of" (a leader), too. We might add that Vināyaka was thus indeed either a "distinguished" (*vi* = *viśiṣṭa*) individual leader or else a plurality of a group without a leader.[40] At any rate, unlike "Gaṇapati" and "Gaṇeśa," which convey the sense of individual leadership or lordship, "Vināyaka" conveys different and multiple meanings depending upon whether used in singular or plural number; the ambivalence cannot be denied.

The name Vināyaka occurs first in the *Mānava Gṛhyasūtra;* it is used there in the *plural* number to refer to a group of four spirits or lesser gods, namely Sālakaṭaṇkaṭa, Kuṣmāṇḍarājaputra, Uṣmita, and Devayajana, and not for Gaṇeśa.[41] The name also appears in *Baijavāpagṛhya* as preserved in extracts quoted in the commentaries of Aparārka and Śūlapāṇi on *YS.*[42] But in these two sources the *vināyakas* are neither connected with Rudra-Śiva nor called leaders of *gaṇas*. Also, they are not described as having an elephant's face. It may be noted further that Bṛhaspati is regarded as a distinct deity like Agni, Indra, Soma, Varuṇa, Vāyu, and Viṣṇu.[43] In the *Mahābhārata,* too, the *vināyakas* are looked upon as unfriendly, malignant demons like *bhūtas, rākṣasas,* and *piśācas,*[44] and their number is taken as more than two.[45] Vināyaka is included in a long list of names of doubtful authenticity in the *Baudhāyana Dharmasūtra*. The list, which includes, among others, the names of deities to whom *tarpaṇa* was to be made in a funerary rite (*śrāddha*), has also Vighna, Vīra, Sūra, Varada, Hastimukha, Vakratuṇḍa, Ekadanta, Lambodara, and Gaṇeśa, as well as the groups of *vighnapārṣadas* and the *vighnapārṣadīs*.[46] But in the later work *Bodhāyana Gṛhyaśeṣasūtra*, in the *Vināyakakalpa*,[47] there is a reference to Devayajana, and so forth, as well as to Vighna, Vīra, Sūra, Ugra, Bhīma, Hastimukha, Varada, and the *vighnapārṣadas* and the *vighnapārṣadīs*, but not to Gaṇapati, Vakratuṇḍa, Ekadanta and Lambodara as in the *Baudhāyana Dharmasūtra*.

On the other hand, the names Vighneśvara and Gaṇeśvara are mentioned as perhaps synonyms of Vināyaka.[48] It is true that later in the *Yājñavalkyasmṛti*, Vināyaka is referred to in the *singular* number and for the first time perhaps recognized as "one" god[49] and reported to have been appointed (*viniyukta*) by Rudra and Brahmā to lord it over the *gaṇas*.[50] However, it is not clear from the text if a merger of the identity of the four *vināyakas* had already taken place under the lordship or leadership of *one* of them,[51] and if Vināyaka had thus been elevated to become a Gaṇapati, or Gaṇeśa.[52] In any case he is not given the elephant face. Nor are deities like Hastimukha, Ekadanta, Vakratuṇḍa, and Lambodara denied their independent existence. It is also relevant to note here that the statement made by R. G. Bhandarkar, and followed by others, that Ambikā was known as the mother of Vināyaka in this text, is not correct.[53] The text actually appears to ask for the adoration of the mother of Vināyaka and then (*tataḥ*) of Ambikā, in order to propitiate him. It does not specify Ambikā as his mother.[54] In fact, the commentary of Viśvarūpācharya equates Ambikā with either Buddhi (i.e., wife of Vināyaka-Gaṇeśa) or Rudrapatni, but *not* as mother of Vināyaka.[55]

Related to Vināyaka are also names like Vighneśa, Vighneśvara, and Vighnahartā, all commonly used for Gaṇeśa. These names are directly related to *vighna* (*vi-ghna* = obstacle). While Vighneśa and Vighneśvara mean the "lord of obstacles" and Vighnahartā means the "remover (*hartā*) of obstacles,"[56] the word *vighna* itself has been used as a proper noun to personify a demigod who was a "breaker or destroyer."[57] In all these *vighna*- related names a dual role, the negative one of malevolence and the positive one of benevolence, is indicated. As in the case of Vināyaka, the first two (Vighneśa and Vighneśvara) indicate the lordship or leadership and the third one (Vighnahartā) the quality of driving away or dispelling evil or obstacle.

Now, quite in a different category belong such popular names of Gaṇeśa as Gajānana, Vakratuṇḍa, and Ekadanta.[58] They are specifically related to the elephant and convey its physical characteristics. The first name is simple enough in its meaning to indicate the elephantine face (*gaja* +

anana). The second one refers to the elephantine trunk of the god in a curved position (*vakra*) in which it is generally depicted in art, although there are many examples where it is shown straight with only the tip curled up.[59] The third name is curiously enough taken to specify only one of the elephantine tusks (*ekadanta*) of the god, supposedly for significant reasons.[60] But the word *ekadanta* can as well mean the one having the "great," "supreme," or "unique" tusk, like the words *ekavrātya* used for Śiva and *ekarāt* used for a great or supreme king.

Of the names of Gaṇeśa mentioned above as related to the elephant's physical characteristics, none has been referred to in the *Ṛgveda*. But names of certain theriomorphic deities that are related indirectly, or partly, to the elephant's face occur in some later Vedic texts. For example, Karāṭa (one with the cheek of an elephant), Hastimukha (one having the face of an elephant), and Dantin (one with tusks) in the *Maitrāyaṇīya Saṁhitā*,[61] and Vakratuṇḍa (one having a curved trunk) and Danti in the *Taittirīya Āraṇyaka*.[62] But there are as many as four elephant-related names mentioned in *Baudhāyana Dharmasūtra*[63] in connection with *śrāddha tarpaṇa;* these are Hastimukha, Vakratuṇḍa, Ekadanta, and Lambodara. But of these only Hastimukha is mentioned in the *Bodhāyana Gṛhyaśeṣasūtra*.[64] It appears to me that while Hastimukha and Vakratuṇḍa are early and often-repeated names, the other two are later interpolations.[65] Moreover, there is no ground to consider these elephant-related names of the lists as synonyms of Gaṇeśa as the name "Gaṇeśa" is not included in them.[66] And it may be noted that the inclusion of Gaṇapati there, as a personal name, has been considered to be of doubtful authenticity.[67]

In any case, there is no evidence in the texts we have just discussed for either Gaṇapati or Vināyaka having any of the physical characteristics of an elephant. I doubt very much if the elephant-related names of these texts have anything to do with our Gaṇapati or Gaṇeśa, or even Vināyaka.[68] On the contrary these names indicate the independent status of the theriomorphic elephant-deity in the centuries before Christ. The names appear to highlight the very distinguishing physical characteristics of this deity who is worshiped in his own right. This was probably what would be known later in Patañjali as a *laukika devatā*,[69] or simply a *deva* as mentioned in the Buddhist sources.[70] Though outside the Vedic pale, they had received recognition in the Brahmanic system as a result of the interactions between the Vedic and the non-Vedic cultures.[71]

By the time of Aśoka, the elephant had become a popular sacred symbol and was labeled as *Gajatame*.[72] The reference to *Hastidasanā* in Aśokan edicts, too, might be taken as another indication of the elephant as a worshiped or divine object.[73] So also a *Hatthimaha* was known to the *Aṭṭhakathā* of a Jātaka story as a folk feast or festival in honor of a *laukika de-*

vatā, the sacred elephant.[74] In the Pali Buddhist text, *Mahāniddesa*, the devotees of this sacred elephant (*Hatthivatika*) are included in a list that includes those of several other sacred animals as well as those of Vāsudeva, Baladeva, Puṇṇabhadda, Maṇibhadda, Aggi, *nāgas*, *supaṇṇas*, *yakkhas*, *asuras*, *gandhabbas*, *mahārājas*, Canda, Suriya, Inda, Brahmā, Deva, and Disa.[75]

Now finally, there are names of Gaṇeśa in languages other than Sanskrit that should be noted. For example, the Tamil name for Gaṇeśa is Piḷḷaiyar. In the Dravidian family of languages *pallu*, *pella*, and *pell* signify specifically "tooth or tusk of an elephant," but more generally "elephant."[76] In the Tamil country *piḷḷe* means a "child" and *piḷḷaiyar*, a "noble child"; originally, it probably meant "the young one of an elephant."[77] In the *Pāia Sadda Mahāṇṇavo* the word *pīlu* means "elephant," and *pīlua*, *pīluka*, "the young one." In Pali, too, the word *pillaka* has the same meaning.[78] According to R. Caldwell[79] it is a word of Scythian origin to be compared with Latin *pullus* meaning "young of an animal."[80] Sylvain Levi noted the Dravidian link in explaining the identity of Dantapura with Paloura of Ptolemy.[81] But it is also interesting to note that J. Przyluski thought this word as of Austric origin and even pre-Dravidian.[82] But it is significant that in Sinhalese, an Indo-European language but geographically next door to Tamil, the word *pulleyar* does not mean "the son" as in Tamil but, as applied to Gaṇeśa, "the elephant lord of the forest."[83] Similarly, in the Aramaic in the northwest, the word *pil* meant "elephant."[84] Some scholars believe that the Dravidian word *pillaiyar* was derived from the Sanskrit word *piluśāra*, because even in Sanskrit the word *pila* or *pilu* means "elephant." It is no doubt feasible linguistically, because Sanskrit *sa* or *śa* could change into *ya* in Tamil. Be that as it may, it is worth notice that the Chinese pilgrim Xuanzang refers to *Pi-lo-sho-lo* (Piluśāra, "elephant-solid" or "elephant-essence") as the name of the local elephant-shaped mountain deity of Kapiśa.[85] There are other elephant-related names of places and peoples in the northwest provided by Xuanzang's account, as well as by the earlier accounts of Alexander's expedition in the region, that strengthen the recognition of the elephant in a supernatural role.[86]

III. A Survey of Early Theriomorphic and Therianthropomorphic Representations of the Sacred Elephant

It is generally agreed that no visual representation of our Gaṇeśa, per se (and for that matter of Vināyaka, too, before he became Gaṇeśa), is known that can be placed unquestionably earlier than the fifth century.[87] One or two representations of him have been dated a century or so earlier based essentially on artistic style, which may or may not be acceptable to all.[88] So also attempts have been made to discover prototypes that might have inspired the evolution of the classic form of Gaṇeśa.[89] A few therianthropomorphic examples that are not necessarily recognized as Gaṇeśa of the orthodox Brahmanic pantheon and that may be dated to times earlier than the fourth or fifth century A.D. have been identified. One of them has been noticed by Jouveau-Dubreuil and Coomaraswamy on one of the Amarāvatī railings datable in the first century A.D.[90] However, Getty has rightly pointed out that the head of this crouching personage is "unquestionably that of an elephant: that is, the eyes, ears, and the lower lip; but as the image has neither trunk nor tusk, it is questionable whether it is really a prototype of Gaṇeśa."[91] In this category perhaps also belongs a fragmentary Mathurā relief, referred to above in note 6, with five elephant-headed figures.[92] Getty's remark in respect of the Amarāvatī specimen is valid, in my opinion, also for this Mathurā example. It is difficult to justify P. K. Agrawala's comparison of the central figure in this relief with the developed Gaṇeśa figure from Mathurā and elsewhere belonging in the Gupta period.[93] The Amarāvatī and Mathurā specimens may or may not be considered as examples of a *Gaja-śirṣa "Yakṣa,"*[94] but they do not appear to me as examples of therianthropomorphic representations of the sacred elephant.

For two other examples of therianthropomorphic images with elephant heads that are pre-Gaṇeśa we must cross the boundaries of modern India. The first of these was noticed by S. Paranavitana in a frieze of *gaṇa*s on a stupa near Mihintale in Sri Lanka.[95] One of the *gaṇa*s here was clearly the face of an elephant, complete with trunk and tusk. While Paranavitana believes this sculpture to be of a later period, Getty thinks that it "may be unquestionably ascribed to the first centuries of our era," and she further concluded that

> as it is the only one of its kind and is in a group of other *gaṇa*s, it could hardly have struck the popular imagination deeply enough to inspire the forms of Gaṇeśa which appeared in India in the Gupta period. Thus, seemingly without transitional stage, the most ancient representations of Gaṇeśa are the *completed* type: two or four-armed, holding the axe, the broken tusk, a modaka (or is it a *jambu?*), or a bowl of cakes.[96]

The second extra-India example was brought to scholarly notice by me on an Indo-Greek coin of Hermaeus.[97] On this unique coin the seated figure is clearly endowed with the trunk of an elephant. This example may be dated around 50 B.C. or a little earlier, and thus it remains so far the earliest representation of a therianthropomorphic elephant deity, probably an incipient Gaṇeśa. I have discussed elsewhere in detail the gradual evolution of this type of representation in the northwest, in what are now Afghanistan and Pakistan.[98]

Now, unlike the late appearance of the therianthropomorphic Gaṇeśa, the visual representations of the independent theriomorphic elephant deity can be seen from even before the Vedic times. It is well known that many animals are depicted on the seals pertaining to the Harappa culture with its center in the northwestern parts of South Asia. While it is difficult to say if all of the animals depicted on the Harappa seals were sacred in character, some of them clearly were. Among the possibilities we may safely include, along with the bull, the elephant. When the authors of the Vedic texts began to make a note, albeit marginally, of such cult deities as the Hastimukha, the Dantin, and the Vakratuṇḍa, perhaps they were at that time represented in perishable material for temporary rituals and so they did not survive to later times.[99] But "images" or "representations" of the sacred elephant in durable materials appear to have existed in the northwestern parts of South Asia. If ideas traveled in the Achaemenid period of domination over this region and extended to the Western world, it is interesting to find on a Sicilian coin of the fourth century B.C. a deity wearing an elephant scalp on the obverse.[100] After Alexander's encounter in 323 B.C. with the elephants of Porus, the fascination with elephants of the Greeks and others in the West so increased that Seleucus regarded the possession of elephants as more valuable than that of territories; and thus, after Seleucus's victory over Antigonas, it is no wonder that the elephant came to be considered by the Greeks, too, as a symbol of success. Thus among the Greeks of Bactria, Demetrius and several other kings used the elephant scalp as their headdress.[101] It is very interesting that Demetrius issued a coin type with the head of an elephant wearing a bell around the neck.[102] This was exactly copied later by the Śaka king Maues.[103] The significance of the bell around the neck of the elephant not only confirms the elephant's special status but also offers a link to one of the later legends about the origin and role of Gaṇeśa.[104]

Two other Greco-Bactrian kings, Antimachus Theos and Apollodotus, issued coins with the figures of full-bodied elephants.[105] In addition, we have a series of coin types of Antialcidas showing the forepart of the sacred elephant in association with the Greek god Zeus holding Nike, the goddess of victory, and particularly one where Zeus is made to walk alongside a large, full-bodied elephant with Victory over the head, which easily reminds one of the coins of the later Kuṣāṇa king Wima Kadphises showing Śiva walking alongside a full-bodied bull.[106] Finally we have the unique coin of Hermaeus, which I have discussed elsewhere to show how the Greeks of Bactria and India honored the sacred elephant and gave recognition not only to a local cult of the elephant deity of Kapiśa but also to the first therianthropomorphic figure of this deity.[107]

Theriomorphic representation of the elephant was already known from the *karshapanas* (punch-marked coins) of Mauryan India.[108] It appears that before orthodox Brahmanic Hinduism recognized the sacredness of the elephant, the Buddhists had already included it in their religious thinking by associating it with the conception of the Buddha. Thus, Aśoka places the sacred elephant on his pillars (*dharmastambhas*), and at Kalsi a line drawing of the elephant belonging to his times is labeled as the *Gajatame* (the best or the supreme elephant). At Bhārhut and Sāñcī and in other post-Mauryan monuments, examples of the sacred elephant appearing in positive roles related to the Buddha are not difficult to find.[109] Theriomorphic representation of the sacred elephant was thus not uncommon in Buddhist contexts in South Asia before the beginning of the Christian era. It may be noted that in Sri Lanka, too, the Pulleyar of the Buddhists is not a son of Śiva like the Tamil Piḷḷaiyar, but an independent *devatā*, with functions different from those of the Tamil one.[110] So also it is interesting that a therianthropomorphic representation of the sacred elephant was made in China, again in the Buddhist context, as early as 531 A.D.[111]

It may not be out of place here to refer to two examples of elephant-faced female figures, one from Mathurā and the other found at Rairh in Rajasthan.[112] They have been dated from the first century B.C. to the second century A.D. and have been identified as the goddess Jyeṣṭhā, supposedly early examples of the female Gaṇeśa, who was known in later times by such names as Gaṇeśāni, Gaṇeśi, and Vaināyakī. Without going into the dating of these two figures, which is itself problematical, I find hardly any specific reason to identify them with the female goddess Gaṇeśāni or Vaināyakī. There is no justification to identify Jyeṣṭhā with Hastimukha mentioned in the *Bodhāyana Gṛhyaśeṣasūtra* in the same way as there is no reason, as discussed above, to identify Vināyaka with Hastimukha. I believe that Hastimukha was an independent *laukika devatā*, and therefore Hastimukha was perhaps the female counterpart of the male Hastimukha known from as early as the Vedic times, but not of Jyeṣṭharāja (an epithet of Bṛhaspati of the *Ṛgveda*) or of Vināyaka. If these elephant-faced female figures have any relation at all to the later example of an elephant-headed *yoginī* at Bheraghat, the inscription on the pedestal there reads clearly *Śrī Ainginī*.[113]

IV. Plurality of Traditions and Their Convergence

It is obvious from what we have discussed above that we are dealing with plural traditions and a complex process of interactions spread out over a vast period of time and space. One of the traditions no doubt is the Vedic. The Gaṇapati idea related to wisdom and learning, leadership or lordship, belongs here. But it may be noted that *gaṇapati* of the Vedic sources is not the personal name of a god. *Gaṇapatitva* is a concept that is applied to Bṛhaspati and to Indra and later extended even to Rudra-Śiva. The other traditions we are concerned with here belong in fact to the pot-pourri of the diverse non- and pre-Vedic traditions. Vināyaka represents one of them only. This was governed by the dichotomy of malevolence and benevolence arising out of the age-old primitive concept of fear of the unpredictable moods of nature and therefore the necessity of propitiation for harmonious coexistence with it. The Vināyaka tradition might be a part of the same non- and pre-Vedic traditions to which Rudra-Śiva belonged. The third tradition relevant for us here is the theriomorphic one, which was also at once non- and pre-Vedic. But unlike the Vināyaka idea, this was not based on the dichotomy of malevolence and benevolence and their resolution by propitiation. On the contrary, this was based on positive grounds. Perhaps the theriomorphic concept was less primitive in origin than the Vināyaka idea and dated from the time when animals, like the elephant and the bull, became domesticated and were assigned friendly, positive, and participatory roles in human life and activities. This tradition recognized the power, the majesty, and the usefulness of the physical qualities of these animals and therefore related probably to a practice of totem worship and agrarian rites. This tradition might or might not necessarily, at least to begin with, be associated with the same non- and pre-Vedic tradition to which also belonged the Rudra-Vināyaka idea.[114] To these non- and pre-Vedic traditions we must add the fourth of such external traditions, those originating from the West and from central Asia at different times, like the Greek, the Iranian, and the diverse inner Asian.

A large variety of sacred symbols, deities, and cults that belonged thus in the diverse non-Vedic and non-Brahmanic traditions was labeled as *laukika devatā*s in such Brahmanic sources as those of Pāṇinī and Patañjali, as *vyantara devatā*s in the Jain texts, and as *deva*s in the Buddhist. Their number was naturally much larger than the elite deities, and their list included, among others, not only the various imps and evil spirits, along with a retinue of obstacles personified (*vighna*) in both genders, and celestial beings, but also rivers, mountains, trees, and animals (such as the bull and the elephant). Their vitality never diminished, and their ever-renewing capacity endured the vicissitudes of time and culture.

By about the second century B.C. and onward, these traditions come closer to each other and do not shy away from more open intermingling. Experiments are being made in new adjustments and accommodation. Ideas are exchanged and wherever possible even internalized. Eclecticism and syncretism become the order of the day. Deities belonging in different traditions are provided with equations and receive new recognitions. In all these activities people of various ethnic and cultural origins making the melting pot of India, and enriching it time and again, participated. The credit goes to all.

It has already been noted that in the *Mānava Gṛhyasūtra* certain imps and evil spirits, such as Sālakaṭaṁkaṭa, Uṣmita, Kuṣmāṇḍarājaputra, and Devayajana, are collectively described as *vināyaka*s who were prone to possess men and women, make them failures in life, and put obstacles in the way of their performance of good deeds. The texts also lay down various ways of propitiating these spirits and thus freeing oneself from their possession. Thus the *vināyaka*s were known in the non-Vedic Brahmanic tradition for their dual role of producing obstacles (*vighnakartā*) and of removing obstacles (*vighnahartā*). They were thus in their own way the regulators of order and discipline (*vināya*) in society by first injecting elements of fear and then promising to remove them for an offering. During the post-Mauryan period, arising out of the interaction again, for the second time,[115] between the indigenous and the newly arrived foreign elements, a movement for rapprochement between the elite Vedic-Brahmanic and the folk non-Brahmanic traditions received a fillip. A process of syncretism led to a synthesis and incorporation of elements of popular belief-systems in the mainstream of Indian culture.[116] As a part of this process, the malignancy of Vināyaka as a *vighnakartā* was removed, and from Vighneśvara he became a *vighnahartā*, Gaṇeśvara.[117] First, Vināyaka was assigned a positive role and elevated as a *bhagavat* to whom offerings could be made by those desirous of *siddhi* (success), *ṛddhi* (prosperity), and *paśu* (wealth).[118] He was praised as a *bhūpati* and *bhuvanapati* as well as *bhutānaṁ pati*.[119]

But it should be noted that no "*laukika devatā*" of the elephant group was included in the list of the *gaṇa*s of Vināyaka. Probably their number still remained as four. Hastimukha maintained a separate identity for purposes of *svāhā*.[120] In fact there is a reason to believe that the elephant-related *devatā*s belonged clearly in a different group. On the other hand, either the leaderless (*vi* = "deprived of" + *nāyaka*) group of *vināyaka*s (in plural), or Vināyaka himself (in singular) as the lord of his group, were inducted into the team of Śiva.[121] Nay, probably the elephant deity had something to do with the very process that removed the malevolence of Vināyaka and gave to him a guardianship role that would be later transferred to the Purāṇic Gaṇeśa. For it is significant that in the *Bodhayāna Gṛhyaśeṣasūtra,* as part of the ritual of propitiation and offerings, after the visualization of Devayajana, a *hastimukha* (elephant-faced) Brāhmaṇa or a Brāhmaṇa probably wearing an elephant-face mask, was made to sit facing the south for performing the propitiatory ritual.[122] Thus far no statement is made that Vināyaka-Gaṇapati had an elephant-face or any other elephantine attribute.

In the *Yājñavalkyasmṛti* (ca. fourth century A.D.?), one Vināyaka is assigned the role of lordship of the *gaṇa*s by Rudra and Brahmā. He is supposed also to be associated, rather ambiguously, in this text with Ambikā as his mother. Obviously this was to bring Vināyaka into line with, or into the family of, the major cult deities Śiva and Śakti, who were albeit of non-Vedic origins but already well established in the Brahmanic system. Banerjea[123] rightly states that "this was the beginning of the very confused mythology about the origin of Gaṇapati to be found in later literature." The so-called earliest iconographic description of Gaṇapati in the chapter on *Pratimālakṣanaṁ* of the *Bṛhat Saṁhitā* of Varāhamihira (sixth century A.D.) has already been considered by all concerned as an interpolation.[124] If that is so, Bāṇabhatta (seventh century A.D.),[125] and Bhavabhūtī (eighth century A.D.)[126] are probably the earliest to provide textual references to the elephantine head of Vināyaka,[127] though such images were being already made, whether or not acknowledged as that of our Gaṇeśa.

The most striking visual characteristic of Gaṇeśa is no doubt his elephant's face. And as I have stated above, the many myths that surround Gaṇeśa do not appear to reveal the source for this identifying feature. The disagreement and diversity in the stories detailing the birth of Gaṇeśa do provide a temptingly fertile ground for speculations, but the fact remains that none of the Purāṇic accounts tell us that he was born with an elephant's head. And if the accounts agree on one point, it is that the elephant's head was a grafting done to restore or produce a new life, and that the elephant's head was a borrowed item. Thus, prima facie, there is a very clear indication to posit a separate and independent identity of *the* sacred elephant, on the one hand, and that of a son of Śiva and/or Pārvatī on the other, before the merger takes place. Courtright's summary statement that "there is no independent evidence for an elephant cult or a totem; nor is there any archaeological data pointing to a tradition prior to what we see already in place in the Purāṇic literature and the iconography of Gaṇeśa"[128] is not so absolute as he thinks, and it need not discourage a search for this elephant cult. Foucher is right in suggesting that "when dealing with a therianthropomorphic figure of Gaṇeśa's type, we can easily trace it back to the animal prototype from which it came," and in stating that "an objective analysis of the figure of Gaṇeśa and the convincing analogy provided by every ancient form of religion lead us to admit that he made his entry into the world of things sacred under the guise of an elephant."[129] During the period of transformation from a theriomorphic stage to a therianthropomorphic one, morphological compromises of all kinds were imagined by artists and devotees.

Unfortunately, the Purāṇas, which record the textual birth of Gaṇeśa, do not help in the understanding of the details of the process leading to it. While we do not have to go to Egypt as suggested recently by Y. Krishan to import the concept of an elephant-headed god,[130] the questions remain as to when and how the classic image of an elephant-faced Gaṇeśa came into being. Elephants are indigenous to India, and there is hardly any historical basis to establish a sufficiently strong political or cultural link with Egypt to produce the wanted result. And also, in the formulation of the Hellenistic impact in South Asia, it is more reasonable to think of the Iranian input than of the Egyptian.

It is fair to assume that a considerable time elapsed, firstly, between the earliest visual representation of the sacred elephant as an object of worship and the earliest references to it in any literature, and then secondly, between the earliest attempts to produce an elephant-faced deity and the first iconographic description and identity of the elephant-faced Gaṇeśa in literary sources. The question also arises, as Getty has asked, "whether the original form of the elephant-faced deity was conceived in north or in south India."[131] But before we discuss this question we would like to recall Foucher's warning:

> The almost complete absence of ancient documents relating to Gaṇeśa is somewhat disconcerting, for it is evident that without them no historical reconstruction is possible. Yet must one necessarily succumb to the habitual failing of the philologist whose learned candour leads him to infer that all things have their beginning from the time of their first mention in the texts? Such a conclusion would be absurd, for in any given place and moment there are always many more social facts than those recorded in writing.[132]

It should be evident from what we have discussed above that the sacredness of the elephant in South Asia was first recognized in its northwestern regions. Once we leave the material remains of the Harappa culture, the visual evidence for the sacred elephant in the northern and northwestern regions does not appear before the time of Aśoka. About two millenia after the earliest depiction of the theriomorphic elephant on the Harappa seals, it is visible again in the same northwestern region under the patronage of the Greco-Bactrians and the Indo-Greeks; as I have shown in my earlier writings on the subject, the first attempt at therianthropomorphization of an elephant deity took place during their times and under their patronage. In the Harappa culture the basis of the elephant's sacredness is not clear when it appears individually and independently on the seals. However, the elephant's inclusion among the four animals that surround a seated figure, sometime called "Paśupati," on a seal may indicate its associative, or a subordinative, role to a major god. *If* the central figure on the seal is Paśupati Śiva, one may see a parallel association in the Purāṇic stories of the elephant deity Gaṇeśa with Śiva.

But the reasons for the sacredness of the elephant would assumedly vary according to time and space contexts, and by the time the therianthropomorphic Gaṇeśa receives the classic form, these reasons would help to make him not only a pan-Indian, but a pan-Asian, god.

During the later Vedic times, inclusion of theriomorphic elephants in the *Maitrāyaṇī Saṁhitā* and *Taittirīya Āraṇyaka* in the list for *gāyatrī* invocation tells us that the three distinguishing elements of the elephant physique—namely, the face, the curved trunk, and the tusk—are sufficiently sacred to be incorporated in a *gāyatrī japa* and treated on par with some of the well-known Vedic-Brahmanic deities. This status of the elephant-related deities, such as the Hastimukha, might well have been related to totem and ancestor worship, or agrarian rites, of some of the local communities outside the Vedic pale. The association of the elephant Airāvata as a vehicle of Indra had not taken place in the early Vedic period. In any case, Indra and Airāvata were not strong enough to have a cult around them and find a place in the *pañcāyatana*.[133]

The Buddhists, on the other hand, were also naturally eager to give recognition to the sacredness of the elephant, and that resulted in the legends related to the conception of the Buddha. For in them the *deva*s select the elephant to herald the coming of the Buddha, at once the world conqueror and the world renouncer, a universally beneficent role for the happiness and well-being of the people. The elephant was associated with fertility because of its being a symbol for rain in the form of a cloud,[134] and because of this association with fertility it could be used to denote conception.[135] Aśoka not only adored the Excellent Elephant, *Gajatame*, but also included *Hastidasanā* in the pageants of divine spectacles (*divyānī rūpānī*) he organised for the inculcation of his *Dhamma*, which, as he claimed, made it possible for human beings and the *deva*s to commingle (*missībhūtā*).[136] Early Pali Buddhist literature contains references to the group of people, known as the *Hatthivatikas*, who were followers of a belief system (*vata* = *vrata*) that considered the elephant as sacred.[137] A Jātaka story refers to a *Hatthimaha*, a festival dedicated to the sacred elephant.[138]

In much of the northwestern regions of South Asia there is evidence to indicate that the positive and beneficent role of the sacred elephant was associated with the cities and the suburbia on the one hand and with the symbols of mountains, rocks, and stones on the other. Probably the natural rock formations in that region, sometimes taking the shape of an elephant, particularly the frontal part of it, helped in visualizing the majesty and the divinity of this great animal. In this connection we have discussed elsewhere in detail the evidence of the Chinese pilgrim scholar Xuanzang and that of the Indo-Greek coinage.[139] This association with mountains explains incidentally the linguistic equations of the Chinese name *pi-lo-sho-lo*, the Sanskrit *piluśāra*, and the ancient Tamil *piḷḷaiyar.* Perhaps the much later tradition, according to which Gaṇeśa, like Śiva, was popularly worshiped impersonated by a formless (or almost formless) stone called *svayaṁbhū mūrtī*, the most celebrated examples of which are to be found in Kashmir,[140] may have something to do with the idea of the mountain association of the sacred elephant in the northwest. There are three such famous and most powerful *svayaṁbhu mūrtīs* in the Kashmir region, which from ancient times have drawn pilgrims to their shrines.[141] One is near the village of Ganes-bal, in the river Lidar near its right bank. The second is a rock at the foot of the hill Hariparbat near Srinagar. The third and the most remarkable of these *svayaṁbhū mūrtīs* in Kashmir is the one on a cliff along the Kishen-Ganga known as Ganeś-Ghāti.[142]

This mountain association of the elephant in the northwest is also indicated by the later but widely spread Asian traditions regarding Śiva and Gaṇeśa. One may even venture to suggest that when, in the Purāṇic myth, Śiva ordered the gods to bring the head of the first living being they should meet with in the *northern quarter,* which proved to be that of an elephant, he was probably using the expression *north* in a broader sense to include the northwest.[143] It may also be noted here that in the earlier Brahmanic tradition the role models or the ideals came from the northern areas like Uttarakuru and Śvetadvīpa. Mitra thought that "probably Gaṇeśa worship arose in the regions of Northern and North-western India which form the habitat of the elephant."[144]

Thus the origin of Gaṇeśa's most striking feature, his elephant's face, must be sought in the northwest (or the north in general), where elephants are associated with mountains (or rocks or stones). Rather than looking to the Vedic-Brahmanic or any other elite tradition for the source of Gaṇeśa's elephant face, we should look to the popular worship of the elephant in the northwest. This association of the elephant deity with mountains could also help to explain the relevance of the traditions regarding Gaṇeśa in Southeast Asia and East Asia.[145]

It is against this background that the coin types of the Greco-Bactrian and Greco-Indian kings ending with Hermaeus, which we have referred to above, should be viewed. It is indeed surprising how the coins issued by these kings and their Śaka-Pahlava successors in the northwest exhibit several other iconographic attributes and ideas associated with the classic Gaṇeśa of later times. I have already drawn attention to the bell around the neck of the elephant on the coins of Demetrius as well as on those of Maues.[146] This may easily remind one of the Tibetan tradition assigning Gaṇeśa a role of the doorkeeper of Vaiśali.[147] It is interesting to note that on the other side of these very coin types showing the elephant's head with the bell there is a caduceus, showing the two entwined snakes around Apollo's wand.[148] This again would remind one of the *nagabandha,* of the serpent entwined round the belly, of Gaṇeśa.[149] Curiously the ideas of "success," "victory," and "lordship," the well-known qualities attached to the developed Gaṇeśa, may also be noted from these coins. For example, a Demetrius described as "Aniketos" on a square copper coin type is shown wearing an elephant scalp.[150] On the coins of Antialcidas the elephant is shown not only in association with Nike but also as walking victoriously holding the wreath by its trunk.[151] So also, finally, in the elephant's face of Zeus on the unique coin of Hermaeus the idea of lordship acquired from Zeus is indicated; Hastimukha indeed takes over the throne. On the other hand attention may also be drawn here to the coin of the Pahlava king Azilises, where two elephants are shown consecrating a female divinity.[152]

V. Conclusion

The appearance of the elephant-faced Gaṇeśa in history was not a result of transformation of an evil genius into a benign divinity. The elephant, either as a sacred animal or as a theriomorphic deity, is never shown in visual representations or in related textual references as dreadful, ferocious, or with malign intentions. The Hastimukhas and the Dantins of the earliest texts do not find a place in the lists of the *yakṣa*s, the *rākṣasa*s, or the *piśāca*s. They were tutelary deities to be invoked as part of *gāyatri japa* for regeneration, protection, and success. The Excellent Elephant (*Gajatame*) is chosen to herald the coming of the Buddha and to annoint (*abhiṣeka*) the female divinity Śri or Mahāmāyā. In Kapiśa and elsewhere in the northwest it was honored as presiding over cities (*nagara devatā*) or as a mountain deity overseeing the highways of trade. It is well acknowledged that the name Gaṇeśa is not found in any of the lists, literary or epigraphic, of the *yakṣas*. But curiously it is taken for granted that an elephant deity, Hastimukha, was a *vināyaka*. This is not correct, for the names of all the *vināyakas* are mentioned in the relevant texts, and no name indicating elephantine physique is included either in the group of four or even in that of the expanded six. Therefore, while it is one thing to recognize the transformation of the evil *vināyakas* into a Gaṇapati endowed with benign qualities, it is quite another to push the god of the *Hatthivatikas*, the elephant *bhagavat*, into a process that implies two stages of development—*first* degrading it to an evil *vināyaka*, a *vighnakartā*, and *then* transforming it along with the other *vināyakas* into a *vighnahartā* Gaṇapati, in order to create an elephant-faced Gaṇeśa.

This process, however, is not warranted by the evidence we have. It is not that there are no examples of such transformations of evil genii belonging in the "other" group into benign and acceptable gods and goddesses in the religious history of India, for there are such well-known examples as of Rudra and Hārītī. My point is that the elephant-faced (Hastimukha or Gajānana) Gaṇeśa did not go through that process. The transformation of Vināyaka no doubt followed the precedents of Rudra, but the elephant deity, the Hastimukha, had already proven itself as an independent popular deity in South Asia in its own right as endowed with positive qualities before it was identified with the Vedic Gaṇapati and non-Vedic Vināyaka ideas, on the one hand as Bṛhaspati, the Brahmanic god of wisdom, and on the other as Vināyaka-appointed Gaṇeśvara. And a new name Gaṇeśa, not used earlier, was coined for this new god.

I sum up as follows:

1. Gaṇeśa did not originate in the Vedic tradition.
2. Gaṇeśa's origin is primarily related to pre- and non-Vedic traditions of elephant worship prevailing in the northwest, or broadly in the north.
3. Gaṇeśa did not start as a *yakṣa*.
4. The sacredness of the elephant, among other things, was related to mountains.
5. Gaṇeśa was not a *vighnakartā* or *vighneśa* to start with.
6. Gaṇeśa's *gaṇapatitva* was inherited from Vināyaka, who in turn had acquired it from Rudra after having been converted from a malevolent status to a benevolent one.
7. Gaṇapati and Vināyaka did not have the elephant face until they got one after their merger with Hastimukha to make the new god Gaṇeśa.

8. While the earliest theriomorphic representation of the elephant may be dated from the times of the Harappa culture in the second to third millennia B.C., the earliest attempt at therianthropomorphization was made during the first century B.C. under the patronage of the Indo-Greeks.
9. While the sacred elephant and its role were recognized in various ways during the times that followed that of the Indo-Greeks and found expression in extended areas of South Asia in a variety of representations, no example of our Gaṇeśa can be confidently dated before the fourth and fifth centuries A.D. The Kuṣāṇas, who were well known for their numismatic documentation of a large number of gods and goddesses belonging to various cultures, did not select Gaṇeśa.
10. Apart from the elephant face, some of the other iconographic attributes of Gaṇeśa, such as the bell and the *nāgabandha*, may be traced back to the Indo-Greek times of the second to first centuries B.C. So also some of the divine qualities of Gaṇeśa, such as bestowing victory or success, auspiciousness, fertility, and prosperity, were already recognized from pre-Christian times. While none of the ideas and iconographic attributes mentioned above can be specifically related to a Vedic or Purāṇic Brahmanic context of Gaṇeśa, it is not difficult to relate them to non-Brahmanic ones.

ABBREVIATIONS

AB *Aitareya Brāhmaṇa* of the *Ṛgveda*, with commentary of Sāyana Āchārya, edited by Pandit Satyavrata Samasrami, vol. 1, Bibliotheca Indica, Calcutta (Asiatic Society of Bengal), 1895.

AV *Atharva Veda Saṁhitā*, edited by S. D. Satavalekar, Delhi.

AVj. *Angavijjā*, vol. 1, edited by Muni Shri Punyavijayaji, Prakrit Text Society, Banaras, 1957.

BGS *Bodhāyana Gṛhya Sūtra*, edited by R. Shama Sastri, Mysore, 1920. Reprint Delhi, 1982.

BGSS *Bodhāyana Gṛhyaśeṣa Sūtra*, edited by R. Shama Sastri, Mysore, 1920. Reprint Delhi, 1982.

BDS *Baudhāyana Dharma Sūtra*, with *Vivaraṇa* commentary by Sri Govinda Svami, edited with critical notes by A. Chinnaswami Sastri, Varanasi, 1934. Reprinted with Hindi translation, etc., by Umesh Chandra Pandeya, Varanasi (Chowkhamba Sanskrit Series), 1972.

BS *Bṛhatsaṁhitā* of Varāha Mihira, edited by H. Kern, Calcutta (Bibliotheca Indica), 1865.

Jātaka *The Jātaka*, edited by V. Fausboll, London, 1963 (reprint edition).

LP *Linga Purāṇa*, edited by Shri Rama Sharma, Bareli, n.d.

MBH *Mahābhārata*, edited by V. S. Sukthankar et al., Poona, 1933–69.

MDS *Mānavadharma Śāstra*, with commentary of Medhātithī, Bibliotheca Indica, Calcutta, 1932.

MGS *Mānava Gṛhya Sūtra*, with commentary of Aṣṭāvakra, edited by Friedrich Knaner, St. Petersburg, 1897.

MNds *Mahāniddesa*, edited by Louis de la Vallee Poussin and E. J. Thomas, (PTS ed.), parts 1 and 2, London, 1916–17. Reprint, 1978.

MP *Milindapañho*, edited by V. Trenckner, London/Edinburgh, 1880.

MS *Maitrāyaṇī Saṁhitā, Die Saṁhitā der Maitrāyaṇi-Śākhā*, edited by Leopold von Schroeder, Wiesbaden, 1881. Reprint, 1970. Also reprinted by Ramakrishna Harshaji Sastri, Delhi, 1982.

RV *Ṛgveda Saṁhitā*, together with commentary of Sāyanāchārya, edited by F. Max Müller, 2d ed., London, 1892. Reprint Varanasi, 1966.

TA *Taittirīya Āraṇyaka*, with commentary of Sāyanāchārya, edited by Rajendralala Mitra, Bibliotheca Indica, Calcutta, 1872. Anandasrama Series, no. 36. Poona, 1897–98.

TB *Taittirīya Brāhmaṇa.*

TS *Taittirīya Saṁhitā.*

YS *Yājñavalkya Smṛtī*, with commentary *Bālakrīḍā* of Viśvarūpāchārya, edited by T. Ganapati Sastri, Trivandrum, 1921 – 22. Reprint Delhi, 1982.

NOTES

1. This is in continuation of my earlier presentations and papers on the subject. My first statement on this was made in 1973 at Paris in a paper read at the Twenty-Seventh International Congress of Human Sciences in Asia and North Africa, and later at Varanasi in my "Presidential Address at the Diamond Jubilee Conference of the Numismatic Society of India 1973," *The Journal of the Numismatic Society of India*, 36 (1974):180–91. Later two short articles were published in 1978 and 1982: "On the Earliest Gaṇeśa," in *Senart Paranavitana Commemoration Volume*, ed. Leelananada Prematileke Karthigesu Indrapala and J. E. van Lohuizen-de Leeuw (Leiden: Brill, 1978), 162–66; and "Ganesa on Hermaeus' Coin," *Numismatic Digest* 6 (1982):26–29. An expanded version, analyzing and elaborating the numismatic evidence, was presented at the Thirty-Sixth Annual Conference of the Association of Asian Studies at Washington, D.C., in 1984 and published later in 1988 [A. K. Narain, "Iconographic Origins of Gaṇeśa and the Evidence on Indo-Greek Coin-

age," *Orientalia Iosephi Tucci Memoriae Dicata,* ed. G. Gnoli and L. Lanciotti, Serie Oriental Roma, 56, no. 3 (Rome: Instituto Italiano per il Medio ed Estremeo Oriente, 1988):1007–19].

2. For standard surveys see Alice Getty, *Gaṇeśa: A Monograph on the Elephant-faced God* (Oxford: Clarendon Press, 1936); Paul B. Courtright, *Gaṇeśa: Lord of Obstacles, Lord of Beginnings* (New York: Oxford University Press, 1985); R. G. Bhandarkar, *Vaiṣṇavism, Śaivism, and Minor Religious Systems* (Varanasi: Indological Book House, 1965); and Ananda Coomaraswamy, "Gaṇeśa," *Bulletin of the Museum of Fine Arts* 34 (1978):30–31.

3. Courtright, *Gaṇeśa,* 218–20.

4. Courtright, *Gaṇeśa,* 252.

5. The aspect of "suddenness" of his appearance has been noted by many scholars. See, for example, Coomaraswamy, "Gaṇeśa," 30; Getty, *Gaṇeśa,* 13, 25; and Courtright, *Gaṇeśa,* 8.

6. Claims of an earlier date have been made for some examples found in Mathurā and Afghanistan, but they are essentially based on stylistic considerations, and there is no scholarly consensus. D. B. Diskalkar ["Some Brahmanical Sculptures in the Mathura Museum," *Journal of the U. P. Historical Society* 5, pt. 1 (1932): 45–47] was the first to draw attention to three examples in the Mathurā Museum (nos. 792, 964, 1170) and stated that "these images seem to have belonged to a period from the 1st to 3rd century A.D." He neither illustrated them [see Brown, infra, figs. 5 (no. 964) and 6 (no. 792)] nor gave any reasons for his dating; presumably he dated them on stylistic considerations. A specimen in the typical Mathurā red sandstone found in the Fatehgrah district is referred to and illustrated in Getty [*Gaṇeśa,* 26, pl. II.2a] as "the most ancient representation of the god in stone as yet discovered." But Getty does not specify the date. Vasudeva S. Agrawala [*Mathura Museum Catalogue, Part 3: Jain Tirthankaras and Other Miscellaneous Figures* (Varanasi: Prithivi Prakashan, 1963), 106–7] refers to "five elephant-headed Yakshas showing the earliest representation of the Gaṇeśa figure in Mathura art, perhaps an offshoot of Kubera iconography" and dates them to the Kuṣāṇa period.

M. K. Dhavalikar ["A Note on Two Gaṇeśa Statues from Afghanistan," *East and West,* 21 nos. 3–4 (1971):333–36] thought the Sakar Dhar image (see Dhavalikar, infra, fig. 2) the earliest Gaṇeśa (about the middle of the fourth century A.D.) and noted that another example from Salempur (Mathurā Museum no. 758, see Brown, infra, fig. 8) should be assigned to circa fifth to sixth century A.D. He dates the Gardez image (see Dhavalikar, infra, fig. 1) to the second half of the fifth. (Dhavalikar reconfirms these dates in his article in this volume.) These dates agree with those of T. N. Ramachandran and Y. D. Sharma in *Archaeological Reconnaissance in Afghanistan. Preliminary Report of the Indian Archaeological Delegation* (New Delhi, 1956; for private circulation), who date the Sakar Dhar image to the fourth century and the Gardez image to the latter half of the fifth century or early sixth (on the basis of the paleography of its inscription). (For the inscription see EI XXXV 1963–64, 44–47.) Also see Giuseppe Tucci, "Preliminary Report on an Archaeological Survey in Swat," *East and West* 9, no. 4 (1958):279–328; and R. C. Agrawala, "Ūrdhvaretas Gaṇeśa from Afghanistan," *East and West,* 18, nos. 1–2 (1968):166–68.

An architectural fragment in the Mathurā Museum (no. 509) showing a "two-armed Gaṇapati standing in a spirited pose in profile to his right on a cluster of lotus buds whose triple stalk rises from below" has been dated in the "Gupta Period'' by V. S. Agrawala [''Catalogue of the Mathura Museum Architectural Pieces,'' *Journal of the U. P. Historical Society* 24–25 (1951–52):96].

I do not feel confident in dating the Mathurā specimens mentioned above as belonging to the Kuṣāṇa period only on stylistic grounds. Firstly, the numismatic documentation of the gods and goddesses provided by the Kuṣāṇas is so large, and the Kuṣāṇas were so eclectic in their religious beliefs, that Gaṇeśa's conspicuous absence on their coins indicates that his images were yet to be made in Mathurā. Secondly, even if the examples mentioned above can be dated in the second to third century A.D., the crude workmanship and other features, like exhibiting the genitals, indicate in fact that the popular elephant-deity (Hastimukha?) had not yet become Gaṇeśa.

Yet one final identification of an early Gaṇeśa image is made by Getty (*Gaṇeśa*, 26), who refers to ''a small terra-cotta bas-relief which was found at the ancient site of Akra, NWFP, where pre-Gupta objects as early as the 2nd century have been discovered,'' as ''probably one of the earliest images of Gaṇeśa.'' She adds, nevertheless, that the figure of Gaṇeśa is certainly not earlier than the fifth century.

For a somewhat different opinion from my own regarding the early date of Gaṇeśa images, see Robert L. Brown's introduction (supra) and article (infra).

7. Among the important ones see, for example, Bhandarkar, *Vaiṣṇavism;* Coomaraswamy, ''Gaṇeśa''; Getty, *Gaṇeśa;* Alfred Foucher, ''Introduction'' in Getty, *Gaṇeśa;* Narain, ''Iconographic Origins of Gaṇeśa,'' 1007–19; M. K. Dhavalikar, ''Antiquity of Gaṇeśa: The Numismatic Evidence,'' *Indologica Taurinensia* 8–9 (Torino, 1980–81):137–45; Dhavalikar, ''Two Gaṇeśa Statues,'' 331–36; Y. Krishan, ''Origins of Gaṇeśa,'' *Artibus Asiae* 43 (1981–82):285–301; Courtright, *Gaṇeśa*, 3–13; Herbert Risley, *The People of India*, vol. 2 (repr., Delhi: Oriental Books Reprint, 1969), 113; William Crooke, *Popular Religion and Folklore of Northern India*, vol. 1 (New Delhi: Munshiram Manohar Lal, 1968), 184; D. D. Kosambi, *Myth and Reality* (Bombay: Popular Prakashan, 1962), 25; and G. S. Ghurye, *Gods and Men* (Bombay: Popular Book Depot, 1962), 51–90.

8. Courtright, *Gaṇeśa*, 12.

9. Some scholars have argued that Śiva was within the Vedic fold. See Doris M. Srinivasan, ''Vedic Rudra-Śiva,'' *Journal of the American Oriental Society* 103, no. 3 (July–September 1983):543–56.

10. See for example, Edmund R. Leach, ''Pulleyar and the Lord Buddha: An Aspect of Religious Syncretism in Ceylon,'' *Psychoanalysis and the Psychoanalytic Review* 49, no. 2 (1962); Wendy O'Flaherty, *Ascetism and Eroticism in the Mythology of Śiva* (Oxford: Oxford University Press, 1973); Wendy O'Flaherty, *Hindu Myths* (London: Penguin, 1976); Wendy O'Flaherty, *Women, Androgynes and Other Mythical Beasts* (Chicago: University of Chicago Press, 1980); and Courtright, *Gaṇeśa.*

11. In *Mudgala Purāṇa*, Gaṇeśa is given thirty-two names, and in the *Śāradātilaka* there are fifty-one *dhāraṇīs* where he is invoked under different names representing different aspects. Again, a variety of images described in later iconographic texts provide another subvariety of names depending upon various attributes, roles, and legends. See Getty, *Gaṇeśa*, 13 and her selection of various names on p. xxiv.

12. M. Monier-Williams, *An English-Sanskrit Dictionary* (Oxford: Clarendon Press, 1899), 343.

13. *yathā vā pana mahārāja mahīyā gaṇa vattanti, seyyathīdam . . . Maṇibhada Puṇṇabaddha . . . Sivā Vasudevā . . . Milindapañho*, ed. V. Trenckner (London/Edinburgh: Williams and Norgate, 1880), 191; cf. also I. B. Horner, *Milinda's Questions*, vol. 1 (London: Luzac, 1963), 271–72; and V. S. Agrawala, *Ancient Indian Folk Cults* (Varanasi: Prithivi Prakashan, 1970), 11.

14. Monier-Williams, *Dictionary*, 343.

15. *RV* 2.23.1 (*gaṇānaṁ tvā gaṇapatim havāmahe*). Here *gaṇa* means the assembly of gods, and *gaṇapati*, the divine priest, the Vedic god of wisdom, Bṛhaspati; cf. Bhandarkar, *Vaiṣṇavism*, 149.

16. *RV* II.23.1,4,6,14 and 15; I.40.3. Bṛhaspati and Brahmaṇaspati are identical and not different from each other. For a comprehensive study of Bṛhaspati in the Vedas and Purāṇas see Saraswati Bali, *Bṛhaspati in the Vedas and the Purāṇas* (Delhi: Nag Publishers, 1978).

17. Jyeṣṭha and Jyeṣṭharāja are known as epithets of Gaṇeśa in the Purāṇas and subsequent literature (e.g., *SKP Kāśīkhaṇḍa*, 57.102; *Bṛhatstotraratnākara*, 15th ed., Bombay, 1963:25,27,32). P. K. Agrawala, *Goddess Vināyakī, the Female Gaṇeśa* (Varanasi: Prithivi Prakashan, 1978), 6–7, has argued on the basis of the *Sarvānukramaṇī* that Jyeṣṭharāja (i.e., Gaṇapati) is mentioned in another later passage of the *Ṛgveda* (X.155.1–4), in connection with the destruction of Alakṣmī, and links him with Vināyaka on the basis of the *Sarvānukramaṇī* of *AV* I.18.1–4. But it would be anachronistic for our purposes here to take this into account, and it may be noted that now in some of the critical editions of the Vedic texts the *Sarvānukramaṇī* is not included.

18. *RV* II.23.3,17; II.24.8; IV.50.1,4; V.43.12; VII.97.8. For more references and study, cf. Bali, *Bṛhaspati*, 12–13.

19. *Linga Purāṇa*, vol. 11, 117, verse 11. cf. Bali, *Bṛhaspati*, 176.

20. *RV* X.112.9; III.35.7,9.

21. *RV* VI.21.12; X.111.3.

22. *AB* I.21.

23. *TS* 4.1.2.2; *MS* 2.7.2, 3.1.3.

24. A. B. Keith and A. A. Macdonell, *Vedic Index of Names and Subjects*, vol. 1 (repr., Varanasi: Motilal Banarsidass, 1958), 217–49, do not list Gaṇapati as a personal name.

25. *AV* XI.5.1–23; also V. S. Agrawala, "Catalogue," 3–7.

26. *BDS* II.9.7.

27. Cf. *BGS* II.8.9. It occurs in the same list that includes many deities individually like Agni, Soma, Isana, Jayanta, Dharma, Dhanvantari, Ambikā, etc., as well as some mentioned in groups like the *gaṇas*, *devas*, etc.

28. R. C. Hazra, "Gaṇapati Worship and the Upapurāṇas Dealing With It," *Journal of the Ganganatha Jha Research Institute* 5 (1948):271, nn. 33–34, has noted that this is found only in Chowkhamba Sanskrit Series editions.

29. The reference to Gaṇeśa as a scribe of Vyāsa (*MBH* I App. 1, lines 7–15, 39ff.; also *MBH* 1862 I.I.65–73) is generally considered by scholarly consensus as a later interpolation.

30. *MBH* I.74.75; III.1629.

31. Cf. *MBH* XIII. 150.25, "*Isvaraḥ sarva-lokānaṁ gaṇeśvara-vināyakāḥ.*" It may be noted that there is no reference to an individual and benevolent Vināyaka here; this is a reference to the numerous malevolent evil spirits. See also Hazra, "Gaṇapati Worship," 267.

32. Monier-Williams, *Dictionary,* 343.

33. *BGSS* II.10.9.

34. The passage reads, "*viprānāṁ daivataṁ Śambhūḥ kṣatriyāṇāṁ tu Mādhavaḥ, vaiśyānāṁ tu bhaved Brahmā śūdrāṇām Gaṇanāyakah.*" M. Monier-Williams, *Brahmanism and Hinduism* (London: J. Murray, 1887), 212n., and Getty, *Gaṇeśa,* 2.

35. This text is not found in the present scholarly editions of *Manusmṛti.* Hazra, "Gaṇapati Worship," 268, calls it "quite a modern forgery," and this appears to be the scholarly consensus.

36. Monier-Williams, *Dictionary,* 971–72.

37. Monier-Williams, *Dictionary,* 971–72. In this sense a spiritual preceptor, such as a Buddha, could be Vināyaka.

38. Monier-Williams, *Dictionary,* 971.

39. For Viśvarūpa's commentary *Bālakrīḍā* on *YS,* cf. T. Gaṇapati Sastri, ed., *Yājñavalkya Smṛti* (Trivandrum, 1921; repr., Delhi: Maunsirama Manoharalala, 1982):174.

40. Monier-Williams does not give these meanings, but depending upon the *upasarga,* change in the meaning is not unusual.

41. *MGS* II.14. But cf. R. G. Bhandarkar, *Vaiṣṇavism,* 148, where he states that the *YS* refers to six instead of four names and these are said to be different names of the Vināyaka.

42. Hazra, "Gaṇapati Worship," 263–64.

43. *MG* II.14.26. There is no mention of the use of the *Ṛgvedic mantra, "gaṇānāṁ tvā gaṇapatim . . . ,"* which is addressed to Bṛhaspati in the *RV* 2.31.

44. *MBH* XII.284.131, "*na rākṣasā na piśācā na bhuta na Vināyakaḥ. vighnaṁ kuryrghe tasya yattrāyaṁ paṭhyate stavaḥ.*"

45. *MBH* III.65.23; XII.284.131; XIII.150.25.

46. *BDS* II.9.7. This text is considered as a later interpolation. P. V. Kane, *History of Dharmeśāstra,* vol. 2, pt. 7 (Poona: Bhandarkar Oriental Research Institute, 1941), 214; Hazra, "Gaṇapati Worship," 271. In any regard, we will not be surprised if at least some of the names like Lambodara, Ekadanta, and even Gaṇapati prove to be later interpolations in the text.

47. *BGSS* III.10.

48. *BGSS* III.10.2,9.

49. *YS* I.11.267.

50. *YS* I.11.267. The passage does not assign the name Gaṇapati to Vināyaka. Also, he does not appear to have been freed from the negative roles unless propitiated and/or purified (*pāvanaṁ kṛtaṁ*) by the grace of Varuṇa, Surya, Bṛhaspati, Indra, Vāyu, and the Saptarṣīs (I.11.277–9). Moreover, the text does not recommend doing away with the *homa* offerings to the four *vināyakas*: Mita, Sammita, Sālakaṭaṇkaṭa, and Kuṣmāṇḍarājaputra (I.11.281). It may be noted further that this list varies from the one in the *Mānava Gṛhyasūtra* mentioned above in as much as

Mita and Sammita have replaced Uṣmita and Devayajana. But the number of *vināyakas* remains as four in the *YS* as well as in the later text of the *Viṣṇudharmottara* (II.105.19). As Hazra has pointed out ("Gaṇapati Worship," 265–66) it was Vijñāneśvara who broke up the four names into six without any authority, and his version was followed with minor changes in *Garuḍa Purāṇa, Bhaviṣya Purāṇa,* and *Devī Purāṇa*. Hazra considers this incorrect. But J. N. Banerjea, *Pauranic and Tantric Religion (Early Phase)* (Calcutta: University of Calcutta, 1966), 152, has counted the number of these *vināyakas* as six, although it is clearly stated, even by the commentator Viśvarūpa, "catvāro Vināyakamantrāḥ"; cf. Ganapati Sastri, ed., *Yājñavalkya Smṛti,* 177; perhaps Banerjea chose to be guided by the version of Vijñāneśvara.

51. In the *Śri Gaṇapati Atharvaśirṣa,* a Rudra is known as one of the *vināyakas*. But this text is a very late one; it has been dated from the sixteenth century to as late as even the nineteenth century A.D. See Courtright, *Gaṇeśa,* 252.

52. See for example Getty, *Gaṇeśa,* 3, and Banerjea, *Pauranic,* 152.

53. See Bhandarkar, *Vaiṣṇavism,* 148; Getty, *Gaṇeśa,* 3; Banerjea, *Pauranic,* 152; and J. N. Banerjea, *The Development of Hindu Iconography,* 2d ed. (Calcutta: University of Calcutta, 1956), 355.

54. *YS* I.11.285. "*Durvāsarṣapakalkena dattvārghyaṁ pūrmāñjaliṁ. Pūrvamantraireva. Vināyaka jananimupatiṣthet tato>mbikāṁ.*"

55. Cf. *YS* 1982:178. The commentary reads, "*Ambika cattra Buddhirucyate. sa hyasubhnimittam lobhādim janayati. yadvā, devyevambikā rudrapatnī, adhikaranityatvenetyubhayathapyadoṣah.*"

56. Monier-Williams, *Dictionary,* 957.

57. Monier-Williams, *Dictionary,* 957.

58. See the list in Getty, *Gaṇeśa,* xxiv.

59. See for example Getty, *Gaṇeśa,* pl. 4b.

60. See for the Purāṇic accounts, Getty, *Gaṇeśa,* 3–7, and Courtright, *Gaṇeśa,* 74–90, 117.

61. *MS* II.9.1. Note the word *Karāṭa,* etc.

62. *TA* X.1.5 In the same passage there is another word, *cakratuṇḍa,* that has been ignored by scholars. This refers to the sacred bull.

63. *BDS* II.9.7. The four names are Hastimukha, Vakrataṇḍa, Ekadanta, and Lambodara. See also II.5.83 – 90 for a rite called *deva-tarpaṇa,* quoted in Hazra, "Gaṇapati Worship," 271 and according to him of doubtful authenticity.

64. *BGS* III.10.2.6.

65. See Hazra, "Gaṇapati Worship," 271, nn. 33–34. In regard to this passage from the *BDS* and another from the *BGSS* Hazra states that "these portions of the two works are of doubtful authenticity." There is no doubt that at least names like Ekadanta and Lambodara must have been included in the list of *Baudhāyana Dharmasūtra* only after the elephant-faced Gaṇeśa idea and form materialized.

66. It is also very clear from going through the entire khaṇḍa that the names mentioned in various passages are mostly not used as synonyms for one and the same god but as names of individual gods in their own rights.

67. Hazra, "Gaṇapati Worship," 271, has drawn attention to the fact that this name, as well as that of Vināyaka, in these texts are found only in the editions of the Chowkhamba Sanskrit Series.

68. But see Banerjea, *Hindu Iconography,* 576–77.

69. While commenting on *Varttika 2 of Pāṇinī' Sūtra VI.3.26 (Devatādvandve ca),* Patañjali in his *Mahābhāṣya* appears to distinguish between two different types of divinities, namely, *Vaidika* and *Laukika*. Cf. Banerjea, *Hindu Iconography,* 337.

70. Cf. *Milindapañho.*

71. See Banerjea, *Hindu Iconography,* chap. 9; also A. K. Narain, "First Images of the Buddha and Bodhisattva," *Studies in the Buddhist Art of South Asia,* ed. A. K. Narain (New Delhi: Kanak Publications, 1985):2–3. It is not necessary here to go into the question of whether the non-Vedic element was of Dravidian or of Austric (Munda) origin.

72. For illustrations and reference see Radha Kumud Mookerji, *Aśoka* (Delhi: Motilal Banarasidas, 1962), 170, pl. 11.

73. See for example Rock Edict IV: "*Vimānadasanā ca Hastidasanā ca Agikhandhāni ca aññāni divyānī rūpāni dasayitvā. . . .*" [R. G. Basak, ed., *Aśokan Inscriptions* (Calcutta: Progressive Publishers, 1959), 14–21. The Girnar text adds at the end, on the right side, the following isolated sentence: *(Sa)rva sveto hasti sarva loka sukhakaro nāma*. At Kalsi, a figure of an elephant is incised with the legend *gaj(o)tame.* The animal figures carved on the capitals of the Aśokan columns have been taken by some scholars to stand for gods in animal forms; cf. J. N. Banerjea, *Hindu Iconography,* 96–98.

74. Jātaka no. 455, *The Jātaka,* vol. 3, ed. E. B. Crowell, trans. H. T. Francis and R. A. Neil (London: Luzac, 1969), 58–61. "The king had a stone image made in the figure of the Bodhisattva, and great honour he paid to this. There the inhabitants of all India year by year gathered together, to perform what was called the Elephant Festival" (61).

Foucher in "Introduction," xvii, has referred to quite an analogous festival still celebrated at Iradatpur in the Fatehpur district of Uttar Pradesh, at which pilgrims gather every year around a stone image of the eponymous animal.

75. *Mahaniddesa,* chap. 4 in the *Suddhatthakasuttaniddeso,* pp. 89, 92–93, and chap. 13 in *Mahāviyūhasuttaniddeso,* p. 310. Cf. Bhandarkar, *Vaiṣṇavism,* 3.

76. Getty, *Gaṇeśa,* 3.

77. Cf. P. C. Bagchi, "Some Linguistic Notes," *The Indian Historical Quarterly* 9, no. 1 (1933):259.

78. Bagchi, "Some Linguistic Notes," 259. Also T. W. Rhys Davids, *Pali-English Dictionary* (New Delhi: Oriental Books Reprint, 1975), 460.

79. Robert Caldwell, *A Comparative Grammar of the Dravidian or South Indian Family of Languages* (Madras: University of Madras, 1976), 601.

80. Caldwell, *A Comparative Grammar,* 601. Also Bagchi, "Some Linguistic Notes," 258–65. It is interesting to note that in modern Hindi also it means the same, particularly for a dog's puppies.

81. Sylvain Levi, "Notes Indiennes," *Journal Asiatique* (1925):46–57.

82. J. Przyluski, *Bulletin de la Société de Linguistique de Paris* (1926):218–19.

83. Leach, "Pulleyar," 81–83. But we find it difficult to agree with Leach's analysis and conclusions, which are based on assumptions made arbitrarily and which often entail contradictions. Space does not permit here to go into this, as well as some other psychoanalytic studies of Gaṇeśa, but I purpose to deal with them in a separate article elsewhere.

84. Aramaic was in use in the eastern parts of the Achaemenid empire, i.e., in the Kabul-Gandhara region.

85. Thomas Watters, *On Yuan Chwang's Travels in India 629–645 A.D.* (London: Royal Asiatic Society, 1904), 126–29; see Narain, "Iconographic Origins of Gaṇeśa," 1014–19 for discussion of Xuanzhang's account.

86. Watters, *Yuan Chwang's Travels,* 217–18. See also Bagchi, "Linguistic Notes," 259–60. Attention may be drawn to two place names. One, Po-lu-sha, a name supposed to provide the sense of "elephant's trunk" and related to the story in the *Vessantara Jātaka* about Sudanta, the name of the much-prized white elephant that Vessantara gave away. The second is Tan-to-lo-ka, the name of a location near Po-lu-sha. This name is generally restored as Danta-loka, with which another legend of the Bodhisattva's sacrifice is connected. Bagchi states that "in the region's north-western zone in the region of Piluśāra and Palusha a few other place-names also had connection with elephant in some way. The name of Pushkarāvati has probably been preserved in that of modern Hastnagar 'the city of elephant' with which it is identified. Puskara is one of the names of elephant and it is therefore not impossible that in ancient times it really meant the 'city of elephant,' like Hastinapura of the Kurus and Varanāvata of the Pāṇḍavas. It is not without significance that the historians of Alexander mention a king called Astes (Hasti) as ruling over a people called Astacians (Hastikas) living in the region of Puskarāvati." (260)

87. Getty, *Gaṇeśa,* 25.

88. See note 6 above.

89. Coomaraswamy, "Gaṇeśa," 30; Foucher, "Introduction," xxviii–xx; Getty, *Gaṇeśa,* 25–27; Banerjea, *Hindu Iconography,* 359; Narain, "Presidential Address," 190; and Y. Krishan, "Origins of Gaṇeśa," 287–88, 300–1.

90. Coomaraswamy, "Gaṇeśa," 30. For illustration see James Burgess, *The Buddhist Stupas of Amaravati and Jaggayyapeta* (repr., Varanasi: Indological Book House, 1970), pl. XXX, i; and Coomaraswamy, "Gaṇeśa," pl. 23, fig. 1.

91. Getty, *Gaṇeśa,* 25.

92. V. S. Agrawala, *Mathura Museum Catalogue, Part III,* 106–7. See P. K. Agrawala, *Goddess Vināyakī,* 4 and illustration no. 1.

93. Agrawala, *Goddess Vināyakī,* 4.

94. Agrawala, *Goddess Vināyakī,* 4, has used this name as that of a *yakṣa,* but this name is not included in any list of *yakṣa*s.

95. S. Paranavitana, "Mahāyānism in Ceylon," *Ceylon Journal of Science* 4, pt. 1 (London, 1928); see Getty, *Gaṇeśa,* 25, pl. 22, fig. c.

96. Getty, *Gaṇeśa,* 25.

97. See note 1 above.

98. Narain, "Iconographic Origins of Gaṇeśa," 1017–19.

99. The practice of making temporary ritual images and destroying them after the ritual of worship is over is very well known in India. It includes large images of Gaṇeśa and Durgā, as well as smaller ones of gods, goddesses, and sacred animals.

100. Cf. *Sylloge nummorum graecorum* (Copenhagen, 1942–69), pl. 4.172. See also H. H. Scullard, "Hannibal's Elephants," *Numismatic Chronicle* (1948):159.

101. M. Mitchener, *Indo-Greek and Indo-Scythian Coinages,* vol. 1 (London: Hawkins, 1975), 57–58, 61, 79; vol. 2, 142–43.

102. Mitchener, *Coinages*, vol. 1, 60.

103. Mitchener, *Coinages*, vol. 5, 469.

104. Getty, *Gaṇeśa*, 26.

105. Mitchener, *Coinages*, vol. 1, 75; vol. 2, 115–17.

106. P. Gardner, *The Coins of the Greek and Scythic Kings of Bactria and India in the British Museum* (repr., Chicago: Argonaut, 1966), 125–27; pl. 25, 6–7, 11, and 14.

107. Narain, "Iconographic Origins of Gaṇeśa," 1009–19.

108. Banerjea, *Hindu Iconography*, pl. 9.

109. Foucher, "Introduction," xix.

110. Leach, "Pulleyar," 93–98.

111. Getty, *Gaṇeśa*, 68–69; The earliest *dated* sculpture of an elephant-faced deity known in East Asia is the bas-relief in the Buddhist grotto-temple of Kung-hsien, which, according to the inscription, was executed in A.D. 531. According to the Chinese characters he is the "Spirit King of Elephants" and is figured with nine other inferior deities or "Spirit Kings." This same group is also represented on the base of a Buddhist monument dated A.D. 543, now in Boston.

112. For the Mathurā example see Agrawala, *Goddess Vināyakī*, ill. no. 4 and enlargement as frontispiece; and for the Rairh example, ill. no. 5.

113. R. D. Banerji, "The Haihayas of Tripuri and Their Monuments," *Archaeological Survey of India. Memoirs* no. 23 (1931):85. Also see P. K. Agrawala, *Goddess Vināyakī*, 1–3.

114. This will depend upon the identity of the so-called Yogi figure on the Harappa seals. If it is Paśupati-Śiva, then one may argue in favor of this hypothesis. But as there are other theories also in this respect, I would prefer to keep this question open for the time being.

115. The first time was when the authors of the Vedic civilization interacted with the non-Vedic elements in South Asia. The second major interaction took place in the post-Mauryan period, between the indigenous elements, on the one hand, and the Yavana, Śaka, Pahlava, and Kuṣāṇa elements on the other. Although these interactions were an ongoing process in South Asia and contiguous areas, the two major periods of interaction were crucial to the formulation of the Brahmanical system of beliefs and rituals.

116. Banerjea, *Hindu Iconography*, 84ff., 540–63; Narain, "First Images," 2–5.

117. Compare *BGSS* III.10.2, 9. There are other well-known examples of similar transformation, e.g., of that of Hārītī. Ananda Coomaraswamy, *Yakṣas*, pt. 1 (repr., New Delhi: Munshiram Manohar Lal, 1971), 9.

118. *BGSS* III.10.1.

119. *BGSS* III.10.5.

120. *BGSS* III.10.6.

121. Compare the Purāṇic version (*Śiva Purāṇa*, 2.5.13–14) of fight between the *gaṇas* of Śiva and those of Pārvatī. See Courtright, *Gaṇeśa*, 63–65.

122. Cf. *Bodhayānagṛhyaśeṣasūtra* III.10.1–2. "*Athato Vinayākakalpaṁ vyākhyāsyāmaḥ:- māsimāsi caturthyāṁ śuklapakṣaasya pañcamyāṁ vabhyudayādau siddhikāmaḥ ṛddikāmaḥ paśukāmo va bhagavato Vinayākasya baliṁ haret\\ pūrvedyuḥ kṛtaikabhuktaḥ.*"

123. Banerjea, *Hindu Iconography*, 355.

124. *BS* chap. 58, v. 58. But H. Kern [*Bṛhat Sanhita of Varāhamihira* (Calcutta, 1865), 46, 322] thought that it was an interpolation. See also Getty, *Gaṇeśa*, 62, and Banerjea, *Hindu Iconography*, 354.

125. See *Harṣacarit*, 4th *Ucchvāsa*, v. 2, ed. P. V. Kane, 2d ed. (Delhi: Motilal Banarsidass, 1965), 1, in notes section.

126. *Mālatīmādhava*, the opening verse no. 1, See *Bhavabhuti's Malataimadhava with the Commentary of Jagaddhara*, ed. M. R. Kale (Delhi: Motilal Banarsidass, 1967), 1. But note that the text here refers to Vināyaka. It is in the commentary of Jagaddhara that Vināyaka is described as "Gajānana," i.e., as having an elephant's face. Also it may be noted that it is the *cītkāra* (sound expressive of fear) of Vināyaka that is emphasized. See also Bhandarkar, *Vaiṣṇavism*, 159.

127. It is interesting to note that in these references of Bāṇabhaṭṭa and Bhavabhūtī, as well as of others quoted by Hazra, "Gaṇapati Worship," 270–71, the name Gaṇeśa is not used; they use either Vināyaka or Gaṇapati. It seems to confirm that the idea of the fully fledged Gaṇeśa is preceded by two stages, in the first of which Vināyaka is made a Gaṇeśvara or Gaṇapati and admitted to the family of Śiva, and in the second of which this merged Gaṇapati-Vināyaka receives an elephant's face.

128. Courtright, *Gaṇeśa*, 11.

129. Foucher, "Introduction," xvi.

130. Krishan, "Origins of Gaṇeśa," 300.

131. Getty, *Gaṇeśa*, 25.

132. Foucher, "Introduction," xvii.

133. Airāvata became one of the *diggajas*, one of the elephants guarding the eight quarters, subordinate to Gaṇeśa.

134. Courtright, *Gaṇeśa*, 22–23.

135. Courtright, *Gaṇeśa*, 30.

136. Cf. Minor Rock Edict 1, Basak ed., *Aśokan Inscriptions*, 134–35, *"imina ca kālena (a)misā munisā devehi te dāni misibhūtā. pakamasa hi (esa phale)."*

137. *Mahāniddesa*, 89, 92–93.

138. Jātaka, no. 455.

139. Narain, "Iconographic Origins of Gaṇeśa," 1014–17.

140. Getty, *Gaṇeśa*, 22–23.

141. Getty, *Gaṇeśa*, 22. She cites Foucher for information.

142. Aurel Stein, trans., *Kalhana's Rājataranginī: A Chronicle of the Kings of Kashmir*, vol. 2 (Westminster: Archibald Constable, 1900), 311, writes that "on a face of grey limerock, about fifty feet high, nature has formed a long projecting nose which curiously resembles the head of an elephant with the trunk hanging down. . . . This shows plainly where pious tradition places the head of the elephant-faced god which has given its name to the hill." Getty states (*Gaṇeśa*, 23) following this quote from Stein, "In the mythical land of Jambudvipa there was a mountain in the shape of an elephant called Vinataka, often confused with Vināyaka. The result was that in every Buddhist country where there was a hill or mountain which was vaguely in the form of the head of an elephant, the worship of Gaṇeśa was set up and a place of pilgrimage established. Thus, from an unimportant deity, Gaṇeśa, 'Remover of Obstacles,' grew in popularity and was taken up not only by the Buddhist but by all the Hindu sects."

143. *SP* 2.4.17.47. See, for a summary of brief references, Coomaraswamy, "Gaṇeśa," 30; Courtright, *Gaṇeśa*, 34.

144. *Encyclopaedia Brittanica*, 11th ed., s.v. "Himalaya and Elephant," refers to the past and present distributions of elephants in India and also draws attention to the connection of elephants with Gaṇeśa worship as known from Tantric and Śaivāgamika texts from west and south India respectively.

145. Getty, *Gaṇeśa*, 54.

146. See notes 102 and 103, above.

147. See Getty, *Gaṇeśa*, 26–27, for a curious statue of Gaṇeśa found at Bhumra; and Coomaraswamy, *Yakṣas*, 7, 14, for the Tibetan tradition.

148. For illustration of the caduceus see Mitchener, *Coinages*, vol. 1, 60; vol. 5, 469.

149. For the *nāgabandha* see, for example, Krishan, "Origins of Gaṇeśa," fig. 3 among others.

150. Mitchener, *Coinages*, vol. 1, 61; see note 103 above.

151. Mitchener, *Coinages*, vol. 2, 148, Type 273.

152. Mitchener, *Coinages*, vol. 6, 512, Type 785.

2

Gaṇeśa: Myth and Reality

M. K. Dhavalikar*

Gaṇeśa, the elephant-headed god, is one of the most important divinities of the Hindu pantheon. Although he is a very popular god, as he is invoked for success at the beginning of every undertaking—the god being the success grantor, Siddhidātā—his admission into the hierarchy of major divinities was quite late, sometime in the late Gupta times in the sixth century A.D. But he gained importance in a short period of time; so much so, that the cult of Gāṇapatyas came into being in the ninth century A.D. The main reason for this appears to be that the god was first the obstacle creator (*vighna-kartā*) and later became the obstacle averter (*vighna-hartā*). His popularity reached a high point in the early medieval period (ca. eighth century), when even the Buddhists and Jains borrowed the god from the Brahmanical pantheon and began his worship. It was during this period that the worship of Gaṇeśa traveled beyond the frontiers of India into other areas of Asia, including China. He is perhaps one god who can be rightly described as the god of Asia.[1] This fascination for Gaṇeśa has been rightly explained by Wendy O'Flaherty:

> Gaṇeśa has everything that is fascinating to anyone, who is interested in religion or India or both: charm, mystery, popularity, sexual problems, moral ambivalence, political importance, the works. One can start from Gaṇeśa and work from there in an unbroken line to almost any aspect of Indian culture.[2]

Consequently, there are conflicting views about many aspects of the god. The present paper describes some early images of Gaṇeśa and attempts at

*I am thankful to the American Institute of Indian Studies, Varanasi, and the Archaeological Survey of India, New Delhi.

explaining his true character with the help of evidence from numismatics and contemporary literature.

The Artistic Evidence

It was the late Professor R. G. Bhandarkar who first propounded that the antiquity of Gaṇeśa does not go back beyond the sixth century A.D.[3] However, there are certain images that can be dated to pre–sixth century. Among these we can include two images from Afghanistan, of which one can be assigned to the fifth century and the other to the fourth century.[4] The former was discovered at Gardez and was subsequently removed to Kabul, where it is now worshiped by the Hindu residents of Dargah Pir Rattan Nath locality near the Pamir Cinema (fig. 1). This image bears an inscription on its pedestal that records that this great and beautiful image of Mahāvināyaka was consecrated by the renowned Shahi King Khingala, who on the basis of numismatic evidence can be said to have ruled in the fifth century.[5]

The other image, also from Afghanistan, was reported from Sakar Dhar (Shankar Dharā), about sixteen kilometers north of Kabul, from where also come some interesting images of Sūrya and Śiva (fig. 2). It is characterized by rather slender limbs; even the bulging belly is not of huge proportions, as is usually the case. The chest is muscular and reminds us of the Gandhāra statuary. Stylistically, the statue resembles the early Gupta sculptures and can be placed in the early fourth century when the Gupta influence had begun but the Hellenistic was still lingering.

The Gaṇeśa images from several Gupta-period sites, such as Bhumara and Udayagiri (M.P.), are well known. Among the recent discoveries, those on the Ramgarh Hill in Vidisha district, Madhya Pradesh, are noteworthy (fig. 3). Here Gaṇeśa is shown sitting on a raised seat.[6] He is two armed, holding a bowl of sweets in his left hand; the trunk is turned toward the left and is shown resting on the bowl of sweets. He is potbellied and ithyphallic. Stylistically this image is closely related to that in Udayagiri Cave 6 and can therefore be dated to the late fourth or early fifth century. It should therefore be clear that there are Gaṇeśa images, though quite few, that belong to the fourth and fifth centuries. Had they not been there, it would not have been possible for Varāhamihira to prescribe his iconography in the *Bṛhat Saṁhitā,* which is dated to the late fifth or early sixth century.

Still-earlier sculptural representations of the elephant-headed god have been housed in the Mathurā Museum. As far back as 1932, three Kuṣāṇa-period Gaṇeśa images were noticed in the collection of the museum.[7]

One of these (no. 758) is said to have been found in the Yamuna River near some ghat at Mathurā (see Brown, fig. 8, this volume). It is a red-sandstone standing Gaṇeśa whose portion below the knees is missing. Carved in the round, the god has two hands only. Of these, the left holds the bowl of sweets, and the god is eating them with his trunk. The attribute in the right hand is lost. The god is potbellied and wears a *yajñopavita*. He is naked with the genitals prominently indicated, but is not ithyphallic (*ūrdhvameḍhra*) as is shown by several images of Gaṇeśa.

There are two other Mathurā Museum Gaṇeśas (nos. 792 and 964; see Brown, figs. 6 and 5, this volume) carved in the round and similar to the one described above. It should be noted that carving figures in the round was the speciality of the Kuṣāṇa artists of Mathurā. All three images have been assigned to ca. first to third century A.D. There is yet one more image that is originally said to have come from the Sankisya mound. Alice Getty believes this to be the most ancient representation of the god in stone as yet discovered, although she dates it not before the fifth century.[8] It is carved out of the typical mottled red sandstone of Mathurā. It depicts the elephant-headed god standing with two arms, of which the left one holds a bowl of sweets that the god is eating with his trunk. The right hand, slightly curved, holds a pointed object that may be the radish or broken tusk. The ears are inordinately large, and the head is bare. The figure is potbellied and has stumpy legs, but the other limbs are of relatively slender proportions. As with the Gaṇeśa in figure 1, the god is shown nude with the genitals prominently depicted. The image is small and of relatively crude workmanship, suggesting, perhaps, an early attempt at carving representations of the god. The image may reasonably be assigned to the late second or early third century A.D.

Another image of Gaṇeśa that can also be dated to the Kuṣāṇa period displays a number of characteristics similar to those of the Gaṇeśas discussed above (fig. 4).[9] It is a small image, showing the god in a standing posture, with two arms, the left one holding a bowl of sweets, to which the god helps himself by means of his trunk. The right hand rests over the hip. The figure is marked by a protrusion on the forehead (*ūrṇa*), which is one of the marks of great men (*mahā-puruṣa-lakṣaṇa*). A most remarkable feature of this image is that yet another figure is carved on the back. Such addorsed images are a characteristic feature of Kuṣāṇa statuary.[10]

An early terra-cotta image of Gaṇeśa has recently been reported from Andhra Pradesh (fig. 5). In the course of excavations at Veerapuram, District Kurnool, a small terra-cotta figurine was found in the levels of Period III, which is assigned, on the basis of combined evidence of stratigraphy and artifacts, to the time bracket ca. 50 B.C. to 300 A.D. This stratum could be securely dated because of the evidence furnished by some Sātavāhana coins. Hence the Gaṇeśa image can certainly be dated to pre-300 A.D.

The terra-cotta figurine from Veerapuram is unfortunately fragmentary. It represents probably a standing elephant-headed figure of which the legs are broken. It has two arms, but they too are broken. The headdress is mutilated. The trunk is upturned toward the left, probably for eating the sweets from the bowl in the left hand. The sacred thread of the god appears to be a *nāga-yajñopavita*. The lower garment, which is only partly seen on the waist, was probably a short *dhoti* reaching the knees (*ardhoruka*). The figure gives a somewhat gruesome appearance because of the bulging eyes and the corpulent body. This potbellied, *yakṣa*-like figure is undoubtedly that of Gaṇeśa. Although this is the only terra-cotta Gaṇeśa that is securely Sātavāhana in date, the terra-cotta figurines of Gaṇeśa from Akra, which have been referred to by Getty,[11] may also belong to the same period because the site has yielded a number of pre-Gupta antiquities of the second century.

All these early images of Gaṇeśa are characterized by somewhat slender limbs; they are not as corpulent as those of the later period. In some cases even the belly is not shown bulging. They are all dwarfish figures with stumpy legs that suggest the *yakṣa* lineage of the god. There is little doubt that they would have occupied a subsidiary position in a shrine complex, and the god therefore does not seem to have attained an exalted status. We may therefore identify these images as those of Vināyaka, the *vigna-kartā* (obstacle creator) who, if properly propitiated, becomes *vigna-hartā* (obstacle remover) as described in the *Yājñavalkyasmṛiti* (*Gaṇapati-kalpa* section). And as he belongs to the *yakṣa* class, his representations could also occur in Buddhist shrines, as at Amarāvatī and in Sri Lanka.[12]

The Numismatic Evidence

The existence of Kuṣāṇa-period Gaṇeśa images takes the antiquity of the elephant-headed god back to pre-Gupta times. It is indeed enigmatic that his worship should begin in the early centuries of the Christian era, which was not the golden age of Hinduism. This was possibly due to the sanctity attached to elephants in some parts of the Kuṣāṇa empire, most particularly in the Gandhāra region. The elephant was held in great reverence by the citizens of Kapiśā (present-day Begram in Afghanistan), as is testified to by the celebrated Chinese pilgrim Xuanzang, who visited India during 629–45 A.D. During his prolonged journey he spent considerable time visiting Buddhist establishments in Afghanistan and spent a whole summer in ancient Kapiśā. He has recorded a very curious and interesting legend regarding the tutelary deity of the inhabitants of Kapiśā. We can do no better than quote the words of the pilgrim:

> To the southwest of the capital (Kapiśā) was the Pi-lo-sho-lo mountain. This name was given to the mountain from its presiding genius who had the form of an elephant and was therefore called Pi-lo-sho-lo.[13]

The pilgrim's testimony amply demonstrates that during the sixth and seventh centuries the people of Kapiśā were worshiping their tutelary god Piluśāra (Pi-lo-sho-lo), who had the form of an elephant. It is necessary to emphasize that Xuanzang merely records a tradition that was prevalent long before he visited Kapiśā. This tradition is confirmed by the evidence furnished by an important coin type of Eukratides, an Indo-Greek king who ruled about 170–150 B.C. over a part of the Asiatic possessions of Alexander. The coin type is as follows:

> Zeus sitting on throne to front, holds wreath and palm; to the right of throne forepart of elephant and to left a pilos (?); above this indistinct monogram; Kharoshthi legend: 'Kavi (pi)śive nagara-devatā.'[14]

Two of the coin symbols (the head of the elephant and the mountain accompanying the central devise) and the Kharoshti legend are of especial interest in as much as they can be explained with the help of the account of Xuanzang. Rapson was the first to connect the two symbols and the legend, identifying the mountain symbol as representing Mt. Piluśāra (Pi-lo-sho-lo) and the elephant symbol as representing the elephant god of the mountain and of the city of Kapiśā. Eukratides' respect for the god of his subjects is evident from its portrayal on his coins. It is again significant to find the elephant head on some of the copper coins of Demetrius[15] and other Indo-Greek and Śaka rulers like Menander[16] and Maues,[17] which can also be associated with this deity peculiar to Kapiśā and its environs.

The coin evidence points to the existence of the elephant god of Kapiśā well before the second century B.C. The representation of the elephant is quite common on the early series of Indian coinage; it even occurs on the earliest punch-marked coins, where, however, it is represented as a full-bodied animal and not only by its head. In sharp contrast to this, the head of the elephant on the early coin devices of foreign rulers in India[18] are certainly indicative that the elephant god was on the way to assuming an anthropomorphic form. But since he was a god of the mountains, the Greek rulers naturally tried to identify him with their own Zeus, for to Greeks "a mountain god could not well become anything but Zeus."[19] Perhaps this is why the deity of Kapiśā and Zeus were depicted together on coin devices of foreign rulers of India. This then represents a stage between a totem and its anthropomorphic form. It also shows that the god was elephant headed who originated and developed into the elephant-headed deity of the environs of Kapiśā. Foucher too observes that

> when dealing with a therianthropomorphic figure of Gaṇeśa's type, we can easily trace it back to the animal prototype from which it came; and here we plunge into the oldest layer of superstition which our developed minds can grasp: totem worship and agrarian rites.[20]

Kapiśā by its very name, which means "endowed with elephants," suggests an association with elephants. Other place names mentioned by Xuanzang also indicate an importance for elephants in northwestern India. He visited a town called "Polusha" that Cunningham identified with Palo dheri.[21] Furthermore, to the northeast of Polusha rose the hill of Dantaloka ("place of tusk"). A second city the Chinese pilgrim mentions, Puskarāvatī, may also refer to elephants, as one of the meanings of *puṣkara* is "elephant."

The important Gandhāran city of Taxila also supplies evidence of elephants and their worship. Tarn writes:

> There is a story which may bear on the elephant of Taxila. It is known that Philostratus, when he wrote on the life of Apollonius, he had before him a pretty accurate description of Parthian Taxila by some one who had visited it, and he says that at Taxila there was a very old elephant, once belonging to Porus whom Alexander had dedicated in the temple of the Sun and had named Aias, and whom the people used to annoint with myrrh and adorn with fillets. . . . Philostratus attributes many things to Alexander and Porus, but the story might really be evidence for the existence at Taxila of a sacred elephant, the elephant of the coins; the bell round the elephant's neck on the 'elephant head' coin type of Demetrius, Menander and Maues would support this.[22]

Thus Taxila was also known for its sacred elephant in the ancient past. However, J. N. Banerjea is inclined to identify the elephant on coins with the elephant deity of Kapiśā. He states that

> on the basis of our main hypothesis, it will be possible for us to suggest that the device 'elephant's head with a bell round his neck' used by Demetrius on

> some of his copper coins and other Indo-Greek and the Śaka rulers like Menander and Maues was associated with this elephant deity, peculiar to Kapiśā and its environs. We are not certain whether the elephant used as a device on so many coins of these kings is in any way connected with it; but if any connection between the two could be proved, then one could demonstrate the extreme popularity of the device.[23]

An extremely interesting feature of the elephant depicted on these early coins is that it is almost always shown with a bell around its neck. In this connection we may note that the image of Gaṇeśa in the Bhumara temple is shown wearing bells around his neck, which has been taken to be an unusual feature. This has been explained by Coomaraswamy with the help of an ancient Tibetan legend that is connected with the time of Bimbisara, a contemporary of Buddha. According to the story, one of the gatekeepers of Vaishali had died but was reborn as a demon. He requested the inhabitants of the city to confer on him the position of *yakṣa* and hang a bell around his neck so that whenever there was any danger he could ring it. Thereupon the inhabitants made a *yakṣa* statue and hung a bell round his neck and set it up at the gatehouse.[24] This legend is probably fairly late, and one fails to grasp its significance as it relates to Gaṇeśa. Coomaraswamy was attempting to relate Gaṇeśa to what he felt were his *yakṣa* origins, but the special use of a bell by one *yakṣa* hardly argues for its appearance on Gaṇeśa. In fact, it is more plausible to suggest that the presence of bells around Gaṇeśa's neck may possibly be due to their being worn by the already popular and sacred elephant of Taxila and Kapiśā.

In sum, the evidence suggests that the elephant, or a deity in the form of an elephant, was sacred to the people of the Gandhāra region. Hence the Indo-Greeks gave it a place of honor on their coins, and the Indo-Scythians and Indo-Parthians followed them in order to please their subjects. The Kuṣāṇas who succeeded them went a step further; they had statues of various gods and goddesses made for the first time. It must not have been easy to make statues of Gaṇeśa, which obviously required considerable imagination, for in this case it was the representation of a sacred animal. Here the Greco-Roman artists, who were quite active in the Kuṣāṇa empire, more particularly in the Gandhāra region, must have been of great help. The Greeks were adept at fashioning therianthropic representations, such as centaurs, and their experience must have come in handy for carving the first images of the elephant god. This is now amply borne out by the evidence of an Indo-Greek coin type in the British Museum that has on its reverse the representation of Gaṇeśa. Observes A. K. Narain,

> if this [that it is Gaṇeśa] is accepted, surely this would be the earliest representation of Gaṇeśa and a veritable specimen of syncretic tendencies which started operating from the time of the Indo-Greeks and resulted in the formation of many new gods and goddesses. This is also an example of how a local deity was transformed or, if you may like to say, elevated to the respectable status.[25]

It should be noted in this connection that Hermaeus (c. 75–55 B.C.), probably the last of the Indo-Greek rulers, at the end of his career had associated Kujūla Kadphises, the Kuṣāṇa chief, into the administration of his kingdom, as is evident from the joint coin issues that give the names of both in the legend. This should help to explain the occurrence of the images of Gaṇeśa, though few, in the Kuṣāṇa period.

The Literary Evidence

The artistic and numismatic evidence discussed above is to a considerable extent corroborated by literary evidence. It should be noted here that the references to the elephant-headed deity in the *Maitrāyaṇī Saṁhitā* have been proven to be very late interpolations, and thus are not helpful for determining the early formation of the deity.[26] Regarding Gaṇeśa in the epics, M. Winternitz concludes: "It is, however, worth mentioning that (as far as I am able to see) it is very doubtful whether the elephant headed god can claim a place in the Epic pantheon."[27] So far as the legend that the great sage Vyāsa secured the services of Gaṇeśa as scribe for writing the great epic, Winternitz has shown that it is a late legend that was known only from about 900 A.D.[28] The *Mahābhārata* tells us that among the *gaṇa*s of Śiva there were two groups: one group were benevolent deities of nine classes who dwelt on Mt. Kailasa, and a second group were malevolent deities, called *vināyaka*s, who, however, could be propitiated.[29] Propitiatory rites and ceremonies have been mentioned in both the epics.[30] They are also mentioned in the *Mānava Gṛhyasūtra* in the subsection titled *Vināyaka-kalpa* or "The Pacificatory Rites for Vināyakas," where the four names of *vināyakas* appear as Usmita, Devayajana, Śālakaṭankaṭa, and Kuṣmāṇḍa-rājaputra, and the appeasement of the trouble-creating god is prescribed.

The worship of Gaṇeśa is also alluded to in such later Smṛtis as the *Yājñavalkyasmṛti* (I, 271–94). In the *Baudhāyana Gṛhyapariśeṣasūtra* (III, 10), which can be assigned to the same time as the *Yājñavalkyasmṛti*, we come across reference to a single Vināyaka. Herein the group of four *vināyaka*s is addressed as one god, and he is looked upon as the son of Ambikā. This one Vināyaka was appointed by Śiva as Gaṇapati Vināyaka, who may be considered as the earliest form of Gaṇeśa. He is given the role of creating difficulties and obstructions if not properly propitiated.[31] In the *Baudhāyana Gṛhyapariśeṣasūtra* (III, 10), among many invocations to the spirit under various epithets, there is one that speaks of it as *hasti-mukha,* or elephant faced. It is interesting to note that the same epithet has been applied to Vighna and Vināyaka in the *Baudhāyana Dharmasūtra.* In it the spirit or deity Vighna (obstacle) is given most of the epithets of Gaṇeśa, such as Vināyaka, Hastimukha, Vakratuṇḍa, Ekadanta, Lambodara, and so on.[32] Thus it appears from the literary evidence that in the early centuries of the Christian era one Vināyaka had come to supersede the concept of four or more, making his identification with Gaṇapati easier. But his malevolent character is conspicuous, for he is invoked both as Vighna (obstacles) or Vighneśvara (lord of obstacles). G. S. Ghurye writes:

> Only one step further, and that a very radical transformation, was needed to enthrone Gaṇeśa being the 'Lord of Obstacles' as the 'Destroyer or Remover of Obstacles.' Such transformations inhere in the very nature of early religio-magical systems of beliefs. . . . So Vināyaka, the trouble-maker becomes the much prayed to trouble-averter Gaṇeśa.[33]

This transformation in all probability was completed long before the fifth century and hence the occurrence of the images of Gaṇeśa in the late Kuṣāṇa period.

Two Important Kuṣāṇa-period Mathurā Sculptures

Two more sculptures in the Mathurā Museum are of importance to our discussion. One of these is a frieze (no. 2335) carved with three horizontal bands of which the upper one has a railing and the middle one contains six arches showing worshipers. In the band at the bottom, which is partly preserved, are depicted five elephant-headed figures (fig. 6). V. S. Agrawala identifies each as a *yakṣa,* which according to him is "the earliest representation of Gaṇeśa figure in Mathurā art, perhaps an offshoot of Kubera iconography."[34] We are also inclined to identify these figures as representations of Gaṇeśa, more particularly *vināyaka*s, although P. K. Agrawala has expressed doubts about their identification.[35] They rather appear to be the prototypes of the Pañcha-Gaṇeśa images of the later period. As already discussed, the *vināyaka*s are usually mentioned as four, and the earliest reference to them is to be found in the *Mānava Gṛhyasūtra,* which is supposed to be one of the earliest *Gṛhyasūtra*s, dating back to about the second century B.C. The four *vināyaka*s are said to have been invoked under four separate formulae in the *Mānava Gṛhyasūtra* (II, 14, 47), and they again appear in the *Yājñavalkyasmṛti* (I, 285). The elephant-headed figures in the Mathurā frieze have also been identified as *vināyaka*s by P. K. Agrawala, who observes:

> In the art of Amaravati and Mathura during the first three centuries of the Christian era the portrayal of Vināyakas—who were originally a team of attacking beings of evil disposition—appears possibly to render them as elephant-headed demons or *Yakṣas*. The Mathura relief . . . may be identified as Vināyakas or Gaṇeśa figures. The presence of *five* such beings on this fragmentary relief is more or less certain.[36]

It may, however, be stated that five *vināyaka*s have been mentioned in the *Gaṇapati-kalpa* section of the *Yājñavalkyasmṛti* (I, 285). They are Mita, Sammita, Śālakaṇṭaka, Kuṣmāṇḍa, and Rājaputra.[37] The increase in number from four to five is due to the separate mention of Kuṣmāṇḍa and Rājaputra, who, as already seen, have otherwise been referred to as one Kuṣmāṇḍa-rājaputra. Again Mita and Sammita are phonetically similar to Usmita, which occurs in the *Mānava Gṛhyasūtra*. But Devayajana, which occurs in the *Mānava Gṛhyasūtra*, has been dropped in this list. Be that as it may, it appears that the concept of five, as well as four, *vināyaka*s was prevalent in the early centuries of the Christian era.

The second Mathurā sculpture depicts Gajalakṣmī flanked by Gaṇeśa on the right and Kubera on the left. B. N. Sharma observes that

> Shri V. N. Srivastava, the Curator of the Mathura Museum, says that there are three such sculptures in his Museum. Of these, one belongs to the Kushan period and the other two to the Gupta period.[38]

For us, Sharma's dating of the one sculpture to the Kuṣāṇa period helps support our contention that in the Kuṣāṇa period Gaṇeśa was becoming popular. His association with Lakṣmī and Kubera is not without significance. Both Lakṣmī and Kubera are deities of wealth. Kubera, a *yakṣa* who is referred to as Dhanada ("wealth-giving") has many features in common with Gaṇeśa. Both are grotesque in appearance and potbellied. Even Coomaraswamy has noted this similarity, for he says that

> Gaṇeśa is undoubtedly a *yakṣa* type by his big belly and general character; but he is not cited by name in any lists. He is effectively and perhaps actually equivalent to Kubera or Maṇibhadra.[39]

Perhaps that is why the artist selected Kubera and Gaṇeśa to flank the goddess in the center to balance the sculpture. But in doing so, he was unconsciously elevating Gaṇeśa, who was an obstacle creator, to the level of a divinity, ranking him with Gajalakṣmī and Kubera in importance. Both Kubera and Gaṇeśa were *yakṣas* first, but the former remained a *yakṣa*, whereas Gaṇeśa attained divine status.

Conclusion

The foregoing discussion makes it clear that the worship of Gaṇeśa came into vogue in the Mathurā region during the Kuṣāṇa period. The sacred elephant, which originally may have been the totem of some tribe like the Hastināyanas or the Hastikas in the Gandhāra country, later came to be depicted on the coinage of Indo-Greeks and other foreign rulers. The credit of giving the deity the therianthropic form has to be given to the Indo-Greeks. With the Kuṣāṇas, his worship came to Mathurā, but still Gaṇeśa was only a demigod and can be identified as Vināyaka of the Brahmanical literature; earlier there were four *vināyaka*s who were later merged into one. Originally a creator of obstacles, he came to be worshiped as an obstacle remover. We have sculptural representations of the five *vināyaka*s in the Kuṣāṇa period and single images slightly later that look more like those of *yakṣas*.[40] That the elephant-headed god was known more as Vināyaka than as Gaṇeśa is amply clear from literary references, and that he continued to be known as such is clearly demonstrated by the inscribed Kabul Museum statue that records his name as Mahā-Vināyaka. In fact it appears that the god was not known as "Gaṇeśa" in the early period, for a repertoire of early personal names shows that the earliest occurrence of it is to be found in the early Gupta period in the Allahabad *praśasti* of Samudragupta, which mentions one Gaṇapatināga. Slightly earlier, however, in the *Yākhñavalkyasmṛti*, the propitiatory rites for the god have been described in the section called *Gaṇapati-kalpa*, whereas in the much earlier *Mānava Gṛhyasūtra* it is entitled *Vināyaka-kalpa*. Even Bharata in his *Nātyaśāstra*, which has been placed between 200 and 400 A.D., also refers to Gaṇeśa as one of the lesser gods.[41] Thus sometime in the late Kuṣāṇa and the early Gupta period, the god came to be known as "Gaṇeśa," and he seems to have become popular in the Gupta period, during which quite a number of images of the god came to be carved. That is why it could be possible for Varāhamihira to describe the iconography of Gaṇeśa. We may therefore reasonably conclude that the worship of Gaṇeśa came into vogue much earlier than the sixth century, as was earlier thought; it begins, as the Mathurā evidence shows, in the Kuṣāṇa period in the early centuries of the Christian era.

NOTES

1. M. K. Dhavalikar, "Gaṇeśa beyond the Indian Frontiers," in *India's Contribution to World Thought and Culture. Vivikanada Commemmoration Volume,* ed. Lokesh Chandra, et al. (Madras: Vivekananda Rock Memorial Committee, 1970), 1–16.

2. Wendy O'Flaherty, "Forward," in Paul B. Courtright, *Gaṇeśa: Lord of Obstacles, Lord of Beginnings* (New York: Oxford University Press, 1985), vii.

3. R. G. Bhandarkar, *Vaiṣṇavism, Śaivism and Minor Religious Systems* (Strassburg: K. J. Trübner, 1913), 147–48.

4. M. K. Dhavalikar, "A Note on Two Gaṇeśa Statues from Afghanistan," *East and West* 21, new series (1971):331–36.

5. Dhavalikar, "Two Gaṇeśa Statues," 331–32.

6. Carmel Berkson, "Some New Finds at the Ramgarh Hill, District Vidisha," *Artibus Asiae,* 40 (1978):216.

7. D. B. Diskalkar, "Some Brahmanical Sculptures in the Mathura Museum," *Journal of the U.P. Historical Society* 5, pt. 1 (1932):45–47.

8. Alice Getty, *Gaṇeśa: A Monograph on the Elephant-faced God* (1936, reprint, Delhi: Munshiram Manoharlal, 1971), 26, pl. 2a.

9. The image is in the collection of Mr. and Mrs. James W. Alsdorf, Chicago, Illinois, USA. See Stella Kramrisch, *Manifestations of Śiva* (Philadelphia: Philadelphia Museum of Art, 1981), 75, fig. 61.

10. For example, John M. Rosenfield, *The Dynastic Arts of the Kushans* (Berkeley and Los Angeles: University of California Press, 1967), fig. 21.

11. Getty, *Gaṇeśa,* 26.

12. Getty, *Gaṇeśa,* 25–26. For a recent discovery of an elephant-headed figure at Amarāvatī that has been identified—incorrectly, in my opinion—as Gaṇeśa, see I. K. Sarma, "A Unique *Usnisha* (Coping Stone) from Amaravati," *Journal of the Andhra Historical Society, Somasekhara Sarma Volume* 35 (1975–76):279–84.

13. Thomas Watters, *On Yuan Chwang's Travels in India,* vol. 1, 1st Indian ed., (Delhi: Munshiram Manoharlal, 1961), 129.

14. A. N. Lahiri, *Corpus of Indo-Greek Coins* (Calcutta: Poddar Publications, 1965), pl. XVI, i. For different opinions regarding the representation of the deity see M. K. Dhavalikar, "Antiquity of Gaṇeśa: The Numismatic Evidence," *Indologica Taurinencia, Prof. Ludwig Sternback Volume* 8–9 (1980–81):141–42.

15. Percy Gardner, *Coins of Greek and Scythic Kings of Bactria and India in British Museum* (reprint, Chicago: Argonaut, 1966), pl. III, 2.

16. Gardner, *Coins,* pl. XII, 6.

17. Gardner, *Coins,* pl. XVI, 1.

18. J. N. Banerjea, "Indian Elements in Coin Devices of Foreign Rulers of India," *Indian Historical Quarterly* 14 (1938):300–1.

19. W. W. Tarn, *The Greeks in Bactria and India,* 2d ed. (Cambridge: Cambridge University Press, 1951), 138.

20. Alfred Foucher, "Introduction," in Getty, *Gaṇeśa* (reprint, New Delhi: 1971), xvi.

21. Surendranath Majumdar Sastri, *Cunningham's Ancient Geography of India* (Calcutta: Chuckervertty, Chatterjee and Co., 1924), 60.

22. Tarn, *The Greeks,* 164.

23. Banerjea, "Indian Elements in Coin Devices," 300–1.

24. Ananda Coomaraswamy, *Yakṣas,* pt. 1 (reprinted ed., New Delhi: Munshiram Manoharlal, 1971), 14–15.

25. A. K. Narain, "Presidential Address," *Journal of the Numismatic Society of India* 36 (1974):190.

26. J. N. Banerjea, *Development of Hindu Iconography,* 2d ed. (Calcutta: University of Calcutta, 1956), 574–78.

27. M. Winternitz, "Gaṇeśa in the Mahābhārata," *Journal of the Asiatic Society* (1898):382.

28. Winternitz, "Gaṇeśa in the Mahābhārata," 382.

29. *Mahābhārata* XII, 284, 131.

30. *Mahābhārata* III, 65, 23; *Rāmāyaṇa* VI, 128, 113.

31. *Yājñavalkyasmṛti* I, 271–94.

32. Georg Buhler, *The Sacred Laws of the Aryans,* pt. 2 (Oxford: Oxford University Press, 1882), 254, II, 5, 9(7).

33. G. S. Ghurye, *Gods and Men* (Bombay: Popular Book Depot, 1962), 61.

34. V. S. Agrawala, *Mathura Museum Catalogue, Pt. III: Jaina Tirthankaras and Other Miscellaneous Figures* (Lucknow: U.P. Historical Society, 1952), 106.

35. Prithvi K. Agrawala, "Some Varanasi Images of Gaṇapati and Their Iconographic Problem," *Artibus Asiae* 39, no. 2 (1977):139.

36. Agrawala, "Some Varanasi Images," 139.

37. The late Sir R. G. Bhandarkar took them to be six in number; see his *Vaiṣnavism,* 139.

38. B. N. Sharma, "A Rare Image of Gajalakshmī from Mathura in the National Museum, New Delhi," *Bulletin of Ancient Indian History & Archaeology* 2 (1968):74, n. 2.

39. Coomaraswamy, *Yakṣas,* pt. 1, 7.

40. It is noteworthy that among the gods to be invoked to propitiate *vināyakas*, *yakṣas* are also mentioned. See *Mānava Gṛhyasūtra* II, 14, 29.

41. Manomohan Ghosh, "The Date of the Bharata-*Nāṭyaśāstra,*" *Journal of the Department of Lettres, University of Calcutta* 25 (1934):41–42.

Fig. 1. Gaṇeśa, stone (marble), H:71 cm. Fifth century A.D. Presently Dargah Pir Rattan Nath, Kabul. (Photo: Archaeological Survey of India)

Fig. 2. Gaṇeśa, stone (marble). Fourth century A.D. From Sakar Dhar; presently Shor Bazar, Kabul. (Photo: Archaeological Survey of India)

Fig. 3. Gaṇeśa, stone. Late fourth, early fifth century A.D. Ramgarh Hill, Madhya Pradesh. (Photo: American Institute of Indian Studies)

Fig. 4. Gaṇeśa, stone, H:18.4 cm. Kuṣāṇa period. Collection Mr. and Mrs. James W. Alsdorf, Chicago. [Photo: after Stella Kramrisch, *Manifestations of Shiva* (Philadelphia: Philadelphia Museum of Art, 1981), pl. 61.]

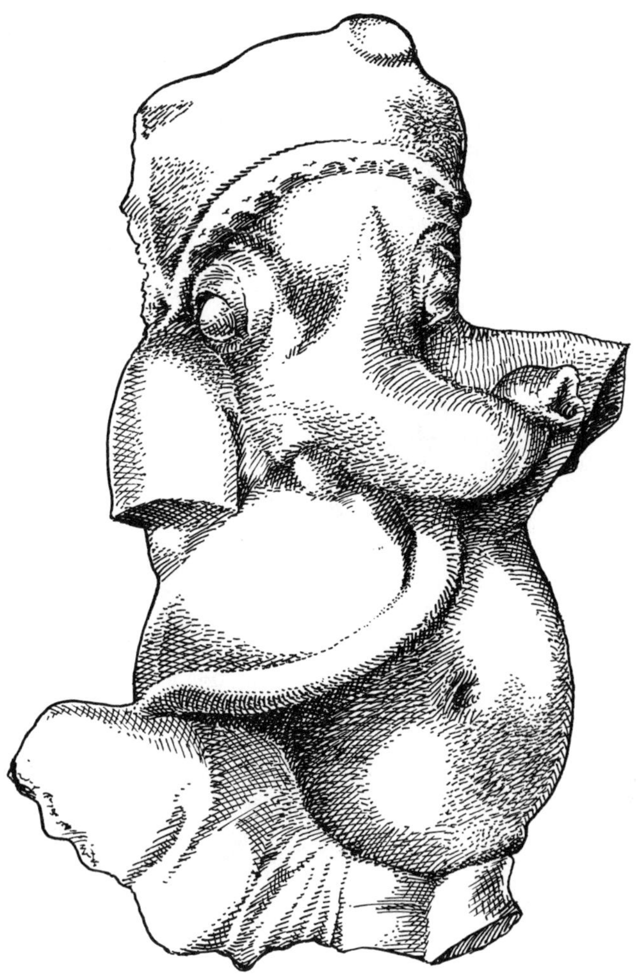

Fig. 5. Gaṇeśa, terra-cotta, 7 cm. 50 B.C.–300 A.D. Veerapuram District, Kurnool, Andhra Pradesh.

Fig. 6. Stone relief, 30.5 × 68.5 cm. From Mathurā; presently Mathurā Museum. (Photo: Mathurā Museum)

3

Gaṇeśa's Rise to Prominence in Sanskrit Literature

Ludo Rocher

Scholars who have studied Gaṇeśa and the Gaṇeśa cult in India often express surprise concerning two facts that are seemingly difficult to reconcile. On the one hand, there is Gaṇeśa's enormous popularity, at least in modern times: he "was, and still is, the most universally adored of all Hindu gods." On the other hand, there is the fact that he appears rather late on the scene in Indian religion; Gaṇeśa was "among the latest deities to be admitted to the Brahmanic pantheon."[1]

Gaṇeśa's true rise to prominence, as far as Sanskrit literature is concerned, is connected with the Purāṇas.[2] Not only does he make occasional appearances in a large number of Purāṇic texts; some Purāṇas reserve entire sections for him, and two Purāṇas are exclusively devoted to the Gāṇapatya cult.

Surveying the entire Purāṇic literature dealing with Gaṇeśa would require more than an article. Before touching on some of these materials, I will first concentrate on some rare references to Gaṇeśa in that section of Indian literature that is generally considered to be older than the Purāṇas.

The term *gaṇapati* appears as early as the Vedic Saṃhitās. In fact, it appears twice in the oldest of all Vedic texts, the *Ṛgveda.* I am convinced, though, that neither passage has any connection with god Gaṇeśa. One passage (2.23.1),

> gaṇā́nāṃ tvā gaṇápatiṃ havāmahe
> kavíṃ kavīnā́m upamáśravastamam
> jyeṣṭharā́jaṃ bráhmaṇāṃ brahmaṇaspata
> ā́ naḥ śṛṇvánn ūtíbhiḥ sīda sā́danam,[3]

clearly refers to Bṛhaspati—who is the *devatā* of the hymn—and Bṛhaspati only. The second passage (10.112.9),

ní ṣú sīda gaṇapate gaṇéṣu
tvā́m āhur vípratamaṃ kavīnā́m,[4]

equally clearly refers to Indra. Expressions such as *gaṇānāṃ gaṇapatim* or *gaṇapate gaṇeṣu* — as well as *brahmaṇāṃ brahmaṇaspate* at *Ṛgveda* 2.23.1 — are well known in the Veda. They mean nothing more than that Bṛhaspati[5] and Indra[6] were heads of *gaṇa*s. They do not imply that either Bṛhaspati or Indra were ever given the name Gaṇapati.[7]

Even though, from a strictly historical point of view, within the context of the *Ṛgveda* these passages have no connection whatever with Gaṇeśa, they had to be mentioned—for, as far as I know, at least the first one is quoted repeatedly in later Gāṇapatya literature. When the authors of more recent Gāṇapatya texts look for Vedic respectability for their deity, they do so by quoting the *Ṛgvedic* verse *ganāṇāṃ tvā gaṇapatiṃ havāmahe.*[8]

Far more important for the study of Gaṇeśa in early Indian literature are two texts belonging to the *Black Yajurveda*. Both the *Maitrāyaṇīya Saṃhitā* and *Taittirīya Āraṇyaka* exhibit a series of *gāyatrī*s. These *gāyatrī*s, however, are not addressed to Savitṛ, as was the case in the original *gāyatrī* in the *Ṛgveda* (3.62.10), but to such deities as Rudra, Garuḍa, Durgā, and Viṣṇu. One *gāyatrī* in particular is addressed to a deity called "Danti" or "Dantin." Thus, in the *Maitrāyaṇīya Saṃhitā* (2.9.1):

tát karā́ṭāya vidmahe
hastimukhā́ya dhīmahi
tán no dántī pracodáyāt;

and in the *Taittirīya Āraṇyaka* (10.1):

tát púruṣāya vidmahe
vakratuṇḍā́ya dhīmahi
tán no dántiḥ pracodáyāt.

Both texts clearly appeal to a deity Danti(n) "the tusked one," who, moreover, is called *hastimukha* "elephant-faced" in one text, and *vakratuṇḍa* "with a curved trunk" in the other. These terms are, indeed, very suggestive of Gaṇeśa. As a matter of fact, Sāyaṇa explicitly establishes the identification in his commentary on the *Āraṇyaka.*[9]

I now proceed to the next "period" in early Sanskrit literature: the Sūtras and Śāstras. The *Mānava Gṛhyasūtra* devotes an entire chapter (2.14) to four *vināyaka*s: Śālakaṭaṅkaṭa, Kuṣmāndarājaputra, Usmita, and Devayajana. It describes, at length, the sufferings of those who are possessed by these dreadfully malignant creatures. The text, subsequently, prescribes the necessary rites to propitiate them, including offerings of raw and cooked fish and meat.

Even though, at some time, Vināyaka became a name of Gaṇeśa, there is little in the *Mānava Gṛhyasūtra* to suggest that its *vināyaka*s are connected with him. The passage, however, becomes important when we compare it to a passage from the *Yājñavalkyasmṛti* (1.271–94).[10] The verses in the *Yājñavalkyasmṛti* are very similar to—occasionally identical with—the text of the *Mānava Gṛhyasūtra*. *Yājñavalkya* enumerates the same four *vināyaka*s, although in the *Mitākṣarā* version[11] their number has been increased to six: Mita, Sammita, Śāla, Kaṭaṅkaṭa, Kuṣmānda, and Rājaputra. The signs of being possessed by the *vināyaka*s are similar to those listed in the *Gṛhyasūtra*, and so are the means of propitiating them, although these now include such items as radish (*mūlaka*), cakes, and sweetmeats (*modaka*). But there are also significant differences between the two texts. First, the four—or six—*vināyaka*s of the *Yājñavalkyasmṛti* are said to be only different manifestations of one single Vināyaka, *the* Vināyaka. Second, this single Vināyaka was appointed by Brahmā and Rudra as the remover of obstacles and as the lord of *gaṇa*s (*gaṇāṇām ādhipatye*). Third, the Vināyaka of the *Yājñavalkyasmṛti* is, explicitly, called "Mahāgaṇapati," and the text reveals the name of his mother: Ambikā.[12]

Some of the data examined so far—a god Danti(n) called *hastimukha* and *vakratuṇḍa* in the *Black Yajurveda*, and the Vināyaka of the *Yājñavalkyasmṛti*—might seem sufficient to conclude to a relatively early date for the appearance of Gaṇeśa in Sanskrit literature. This conclusion is, however, jeopardized by the place Gaṇeśa occupies in the epics.

The *Mahābhārata* knows the *vināyaka*s,[13] but they are malignant demons, even as the *bhūta*s, *rākṣasas*, and *piśāca*s. The *Mahābhārata* also knows the terms *Gaṇeśa*, *Gaṇādhipa*, *Gaṇakāra*, *Gaṇakṛt*, and *Gaṇapati*, but they invariably refer to Śiva.[14]

The single passage in which the real Gaṇeśa appears in the epic has not fared well with *Mahābhārata* scholars. I am referring here to the passage in which Gaṇeśa is said to have written down the entire *Mahābhārata* at the dictation of Vyāsa. Gaṇeśa mischievously accepted to do so on one condition, that Vyāsa never stop dictating. Vyāsa, in turn, accepted Gaṇeśa's challenge on the condition that he only write down if and what he understands. Vyāsa then dictated such complicated sentences that Gaṇeśa could not help halting and, thereby, provide Vyāsa with the pauses he needed.

Moriz Winternitz was first to draw attention to one of the distinctive features of the Southern manuscripts of the *Mahābhārata*: "A remarkable omission is that of the legend of *Gaṇeśa*, who, at the request of Vyāsa, writes down the whole of the Mahābhārata."[15] The story appears in the introductory scene of Rājaśekhara's *Bālabhārata* or *Pracaṇḍapāṇḍavanāṭaka*—in which Vyāsa and Vālmīki inquire from each other about the progress of their respective works. On the other hand, it is absent from Kṣemendra's *Bhāratamañjarī,* so Winternitz was prepared to accept that the story was *known* ca. 900 A.D., but he also maintained that it was not *part* of the *Mahābhārata* in Kṣemendra's time, some 150 years later. He concluded, even more generally, "that (as far as I am able to see) it is very doubtful whether the elephant-headed god can claim a place in the Epic Pantheon."[16]

To Winternitz's arguments we may add that the story was known to al-Bīrūnī:

> Vyasa asked Brahman to procure him somebody who might write for him the *Bharata* from his dictation. Now he entrusted with this task his son Vinayaka, who is represented as an idol with an elephant's head, and made it obligatory on him never to cease writing. At the same time Vyasa made it obligatory on him to write only that which he understood. Therefore Vyasa, in the course of his dictation, dictated such sentences as compelled the writer to ponder over them, and thereby Vyasa gained time for resting awhile.[17]

Whatever the case may be, the editors of the critical edition of the *Mahābhārata* seem to have agreed with Winternitz. The twenty-line passage has been relegated not only to an appendix—the normal procedure for suspect passages—but to a footnote to an appendix.[18] In doing this, V. S. Sukthankar clearly underscored his belief that the *Mahābhārata* — the "Encyclopaedia Brahmanica" as he called it—did not know Gaṇeśa. Even if his decision ultimately proved to be wrong, and even if the passage about the dictation of the *Mahābhārata* could indeed be claimed as an integral part of the epic, the fact remains that a single reference to Gaṇeśa in the *itihāsa* is in sharp and as yet inexplicable contrast with the important role Gaṇeśa plays in the Purāṇas, to which we now turn our attention.[19]

As far as the Mahāpurāṇas are concerned, as could be expected, Gaṇeśa appears in those texts that the tradition classifies as *tāmasa*—or Śaiva —Purāṇas. He does, indeed, appear in the *Śiva,*[20] *Liṅga,*[21] *Skanda,*[22] and *Agni Purāṇas.*[23] Gaṇeśa plays no role in such *sattva* — or Vaiṣṇava — Purāṇas as the *Viṣṇu* or the *Bhāgavata Purāṇa,*[24] but he is present in the *Varāha Purāṇa.*[25] The *Garuḍa Purāṇa* includes him among the major gods,[26] and the *Padma Purāṇa* describes his cult.[27] Among the *rājasa* Purāṇas Gaṇeśa appears in the *Bhaviṣya,*[28] *Brahma,*[29] *Brahmāṇḍa,*[30] and *Vāmana Purāṇas.*[31] More important, he is the sole object of the entire *Gaṇeśa* or *Gaṇapatikhaṇḍa* of the *Brahmavaivarta Purāṇa,* in forty-six chapters.[32]

Several Upapurāṇas[33] deal with Gaṇeśa, including two that are entirely devoted to him. The *Gaṇeśa Purāṇa*[34] consists of two parts: the *Upā-*

sanakhaṇḍa, with 92 chapters, and the *Krīḍākhaṇḍa* (also called *Uttarakhaṇḍa* in the colophons), with 155. Chapters 138–48 of the second part constitute the *Gaṇeśa Gītā*,[35] a shorter version of the *Bhagavad Gītā*, displaying a number of verses practically borrowed from the latter, but adapted to relay a new message. The *Mudgala Purāṇa*, a complete edition of which appeared only recently,[36] is a much longer text. It is divided into nine khaṇḍas, with a total of 428 adhyāyas, each khaṇḍa being devoted to the story (*carita*) of a different manifestation of Gaṇeśa: Vakratuṇḍa, Ekadanta, Mahodara, Gajānana, Lambodara, Vikaṭa, Vighnarāja, Dhūmravarṇa, and Yoga (a combination of different forms of Gaṇeśa).

As I indicated earlier, this article is not the place for an exhaustive survey of the vast Purāṇic literature connected with Gaṇeśa. In the following pages I will restrict myself to pointing out a number of general trends I have perceived in the course of extensive but as yet incomplete readings of Purāṇic Gaṇeśa materials.

Above all, one cannot help being struck by the fact that the numerous stories surrounding Gaṇeśa concentrate on an unexpectedly limited number of incidents. These incidents are mainly three: his birth and parenthood, his elephant head, and his single tusk. Other incidents are touched on in the texts, but to a far lesser extent.

For instance, the Purāṇas, like iconography, know that Gaṇeśa's mount is a rat. Gaṇeśa is called *adhasthān mūṣakānvitam*.[37] When all the gods offered him presents after his name-giving ceremony, the Earth gave him a rat to serve as his vehicle.[38] Yet even the story in the *Gaṇeśa Purāṇa* (2, ch. 134) that, in the *dvāparayuga*, Vāmadeva cursed the Gandharva Krauñca to become a rat, which, to punish it for its misbehavior, Gajānana made into his own *vāhana*, does not explain the special connection between both. Hence modern speculations that Gaṇeśa did so "because of its mischievous character," or that Gaṇeśa in some way became connected with agriculture and that "some agricultural deity, riding a rat, was identified with him."[39] Or, since *mūṣaka* also means "thief," the rat as Gaṇeśa's vehicle "implies that he is riding over the thief of the field (field rat)."[40] Elsewhere the rat is "the animal that finds its way to every place."[41] One scholar reminds us that the rat "is a totem of at least one Dravidian tribe, the Oraons," and uses this argument to claim Dravidian origin for Gaṇeśa.[42]

Similarly, very little attention is paid to the question whether or not Gaṇeśa is married, and, if he is, to the name and identity of his wife—or wives. To quote Venkatakrishna Rao,[43] the texts "are not agreed as to whether he is married or not." There are texts that describe Gaṇeśa's wedding to Siddhi and Buddhi,[44] the daughters of Prajāpati Viśvarūpa. On the other hand, descriptions of Gaṇeśa as *siddhi-buddhi-samanvita* "accompanied by, followed by *siddhi* and *buddhi*," often seem to mean no more than that, when Gaṇeśa is present, *siddhi* "success" and *buddhi* "wisdom" are not far behind. Such may well have been the original conception, of which the marriage was a later development.

The relatively few incidents in Gaṇeśa's life that are told in the Purāṇas display two principal trends. First, not only are they told again and again; they are also told in an infinite variety of ways. The Gaṇeśa stories are a perfect illustration of the "variants and multiforms"[45] that are characteristic of Purāṇa literature generally. In this particular case the composers of the Purāṇas were obviously aware of the situation, and they formulated their own justification for it:

> The story of how Gaṇeśa came into being is told differently in different *kalpas*. Sometimes his head was cut off when Śani looked at him. Here we will tell the story of Gaṇeśa as it is told in the Śveta(vārāha)kalpa, and according to which his head was cut off by the merciful Śiva.[46]

The second trend I perceive in the Purāṇic Gaṇeśa stories in some ways counterbalances the one just mentioned. The point is that, behind the many variants and multiforms of each of the principal incidents in Gaṇeśa's life, there are certain basic, unifying ideas. To be sure, we meet with rare stories that are totally isolated from the mainstream; in general, however, the variants and multiforms are based on some common denominator. I will now illustrate the interaction between these two trends for the Purāṇic stories dealing with the three main events in Gaṇeśa's life.

Although the stories surrounding his birth vary greatly, there is, without doubt, one common element that underlies most of them.

Only in very exceptional cases is it Śiva who takes the initiative to create Gaṇeśa. In the *Liṅga Purāṇa*[47] Śiva himself created Gaṇeśa at the request of the *devas*, to remove the obstacles the gods were subjected to on the part of the *daityas*. Ambikā, like the other gods, praised the newborn lord of the *gaṇas*. Or, again at the request of the gods, Śiva created, from his laughter (*hasataḥ*), a being endowed with all the qualities of lord Parameṣṭhin, truly a second Rudra.[48]

In most birth stories, however, it is Pārvatī, not Śiva, who is anxious to have a son. It is she who tries, hard but unsuccessfully, to convince Śiva to have a son with her. For this reason Gaṇeśa becomes the son of Pārvatī alone, not of Śiva. Even though this may, in last resort, have more to do with the nature of Śiva than the nature of Gaṇeśa, Gaṇeśa's status is, nevertheless, very much determined by it.

For example, in one text,[49] in answer to Pārvatī's insistent request, Śiva makes it clear to her that he does not want, in fact does not need, a son. Sons are necessary for householders who will eventually die and need sons to perform the ritual for the dead (*putrāḥ piṇḍaprayojanāḥ*). He, however, is not a householder; he is immortal.

> I am not subject to death, so I do not need a son, o Devī. When there is no illness, what is the use of taking medicine against it?[50]

In another text Śiva himself is made to tell Pārvatī that Gaṇeśa is *her* son; and he explains that Gaṇeśa will be called "Vināyaka" because he was born *nāyakena vinā*, "without the intervention of a husband."[51]

In the case of Gaṇeśa's birth, this first common denominator—the fact that he is not really Śiva's son—finds its counterpart in a second one. Most texts insist, often with words put in the mouth of Śiva himself, that Śiva fully approves of Umā's child, and that he is pleased to have him as a son.

For instance, in the aforementioned passage from the *Vāmana Purāṇa* Śiva is said to have been pleased when he saw the child;[52] and immediately after his etymological explanation of the name Vināyaka as *nāyakena vinā*, he proudly predicts:

> Vināyaka will create thousands of obstacles for the gods and everyone else; and, o Devī, the worlds, both movable and immovable, will worship him.[53]

Also, there are numerous indications in the texts to the effect that Gaṇeśa resembles Śiva, in fact that Śiva wants "his son" to be exactly like himself.[54]

Against the background of these two common elements the birth stories of Gaṇeśa go in different directions. In several stories Gaṇeśa is born from the *mala* of Pārvatī's body, which she rubs off during or after a bath. Sometimes[55] Pārvatī creates this son because Nandin proves to be an inadequate gatekeeper while she is taking her bath; Śiva just has to rebuke Nandin to be allowed in and disturb Pārvatī's bathing. The goddess then decides to create her own gatekeeper who will listen to her orders and to no one else's. Gaṇeśa, indeed, becomes the ideal gatekeeper, who fights off the *gaṇa*s and Śiva himself.

In a variant on this story[56] Śiva and Pārvatī are engaged in *mahāmoha*, so much so that the gods become afraid that the son born of their union will be imperishable, and deprive them all, including Indra, of their exalted positions. They go to Śiva and have him agree to have his semen drunk by Agni, rather than having a son with Pārvatī. Pārvatī is angry, bathes,[57] and out of her *mala* creates Gaṇeśa. The text even calls him *malapuruṣa* (v. 65b).

In another text[58] Pārvatī beholds Kṛṣṇa and desires a son like him. Her subsequent lovemaking with Śiva is interrupted by Viṣṇu in the disguise of a beggar. As a result, Śiva's semen does not enter Pārvatī's womb, but falls on the bed. At the end of a long discourse by the beggar, Viṣṇu suddenly disappears, hastily takes on the form of a newborn boy, and mixes himself with Śiva's seed. A voice from the sky announces to Pārvatī that Kṛṣṇa has manifested himself in her house as her son. Pārvatī, Śiva, and all the other gods rejoice in the birth of Gaṇeśa.

Elsewhere[59] a very different story is told. Śiva, upset because of Pārvatī's incessant requests to have a son, finally promises that he will make one for her to kiss.[60] He pulls Pārvatī's clothes off and shapes them in the form of a child.[61] Pārvatī, in disbelief, takes the doll on her lap; it falls on the floor, comes to life, and addresses her, "*māṃ, māṃ*" (v. 29d).

I now pass on to the second major element in the mythology of Gaṇeśa, the fact that we are dealing with a deity with the head of an elephant.

There are Purāṇic stories according to which Gaṇeśa was actually born in that form. For example, when Śiva agreed to have his semen drunk by Agni rather than deposit it in Pārvatī's womb, Umā was, understandably, angry, and she created a son out of the dirt of her body. The text explicitly says: *malāc cakre gajānanam*.[62] The possibility that we might have to interpret the term *gajānana* as merely anticipatory — "a son who *later* would be called Gajānana"[63] — is eliminated later in the chapter. When Śiva and Pārvatī were again united on the throne, with the *malapuruṣa* at their feet, Umā realized "the wonderful thing that, from the dirt of her body, she had produced a divine being that was elephant-headed."[64]

The expression *naraṃ cakre gajānanam* also appears in other texts. According to one story[65] Pārvatī rubbed scented oil mixed with powder over her body and, with the dirt of her body, "produced a male being with an elephant's head." Sportingly she threw her son in the Gaṅgā, where his body expanded enormously, until he eventually filled the entire world. Pārvatī called him "son," but so did Gaṅgā, whence his name Gāṅgeya. The gods worshiped him, and Brahmā appointed him as the lord of the *gaṇa*s.

Although there are, therefore, texts according to which Gaṇeśa was born elephant-headed,[66] these are the exceptions. As a rule, Gaṇeśa acquired the head of an elephant at a later stage only, be it in different ways.

I referred earlier to the story of Śani, "Saturn." According to this legend,[67] when Gaṇeśa was born, Pārvatī proudly wanted to show him to

Śani. Śani, however, the *krūradṛś* ("evil-eyed") was cursed that anything he would look at would be burned to ashes. When he was encouraged to look at Gaṇeśa, he did so reluctantly, with one eye only. Gaṇeśa's head was, nevertheless, reduced to ashes. Viṣṇu immediately mounted Garuḍa and flew northward. There he found an elephant exhausted from intercourse with his mate; he cut off his head, and returned to join it to the body of Gaṇeśa.

Notwithstanding this story of Śani, in which Śiva plays no role, in the vast majority of cases Gaṇeśa is beheaded by Śiva, who then replaces—or orders replaced—the missing head with that of an elephant. The stories, again, vary in detail, but there clearly is one single, broad motivation behind them. Whenever Gaṇeśa is beheaded by or through Śiva, this happens "because he has come between Śiva and Pārvatī in some way."[68]

In one story,[69] after Śiva killed and beheaded Gaṇeśa—as Pārvatī's doorkeeper—in a fierce battle, the goddess became so angry that the gods feared an untimely world destruction. She threatened that only if her son be brought back to life would there again be peace in the worlds. Śiva then sent the gods to the northern region, with the order to cut off the head of the first being they met. This happened to be a single-tusked elephant. They brought the head with them, attached it to Gaṇeśa's body, and Śiva revived him.

Elsewhere[70] Gaṇeśa is said to have been born from Prakṛti—obviously, here, the Paraśakti of Śiva. Śiva, who does not know him, engages in a battle with him. The interesting point here is that Gaṇeśa is said to be "mounted on an elephant" (*gajārūḍha*) and that Śiva uses his *triśūla* to kill both Gaṇeśa and his elephant. The Paraśakti praises Śiva and obtains a boon. She then tells Śiva that he has killed her son and asks him to bring him back to life. Śiva revives the *māyāputra* and attaches the elephant's head to the body of Gaṇeśa.[71]

In the story from the *Varāha Purāṇa,* in which Śiva created Gaṇeśa from his laughter, he soon became jealous and afraid that his son might allure the ladies. He himself cursed Gaṇeśa to become elephant-headed, to have a protruding belly, and to carry a garland of serpents around his neck.[72]

The question why Gaṇeśa's head was replaced with that of an elephant rather than that of any other living being is, as far as I know, not addressed in the texts. The one form of the legend that establishes a connection between Gaṇeśa and the elephant that was his mount prior to his death, seems to be a rationalization rather than an explanation. It might be worth noting that, in some cases at least,[73] the elephant whose head was to replace Gaṇeśa's was none else than Indra's mount, Airāvata.

There has been quite some speculation among modern scholars on the date—and the reason why—Gaṇeśa was provided with the head of an elephant. According to Bhandarkar,[74] "When and how the god came to have an elephant's head, is difficult to determine." Based on the first stanza in Bhavabhūti's *Mālatīmādhava* he considered the beginning of the eighth century as the only certain *terminus ante quem.* Hazra[75] examined a wider variety of sources and concluded that the elephant head "must have been added to him at a comparatively late date," however "earlier than the sixth century A.D." As to the reason why this happened, Hazra suggests either that it "may be due . . . to the mediaeval idea about the queer forms of Śiva's Gaṇas," or, based on *Gaṇeśa Purāṇa* passages (1.46.48,72–73), "to his identification with some popular deity conceived and worshiped for immunity from havoc created by wild elephants."[76]

Without pursuing the problem any further in this paper, I would like to suggest two approaches toward a possible solution. First, there is in Hindu mythology a parallel case in which the burnt head of Dakṣa is, at Śiva's command, replaced with that of a goat. Understanding the symbolism that made Śiva relate the figure of Dakṣa to a goat might help us understand the reason why Gaṇeśa's head was replaced with that of an elephant.[77] Another possible approach to understanding Gaṇeśa's elephant head might be through further investigation into the role and meaning of the elephant in classical India — and elsewhere.[78] Writers on this subject notice that "from the most ancient classic times this sagacious and most useful animal has been known."[79] Elsewhere too, "the elephant's head is the emblem of sagacity."[80] Or, "in India at any rate the idea of hugeness is conveyed by comparison with an elephant, the biggest animal known."[81] The elephant is "the greatest and most interesting of Indian animals."[82]

The third prominent element in the Gaṇeśa myths is the fact that his elephant head only has a single tusk. The explanations in the texts of how this unusual situation came about are, once again, very different. Either Gaṇeśa's elephant head was single tusked from the time he acquired it, or one tusk was lost at a later stage. Both alternatives appear in the literature.

In the story from the *Śiva Purāṇa* referred to earlier, Śiva, after beheading Gaṇeśa, sent the gods northward with the order to cut off the head of the first living being they would encounter, which happened to be a single-tusked elephant.[83]

It seems, however, that, even as with Gaṇeśa being born with an elephant's head, his being single tusked from the beginning is the exception rather than the rule. It is my impression that Hindu mythology prefers him to lose one of his original two tusks, although those responsible for it may be different. In one Purāṇic story[84] it is Paraśurāma who cuts off a tusk, when he comes to visit his teacher, Śiva, in Kailāsa. Gaṇeśa, in his role as gatekeeper, refuses him entrance because Śiva is resting. In the ensuing battle Paraśurāma cuts off one tusk. But there are also stories in which Rāvaṇa cuts off the tusk,[85] or in which Gaṇeśa loses his tusk because of a wager with Skanda on who could go most quickly around the earth.[86]

In conclusion, there is no doubt that in classical Indian literature Gaṇeśa comes to real prominence in the Purāṇas, which are considered to be relatively late texts. Admittedly, the fact that a particular element appears in the texts at a certain moment does not prevent it from having existed earlier, even much earlier. In the case of Gaṇeśa the *gāyatrī*s to Danti(n) in texts belonging to the *Black Yajurveda* might be taken as an indication that he, by far, antedates the Purāṇas. This does not, however, solve the problem of Gaṇeśa's absence from the epics, especially the *Mahābhārata,* which deals with anything imaginable. The story of his writing down the *Mahābhārata* at the dictation of Vyāsa looks like an effort, ex post facto, to connect Gaṇeśa with the epic, even an effort to do so in a big way.

NOTES

1. Both quotations are from Alice Getty, *Gaṇeśa: A Monograph on the Elephant-faced God* (1936; reprint ed., Delhi: Munshiram Manoharlal, 1971), 1. Among those who claim an early origin for Gaṇeśa are Auguste Barth, *The Religion of India* (London: Kegan Paul, 1921), 197, with a—casual and undocumented—statement on Gaṇeśa as a god "whom we meet with early as the god of arts and letters"; and Haridas Mitra, "Gaṇapati," *The Vishva-bharati Quarterly* 8 (1930–31):461–81, who argues that "the beginnings of Gaṇeśa worship must be pushed back at least to the Indo-Skythian and Indo-Parthian periods of Indian History, or perhaps even earlier."

2. This paper was written for the Gaṇeśa conference, prior to the publication of Paul Courtright's study *Gaṇeśa: Lord of Obstacles, Lord of Beginnings* (New York: Oxford University Press, 1985). On Gaṇeśa's rise in relation to Skanda/Kārttikeya, see Juan Roger Riviere, "The Problem of Gaṇeśa in the Purāṇas," *Puranam* 4 (1962):96–102.

3. Trans. Griffith: "Lord and Leader of the heavenly hosts"; Geldner: "dich, den Herrn der (Sänger)scharen."

4. Trans. Griffith: "Lord of the hosts, amidst our bands be seated"; Geldner: "Setz dich fein nieder, du Herr der Schar, unter den (Sänger)scharen."

5. Cf. *Ṛgveda* 4.50.5, which says of Bṛhaspati: *"sā suṣṭúbhā sá ŕ̥kvatā gaṇéna valāṃ ruroja."* Sāyaṇa: *"gaṇena aṅgirasām."* See also *Aitareyabrāhmaṇa* 1.12.1, etc.

6. Cf. *Ṛgveda* 6.40.1: *"utá prá gāya gaṇá ā niṣádya. . . ."* Sāyaṇa: *"gaṇe 'smatstotṛsaṃghe."*

7. Cf. the expression *rudrasya gāṇapatyam,* "Rudra's leadership," in several Yajurvedic texts (*Taittirīya Saṃhitā* 4.1.22; 5.1.23; *Vājasaneyi Saṃhitā* 11.15; etc.).

8. I am, therefore, not convinced by R. G. Bhandarkar's conclusion in *Vaiṣṇavism, Śaivism and Minor Religious Systems* (1913; reprint ed., Varanasi: Indological Book House, 1965), 149: "Gaṇapati's reputation for wisdom is, I believe, to be attributed to the confusion of him and Bṛhaspati, who in *Ṛgveda* II,23,1 is called Gaṇapati. Bṛhaspati, of course, is the Vedic god of wisdom, and is called the sage of sages."

9. He introduces the *gāyatrī* to Danti as follows: "*bījapūragaḍekṣukārmuka ity āgamaprasiddhamūrtidharaṃ vināyakaṃ prārthayate.*"

10. For a textual comparison of the Vināyakaśānti in the *Yājñavalkyasmṛti* with the *Agni* and *Garuḍa Purāṇas*, see Hans Losch, *Die Yājñavalkyasmṛti* (Leipzig: Harrassowitz, 1927), XX–XXII, 33–36.

11. In their commentaries on the *Yājñavalkyasmṛti* Aparāditya and Śūlapāṇi quote passages from a *Baijavāpagṛhya*, also with four *vināyaka*s.

12. Comparison of the *Mānava Gṛhyasūtra* and the *Yājñavalkyasmṛti* has led scholars to some far-reaching conclusions. See Bhandarkar, *Vaiṣṇaivism*, 148, who was followed, with more than one confusion, by S. Bhattacharji, *The Indian Theogony* (London: Cambridge University Press, 1970), 183, who concluded, on the basis of the *Gṛhyasūtra*, "that the Vināyakas had come to be objects of faith before the Christian era." The cult of one Gaṇapati-Vināyaka exhibited in the *Dharmaśāstra*, on the other hand, was more recent; it "was introduced about the sixth century" (150). The result is that, in his opinion, the *Yājñavalkyasmṛti* "must have been written not earlier than the sixth century." [Regarding Ambikā being Gaṇeśa's mother, see Narain's article, p. 23, ed.]

13. Cf. R. C. Hazra, "Gaṇapati Worship and the Upapurāṇas Dealing with It," *Journal of the Ganganatha Jha Research Institute* 5 (1948):267.

14. See S. Sørensen, *An Index to the Names in the Mahābhārata*, (1904; reprint ed., Delhi: Motilal Banarsidass, 1963).

15. Moriz Winternitz, "On the Mahābhārata MSS. in the Whish Collection of the Royal Asiatic Society," *Journal of the Royal Asiatic Society of Great Britain and Ireland* (1898):147.

16. Moriz Winternitz, "Gaṇeśa in the Mahābhārata," *Journal of the Royal Asiatic Society of Great Britain and Ireland* (1898):382. Gaṇeśa is absent from the index to E. W. Hopkins's *The Great Epic of India* (1901; reprint ed., Calcutta: Punthi Pustak, 1969). Hopkins refers to the Gaṇeśas (115), "the god himself belonging only to the pseudo-epic introduction, and very likely interpolated there, as has been shown by Dr. Winternitz."

17. Edward C. Sachan, *Alberuni's India* (1888; reprint ed., Delhi: S. Chand, 1964), vol. 1, 134.

18. *Mahābhārata*, critical edition, vol. 1, part 2, 884.

19. For a good survey of Purāṇic—and other—references to Gaṇeśa, see Amarendra Gadgil, *Śrīgaṇeśakośa* (Puṇe: Śrīgaṇesa Kośa Maṇḍala, 1968). Khaṇḍa 1: "Gaṇeśa grantha," 1–91 (in Marathi).

20. *Śiva Purāṇa* 2.4.chaps.13–20.

21. *Liṅga Purāṇa* 1.chaps.104 – 5. Cf. N. Gangadharan, *Liṅgapurāṇa. A Study* (Delhi: Ajanta Publications, 1980), 75–76.

22. *Kāśīkhaṇḍa, Uttarārdha*, chaps. 55 – 57. A *Gaṇeśakhaṇḍa* claims to belong to the *Skanda Purāṇa* (Bodl. Ms. Mill 79).

23. *Agni Purāṇa* Chaps. 71, 179, 313, 318, 348.

24. Yet, at *Bhāgavata Purāṇa* 8.7.8, Vighneśa is responsible for mount Mandara's sinking in the ocean and for Viṣṇu taking the form of a tortoise. At 11.27.29 Vināyaka is one of the gods to be worshiped during the *kriyāyoga*.

25. *Varāha Purāṇa*, critical edition, chap. 23.

26. *Garuḍa Purāṇa Sāroddhāra* 15.79 [ABEGG: *Pretakalpa;* Wood and Subrahmanyam, *Sacred Books of the Hindus*, vol. 9 (New York: AMS Press, 1974) 9].

27. *Padma Purāṇa Sṛṣṭikhaṇḍa*, chaps. 61–63 (ĀnSS Extra No., 1893–94). A Gaṇeśasahasra-nāmavyākhyā claims to belong to the *Padma Purāṇa* (Asoke Chatterjee, *Padmapurāṇa. A Study* (Calcutta: Sanskrit College, 1967), 205–6.

28. *Bhaviṣya Purāṇa*, 4 (Uttaraparvan), chaps. 32–33 (Veṅkaṭeśvara ed., 2nd ed., 1910). See also Raj Kumar Arora, *Historical and Cultural Data from the Bhaviṣya Purāṇa* (Delhi: Sterling, 1972), 79–82 (Gaṇeśa-worship).

29. *Brahma Purāṇa*, Chap. 39. See also Surabhi Seth, *Religion and Society in the Brahma Purana* (Delhi: Sterling, 1979), 206–8 (Gaṇapati).

30. See *Śrīgaṇeśakośa*, 80 – 86: five chapters on Satyavināyakavratakathā (not identified in the text).

31. *Vāmana Purāṇa*, critical edition, chap. 28.

32. There are no separate editions or studies of the *Gaṇeśakhaṇḍa*. For occasional references, see C. MacKenzie Brown, *God as Mother. A Feminine Theology in India. An Historical and Theological Study of the Brahmavaivartapurāṇa* (Hartford, VT: Stark, 1974); Adalbert Gail, *Paraśurāma Brahmane und Krieger* (Wiesbaden: Harrassowitz, 1977), especially 121–37: Paraśurāma im *Brahmavaivarta Purāṇa*.

33. For Hazra's survey, see n. 13; also *Śrīgaṇeśakosa*, 86–92.

34. *Gaṇeśa Purāṇa* (Bombay: Jagaddhitecchu Press, 1876); (Bombay: Gopal Narain, 1892). See also Rev. Dr. Stevenson, "Analysis of the Gaṇeśa Purána, With Special Reference to the History of Buddhism," *Journal of the Royal Asiatic Society of Great Britain and Ireland* 8 (1846):319–29; R. C. Hazra, "The Gaṇeśa-purāṇa," *Journal of the Ganganatha Jha Research Institute* 9 (1951–52):79–99.

35. *Gaṇeśa Gītā*, with Nīlakaṇṭha's comm., *Ānandāśrama Sanskrit Series* 52, 1906; trans. Kiyoshi Yoroi (The Hague: Mouton, 1968). Cf. also H. von Glasenapp, "Über vier purāṇische Nachbildungen der Bhagavadgītā," *Aus Indiens Kultur. Festschrift Richard von Garbe*, ed. Julius von Negelein (Erlangen: Palm & Enke, 1927) 140–42; G. Sitaramiah, "Śrī-Gaṇeśa-Gītā. Its Religious and Philosophical Significance," *All-India Oriental Conference* 22 (1965):2:241–45.

36. *Mudgala Purāṇa* (Bombay: Nirṇayasāgara Press, 1976). Cf. also G. Caturvedi, "Mudgalapurāṇaviṣayasamālocanam," *Puranam* 4 (1962):339–50.

37. *Matsya Purāṇa* 260.55.

38. *Brahmavaivarta Purāṇa* 3.13.12cd: *"vasundharā dadau tasmai vāhanāya ca mūṣikam."*

39. Both explanations are suggested by Hazra, "Gaṇapati Worship," 275.

40. B. A. Gupta, "Harvest Festivals in Honour of Gauri and Ganesh," *Indian Antiquary* 35 (1906):63.

41. H. Jacobi: "Brāhmanism," *Encyclopaedia of Religion and Ethics*, ed. James Hastings, 2 (New York: Scribners, 1910):807.

42. G. A. Grierson, "Gāṇapatyas," *Encyclopaedia of Religion and Ethics*, ed. James Hastings, 6 (New York: Scribners, 1913):176.

43. U. Venkatakrishna Rao: "The Gaṇapati Cult," *Quarterly Journal of the Mythic Society* 41 (1950):95.

44. *Śiva Purāṇa* 2.4.chaps.19–20.

45. Cf. Wendy D. O'Flaherty, *Asceticism and Eroticism in the Mythology of Śiva* (London: Oxford University Press, 1973), 16–21.

46. *Śiva Purāṇa* 2.4.13.5–6.

47. *Liṅga Purāṇa* 1.chaps.104–5.

48. *Varāha Purāṇa*, critical edition, ch. 23; "*parameṣṭhiguṇair yuktaḥ sākṣād rudra ivāparaḥ*" (v.13cd).

49. *Bṛhaddharma Purāṇa* 1.60.10–13.

50. "*na me 'sti maraṇaṃ devi na me putre prayojanam / vyādhir na vidyate yarhi kiṃ tarhi kāryam auṣadhaiḥ*" (*Bṛhaddharma Purāṇa* 1.10.13). A passage to the same effect in the *Kathāsaritsāgara* (3.6.60–73; cf. O'Flaherty, "Asceticism and Eroticism," 163) has Śiva, at the insistence of Pārvatī, agree to have a son with her, but not in the ordinary way. "I do not require the might of love in order to have offspring as mortals do" (trans. Penzer 2:101; "*na hi me madanotsāhahetukā lokavat prajā*").

51. *Vāmana Purāṇa*, critical edition, 28.71cd–72ab.

52. *Vāmana Purāṇa*, critical edition, "*apatyaṃ hi viditvā ca prītimān bhuvaneśvaraḥ*" (28.66cd).

53. "*eṣa vighnasahasrāṇi surādīnāṃ kariṣyati / pūjayiṣyanti caivāsya lokā devi carācarāḥ*" (*Vāmana Purāṇa*, critical edition, 72cd–73ab).

54. "*yathārūpaḥ śivaḥ sākṣāt tadrūpo hi gaṇeśvaraḥ*" (*Skanda Purāṇa* 1.1.10.28cd). Cf. Śiva's words when all the gods bless the newborn Gaṇeśa: "*dātā bhava mayā tulyo haribhaktaś ca buddhimān / vidyāvān puṇyavān śānto dāntas ća prāṇavallabha*" (*Brahmavaivarta Purāṇa* 3.10.28).

55. *Śiva Purāṇa* 2.4.13.20.

56. *Vāmana Purāṇa*, critical edition, 28.30ff.

57. Pārvatī's bath water also plays a role in one explanation of Gaṇeśa's elephant trunk, which will be referred to later.

58. *Gaṇeśakhaṇḍa*, chaps. 8–10.

59. *Bṛhaddharma Purāṇa* 1.chap.60.

60. "*putraṃ te kalpayiṣyāmi taṃ cumba yadi te spṛhā*" (*Bṛhaddharma Purāṇa* 1.60.22ab).

61. "*vasanenaiva tenaiṣa putraṃ nirmāya śaṅkaraḥ*" (*Bṛhaddharma Purāṇa* 1.60.23ab).

62. *Vāmana Purāṇa*, critical edition, 28.58.

63. Even as Pārvatī's son is often (e.g., *Śiva Purāṇa* 2.4.chaps.13–17) called "Gaṇeśa" long before he became the head of the *gaṇas* (*Śiva Purāṇa*, chap. 18).

64. "*yat tadaṅgamalād divyam kṛtaṃ gajamukhaṃ naram*" (*Vāmana Purāṇa*, critical edition, 28.58.70ab).

65. *Matsya Purāṇa* 154.501–5.

66. The *Suprabhedāgama* is reported to contain a story according to which Śiva and Pārvatī, when they retired to a forest on the slopes of the Himālayas to enjoy

themselves, saw two elephants making love. This excited their passion, and they decided to transform themselves into elephants. As a result, Gaṇeśa, too, was born with the face of an elephant. See T. S. Gopinath Rao, *Elements of Hindu Iconography,* (1914; reprint ed., Varanasi: Indological Book House, 1971), 1.1:44–45. According to Jayaratha's *Haracaritacintāmaṇi* (chap. 18) Gaṇeśa was born, not with one but with five elephants' heads, which were later reduced to one by Śiva. See *Encyclopaedia of Religion and Ethics,* ed. James Hastings, 2 (New York: Scribners, 1910):807–8.

67. *Brahmavaivarta Purāṇa* 3.chaps.11–12.

68. O'Flaherty, "Asceticism and Eroticism," 150. See also there for some other versions of the myth: (1) Śiva beheads Gaṇeśa when he finds him playing with Uṣā, who is said there to be Śiva's daughter [from Shakti M. Gupta, *Plant Myths and Traditions in India* (Leiden: Brill, 1971), 103–4]; (2) Gaṇeśa made love to Pārvatī and was castrated by the angry Śiva [from Philippus Baldaeus, *Naauwkeurige beschrijring van Malabaren en Choromandel* (Amsterdam: J. Janssonius van Waasberge & J. van Someren, 1672), 21].

69. *Śiva Purāṇa* 2.4.chap.17.

70. *Skanda Purāṇa* 1.1.10.27ff.

71. *"sindhuravacanenaiva mukhe sa samayojayata"* (*Skanda Purāṇa* v. 34cd).

72. *"kumāra gajavaktras tvaṃ pralambajaṭharas tathā / bhaviṣyasi tathā sarpair upavītagatir dhruvam"* (*Varāha Purāṇa*, critical edition, 23.17).

73. *Bṛhaddharma Purāṇa* 1.60.51ff.

74. Bhandarkar, *Vaiṣṇavism,* 149.

75. Hazra, "Gaṇapati Worship," 269, 272.

76. H. Heras, "The Problem of Gaṇapati," *Tamil Culture* 3 (1954):151–213, speculates that "the appearance of the head of an elephant seems to have been due to the action of the Nāgas" (213).

77. For the symbolism of the goat, see O'Flaherty, "Ascetism and Eroticism," 128.

78. Cf. H. H. Scullard, *The Elephant in the Greek and Roman World* (London: Thames and Hudson, 1974). For India, see Jean Deloche, *La circulation en Inde avant la révolution des transports* (Paris: École Française d'Extrême-Orient, 1980), vol. 1, 237–40.

79. George Watt, *The Commerical Products of India* (1908; reprint ed., Delhi: Today & Tomorrow, 1966), 696–97 ("The Elephant"). Contains a useful survey of ancient and more recent visitors to India who wrote about elephants.

80. K. Srikanta Iyer, "The Popular View of Gaṇeśa in Madras," *Indian Antiquary* 30 (1901):255.

81. B. A. Gupta, *Plant Myths,* 63.

82. Franklin Edgerton, *The Elephant-Lore of the Hindus* (New Haven, CT: Yale University Press, 1931), xii.

83. *Śiva Purāṇa* 2.4.19.49cd: *"prathamaṃ militas tatra hastī cāpy ekadantakaḥ."*

84. *Gaṇeśakhaṇḍa,* chap. 43. Cf. *Brahmāṇḍa Purāṇa* 3.chaps.41–42.

85. E.g., *Śísupālavadha* 1.60.

86. *Haracaritacintāmaṇi* 18.23 – 24 [*Kāvyamālā* (Bombay: Nirṇayasāgara Press, 1897), 61.]

4

Gaṇeśa as Metaphor: The *Mudgala Purāṇa*

Phyllis Granoff

I. Introduction

Modern scholars pondering the question "Who is Gaṇeśa?" are only the most recent representatives of a long line of seekers who endeavored to fathom the mysteries that lay behind the elephant-headed god. For the classical Indian tradition not only sang the god's praises, lovingly represented him in art, and wove intricate narratives about his deeds and powers; it also strove to understand the hidden and symbolic meaning that so greatly contributed to the awe that Gaṇeśa could inspire. In many ways, the modern and the traditional scholar have approached Gaṇeśa in strikingly parallel fashion; each has told and retold Gaṇeśa's stories, and each has sought to analyze those stories within a recognizable intellectual context and framework that would make apparent the unconscious motifs and structures that ultimately shaped the stories told. But here the similarities end, for the intellectual context of the modern scholar differs greatly from that of the traditional reader. Where the modern scholar can call upon theories of psychoanalysis and anthropology, just to name a few of the tools available, the traditional scholar moved in an intellectual world that provided very different models for understanding.[1]

At least one group of traditional scholars who asked, "Who is Gaṇeśa?," were philosophers, and they sought their answer in creative transformations of the models that classical Indian philosophy offered for the understanding of the visible world and ultimate reality. They had at their disposal core texts from their tradition, which provided them with a fixed point of reference for their speculation. What is remarkable is the freedom with which they could manipulate and interpret these texts to arrive ultimately at a new synthesis and a new understanding of these fundamental texts. It was through their reinterpretation of standard philosophical concepts that they ultimately also created a distinctive understanding of Gaṇeśa.

The philosophers who speculated on the nature of Gaṇeśa in medieval India remain largely anonymous. They have left us the record of their thoughts not in systematic treatises, but in texts that carefully combine storytelling with philosophical discourse and often divulge their philosophical content through images and metaphors and through the medium of hymns of praise and allegorical tales, rather than through the philosopher's tools of rigorous argument and debate. The main text we have today that tells us of the philosopher's quest to understand Gaṇeśa is the *Mudgala Purāṇa*. Nothing is known of its date or provenance, and little work has been done on any aspect of the text, although it would clearly repay a full-length study.[2]

This paper is meant as a first step in studying this text, and its approach will be to describe two of the reinterpretations the *Mudgala Purāṇa* offers of fundamental philosophical texts in its tradition: of the scriptural statement *tat tvam asi* from the *Chāndogya Upaniṣad*, 6.8.7, and of the system of yoga that was first codified in the *Yogasūtras* of Patañjali. Perhaps if we can begin to understand how the *Mudgala* engages other medieval philosophers, we can begin to reconstruct its context and arrive at a meaningful understanding of its time and place and position in the history of Indian philosophy. The *Mudgala* can also teach us much about the diversity of philosophical speculation in medieval India, a diversity that is not always obvious to a student who concentrates solely on the systematic treatises and is unaware of texts like this Purāṇa with its own contributions to scriptural exegesis and the practical religious quest. In a brief concluding section the paper will suggest directions for continuing research on the text.

II. The *Mudgala Purāṇa* and *tat tvam asi*

The *Mudgala Purāṇa* offers more than one interpretation of the scriptural statement *tat tvam asi*, in a striking departure from the usual practice of medieval philosophers, which was to settle on one meaning of any given scriptural statement through a strict reliance on a fixed set of rules that govern scriptural interpretation. This phrase in the *Chāndogya Upaniṣad* had always been central to the system of Advaita Vedānta, for it was one of the key statements or *mahāvākya*s from which Advaita sought the necessary scriptural authority for its doctrine of nonduality. To the Advaitin the statement meant "That Thou art," and it propounded the unity of the individual soul with the highest real, Brahman. Every subsequent school of theistic Vedānta was also compelled to deal with this line from the *Chāndogya Upaniṣad* in order to refute the Advaitin claim that their system was firmly supported by this and other similar statements in the sacred texts.[3] In the debates that ensued over the meaning of *tat tvam asi* we can in fact see something of the extreme flexibility that existed in classical Indian hermeneutics. Madhva would argue in his commentary to the *Chāndogya Upaniṣad* that the statement should be read *atat tvam asi,* adding a negative to mean, "You are different from the absolute."[4] Vallabha would offer still another interpretation, arguing that the *tvam* was an abstract suffix and not a personal pronoun and that the statement was intended to prove that the individual souls are a part of God.[5] Rāmānuja offered yet a different interpretation. And between themselves the supporters of these interpreters debated vigorously the significance of this one seemingly simple line.[6] But where they all converged was in agreeing that the statement had one fixed meaning; the individual words in the context in which they appear in the *Upaniṣad* each had a specific referent, and that referent could be determined by recourse to the well-established rules for determining the meaning of a statement that were part of the Mīmāṃsaka tradition.

It comes therefore as something of a surprise to see the *Mudgala Purāṇa* enter this debate with a very different assumption: *tat tvam asi* is not one statement but many; each term has a plurality of meanings, even within the one unchanging context of the *Chāndogya Upaniṣad,* and no one combination of these words and their meanings can be privileged above any other. In fact the statement that sets forth a term *tat,* another term *tvam,* and the copula that unites them, *asi,* is a mirror image of the elephant-headed god himself, who bears the body of a man (likened to the term *tvam*) and the head of an elephant (equated with the term *tat*) and is himself the unifier of both these disparate terms (as is the copula, *asi*). Gaṇeśa and this scriptural statement with which Gaṇeśa is identified both have many meanings and explanations.[7]

Gaṇeśa and the scriptural statement are not single, unvarying, fixed entities. Instead both serve as symbols that elucidate the complex nature of reality. They function as metaphors for reality that this text understands as unfolding from an absolute that is its source in a process of bifurcation or multiplication and synthesis. Gaṇeśa, in having both elephant head and human body, stands as a perfect symbol for the concept that reality is always a combination of seemingly disparate building blocks or constituents. And in an exactly analogous fashion the statement *tat tvam asi* signals that reality is made up of seemingly incompatible units, *tat*s and *tvam*s, but is their sum total or the synthesis that can be achieved between them.

The possibilities for analyzing the world are virtually infinite, and so the meanings of the individual words *tat* and *tvam* and their synthesis *asi* are also infinite. Gaṇeśa, who is this synthesis, this *asi,* is also infinite in his incarnations or *avatāras*, but the text settles on eight primary forms, and I should like to look at some of these in order to make clearer how the *Mudgala Purāṇa* understands Gaṇeśa and how it interprets this famous scriptural statement.[8]

The eight incarnations of Gaṇeśa are first named in 1.17.24–28, and the text is subsequently organized so that it devotes separate sections to each of the incarnations, detailing their exploits in stories that are often clearly allegorical, and also providing philosophical commentary in the form of hymns and direct discussion. In most cases a specific reference is also made to the scriptural statement *tat tvam asi,* and the exact meaning of *tvam,* which is Gaṇeśa's body, and *tat,* which is his head, are given, while the incarnation under discussion is equated with the word *asi,* the union of the two separate terms and body parts.

Each incarnation in fact represents a particular stage of the absolute as it unfolds into creation. Essential to the philosophy of the *Mudgala Purāṇa* is the belief that Gaṇeśa is the physical world; that the absolute is both *sarvākāra,* by very nature the world in all its diversity, and *nirākāra,* the soul as its stands aside from the movement of creation and dissolution of the universe.[9] The *Mudgala Purāṇa* offers a distinctive understanding of how the absolute unfolds as the world, and some brief introduction to the description of creation in the *Mudgala Purāṇa* is required if we are to understand its doctrine of the eight incarnations of Gaṇeśa as embodiments of the scriptural statement *tat tvam asi* and paradigms of understanding reality.[10]

The *Mudgala Purāṇa* in a way may be understood to frame its narratives with a discussion of creation; it first introduces the discussion of creation in book 1, chapter 6, and the last book repeats the description with slight variation, in 9.1. The topic in fact comes up again and again in the text, as if to underscore its importance. As is the case with many of the philosophical concepts in the text, creation is not only described directly in a dialogue that is taking place between various individuals. It is also described in hymns, in which Gaṇeśa is praised as a variety of entities that represents the various stages of the absolute as it unfolds in the world. These entities are listed in the order in which they appear in creation, and it thus becomes possible to reconstruct the process of creation from the hymn.[11] What follows here is a summary of some of the essential steps in creation that are critical for an understanding of the incarnations of Gaṇeśa.

The absolute prior to creation is devoid of distinction (1.6.7). The first step in the creative process is a twofold change in the absolute that becomes *svata utthānaka,* a term that means something like "awakening on its own," and *parata utthāna,* which might be loosely translated as "aroused by another."[12] These terms carry very specific meanings in this system, meanings that are not obvious from the names of the terms.

The *svata utthāna brahma,* the absolute that has awakened to creation of its own accord, is in fact the entity responsible for creation. It begins to wonder about itself, to ponder its own nature, and through the power of its thought (*vikalpa*) it becomes twofold. It becomes a cognizer, and it becomes that which is cognized, both, however in an undifferentiated state (1.6.9–11); in other language, it becomes both the body (*deha*) and the embodied soul (*dehin*).

The cognizer is considered to be formless, *nirākāra,* while the absolute as the potential object of cognition, the visible and invisible physical world, has everything as its form, and is *sarvākāra* (1.6.14). The text stresses that the absolute as soul and as visible world are on the same ontological footing; both are stages in the process of creation; both are the result of the cosmic delusion that sets off the entire creative process (1.6.15–16).

At this point in the creative process, then, the absolute exists in several different manifestations. From the initial stage came an entity that would be involved in creation, the *svata utthāna,* and an entity that stood aloof from creation, the *parata utthāna.* The actual creation of the world will proceed naturally from the *svata utthāna.* More specifically, it will proceed from the undifferentiated unity of potential physical objects, which are seen as in fact four different types of bodies. This undifferentiated unity of the four bodies is termed the *bindu.* The process will require as well an undifferentiated unity of cognizers, which the text describes as *"so 'ham,"* an awareness, "I am," and which also comes into being from the *svata utthāna.*[13] The *bindu* is equated with *prakṛti,* primordial matter of the Sāṃkhya system, while the unity of souls is equated with *puruṣa,* and together they will create the world of souls and bodies. But more important for our discussion, the text begins here to establish its main principle of analysis and to set forth its doctrine that ultimately reality lies in a synthesis of the diverging elements. For it stresses that in order for the creative process to occur there must be something that brings these two things together, and this is Gaṇeśa, who joins the two units and allows them to proceed with creation (1.6.19–20).

At the same time, there is another important process that takes place. The absolute exists not only as *svata utthāna,* which divides into two parts that Gaṇeśa joins together. It also exists as *parata utthāna*, but it is a cardinal principle of our text that units never function except through synthesis. If we turn to the account of creation in 1.16, we begin to see how Gaṇeśa is not only the synthesis of the undifferentiated collocation of souls and bodies; Gaṇeśa is also the synthesis of the two absolutes that arise at the first moment of creation, the synthesis of *svata utthāna* and *parata utthāna* (1.16.5). This is Gaṇeśa as the source of the Purāṇic gods, Śakti, Sūrya, Viṣṇu, and Śiva. Gaṇeśa, then, as the synthesis of differentiated units, is responsible for the appearance of the entire universe: of its physical elements from the *bindu*, of its individual souls from an undifferentiated unity of souls, and of its major deities.

We are now ready to examine the eight incarnations of Gaṇeśa, each of which represents the absolute at some stage in the evolutionary process, and each of which is also a synthesis of disparate elements. First in the series is Vakratuṇḍa, "the one with a crooked trunk." Vakratuṇḍa is the absolute as the aggregate of bodies, what we have called above the *bindu brahma*. His body is the three physical bodies that are made up of the qualities *sattva, rajas,* and *tamas,* familiar from Sāṃkhya thought; this is the *tvam* of the scriptural statement *tat tvam asi.* His head is the fourth body, the *turīya* or *nāda,* which stands beyond these three physical bodies (9.3.92). This is the term *tat* of the scriptural statement, while Vakratuṇḍa, their combination, is *asi.* The next incarnation is Ekadanta, "the one with the single tusk." Ekadanta corresponds with Vakratuṇḍa in representing the sum total of individual souls, as Vakratuṇḍa was the sum total of bodies. It is to be recalled that in creation the *svata utthāna* absolute differentiates itself into a sum total of bodies (*bindu*) and a sum total of souls. For Ekadanta the text similarly makes an analogy with the scriptural statement, with *tvam* as the body and *tat* as the head. Here the body is the individual soul, subject to delusion, the *jīva,* while the head is the soul who is not subject to false identification of the body—the *sākṣin,* or witness consciousness, a term clearly borrowed from Advaita Vedānta (9.3.94).

The next incarnation, Mahodara, is a synthesis of both Vakratuṇḍa and Ekadanta. It corresponds to the absolute *svata utthāna,* which becomes differentiated into the aggregate of bodies on the one hand and souls on the other hand. Here the *tvam* or body of Gaṇeśa is the *bindu,* the sum of bodies, while the *tat* or head is the consciousness or the soul, described as *so 'ham,* "I am" (9.3.104).

The next incarnation, Gajavaktra, "the one with the elephant head," is the counterpart to Mahodara. Mahodara is the absolute as it enters the creative process; this is the *parata utthāna,* the absolute that is aloof from creation. It stands somewhat outside the normal equation the scriptural statement *tat tvam asi* makes because it remains untouched by the created world of relationships (4.1.15–17). It has no equation of its own, but it is present in the terms of the equation that mark Mahodara, for the *parata utthāna* is conceived as a kind of response to the *svata utthāna*. Thus the parts of its body are the same as the parts of the Mahodara; it exists in and through them and yet outside them.

The next four incarnations bring us into the stages where the Purāṇic gods are created. They are created from the Gaṇeśa that combines the *svata* and *parata* absolutes; their head is the *parata* and their body the *svata utthāna*, and they are as follows: Lambodara, corresponding to Śakti; Vikaṭa, corresponding to Sūrya; Vighnarāja, corresponding to Viṣṇu; and Dhūmravarṇa, who corresponds to Śiva.

While the *Mudgala Purāṇa* takes delight in detailed descriptions of the deeds and wonders of each of these incarnations, this brief description should make clear that to the *Mudgala Purāṇa* Gaṇeśa is a multivalent symbol in a complex philosophical system. It interprets Gaṇeśa and the scriptural statement with which Gaṇeśa is identified in a plurality of ways, only some of which I have given. Indeed the text does not seem bothered when even at the same stage of reality different interpretations are given for Gaṇeśa and for the scriptural statement, so long as the basic principle remains unchallenged.[14] Gaṇeśa and the scripture that validates him serve more as metaphors than as single direct statements. They make known the nature of reality, indicating that reality itself is a complex process that involves replication and synthesis, with synthesis always at the beginning and end of the creative process.

III. Gaṇeśa as Yoga: Beyond the Creative Process

Through the preceding discussion of the accounts of creation the *Mudgala Purāṇa* offers, we have tried to understand how the text provides both a distinctive understanding of Gaṇeśa as the absolute reality and an unusual way of looking at scriptural statements. We emphasized that Gaṇeśa was regarded as a synthesis, a combination of distinct units. The *Mudgala Purāṇa* extends this paradigm for understanding reality to the practical aspect of its teachings as well. The true path by which we may come to understand the nature of Gaṇeśa, the nature of reality, is also a synthesis and not a single option.

In its discussion of the means to achieve knowledge of the truth and thus to free oneself from the bondage of worldly existence, the *Mudgala Purāṇa* offers a distinctive interpretation of traditional yogic practices that were formally codified in the *Yogasūtras*. In much the same way as it acted as a commentary to the *Chāndogya Upaniṣad* in its discussion of *tat tvam asi,* the *Mudgala Purāṇa* acts as well as a commentary to the *Yogasūtras* and their standard commentaries. It deviates from the *sūtras* themselves and from the *Bhāṣya* at a number of points, but its most significant point of difference is in its understanding of what must be the content of yogic meditation and the nature of the philosophical realization that is behind yoga.

The philosophical background to the *Yogasūtras* is Sāṃkhya. The *sūtras* define a process of internalizing the philosophical truths of that system. The *Mudgala Purāṇa* borrows the terminology of the *Yogasūtras* and the *Bhāṣya,* but it greatly modifies the meaning of the terms it uses.[15] It keeps strictly to the paradigm for understanding reality that we have outlined in the section above; the true yoga, like the true reality, must be a combination of factors. Indeed Gaṇeśa is yoga, *śānti yoga,* "the yoga of peace," or *pūrṇa yoga,* "the full yoga."[16] This full yoga represents the synthesis of two alternative understandings of reality; it also represents the synthesis of two features that hold true for reality. And in synthesizing the individual paths, it also transcends them to find a truer religious meaning.

The text here provides its own terminology for the two practices that combine to make the full yoga. It calls them *saṃyoga,* a term we might render as "synthesis," and *ayoga,* which might be glossed as "the denial of synthesis." It also less frequently uses technical terms that are found in the *Yogasūtras, bhavapratyaya,* and *upāyapratyayasamādhi,* although it gives these terms a new meaning.[17]

Fortunately for those of us who must read the text without the benefit of a spiritual guide, the *Mudgala Purāṇa* describes in detail what *saṃyoga* and *ayoga* involve.[18] *Saṃyoga* consists of eight stages in which the seeker identifies himself with Gaṇeśa, or absolute reality, at the various stages of the creative process. We recall that at creation the absolute begins to stir of its own accord (*svata utthāna*). This awakened entity then begins to wonder about itself, to ask what it is, and from its imaginings it conceives a body that is the undifferentiated causal state of the four bodies that will eventually evolve (*bindu*). It also conceives a soul for those bodies, that again at this stage exists as an undifferentiated whole (*so'ham*). The aspirant in the synthesis yoga begins by identifying himself with the *bindu* (9.6.3–9). The process of identification is described in some detail; the aspirant must concentrate on the fact that he is not the body, not the gross body, nor the subtle body, nor their combination; he is also not the fourth body (9.6.3; 9.6.6). What he is doing is denying that he is the differentiated products of the *bindu;* by implication he is their undifferentiated unity.

At the next step the aspirant identifies himself with the second product of the *svata utthāna,* with the souls as they exist in an undifferentiated whole (9.6.9–9.6.19). In the third stage he identifies himself with the *svata utthāna* stage (to verse 28), while in the fourth stage he identifies himself with the *parata utthāna* (to verse 42). In the fifth stage he begins to identify himself with the combination of the *svata* and *parata utthāna,* which is Gaṇeśa as he divides himself into the major gods of Hinduism, Śakti, Sūrya, Viṣṇu, and Śiva. Stages five, six, seven, and eight involve an identification with these gods. The ninth stage, which goes beyond all of these, is the identification with Gaṇeśa, who unites in himself all of these differentiating entities.

The stages of *saṃyoga* meditation parallel exactly the eight incarnations of Gaṇeśa and mark an identification of the individual with the creative process and the absolute reality that underlies this process. Over and against this, the *Mudgala Purāṇa* now sets the next category of yoga, which it calls *ayoga,* and in which the aspirant is asked to deny the creative process and recognize the immutability of the soul. The process is described in 9.6.105ff. There are three stages to this meditation, in which the aspirant denies that the absolute awakens by itself (*svata utthāna*); he denies that it is aroused by another (*parata utthāna*); and he denies that it is a synthesis of these two entities (9.6.116ff). What he meditates upon is a pure abstraction, removed from connection with the world, something that cannot be subjected to logical scrutiny and that is beyond normal means of knowledge (9.6.106).

The *Mudgala Purāṇa* remains content with neither of these single alternatives. Gaṇeśa, as the metaphor for the truth, tells us clearly that truth is embodied in a combination of alternatives and is never conveyed by single exclusive viewpoints. Thus both *saṃyoga* and *ayoga* are to be transcended. And what transcends them is Gaṇeśa as the true yoga, the full or complete yoga that this text was written to celebrate. It embraces both the truth of creation and the truth of eternality, but leaves them both behind in a mystical realization of a unity that defies characterization into polar opposites, that defies analysis as either evolving into creation or not participating in creation, the two alternatives of the *saṃyoga* and *ayoga* meditations (9.6.127ff.).

IV. Conclusions

This paper has given a brief synopsis of only a few of the doctrines described in the *Mudgala Purāṇa.* It has attempted to see the text as participating in the long and venerable context of commentaries that were written on core texts within the Indian tradition. It highlighted only two areas in which the *Mudgala* can be seen to have served as commentary, the famous line from the *Chāndogya Upaniṣad*, and the *Yogasūtras* and their standard commentaries. There is really nothing unusual for a text like the *Mudgala Purāṇa* to offer such reinterpretations of well-known works in the tradition. Not all commentaries called themselves "commentaries"; some of them, like the *Mudgala Purāṇa*, called themselves "Purāṇas," but in retelling the stories that were central to earlier texts they provided implicit if not explicit commentary on those earlier texts. Indeed the *Bhāgavata Purāṇa* offers significant commentary on the *Mahābhārata* as it retells the epic, and the *Mudgala Purāṇa* should also be regarded as commenting on the *Bhāgavata Purāṇa*, many of whose stories it retells as well. But just to identify the general mode in which the *Mudgala Purāṇa* operates is to open more questions and to answer none.

The questions become clearer if we look specifically to the sources of the system of yoga offered by the *Mudgala Purāṇa* as an example. There is no question that the *Mudgala Purāṇa* was not alone in offering its own interpretation of the *Yogasūtras*. This seems to have been a common practice in medieval India. The *Netra Tantra*, for example, redefines the terms of the *Yogasūtras*, as do the *Pāśupatasūtras*.[19] The *Śiva Purāṇa* also offered a distinctive version of yoga, which in many ways is reminiscent of that given in the *Mudgala Purāṇa*, in that it proposes a yoga that involves a stage of concentration in which first the aspirant concentrates on the ultimate as the universe, then one in which all objects are negated, and finally a greater stage that transcends both of these.[20] But these similarities are superficial, for every system of yoga is intimately tied with an entire system of philosophy, and the challenge that awaits the student is to explore the sources of the thought of the *Mudgala Purāṇa* and place it in its proper philosophical context. Until that is done, the remarkable vision this text provides of Gaṇeśa, combining striking visual imagery with scriptural commentary and meditative practice, all joined together in a coherent system for which Gaṇeśa himself provides the conceptual model, will retain much of its mystery and hold back many of its secrets.

NOTES

1. The most recent monograph on Gaṇeśa, Paul B. Courtright's *Gaṇeśa, Lord of Obstacles, Lord of Beginnings* (New York: Oxford University Press, 1985), provides a good example of the many tools modern scholars employ in their efforts to come to an understanding of Gaṇeśa.

2. The only article I know of that deals exclusively with the *Mudgala Purāṇa* is a short article in Sanskrit by Paṇḍit Giridharaśarmā Caturvedi, "Mudgalapurāṇaviṣayasamālocanam," *Purāṇa* 4, no. 2 (1962):339–50. Caturvedi worked from

manuscripts and seems to have been unaware that the text was published. His article contains some interesting material on allegory in the *Mudgala Purāṇa* but has little to say on either the basic philosophical doctrine of the text or its unusual description of yoga. Alain Danielou, in his article "The Meaning of Gaṇapati," *Adyar Library Bulletin* 18, pts. 1–2 (1954):107–29, has some discussion of Gaṇeśa along the lines offered by the *Mudgala Purāṇa*. I suspect that there might be more scholarship on the text in Indian languages, particularly in Marathi, but I have been unsuccessful in obtaining any Marathi material from libraries in my area.

R. C. Hazra, in his article "The Gaṇeśa Purāṇa," *Journal of the Ganganatha Jha Research Institute* (1951):79–99 suggested that the *Mudgala Purāṇa* is earlier than the *Gaṇeśa Purāṇa*, which he dates to somewhere between 1100 and 1400 A.D. (96). There are problems with this relative chronology; the *Mudgala Purāṇa* specifically mentions the *Gaṇeśa Purāṇa* as one of four Purāṇas that deal with Gaṇeśa. These are the *Brahma*, the *Brahmaṇḍa*, the *Gaṇeśa*, and the *Mudgala Purāṇa* itself. The *Brahmaṇḍa* it says deals with *saguṇa* Gaṇeśa, by which the text means Gaṇeśa as the visible physical world; the *Brahma Purāṇa* treats *nirguṇa* Gaṇeśa, or Gaṇeśa as the soul removed from the process of creation and ordinary cognizing activity; the *Gaṇeśa Purāṇa* tells of their union in concrete physical form, particularly to emphasize the worship of Gaṇeśa in concrete physical form, while the *Mudgala Purāṇa* deals with Gaṇeśa as *saṃyoga*, "synthesis," which I will argue in this paper means a process or a model for understanding the world and absolute reality rather than a fixed designated combination of specific terms. See *Mudgala Purāṇa*, 9.18.23 – 26 and 2.34.29–42. The same distinction between these four Purāṇas appears in the anonymous commentary to the *Atharvaśiras* published in the Ānandāśrama Sanskrit series, vol. 1, Poona, 1919, 4. I am citing the edition of the *Mudgala Purāṇa* that was published with an anonymous commentary in 1822 Sarvari from Kurundavada. Courtright, *Gaṇeśa*, 214, states that the *Mudgala Purāṇa* dates from the fourteenth to the sixteenth century, but he does not give any reason for his dating.

On the basis of internal evidence alone, it is difficult to arrive at an absolute date for the text, although it is not so problematic to suggest a relative chronology of Gaṇeśa texts that would place the *Mudgala Purāṇa* firmly as the last of the philosophical works that treat Gaṇeśa. In addition to the observation that the *Mudgala* names the *Gaṇeśa Purāṇa*, and that there is a degree of convergence in their contents, particularly in their stories, the *Mudgala* also repeatedly mentions the *Atharvaśiras*, specifically as a hymn recited in praise of Gaṇeśa (see for example 1.23.4; 2.31.12; 2.72.5; 2.36.48), and it knows of a commentary to the *Gaṇeśa Gītā* by Gārgya (5.34.11). The *Atharvaśiras* has recently been translated into English by Gudrun Bühnemann in her article "Some Remarks on the Structure and Application of Hindu Sanskrit Stotras," *Wiener Zeitschrift für die Kunde Südasiens* 28 (1984):73–104 and by Courtright, 252 – 54. Courtright states that the *Atharvaśiras* probably belongs to the sixteenth and seventeenth century, which would in fact invalidate his dating of the *Mudgala Purāṇa*. It is of particular interest to a student of the *Mudgala Purāṇa* because it would seem that the commentator to the *Atharvaśiras* in the Ānandāśrama edition and the commentator to the *Mudgala* are either one and the same or that both rely heavily on the same source. I would take the simpler suggestion, namely that they are the same person. (In support of this I cite *Mudgala* 3.47 where the commentator offers almost word for word what is to be found in the opening sections on the *Atharvaśiras*). The commentator to the *Mudgala* is not always a reliable guide to the text, it should be noted; he is at his most detailed in his discussions of the practical aspects of the philosophy, the various types of yoga that are enjoined, and there is no question that he brings to the text a system of yoga that is nowhere to be found within the text itself (see the lengthy commentary to 1.16 and 2.3; similar discussions are repeated elsewhere in the commentary, which should then be contrasted with what the text itself offers in 9.6). The *Mudgala Purāṇa* also seems to know the *Yogavāsiṣṭha*, for in 3.14 it mentions that Vasiṣṭha taught yoga to Rāma.

3. A classic statement of the Advaita position may be found in the *Saṃkṣepaśārīraka* of Sarvajñātmamuni, 1.160ff, p. 161 of the edition edited by Raṅganātha Śāstrī in the Ānandāśrama Sanskrit Series, vol. 83, Poona, 1918.

4. See Madhva's commentary to the *Chāndogya* in *Sarvamūlagrantha*, published from the Akhila Bharata Madhva Mahamandala, 1969, 440.

5. On Vallabha's interpretation see Jethalal G. Shah, *Sri Vallabha: His Philosophy and Religion* (Nadiad, Gujarat: Pushtimargiya Pustakalaya Library, 1969), 134.

6. For Rāmānuja's interpretation see the *Vedārthasaṃgraha*, vol. 16, J. A. B. Van Buitenen (Poona: Deccan College Monograph Series, 1956), 82.

7. That Gaṇeśa is the scriptural statement *tat tvam asi* is also stated in the opening passages of the *Atharvaśiras*.

8. I would not wish to suggest that the doctrine of Gaṇeśa's eight incarnations is unique to the *Mudgala Purāṇa* and the texts that directly influenced it and bore its influence, but it is interesting to note that in the many hymns or *stotras* to Gaṇeśa that have been collected, these eight forms do not figure prominently, as they do, here in the *Mudgala*. More typically the eight forms of Gaṇeśa are interpreted as the five physical elements, the sacrificer, the sun, and the moon, the same eight forms that are associated with Śiva. See Gudrun Bühnemann, *The Worship of Mahāgaṇapati According to the Nityotsava* (Wichtrach: Institut für Indologie, 1988), the hymn marked 4.14. The *Stotraratnārṇava*, ed. T. Chandrasekharan (Madras: Government Oriental Library, 1961) has collected a number of hymns to Gaṇeśa. None of them uses the particular language that the *Mudgala* uses or makes use of the system of eight *avatāras*. Of the hymns in the *Bṛhatstotraratnākara*, ed. Rāmatejaśāstrī (Varanasi: Pandita Pustakalaya, 1967), hymn 11, "Ekadantastotra," stands out from the others in its terminology and its philosophical content. Although Rāmatejaśāstrī does not identify the source of the hymn, it can be found in the *Mudgala Purāṇa*, 2.55.

9. This is repeated throughout the text. See for example 1.6.21, where the absolute is both "*sarvātmaka*," of the nature of the entire visible world, and "*nirākāra*," without distinguishable characteristics. The synthesis of these two opposing poles is the mystery of Gaṇeśa. It is worth noting that these two concepts of the absolute, as the entire universe and as the pure soul, may also be identified with specific philosophical doctrines as well. The doctrine that the absolute is the physical world is central to the school of Vallabha, for example, while the *nirākāra* soul corresponds closely with the standpoint of Advaita Vedānta. On *brahma* as *sarvākāra* in the school of Vallabha see the *Vidvanmaṇḍana* of Vallabha's son Viṭṭhalanātha, edited with four commentaries by Goswami Shrimad Vrajesh Kumarji Maharaj, Shri Vallabha Studies Series, no. 17 (Baroda and Delhi: Shri Vallabha Publications, 1985), 72ff. It is stressed again and again in the *Mudgala Purāṇa* that there exists a multitude of scriptural statements that characterize that absolute in a variety of ways; all

of these are equally true, for the absolute is everything in the universe. The *Mudgala Purāṇa* is meant to convey this message more generally by showing that Gaṇeśa should be understood as not any one absolute truth but as a paradigm for the truth indicating that the truth is a combination of single factors. See *Mudgala Purāṇa,* 1.1.42; 5.10.17; 5.24.25ff; 7.13; 9.14.27ff.

10. Perhaps the greatest challenge that a text like the *Mudgala Purāṇa* poses is the challenge of putting it into an appropriate context. Is the doctrine it propounds unique to it? What were its sources? What was it meant to supplant or criticize? Who was its audience? It is these questions that ultimately make the text interesting, but they cannot so readily be answered. I am not in a position to do more than raise such questions in this paper, but I hope that by describing some of the ideas in the *Mudgala Purāṇa* I can at least tempt others into pursuing the study of the text and trying to answer them. The *Mudgala Purāṇa* description of creation is a perfect example of this challenge of finding the correct context for the text. In its treatment of creation, for example, the *Mudgala Purāṇa* employs terminology that is standard in the Tantric schools, terms like *nāda* and *bindu,* for example. But for the *Mudgala Purāṇa* these terms have no connection with language and the manifestation of speech from the *śabda brahma,* the absolute that unfolds into audible speech. Was the *Mudgala Purāṇa* meant as a criticism of Tantric theories of creation, borrowing their terminology and divesting it of any connection with linguistic speculation? For Tantric use of the terms *nāda* and *bindu* see David Ruegg, *Contributions à l'Histoire de la Philosophie Linguistique Indienne* (Paris: E. de Boccard, 1959); André Padoux, *Recherche sur la Symbolique et l'Énergie de la Parole dans Certains Textes Tantriques* (Paris: Publications de l'Institut de Civilisation Indienne, 1975); Lillian Silburn, *Le Vijñanabhairava, Texte Traduit et Commenté* (Paris: Publications de l'Institut de Civilisation Indienne, 1961), 49ff; Dr. Kanti Chandra Pandey, *Bhāskarī,* vol. 3 (Lucknow: Prince of Wales Sarasvati Bhavana Texts, 1954), 87–94.

11. See for example 2.55; 9.1.19ff.

12. These terms are unusual. I suspect that they are borrowed from yoga. Nīlakaṇṭha, in his commentary to the *Gaṇeśa Gītā,* which is published in the Ānandāśrama Sanskrit Series, from Poona (my edition lacks the title page) discusses the seven stages of yoga that are offered by the *Yogavāsiṣṭha* and distinguishes the last three stages in the following way. In the third to last stage the aspirant can come out of his meditation himself (*svato vyutthāna*); in the next to last stage he needs to be brought out of his meditation by someone else (*parato vyutthāna*); and finally in the last stage he cannot come out of his concentration by himself nor can he be aroused by another. Similarly in the *Mudgala* characterization of the absolute as it involves itself in the creative process, it is aroused to create by itself (*svata utthāna*). But concepts like "by itself" are relative and call to mind immediately "by another." The absolute also at this point appears as the soul that is totally divorced from the process of creation, and the text explains that this is *"parata utthāna"* in that it appears by way of response to the *"svata utthāna,"* the absolute that just naturally becomes involved in creation. (See 9.5.71ff.) The two are then synthesized into a third entity, which cannot be awakened either on its own or by another, exactly as the yogin Nīlakaṇṭha describes in his treatment of the stages of the *Yogavāsiṣṭha.* The *Yogavāsiṣṭha* passages in question can be found in the *utpattiprakaraṇa,* chaps. 117–18. The commentator to the *Mudgala Purāṇa* also mentions them while commenting on 4.13, although they are nowhere evident in the text itself.

13. The four bodies are the subtle, the gross, their combination, and the one beyond those that is aware of them, or in the exact terminology of the text, *sthūla, sūkṣma, sama* and *nāda* (see for example 1.26.31; 9.5.37). These are also equated with the various states of the soul, the waking state or *jāgrat*, dreaming state or *svapna*, state of deep sleep or *suṣupti*, and that state that transcends the state of deep sleep, *turīya* (see 9.5.32ff and 1.9ff). Together, in their undifferentiated potential state, they form the *bindu brahma*. Brahman is described as having four parts in many of the Upaniṣads. In the *Māṇḍukya Upaniṣad*, 8 – 12, these four parts are equated with the states of the soul. H. Luders, "Zu den Upaniṣads, II. Die Ṣoḍaśakalavidyā," *Philologica Indica* (Gottingen: Vandenhoeck and Ruprecht, 1940), 509–26, traces the concept of the quadripartite nature of the absolute in Vedic and Upaniṣadic thought.

14. See for example 9.11, which allows alternate explanations without any difficulty.

15. The relationship between the *Mudgala Purāṇa* and the *Yogasūtras* and its various commentaries deserves a full-length study. This paper can touch on only a few points at which the *Mudgala Purāṇa* modifies the *sūtras* and cannot deal with its relationship to the commentaries. For example the *Mudgala Purāṇa* adopts the five *citta vṛttis* or mental states that are named in the *Bhāṣya* to 1.1 but defines them differently (*Mudgala Purāṇa*, 2.26.18; the text defines these five mental states on several occasions and is consistent in its definitions.) It would be interesting to study late medieval commentaries to the *Yogasūtras* in search of interpretations that might parallel those offered by the *Mudgala Purāṇa*. Such a study might go a long way in helping us to date the text and understand its context.

16. This is probably the statement made most frequently about Gaṇeśa in the text. See for example 3.3.35; 5.13; 6.1.42; 9.5; 9.6.

17. *Yogasūtra*, 1.19–20. I am using the edition with the commentaries of Vācaspati Miśra and Vijñānabhikṣu edited by Śrī Nārāyaṇa Miśra (Varanasi: Bharatiya Vidya Prākasan, 1971). The *Mudgala Purāṇa* regards both of these practices as suitable for all aspirants at a certain stage in their careers, and does not follow the traditional interpretations of the *Bhāṣya* and Vācaspati Miśra, which separated *bhavapratyaya* and *upāyapratyaya*, allowing that *bhavapratyaya* was restricted to gods and souls at the time of universal dissolution. The *Mudgala Purāṇa* seems to ignore the fact that the words in the *sūtra* 1.19 need not all be in the grammatical case; it nonetheless regards the compound at the end as indicating three types of *bhavapratyaya* meditation open to all. For the *Mudgala Purāṇa* on *bhavapratyaya* and *upāyapratyaya* see for example 2.3.30–31; 7.28.61; 8.28.53.

18. See particularly 9.5; 9.6. Both *saṃgoya* and *ayoga* belong to what the *Yogasūtra* calls *asaṃprajñāta samādhi* (1.18). The *Mudgala* does infrequently mention *saṃprajñāta samādhi*, but it is less interested in this stage. It even regards Gaṇeśa as the combination of *saṃprajñāta* and *asaṃprajñāta samādhi* (for example, 4.6.77). For the *Mudgala Purāṇa*, *saṃprajñāta* takes as its object the various individual elements of the creative process as they exist in a differentiated state. It proceeds as far as a realization of identity between the individual soul and the highest soul, between the *jīva* and Śiva, which is described as an understanding of the category *nāda*, the fourth of the individuated bodies that is really the soul connected with those bodies. (See above, note 13). The further understanding of the nature of reality begins with *asaṃprajñāta*, when the seeker realizes that these individual parts exist in an

undifferentiated whole that is Gaṇeśa at the stage of *bindu* and the undifferentiated *so ʾham*. See 9.5, particularly up to verse 41. For the *Mudgala Purāṇa, saṃprajñāta* is also equated with the fourth of the five mental modes, *ekāgra*.

19. See Mark S. G. Dyczkowski, *The Doctrine of Vibration: An Analysis of the Doctrines and Practices of Kashmiri Saivism* (Buffalo: State University of New York, 1987), 209ff. For the *Pāśupata Sūtra*s, see the edition by Haripada Chakraborti (Calcutta: Academic Publishers, 1970).

20. *Śiva Purāṇa, Vāyavīyasaṃhitā, uttarārdha*, ed. Pandeya Rāmatejashastrī (Kasi: Pandita Pustakalaya, 1964), 106ff. Particularly suggestive is the way in which the *Śiva Purāṇa* describes the first stage, *bhavayoga*, in which everything appears to consciousness in an undivided stage, in which the component parts of the world are no longer distinct (37.10, *"vilīnāvayavaṃ viśvaṃ rūpaṃ saṃbhāvyate."* In the *Mudgala Purāṇa* 5.30.60ff, similarly we are told that the world has parts and consists of the four bodies. What transcends or unites them is the *bindu*. In an analogous fashion the individual souls that operate in these bodies seem to be four in number when they are identified by their bodies, and they are also subsumed under a higher category. These higher categories are the focus of meditation in the *saṃyoga* stage. It thus becomes possible to say that in the *saṃyoga* stage for the *Mudgala Purāṇa* the focus of meditation is the visible world, in an undifferentiated state, its component parts no longer distinct. But here the similarity would end, for the basic philosophical constructs of the *Śiva Purāṇa* and the *Mudgala Purāṇa* are widely divergent.

5

Images of Gaṇeśa in Jainism

Maruti Nandan Tiwari and *Kamal Giri*

Gaṇeśa or Gaṇapati, the remover of obstacles and bestower of success (*siddhi*), has been invoked at the beginning of most auspicious ceremonies, and also at several other occasions like death, in Vaidika or Brahminical tradition for over two millennia.[1] During the early medieval times (ca. ninth century A.D.), the Jainas and the Buddhists also incorporated Gaṇeśa into their pantheon and held him in esteem. This assimilation took place only after the development of a separate Gaṇapati cult in the early Gupta period (ca. fifth century A.D.).[2]

In later Buddhism, Gaṇeśa has been conceived as the god of obstacles in place of their remover. Hence in the Vajrayāna and cognate Buddhist art he has frequently been depicted as a subdued god being trampled by Buddhist deities like Aparājitā, Parṇaśabarī, and Vighnāntaka. According to the Buddhist text *Sādhanamālā* (A.D. 1165), the twelve-armed Gaṇeśa, riding a mouse, is endowed with three eyes and one tusk. Gaṇeśa, potbellied (*ghaṭodara*) and in dancing posture, holds an axe, arrow, goad, thunderbolt, sword, spear, pestle, bow, skull-scepter, skull, and his own plucked-out tusk. Another Buddhist text, the *Niṣpannayogāvalī* (twelfth century A.D.), visualizes him with four hands and as carrying trident, sweet-ball (*laḍḍuka*), axe (*paraśu*), and radish (*mūlaka*).[3]

Contrary to the Buddhist conception of Gaṇeśa as obstacle creator, in Jainism he has always been worshiped solely as the remover of obstacles and bestower of success. According to the late Śvetāmbara Jaina work, the *Ācāradinakara* of Vardhamānasūri (S. 1478/A.D. 1412), Gaṇapati is propitiated even by the gods in order to obtain desirable things.[4] It is further mentioned that he is worshiped at the beginning of every auspicious ceremony or new project. This tradition is still very common in the Śvetāmbara community. The text also gives the *pratiṣṭhāvidhāna*, the proper visualization, of the image of Gaṇeśa. The popularity of Gaṇeśa is not met with in the Digambara texts.[5] Excepting two medieval figures carved in the Digambara Jaina caves at Udayagiri and Khaṇḍagiri in Orissa and an early figure from Mathurā, his representation is not found at Digambara Jaina sites. It may be underlined here that the Śvetāmbaras were liberal toward assimilating Brahminical deities into their fold, a fact reinforced by the inclusion of several Brahminical deities and their different forms like Śiva, Brahmā, Gaṇeśa, Vaiṣṇavi, Gaurī (or Ambikā), Kṛṣṇa, and Nṛsiṁha, who were visualized and represented in visual manifestations respectively as Kaparddi, Yakṣa, Brahmaśānti Yakṣa, Gaṇeśa, Cakeśvarī Yakṣī, Mahāvidyā Gaurī (and Yakṣī Ambikā), Kṛṣṇa, and Nṛsiṁha. The episodes from the life of Kṛṣṇa, such as his birth in prison, Kāliya-damana, and his other *bālalīlās*, along with the scene of *Holī* and also the Bali-Vāmana episode are represented in the Vimala-vasahī and Luṇa-vasahī (Delvāḍā, Mt. Ābū, Rajasthan).

The worship of Gaṇeśa in Jainism, judging from the visual evidence, began around the ninth or tenth century A.D. The earliest Jaina Gaṇeśa is from Mathurā, a figure associated with that of an image of Jaina Yakṣī Ambikā and dating to the ninth century A.D. A later (tenth century A.D.) Gaṇeśa is located at the Mahāvīra temple at Ghāṇerāv in Rajasthan. Also dating to the eleventh century are Gaṇeśa images in the small Jaina shrines (*devakulikā*s) at Osiāñ in Rajasthan. The earliest Jaina literary reference to Gaṇeśa is even later, in the *Abhidhānacintāmaṇi* of Hemacandra (ca. the third quarter of the twelfth century A.D.), while his more detailed iconography is enunciated still later, in the *Ācāradinakara* (A.D. 1412).

The *Abhidhānacintāmaṇi* refers to several appellations of Gaṇeśa, such as Heramba, Gaṇavighneśa, and Vināyaka, and visualizes him as elephant-headed with one tusk, potbellied, and bearing an axe while riding on a mouse mount.[6] The *Ācāradinakara* conceives the one-tusked and potbellied Gaṇapati as possessing 2, 4, 18, and even 108 arms, but the attributes of only the 4-armed variety are given in this text. According to this work, Gaṇapati rides on a mouse and makes the boon-conferring gesture (*varada-mudrā*) with one right hand and holds an axe in the other, while the corresponding left hands show the safety-bestowing gesture (*abhaya-mudrā*) and the sweet-ball (*modaka*).[7]

A Survey of the Images

About twelve figures of Gaṇeśa are reported from different Jaina sites. They range in date from the ninth to the fifteenth centuries A.D. and come mostly from western India. Among these western Indian images are seven figures carved in stone and fully in the round. These images function as tutelary deities and are located at the doorframes and the basement (*pīṭha*) of Jaina temples. Their absence on the main facade suggests that in Jaina temples Gaṇeśa has never been given a very prominent position. One independent brass figure of Gaṇeśa (ca. fifteenth century A.D.) from western India may also be Jaina. Apart from these three-dimensional renderings, Gaṇeśa is also carved in the surrounding frame (*parikara*) of the image of the Jaina Mahāvidyā Gaurī in the Vimala-vasahi (Delvāḍā, Mt. Ābū, Rajasthan). Outside western India, we find only three examples of Jaina Gaṇeśa that date before the fifteenth century A.D. Of these, two are carved in the Gaṇeśa and Navamuni caves in Puri District of Orissa, while the remaining one is on the pedestal of an image of Yakṣī Ambikā (of twenty-second Jina Ariṣṭanemi or Neminātha) from Mathurā.

Looking now in detail at these images, the Mathurā (U.P.) image is the earliest example of a Jaina Gaṇeśa, assignable to ca. ninth century A.D. (fig. 1). The image is now on display in the Archaeological Museum, Mathurā (acc. no. D.7). Gaṇeśa occupies the right flank of Ambikā, while on the left there appears Vaiśravaṇa. The two-armed Gaṇeśa sits with right leg dangling down and left folded on the seat (in *lalitāsana*) and shows a safety-bestowing gesture and a pot filled with sweets (*modaka-pātra*). That he has only two, rather than four, arms points to his "early" date. The Jainas have not ignored the fact that Gaṇeśa was "borrowed" from the Brahminical pantheon; he is the son of Ambikā (or Pārvatī or Gaurī), which is why he has been shown with her here. The Brahminical relationship between Gaṇeśa and Pārvatī is reflected again in a second Jaina work, a Gaurī from Mt. Ābū, to be discussed below.

There are several Jaina Gaṇeśas that date to the tenth or eleventh century A.D. One is from Ghāṇerāv, Rajasthan, carved on the northern pillar of the closed hall (*gūḍhamaṇḍapa*) of the Mahāvīra temple. The Gaṇeśa, in *lalita* pose, makes with one hand the *varada-mudrā*, and holds with the other three the goad, lotus (or axe?), and the *modaka-pātra*.[8] Osiāñ (District Jodhpur, Rajasthan) has yielded three eleventh-century figures of Gaṇeśa. All of these figures are carved in the small Jaina shrines (*devakulikā*s) that stand in the foreground of the Mahāvīra temple. Each Gaṇeśa is four-armed and seated in *lalita* pose on a throne (*bhadrāsana*). Two are carved on the doorsills along with Kubera, while the remaining one is on the *pīṭha*. The two doorsill Gaṇeśas on the western pair of *devakulikā*s hold spear, goad, lotus, and *modaka* bowl. The trunk in both cases is turned toward the bowl. In one instance, however, Gaṇeśa rides on an unconventional mount, an elephant. The third example, on the south side of the *pīṭha* of one of the eastern pair of *devakulikā*s, depicts Gaṇeśa with different attributes than those on the western *devakulikā*s, including an elephant tusk (*svadanta*), axe, and flower in the three surviving hands (fig. 2). Gaṇeśa, wearing sacred thread made from a snake (*nāgopavīta*), here is joined by two devotees with their hands folded in supplication.

Kumbhāriā (District Banaskantha, Gujarat) has yielded only one sculpture, carved on the west side of the *pīṭha* of the Neminātha temple (A.D. 1135) (fig. 3). The four-armed and potbellied Gaṇeśa is seated in *lalita* pose on a throne. As usual the mouse is his mount, and the god carries an elephant tusk, axe, lotus bud, and the *modaka-pātra*. The trunk, somewhat mutilated, is touching the *modaka-pātra*. Gaṇeśa is bedecked with *karaṇḍa-mukuṭa, udarabandha*, and the *nāgopavīta*.

Two Gaṇeśa images have been found at Nāḍlāi (Pali District, Rajasthan), both assignable to the twelfth century A.D. Of the two, one is incorporated in the entrance wall of the Neminātha temple, while the other is lying uncared for within the compound wall of the Supārśvanātha temple. The former figure, with his rat vehicle on the left, has four arms, three of which survive. With one hand he makes a gesture, perhaps the *varada-mudrā;* with the other two he holds the lotus and *modaka-pātra*. Surprisingly, the second Nāḍlāi Gaṇeśa (fig. 4) has only two arms, and he holds a mace and a noose respectively in his right and left hands. This Gaṇeśa's vehicle, a ram (*meṣa*), is also unexpected, and we must ask if he is indeed Gaṇeśa or some other, hitherto unidentified, deity or an unknown representation of Vināyaka?[9]

The brass Gaṇeśa, in the collection of the Museum of the Indian Historical Research Institute, St. Xavier's College, Bombay, has eighteen arms and sits cross-legged in *padmāsana* on a lotus seat. The trunk turns toward the right instead of being to the more usual left. The god's hair is piled on top of the head (*karaṇḍamukuṭa*) and wears a *nāgopavīta*. He is accompanied by his śakti, who sits on his left thigh and holds a flower and a flywhisk (*cāmara*). Close to the seat appears his mount, a mouse. Two of Gaṇeśa's hands are in *abhaya-mudrā* while others carry spear, axe, radish, pestle, arrow, mace, rosary, trident, thunderbolt, bow, water vessel, goad, noose, tusk, and fruit. H. D. Sankalia has identified this image as Jaina.[10] Nevertheless, we feel there exists no clear evidence for associating the figure with Jainism. The image, with no definite provenance, does not contain even the usual figure of the Jina at the top to suggest its Jaina affiliation. Moreover, the rendering of śakti along with Gaṇeśa is also a violation of Jaina tradition, wherein no deity has ever been conceived with his śakti.

One small figure of Gaṇeśa is carved in the frame (*parikara*) of an image of Mahāvidyā Gaurī in the Vimala-vasahī at Mt. Ābū (porch ceiling of cell no. 11, twelfth century A.D.) (fig. 5). The sixteen-armed Gaurī, whose cow vehicle lies below, displays features that suggest her association with Pārvatī, Śiva's wife.[11] Her Śaiva relationships include, for example, the

Śiva *gaṇa* and mother goddesses (*aṣṭamātṛkās*) that surround her along with Gaṇeśa. The four-armed Gaṇeśa sits in *lalitāsana* and bears tusk, goad, lotus, and *modaka*.

The two figures of Gaṇeśa from Digambara Jaina sites are found in the Navamuni (at Khaṇḍagiri) and Gaṇeśa (at Udayagiri) caves in Orissa. Both these caves, datable to ca. eleventh or twelfth century A.D., have one figure each of the four-armed Gaṇeśa. The figure in the Navamuni cave is especially interesting. Here Gaṇeśa precedes a row of seven Jaina *yakṣīs*, corresponding in number as well as iconography to the *saptamātṛkās*. The presence of Gaṇeśa here is in accord with the usual Hindu convention of rendering *saptamātṛkās* with Gaṇeśa, though he is usually shown last in the series. Gaṇeśa, sitting in the *mahārājalīlāsana* with the rat below on the pedestal, wears matted hair (*jaṭā-mukuṭa*) and holds a flower, rosary (*akṣamālā*), axe (*paraśu*), and the *modaka-pātra*.[12] The figure in the Gaṇeśa cave likewise carries a flower, axe, and the *modaka-pātra* in his three surviving hands.

Apart from the above-noted figures, the icon type of Pārśva Yakṣa of the twenty-third Jina Pārśvanātha in the Śvetāmbara tradition also has some relationship to Gaṇeśa, at least in respect of his elephant head (with one tusk); sometimes he holds his plucked-out tusk. The Śvetāmbara works, however, conceive Pārśva Yakṣa as elephant headed with a snake canopy overhead, possibly on the analogy of Dharaṇendra Yakṣa of Jina Pārśvanātha in Digambara tradition.[13] The elephant-headed Pārśva Yakṣa usually rides a tortoise (*kūrma*) and holds fruit, snake (or mace), mongoose (*nakula*), and snake. In several representations from Vimala-vasahī, Kharatara-vasahī (Delvāḍā, Mt. Ābū, Rajasthan), and Rohtak (Punjab),[14] the Yakṣa is shown with elephant head and snake canopy. The Yakṣa in four instances from the Kharatara-vasahī, which dates to A.D. 1459, rides either on a tortoise or a peacock and carries a lotus, snake, tusk (or a stick-like object or a second lotus or snake), and fruit.[15] Sometimes, the elephant head has only one tusk (*ekadanta*). In case of the image of Jina Pārśvanātha in Vimala-vasahī (cell no. 4, A.D. 1188), the elephant-headed Yakṣa, riding the tortoise, is provided with a three-hooded snake canopy. The Yakṣa holds a snake, vessel (*pātra*), a second snake, and mongoose-skin purse in his hands. The twenty-third Jina, Pārśvanātha, was born in Vārāṇasī, the abode of Śiva, and his association with Śiva appears in such features as a seven-hooded snake canopy and the attendance of the elephant-headed Pārśva Yakṣa. The Pārśva Yakṣa of Jina Pārśvanātha in Śvetāmbara tradition is thus represented with characteristics that reflect those of Gaṇeśa. The connection of Śiva, Pārvatī, and Gaṇeśa with the Jain tradition was also seen above, in the two examples — one from Mathurā and one from Vimala-vasahī — with Gaṇeśa depicted with Ambikā (Gaurī). It may be finally observed that the Yakṣa of Jina Pārśvanātha in Digambara tradition is Dhraṇendra, the snake king, who, however, does not show any of the features of Pārśva Yakṣa that suggest his association with Gaṇeśa.

Conclusion

On the basis of the above-cited examples, it is apparent that Gaṇeśa in Jaina tradition and art has close parallels to Brahminical Gaṇeśa. The Jaina Gaṇeśa never took on the negative connotations found in later (*vajrayāna*) Buddhism. Jaina texts such as the *Ācāradinakara* give only two attributes (the axe and sweet-ball) to be shown with the images of Gaṇeśa. The rendering of attributes like the lotus, goad, spear, and tusk in the hands of Jaina Gaṇeśas is guided by the prescriptions of the Brahminical works, which invariably conceive the four-armed Gaṇeśa as holding tusk, axe, lotus, and the *modaka* (or *modaka-pātra*).[16] A few other Brahminical works also envisage such attributes as goad, snake, and trident (*triśūla*) for four-armed Gaṇeśas.[17] In concurrence with the textual prescriptions, Gaṇeśa in Brahminical art of Osiāñ, Khajurāho, Ellorā, Bubaneśwara, and elsewhere has usually been carved as riding a rat and showing the *abhaya-mudrā* (or *abhaya-mudrā*-cum rosary, or radish, or tusk), axe, goad (or flower), and the *modaka-pātra*. The rendering of a ram and elephant as the mount of Jaina Gaṇeśa, in two instances respectively from Nāḍlāi and Osiāñ, however, finds no textual support.

From the foregoing discussion, it is clear that Gaṇeśa was assimilated into the Jaina pantheon in about the ninth century A.D. and was thenceforth accorded a favored position in Jaina worship, mainly as a god bestowing success (*siddhi*). In the beginning he was conceived both as two-armed and as four-armed, but by the tenth or eleventh century A.D. he was a prominent Jaina deity and was consequently visualized with six, eight, and even more arms. His conventional mount, the rat, appears for the first time in the twelfth century A.D. in the Jaina context, as evidenced from the instance in the Neminātha temple at Kumbhāriā. In the Śvetāmbara community of western India, Gaṇeśa still occupies an exalted position and is propitiated at different auspicious occasions.

NOTES

1. J. N. Banerjea, *The Development of Hindu Iconography* (Calcutta: Calcutta University Press, 1956), 354–55; Alice Getty, *Gaṇeśa: A Monograph on the Elephant-faced God* (Oxford: Clarendon Press 1936).

2. Banerjea, *Hindu Iconography,* 354 – 55; B. N. Puri, "Gaṇeśa and Gaṇapati Cult in India," *Journal of Indian History* 48, no. 2 (August 1970):405–13.

3. B. Bhattacharyya, *The Indian Buddhist Iconography* (Calcutta: Firma K. L. Mukhopadhyay, 1968), 348–49, 365–66.

4. "sarvārādhanasamaye kāryārambheṣu maṅgalācāre / mukhye labhye lābhe devairapipūjyase deva" [*Ācāradinakara, Gaṇapati Pratiṣṭhā* 3 (Bombay: 1923), 210.]

5. It may be observed that the Digambara sect was never so liberal as compared to the Śvetāmbara one in assimilating deities from other sects, and this is perhaps the reason why Gaṇeśa does not figure in Digambara tradition.

6. "Herambo gaṇavighneśaḥ paraśupāṇirvināyakaḥ / dvaimāturo gajāsyaikadantau lambodarākhugau" [*Abhidhānacintāmaṇi, Devakāṇḍa,* second verse, 207 (Surat: 1946), 30.]

7. "Tatra Ganapatermūrtayaḥ prāsādasthāḥ pūjanīyāḥ dhāraṇīyāśca Vidyāgaṇeśāḥ dvibhujacaturbhujaṣaḍ-bhujanavabhujāṣṭādaśabhujāṣṭottaraśatbhujarūpāḥ ... jayajaya lambodara paraśuvaradayuktāpasavyahastayug/ savyakaramodakābhayadharayāvaka-varṇapītalasika//mūṣakavāhanapīvarajaṅghā-bhujavastilambigurujaṭhare/vārāṇamukhaikarada varada saumya jayadeva gaṇanātha" [*Ācāradinakara: Gaṇapati Pratiṣṭhā,* 1–2.]

8. The attributes here and elsewhere are reckoned clockwise starting from the lower right hand.

9. M. N. P. Tiwari, *Elements of Jaina Iconography* (Varanasi: Indological Book House 1983), 110–12.

10. H. D. Sankalia, "A Jaina Gaṇeśa of Brass," *Jaina Antiquary* 5, no. 2 (September 1939):49–52.

11. The goddess holds thunderbolt, trident, sword, noose, goad, arrow, bow, mace, and shield, among other attributes.

12. Debala Mitra, "Śāsanadevīs in the Khaṇḍagiri Caves," *Journal of the Asiatic Society* 1, no. 2 (1959):127–28.

13. *Nirvāṇakalikā* 18.23; *Trisaṣṭiśalākāpuruṣacaritra* 9.3.362–63.

14. B. C. Bhattacharya, *Jaina Iconography* (Lahore: Motilal Banarasi Dass, 1939), 82.

15. Three figures are carved on three sides of the quadruple image of Pārśvanātha enshrined in the Pārśvanātha temple, known as Kharataravasahī, while the remaining one is carved on the door lintel of the sanctum of the same temple.

16. *Aparājitapṛcchā* 212:35 – 37; *Matsya Purāṇa* (Gaekawada Oriental Series), 260:52–55; *Agni Purāṇa* (Bombay: Venkatesvara Press, 1895), 50:23–26; *Rūpamaṇḍana* (Calcutta: Saraswati Press, 1882), 5:15. See Ramashraya Avasthi, *Khajurāho kī Devàpratimāyen* (Agra: Oriental Publishing House, 1967), 36 (in Hindi).

17. Banerjea, *Hindu Iconography,* p. 358.

Fig. 1. Gaṇeśa (flanking Ambikā), stone, ca. ninth century A.D. Archaeological Museum, Mathurā.

Fig. 2. Gaṇeśa, stone, eleventh century A.D. Mahāvīra Temple, Osiāñ, Rajasthan.

Fig. 3. Gaṇeśa, stone, ca. 1135 A.D. Nemināthа Temple, Kumbhāriā, Gujarat.

Fig. 4. Gaṇeśa, stone, twelfth century A.D. Nāḍlāi, Rajasthan.

Fig. 5. Gaṇeśa (lower left corner, flanking Mahāvidyā Gaurī), stone, twelfth century A.D. Vimala-vasahī, Mt. Ābū, Rajasthan.

6

The Wives of Gaṇeśa

Lawrence Cohen

Introduction

> When I was a child [in Karnataka], we believed Gaṇeśa to be a bachelor. But when I came to Calcutta, Gaṇeśa was with a woman. I asked a man, "Who is that?" He said: "That is Gaṇeśa's wife." I said: "As far as I know, Gaṇeśa is a bachelor."
>
> —*M. B. Talgeri, Bombay*

Mr. Talgeri is not alone. As far as many besides him know, Gaṇeśa is indeed a bachelor, the archetypical divine *brahmacārin*. For others, like Mr. Talgeri's passerby, the elephant-headed son of Pārvatī and Śiva is a married householder. Even within the married camp concord is lacking. At times Gaṇeśa is said to have two wives, here Ṛddhi and Siddhi, there Buddhi and Siddhi. Alternatively he is imaged and worshiped with a single consort, whether she be Sarasvatī, Śarda, Lakṣmī, a banana tree, or a nameless *dasī*, a servant. This diversity of connubial possibilities is heightened by Gaṇeśa's ambiguously structured and mythically dense relationship with his mother, the Goddess as Pārvatī, Gauri, or Durgā; by his androgynous appearance and comic persona; by his drawing on complex mythic and iconographic traditions of elephants, *yakṣa*s, and his divine parents; and by the geographic and ritual breadth of Gaṇeśa's importance in the worship of Hindus.

This essay examines this diversity, suggesting that it be used as a context in which a contemporary reading of Gaṇeśa as iconographic, ritual, and mythological text be situated. My conclusions come from a year (1983 – 84) spent asking many different people in many different places throughout India about the life, worship, and significance of Gaṇeśa. They suggest that the variety of ways in which Gaṇeśa's relationship to women is articulated may itself be structured along regional, class, and sectarian lines. The question of Gaṇeśa's marriage is not central to his mythic cycle as told by laypersons, yet when it is examined in an "all-India" context, coherent traditions emerge that distinguish north-central India from Maharastra, Marwar, south India, and Bengal, and devotees of Gaṇeśa as *iṣṭadevata* from devotees of Murukan̲, tantrics, the business community, and others. Through a focus on the marriage of Gaṇeśa, differences in how individuals and communities structure his divinity become apparent.

I begin with a review of textual and iconographic traditions of the consorts of Gaṇeśa, follow with a summary of observations from my fieldwork, and conclude by examining a variety of approaches to Gaṇeśa's ambiguous relations with women from both within Hindu tradition and without. The paper is based on notes of conversations that occurred as I traveled through India visiting temples of Gaṇeśa; specifically, the work was carried out in Maharastra (the Aṣṭa Vināyak shrines, Aurangabad, Bombay, Chinchwad, Ellora, Ganipatipule, Mahabeleshwar, Nasik, Pune, Shirdi, and Tryambak), Uttar Pradesh (Allahabad, Mathura, Varanasi and surrounding villages, and Vrindavan), Madhya Pradesh (Gwalior and Khajuraho), Punjab (Amritsar, Anandpur Sahib, and Patiala), and Rajasthan (Bikaner, Jaipur, Jaiselmer, and Udaipur) using Hindi or English in conversation, and in West Bengal (Calcutta), Karnataka (Bangalore and Mysore), Kerala (Trivandrum), and Tamil Nadu (Kanniyakumari, Madras, Madurai, Mahabalipuram and Tiruchchirapalli) using English or a third-party translator. My conversations were with *pūjārīs*, *pandits*, pilgrims, and passersby; I am grateful for their kindness and concern in talking with me and sharing their knowledge of Gaṇeśa.

Text and Icon

The story of Gaṇeśa's marriage most often told to me by informants in Uttar Pradesh was that of the *Śiva Purāṇa:*

> Śiva and Pārvatī said to their two sons, "You are both good sons, equal in our eyes. An auspicious marriage will be performed for the son who returns here after having gone around the entire world." When he heard this, Skanda started off immediately to go around the world, but Gaṇeśa pondered in his mind. Then he bathed and placed two seats for the worship of his father and mother. After praising them he circumambulated seven times around their seats, and then said, "Let my auspicious marriage be celebrated

> now." But his parents were surprised at his remark, and so Gaṇeśa replied. "Is it not said in the Vedas and Śāstras that anyone who worships his parents and circumambulates them will derive the merit of circumambulating the earth? Such things are said in the Vedas and Śāstras; are you going to say they are false? If you do, then your forms become false, as do the Vedas themselves. So, let my marriage be arranged quickly."
>
> When Śiva and Pārvatī heard his words they were greatly astonished, but they praised their son for his clever mind. And so Gaṇeśa was married to the daughters of Prajāpati: Siddhi (Success) and Buddhi (Intellect). After some time Gaṇeśa begat two sons: Kṣema (Prosperity) born to Siddhi, and Lābha (Acquisition) born to Buddhi. When Skanda returned and found that he had been tricked by his brother, he went angrily to the Kraunca mountain where he remains, celibate.[1]

This text was utilized as a definitive resolver of arguments over who was the wife of Gaṇeśa; in a small village south of Varanasi, the elder head of a Bhumihar family fetched his copy of the *Śiva Purāṇa* to provide an authoritative answer.

Textual references to the marriage of Gaṇeśa are few. The *Matsya Purāṇa*, in detailing the iconography of Gaṇeśa, envisions him as "the owner of Ṛddhi (success, prosperity) and Buddhi (intelligence)."[2] Here Ṛddhi and Buddhi (as do Buddhi and Siddhi in the *Śiva Purāṇa* and the popular modern pairing of Ṛddhi and Siddhi in Uttar Pradesh) function not as wives or *śakti*s, but as depersonalized emblems on the level of Gaṇeśa's lotus or bowl of sweet *modaka*s. In the *Brahmavaivarta Purāṇa*, Nārada interrupts his narrative of the birth and early life of Gaṇeśa to describe the origin of Kārtika. Kāma gives "the knowledge of the sexual science" to Kārtika; after this "Brahmā chanted the Vedas and married the fair, lovely, good-natured Devasenā (whom the savants called Saṣṭhī) to Kārtika." Only then, "after the lapse of a time, Śiva again invited the above gods, munis &c. and married the magnanimous Gaṇeśa with great eclat to Puṣṭi."[3] The narrative centers on Gaṇeśa, but on the subject of marriage Kārtika's story is interpolated. The incongruous references to Kāma's teaching and to the "fair, lovely, good-natured" bride of Kārtika suggest that Kārtika's marriage is a sexual union, and one in pronounced contrast to Gaṇeśa's.

Alice Getty concluded in her monograph on Gaṇeśa that "there is no trace of a Gaṇeśa cult in India before the fifth century A.D."[4] Balaji Mundkur has more recently supported this conclusion.[5] Possible antecedents to the worship of an elephant-headed lord of obstacles do appear in Vedic literature and pre-Gupta art; some of these deserve mention in the context of the consort of Gaṇeśa. The *Ṛgveda* refers to a "Gaṇapati" and the *Sāmaveda* to "Gaṇeśa."[6] Gaṇapati may be an epithet of Brahmanaspati or Indra,[7] and Gaṇeśa here probably refers to Rudra/Śiva as lord of the *gaṇa*s.[8] What is of interest is the possible link between these Vedic lords of the *gaṇa*s and women — Prithvi Agrawala cites the *Ṛgveda* commentary *Sarvānukramaṇī* to suggest a link between Brahmanaspati/Gaṇapati and Alakṣmī.[9] Brahmanaspati/Gaṇapati is invoked for *alakṣmī-nāśanam*, the removal of the inauspicious antithesis of Lakṣmī. As the more familiar elephantine god comes to take on this role of *gaṇa* lord, his association with dangerous females continues. From at least the fifth or sixth century onward, Gaṇeśa is found with the *saptamātṛkā*s (seven mothers) in temple sculpture, fitting complements to his own ambivalent nature as placer and remover of obstacles.

Mundkur explores the association of "Gaṇeśa" and Rudra/Śiva in the *Sāmaveda* in the context of the origin of the rather mysterious "female Gaṇeśa." He suggests a process through which Śiva's titles such as Gaṇeśa and Gaṇapati were extended to pre-Vedic, often theriomorphic deities, who became the *gaṇa*s.[10] This theory might both explain the Vedic references and origin of Gaṇeśa as well as the parallel incorporation of female elephant-headed *yakṣī*s into the emerging Śaivite cultus.

The earliest evidence of such a "female Gaṇeśa" is a weathered terracotta plaque from Rairh in Rajasthan, dated by Agrawala from the first century B.C.E. to the first century C.E., of what appears to be a standing female figure with an elephant's head. However, the significance and even the identity of this plaque are not clear. Agrawala labels the figure Vināyakī, but he offers little justification for associating it with either later elephant-headed goddess figures or the later Purāṇic references to Vaināyakī and its variants.[11]

Vaināyakī in the Purāṇas is neither described as elephant-headed nor associated explicitly with Gaṇeśa. The sixth-century *Matsya Purāṇa* mentions Vaināyakī amidst a list of two hundred "Divine Mothers" whom Śiva created to drink the generative blood of the demon Andhaka, who wanted to kidnap Pārvatī.[12] The *Liṅga Purāṇa* includes the name in a list of *śakti*s invoked during the mammoth Jayābiṣeka rite that yields the four *puruṣārtha*s.[13] Elephant-headed females who figure prominently in Purāṇic and folk literature are not Vaināyakīs but demonesses or transformed goddesses. Mālinī is an elephant-headed demoness who, in a variant of Gaṇeśa's origin story, drinks Pārvatī's bath water and has a son with five elephant heads, four of which Śiva removes.[14] In an episode from the *Skanda Purāṇa*, Lakṣmī is cursed by a Brahman to have an elephant's head. Brahmā is so pleased by her penance in this form that he declares that she will henceforth be worshiped as Mahālakṣmī.[15] The elephant-headed goddess as Mālinī is mother to Gaṇeśa; Lakṣmī, as will be seen below, is usually associated with Gaṇeśa as consort. Gaṇeśa's connection to elephant-headed females, however tenuous, encompasses these two roles — if we take the "female Gaṇeśa" tradition as a whole, we find within it the same tension that characterizes Gaṇeśa's overall relationship to the Goddess, both his wife and mother.

Aside from the Rairh plaque, all extant images of an elephant-headed goddess date from the tenth century onward. The most famous of these, indeed the only one mentioned by Getty in her classic monograph on Gaṇeśa, is the forty-first *yoginī* in a Causath Yoginī temple at Bheraghat, Jabalpur district, Madhya Pradesh. This *yoginī* is inscribed "Śrī-Ainginī." She is unique in that an elephant-headed male, presumably Gaṇeśa, supports her bent left leg.[16] Mundkur argues that it is unlikely that the Ucchiṣṭa Gāṇapatyas, the Tantric worshippers of Gaṇeśa, envisioned the god with an elephant-headed counterpart as *śakti;* in Gaṇapatya texts when Gaṇeśa is described with a *śakti* she is inevitably anthropomorphic.[17] However, the Bheraghat image does seem to draw upon Śakta tradition in its structuring of the relation between the feminine and the masculine embodied in a totalized — yet split — Gaṇeśa.

Another central Indian image, from Satna (now in the Indian Museum, Calcutta), suggests an alternative structuring of this relationship. It is an image of the boar-headed Vṛṣabhā holding a baby Gaṇeśa in one of her left hands and surrounded by four votive therianthropic goddesses, one of which has an elephant head. Agrawala speculates that

> the Gaṇapati figure in the hand of Vṛṣabhā as her child tends to suggest that this cow-headed Yoginī personification was considered to be the principal divinity of Śaivite nature including in her *parivāra* both Gaṇeśa and his female equal Vināyakī as her children.[18]

Here "Vināyakī" is arguably a sibling to Gaṇeśa, although her presence as one of a therianthropic group suggests her substitutibility for Vṛṣabhā and thus a maternal relationship to Gaṇeśa the child.

Agrawala includes in his survey of female Gaṇeśas two descriptions of hermaphroditic figures. He translates Śrīkumāra's sixteenth-century *Śilparatna,* which details the iconography of "Śakti-Gaṇapati":

> Now Śakti-Gaṇapati, Salutation to the god Gaṇeśa, who is from the neck upwards an elephant and whose lower body is of a youthful female, has vermilion-red colour of the evening, a corpulent belly, the breasts which

> make the bodily frame bow down owing to their weight, and beautiful hips; is shining with two proboscises which are (like) two great chains of molten gold, is of the form of Five Seed-syllables (*pañcabījasvarūpam*) and has ten splendid arms adorned with a citron (*bījapūra*), etc.[19]

The description—a female body, a Siamese head—is certainly unusual, and may reflect Agrawala's misreading of Gaṇeśa imaged with his *śakti* as the two combined. If we follow Agrawala, the two trunks suggest that Śakti-Gaṇapati fuses male and female elephant-headed deities. As with the Bheraghat image, a Śākta orientation appears to define the relation between the elephant-headed goddess and Gaṇeśa. An inscription on the Amareśvara temple at Mandhata, Nimar district, Madhya Pradesh, similarly notes that Gaṇapati, competing with his father's Ardhanārīśvara form, assumed the same form.[20]

Finally, Agrawala offers the Buddhist text *Āryamañjuśrīmūlakalpa*, portions of which he summarizes:

> It is stated that the region of the Vindhya is appropriate for the *siddhi* of Vināyaka. She is the deity causing obstacles to those who mutter religious charms. She possesses the elephant-proboscis (*hastākāra-samāyuktām*) and is one toothed (*ekadantām*). She is of the form of a horse (*aśvārūpā*) and can assume many different forms. She is the divine daughter of Īśāna, is of varying nature and causes obstacles (*vighnakārakām*).[21]

Here the goddess Vināyaka is identified explicitly with Gaṇeśa, unlike Vaināyakī in the Purāṇic lists; she assumes several of his ritual (causer of obstacles), iconographic (elephant's trunk and single tusk), and mythological (daughter of Īśāna, who Agrawala identifies with Śiva) aspects.

The vast majority of images of Gaṇeśa, however, show him with only a human *śakti*. According to Ananda Coomaraswamy, a statue from Bhumara represents the oldest known depiction or Gaṇeśa with a *śakti;* he places it in the sixth century.[22] The goddess sits on Gaṇeśa's left hip, holding a bowl of *batasa*s (flat cakes) or *modaka*s (round sweets) in her lap from which Gaṇeśa with his left-turning trunk takes a sweet. This motif is repeated in other areas and periods; throughout, the consort lacks a distinctive personality or iconographic repertoire.

Far from functioning as iconic deflated phallus, symbol of Gaṇeśa's defeat and emasculation by his father—the classic psychoanalytic interpretation of Gaṇeśa's origin and iconography[23]—his bent trunk vividly contributes in these images to the erotic bond between the god and his consort. With it Gaṇeśa reaches into the consort's lap for the bowl of *mo-*

dakas (Getty equates these with "the germ of life").[24] In the more risqué Ucchiṣṭa-Gaṇapati images, the bowl of *modakas* is dispensed with; Gaṇeśa's trunk descends directly into the goddess's *yoni*.

The connubial, occasionally erotic, imaging of Gaṇeśa and his *śakti* parallels the emergence of the Tantric Gāṇapatya *sampradāya* — the worship of Gaṇeśa above other deities in the pantheon. Courtright places the rise of an identifiable Gaṇeśa cult in the sixth to eighth centuries, and of a developed Gāṇapatya tradition certainly by the tenth.[25] Central to Gāṇapatya practice was the imaging of the deity with his consort. According to Getty, Gāṇapatyas worshiped five and later six distinct forms of "Śakti-Gaṇapati." Symbols of fertility predominate; in addition to the consort's *modakas*, Gaṇeśa himself often holds a pomegranate.[26]

The *Śaṅkaravijaya* of Ānandagiri, which Courtright dates to about the tenth century, has Śaṅkara debate and defeat proponents of various philosophical and religious schools; it provides a description of the six groups of Gāṇapatyas. One of the six, led in the *Śaṅkaravijaya* by Herambasuta, is the left-handed Tantric Ucchiṣṭa Gāṇapatyas. In the text Herambasuta describes the erotic image of Ucchiṣṭa worship, trunk in *yoni*, and glosses "Gaṇapati and Devī are part of one another; just as, though the self [*jīva*] is smaller than the lord [*īśa*], even so they are one." This move toward equivalence of god and goddess is paralleled by the antinomianism of the Ucchiṣṭas:

> First, all men born of different castes are of one caste; second, the women of all castes are the same as the men. There is no sin if there is intercourse between men and women [of difference castes], or separation either, because there is no rule that one woman belongs to one man. If they are united in intercourse while she is menstruous, there is greater bliss [*ananda*] to be experienced, because there is much blood flowing. There is no such arrangement as marriage and all classes [*varna*] are the same.[27]

This union of social and cosmological opposites seems to remain, however, a path for men alone: "The act of enjoyment should be taken by any man who, having Heramba Gaṇapati in his mind, takes a women as his *śakti*."[28]

The antinomian license of the *vamacara* Ucchiṣṭa Gāṇapatyas never came to characterize the mainstream of Gaṇeśa worship, but the Tantric Gāṇapatya tradition did influence later and more orthodox understandings of Gaṇeśa's relationship with women. Getty notes briefly that the Tantric *śakti* of Gaṇeśa was sometimes called "Lakṣmī";[29] she differentiates this Lakṣmī from the Vaiṣṇavite Śrī-Lakṣmī but offers no evidence for the distinction. Both Gaṇeśa and Śrī-Lakṣmī have long traditions of relationships with elephants and the auspicious. The possible relation of Brahmanaspati/Gaṇapati to Alakṣmī and the *Skanda Purāṇa* story of Lakṣmī's transformation into an elephant-headed goddess have already been mentioned. Although no evidence exists to suggest a popular tradition of the joint worship of Lakṣmī and Gaṇeśa as distinct personalities until the recent past, their figuring together in artistic and popular imagination does precede the current era of calendar art and at least keeps open the possibility of partial Tantric origins. Getty in her book includes an undated Rajput miniature of the *abhiṣeka* of Gaja Lakṣmī with various gods in votive attendance.[30] Gaṇeśa is distinguished from the other deities in his position apart from them and directly below the goddess, forming a vertical axis with her. He appears to be the most direct beneficiary of the *prasāda* of the *abhiṣeka* effluence and, given his resemblance to the elephants who bathe Lakṣmī, seems more closely tied to her essence than does Viṣṇu standing to his left.

Gaṇeśa's marriage in the *Śiva Purāṇa* to Siddhi and Buddhi is another central archetype; it can also be viewed within a Tantric context, that of the Aṣṭa Siddhi. *Siddhis*, special and often magical powers or successes, are important in the yoga literature as largely iconic signs of the goal achieved along the path to *mokṣa*. In Tantra their function is more indexical; Mircea Eliade points out that for many Tantric texts *siddhis* are "direct proof of man's gaining divinity."[31] There are many *siddhis*, but texts such as the fourth-century *Vaikhānasasmartasūtra* come increasingly to speak of eight.[32] In the eleventh-century play *Prabodha Chandrodaya*, the antinomian sexual practices of the Kapalikas are said to lead to the attainment of "the eight great *siddhis*."[33] As *siddhis* are powerful indices of godhead attained, a state usually imaged sexually within Tantra, their embodiment as goddesses is not surprising. Eliade's attribution of this personification to the magical worldview of peasants[34] seems unimaginatively naive.

In the cosmopolitan Śākta worship of Gaṇeśa the Aṣṭa Siddhi were also addressed as eight goddesses. In the *Gaṇeśa Purāṇa*, according to the retelling of this work on the walls of the Siddhi Vināyak temple in Pune, these personified Aṣṭa Siddhi are used by Gaṇeśa to attack the demon Devantaka. These eight consorts are fused in a single *devi*, Gaṇeśa's *śakti*, according to Getty.[35] She speculates as to whether the Aṣṭa Siddhis are a transformation of the *saptamātṛkas* with whom Gaṇeśa is often sculpturally represented;[36] their relation to other divine octets like the Aṣṭa Durgā also deserves attention.

Gaṇeśa's entry into the canon of orthodox Brahmanical Smarta worship in south India and then throughout the subcontinent is as a single deity, imaged without a *śakti* or consorts. He is worshiped with Śiva, Pārvatī,

Viṣṇu, and Aditya, the sun. Whether Gaṇeśa occupies a corner of the *maṇḍala* or is worshiped as principal household god in the center of the group, he remains alone. Yet images of Gaṇeśa with a *śakti* on his lap or flanked by two consorts are to be found throughout India. Like the mythological traditions of Gaṇeśa's ambiguously structured relationships with his parents, this complex legacy in text and icon of the relationship of the god to women who are not his mother forms a part of the cultural materials with which contemporary worshipers make sense of Gaṇeśa.

Arrangements

When confronted with an image of Gaṇeśa with a *śakti* or two consorts, a worshiper or passerby may not invest the female images with much significance. Unlike, for example, a goddess in a picture with Śiva—where she will immediately be identified as Pārvatī or another—the goddesses associated with Gaṇeśa often lack a density of meaning. When questioned about such an image, an individual may politely but halfheartedly suggest a name, or state, "I don't know." However, on numerous occasions at shrines or images of Gaṇeśa when I was observing or participating in worship or conversing with *paṇdit*s or *pūjārī*s, people had definite ideas about the identity of these images and the marital status of Gaṇeśa. Not only do such ideas exist, but over the course of hundreds of such conversations I became aware of patterns in responses to the question of Gaṇeśa's consorts. The most prevalent distinction was regional: individuals in Varanasi and other cities in Uttar Pradesh often spoke of Ṛddhi and Siddhi as the two wives of Gaṇeśa, and there was a less pronounced tendency to associate him with Lakṣmī; in Maharashtra, Gaṇapati was also considered to be married but not always to Ṛddhi and Siddhi—more frequently, Sarasvatī and also Śarda were declared to be the wives of Gaṇeśa; in the four southernmost states of India, Gaṇapati or Pillaiyar was almost always *brahmacārin;* and in Calcutta, Gaṇeśa was also unmarried, conceptualized not only as the son of the Goddess as Durgā or Kālī but also as the brother of Lakṣmī and Sarasvatī. In this section I will examine this plurality of approaches to the marriage of Gaṇeśa.

Pārvatī

A Gujarati story revolves around the custom of gambling through the night during the festival of Diwali:

> Śiva and Pārvatī were themselves playing at a game of dice. Śiva lost all that he owned to Pārvatī. Kārtik saw his father dejected and asked Śiva to teach him how to play at dice. Kārtik then challenged Pārvatī to a game of dice and

> won back everything from her. Gaṇeśa saw his mother dejected and asked her to teach him the game; he then won everything back from Kārtik. He returned to Pārvatī with his good fortune, but she still looked dejected. Gaṇeśa asked, "I have won all—why are you not smiling?" Pārvatī replied, "But my son, you have not brought back your father."[37]

Through tales such as this individuals are reminded of the inevitable tension in Gaṇeśa's devotion to his mother. Paul Courtright's detailed examination of Gaṇeśa's relationship with Śiva and Pārvatī in Purāṇic literature and his reading of Sudnir Kakar enable him to tie Gaṇeśa's fractious origins and sexual ambiguity to the psychological and ritual contexts of the transition from female-dominated childhood to male-dominated youth.[38] His interpretation rests in part on an interesting association of the *upanayana* rite of passage with Gaṇeśa's filial conflict. Though speculative at best, Courtright's attempt to offer an Indian frame of analysis for Gaṇeśa's ambiguous sexuality moves away from the category fallacy[39] of more simplistic Oedipal analyses. It is a significant effort to ground the study of myth and divine meanings in a more indigenous psychodynamic.

Yet if reflecting as Courtright suggests the inevitable reality of childhood's end, the stories of Gaṇeśa's birth, beheading, and reintegration did not provoke in any of the many worshipers with whom I discussed them either reactions of irony or discourse expressive of any problematic in the conflict between father and son for Pārvatī. Nor did this conflict seem to emerge in rituals of and for Gaṇeśa, despite the Turnerian capacity of ritual to structure ambiguity. Where irony occasionally did appear in popular myth and ritual was in the recognition that the Goddess may function as both the mother and the consort of Gaṇeśa. Two ritual pairings of Gaṇeśa with a goddess who is and yet is not his mother are especially suggestive of this trope: the worship of Gaṇeśa and Gauri in harvest festivals, and the pairing of the Kala Bo with Gaṇeśa during Durgā Pujā.

In Bengal, Gaṇeśa on Durgā Pujā is associated with a banana tree—the "Kala Bo"—ritually transformed into the Goddess during the festival. According to Haridas Mitra, the Kala Bo is a condensation of the *nava patrika,* nine types of leaves that together form a sacred complex on Durgā Pujā.[40] Each of the plants is associated with a particular manifestation of Devī, and together they symbolize her unity and represent peace. On the first day of Durgā Pujā, the Kala Bo is set up alongside the other gods next to Gaṇeśa and wrapped in a sari. For most who view her, the new sari indicates her role as a new bride; for many with whom I spoke, the Kala Bo is unquestionably married to Gaṇeśa each year.[41] For some Bengalis, this is a marriage of desperation: Gaṇeśa, they say, is, given his appearance and nature, almost unmarriageable. The mute and uncomplaining banana bride is his last — and only — hope. But however unlikely the couple, in Calcutta and surrounding villages the response to a query regarding Gaṇeśa's marital state remained, "He is married to the Kala Bo."

Yet the Kala Bo signifies none less than Durgā herself during the Pujā festival. Durgā in Bengal is the mother of Gaṇeśa. Where the Kala Bo's identity with the Goddess is not widely appreciated, the relationship is not very ambiguous. For individuals knowledgeable in matters of ritual signification, however, a conflict may emerge. One woman in Calcutta, a librarian with whom I spent a delightful morning discussing the Kala Bo, serves as a case in point. She first utilized an apologetic rhetoric of symbolism, explaining that as the tree symbolizes the importance of agriculture, its marriage with Gaṇeśa is merely a "symbol" of the desire for a productive and obstacle-free harvest. Up to this point our discussion had less to do with the ambiguity of Gaṇeśa's relations with women than with the more generally troublesome hermeneutics of post-Orientalist discourse. But when she examined a reference text (Nogindranath Basu's *Vishnu Kosh*) and read of the identity of the tree with Durgā, the librarian suddenly switched from a focus on the symbolism of this marriage to denying its existence, noting that "only illiterate persons see this as the wife of Gaṇeśa." By this denial of the marriage of Gaṇeśa as the ignorance of those without textual references, his ties to the Goddess were rendered unambiguous. But the rejection of irony is incomplete, for it is premised on the denial of a known reality (Gaṇeśa is married to the Kala Bo) given a potent but questionably real fear (the Kala Bo is Gaṇeśa's mother).

In central India, Gaṇeśa and Gauri are traditionally worshiped in the shared context of a harvest festival in which ritual motifs of menstruation and rebirth are integral. This worship has become increasingly tied to Gaṇeśa's festival of Bhādrapad Chaturthī. The immersion of Gaṇeśa's *mūrti* after the Chaturthī is associated with the celebration of Gauri as *śakti*. B. A. Gupte, writing in 1906 in the best Frazerian tradition, ties Gaṇeśa's "death" through immersion to the death of the old harvest season; his association with Gauri both structures this death and leads through the fertility of the Goddess to rebirth. Although Gauri is technically Gaṇeśa's mother, as with the Kala Bo, the Goddess comes to be identified more as consort than as parent.[42]

The potential for ambiguity between wife and mother extends beyond central India. One man in Varanasi originally from Himachal Pradesh noted the potential conflict in the relationship of Gaṇeśa with Gauri, and at first explained it through recourse to a common rhetoric of plurality — different devotees may structure the relationships between gods differently, and therefore Gauri can be either Gaṇeśa's mother or his wife but not both. He paused, and went on to give a more personal answer from his own Śākta perspective: "The father is in the womb of the mother," he noted. Men marry their mothers and recreate themselves. The iconographic relations between gods structure this sexual ambiguity. "If Lakṣmī is on Gaṇeśa's left she is his wife, but if on his right his mother." For this man, the ambiguity is essential; though perceived by few, it is fundamental to the esoteric experience through contemplation of Gaṇeśa of the equivalence of generations and relativity of time.

The conflicting loyalties of a son between mother and wife is a deeply resonant theme in Indian popular culture. Lannoy writes on the primacy of the mother–son relationship in India on into adulthood, suggesting that "the Hindu male tends to seek in his wife not a mate but a mother."[43] Whether the Goddess functions as in the case of the Kala Bo and Gauri as both wife and mother or, as is far more frequently the case, Gaṇeśa's complex relationship to his mother prevents much attention in his mythic cycle from being focused on his own marriage, the structuring of divine relations reflects human realities. Its ambiguity denied, the total relationship of mother to son is celebrated and continually reasserted. The popular Siddhi Vināyak temple in Pune's Saras Bagh is said to sit on a mound of earth scooped from the land at the foot of Pārvatī hill near where it rests, a striking affirmation of Gaṇeśa's bond to the Goddess as mother, a bond that can dwarf all others.

Celibacy

Mr. Talgeri was surprised when he left his native south to find that Gaṇeśa was married. Throughout southern India, Gaṇeśa is envisioned as *brahmacārin*. Even in Varanasi in the north, worshipers at the Chintamani Gaṇeśa temple near Kedar Ghat, frequented chiefly by south Indians, describe Gaṇeśa as celibate and single, but at neighboring shrines with different clientele he remains married. In both north and south, Gaṇeśa's condition is in opposition to that of his brother Kārtika/Murukaṉ. In the south, Murukaṉ can be both ascetic and married; but even where, as at Palani, he is enshrined as an ascetic, for his devotees he still remains unquestionably married. Murukaṉ's courtship and marriage to each of his wives serves as a devotional paradigm for *bhaktas*.[44] Gaṇeśa, however, in the south is solely *brahmacārin*.

In the north, Kārtika is today a minor deity; he was mentioned by informants in Uttar Pradesh and Rajasthan only in the context of his contest with Gaṇeśa, in their telling of a marriage story similar to that in the *Śiva Purāṇa*. The fact that in the south Gaṇeśa is considered celibate and unmarried was only acknowledged in these northern states by transplanted south Indians. Other northerners lacked a sense of the plurality of regional possibilities for Gaṇeśa's marital state; this lack underscores the relative unimportance of a north/south opposition in the construction of north Indian identity.

In Maharashtra and the south, however, the fact that Gaṇeśa would be *either* married or celibate was on many occasions recognized by my informants. The opposition of Gaṇeśa as married and Gaṇeśa as single here helped focus a discourse of regional identity largely phrased in terms of north versus south. A Brahman working in Madurai's Minaksi temple affirmed Gaṇeśa's celibacy and then noted in some consternation the paradox that "in Bombay Gaṇeśa is a family man and Kārtik a *brahmacārin!* Why? I don't know." Alternatively, schoolgirls outside a temple in Nasik in Maharashtra informed me that "in the south, the opinion is that [Gaṇeśa] is not married. But here he is." Through the contrast of Gaṇeśa as single and as married, the girls identify that "here" is different from the south, a statement more significant in Maharastra than the north, given, as Courtright[45] notes, its liminal position between south and north.

The contrast between these two views of Gaṇeśa suggests that myths are tied to regional conceptions of the relationships between gods; their selective use relates to an individual's sense of social identity. People in urban areas come from many parts of India. Though individuals may be aware of different variants of Gaṇeśa's marital status, they make sense of it in a fashion tied to their regional heritage.

In the south, married/single opposition was structured not only in terms of north/south but also a perpendicular Murukan̲/Gaṇeśa (Pillaiyar) opposition. Gaṇeśa's celibacy is justified by pointing out that Murukan̲ is married. The brothers' opposition reveals the fundamental duality of male adulthood obscured through the syntagmatic ideology of *āśramadharma*. Man can be — is perhaps unavoidably — both householder and ascetic, wife-taking and wife-rejecting.[46] This duality is usually read in alternative contexts to the paradigmatic construction of self, whether the historical incompatibilities of *dharma* and *mokṣa*,[47] the ideologically encompassed and encompassing,[48] the moral conflict of particularistic and universal norms,[49] and of course the developmental struggle between paternal and maternal identification,[50] the usual rendition of Gaṇeśa's origin. Whichever of its etiologies is chosen, however, the duality remains a model for comprehension and resolution of the ambiguities of divine and human male sexuality.

Gaṇeśa's state of *brahmacarya* should not be understood as an Indianized sort of Oedipal fixation, despite the critical mass of the god's relationship with Pārvatī. Lannoy notes that "we should be careful not to use the familiar Western model of the mother-dominated son."[51] Even when compared to his powerful and unambiguously masculine married brother, Gaṇeśa is often seen as a locus of unusual strength. He is the embodiment of both his parents, Śiva and Śakti. Though his unusual birth and mutilation are often textually justified as necessary for preventing the cosmic imbalance that would result if a natural son of Śiva and Pārvatī were ever created,[52] several individuals spoke of Gaṇeśa as precisely that microcosmic locus of totality. One man in Varanasi, my Tantric friend mentioned above, in defending Gaṇeśa's celibacy identified the *śakti* of Gaṇeśa with his red color, implying that to speak of the marriage of a god who contains within his corpulent self both male and female would be redundant.

The *Gaṇeśa Purāṇa* stories from the walls of the Siddhi Vināyak temple in Pune offer two versions of the source of Gaṇeśa's color—one external, the spilled blood of a demon, and another internal, the swallowing of a demon whose heat causes Gaṇeśa to develop a raging fever. Many of Gaṇeśa's ritual preferences are explained in terms of his need to be cooled; *dūrvā* grass, for example, is said to be a very cooling substance. Wendy O'-Flaherty has discussed at length the potential for equivalence of erotic and ascetic heat. Gaṇeśa's demonic heat, acquired through the displaced sexual actions of swallowing or the exchange of fluids, becomes ascetic *tapas* through his *brahmacarya* status. The god is daubed in the vermillion of his own *śakti;* contained and containing both male and female, he renders circular the distinction between erotic and ascetic. Fluid cannot be lost; sex equals no sex.

Gaṇeśa's power often remains true to its demonic origin in its liminal and largely negative signification for devotees; Brenda Beck[53] contrasts Gaṇeśa's role in south India as someone "who helps overcome obstacles and inauspicious influences" with his brother's ability "to respond to a devotee's expression of affection and need." Susan Wadley, in describing the delegation of divine powers in the structuring of the pantheon in a western Uttar Pradesh village, notes that in Karimpur Śiva's powers of creation and destruction are divided between Gaṇeśa as destroyer of obstacles and Guru Gorakhnath as source of fertility and controller of snakes.[54]

Gaṇeśa's power can often function generatively, however. Stella Kramrisch discusses the fat *yakṣa* as "the Eater," prefiguring a class of generative deities including Brahmā, Agni, and Gaṇeśa.[55] Given his liminal position Gaṇeśa is uniquely associated with weddings. In Varanasi, on Gaṇeśa's Chaturthīs each month some women observe a *vrata* to acquire sons by fasting until the moon comes out and worshiping at a Gaṇeśa temple. On Māgh Chaturthī couples wishing a son together come to worship

Gaṇeśa. The god's tradition of generativity in Varanasi is prefigured in the *Vayu Purāṇa* story of the king Divodāsa requesting a son from the *gaṇeśa* Nikumbha.[56]

In Madurai, the Gaṇeśa Nataraja temple is well known for its efficacy for childless couples, who come to bathe the image and circumambulate it in the early morning for forty-eight days. One woman in Madurai associated Gaṇeśa's fertility with his control over snakes, reminiscent of Guru Gorakhnath in Karimpur. Gaṇeśa is worshiped in the presence of *nāga*s, themselves signs of fertility, not only in Madurai but in cities throughout the south and at least at one temple in Allahabad.

Another framework for the paradox of Gaṇeśa's fertility is offered by E. Valentine Daniel, who in his ethnology of a Tamil village views Gaṇeśa not in terms of Freudian ambiguity but using a Marriottian scheme of coded substance transactions:

> Ganapathy, by symbolizing both fertility and celibacy, recommends to the mind not indefinite celibacy but controlled sexual transactions so that potential fertility may be enhanced rather than threatened.[57]

In short, the god of fertility is not necessarily a locus of neutered sexuality and weakness. He can be; witness the humor many Bengalis took in his sham marriage. Weakness is part of Gaṇeśa's semiotic repertoire, but so is power, and often it is the nature of superimposed discourses that shape his public image. Compare Tilak's vision of Gaṇeśa as a symbol of a united and empowered India with the self-image of one south Indian in Varanasi, structured again through a north/south opposition:

> We are a south Indian temple, and worship Gaṇeśa as our families' *iṣṭadevata;* but in the north people worship Mahadeo and Hanuman. They are very healthy people as Hanuman is their *iṣṭadevata*—he is very strong.

Paired Consorts

Throughout India, on contemporary poster art Gaṇeśa is portrayed primarily in three situations: alone; with the family group of Śiva, Pārvatī, and Kārtika; or with Lakṣmī, Sarasvatī, or both. However, in temples and over doorways he is almost ubiquitously flanked by two smaller female figures. They often hold fans and may be joined or replaced by paired fish, rats, peacocks, parrots, monkeys, elephants, *yali*s (lions with elephant trunks), the two sons of Gaṇeśa, *yakṣa*s carrying fruit, swastikas, the words *"śubha"* and *"lābha,"* planetary deities, or even other Gaṇeśas.

Throughout north India, these female figures are identified as Ṛddhi and Siddhi. There are no Purāṇic sources for Ṛddhi and Siddhi, but the pairing parallels those of Buddhi and Siddhi in the *Śiva Purāṇa* and Ṛddhi and Buddhi in the *Matsya Purāṇa*. They are depersonalized figures, interchangeable, and given their frequent depiction fanning Gaṇeśa are often referred to as *dasī*s—servants. Their names represent the benefits accrued by the worshiper of Gaṇeśa, and thus Gaṇeśa is said to be the owner of Ṛddhi and Siddhi; he similarly functions as the father of Śubha (auspiciousness) and Lābha (profit), a pair similar to the *Śiva Purāṇa*'s Kṣema (prosperity) and Lābha. Though in Varanasi the paired figures were usually called Ṛddhi and Siddhi, Gaṇeśa's relationship to them was often vague. He was their *mālik,* their owner; they were more often *dasī*s than *patnī*s (wives). Yet Gaṇeśa was married to them, albeit within a marriage different from other divine matches in the lack of a clear familial context.

Such a context has recently emerged in the popular film *Jai Santoshī Mā*. The film builds upon a text, also of recent vintage, in which Gaṇeśa has a daughter, the neophyte goddess of satisfaction, Santoshī Mā. In the film, the role of Gaṇeśa as family man is developed significantly. Santoshī Mā's genesis occurs on Rāksa bandan. Gaṇeśa's sister is visiting for the tying of the *rākhī.* He calls her *bahenmansa*—his "mind-born" sister. Gaṇeśa's wives, Ṛddhi and Siddhi, are also present, with their sons Śubha and Lābha. The boys are jealous, as they, unlike their father, have no sister with whom to tie the *rākhī.* They and the other women plead with their father, but to no avail; but then Nārada appears and convinces Gaṇeśa that the creation of an illustrious daughter will reflect much credit back onto himself. Gaṇeśa assents and from Ṛddhi and Siddhi emerges a flame that engenders Santoshī Mā.[58]

The film articulates the role of Gaṇeśa as *gṛhastha*—as householder. Like his father, he remains an ambivalent householder, not wishing to have another child and not engaging with normal relations with his wives. And yet Gaṇeśa is envisioned with wives, sons, a sister, tying *rākhī*s—images of normative family life. For many in Varanasi, Gaṇeśa was unquestionably married to Ṛddhi and Siddhi; for others, the relationship was less clear. Although Gaṇeśa was seldom considered *brahmacārin,* the identity of his wives was often problematic. Gaṇeśa's relationship with Lakṣmī added an element of uncertainty to his relationship with the far less charismatic Ṛddhi and Siddhi, as will be discussed below.

In Mysore, Madurai, and Tiruchchirapalli, the paired figures were almost always identified as Siddhi and Buddhi. Given local knowledge that Gaṇeśa is *brahmacarya,* they were usually viewed symbolically as the positive fruits of the worship of Gaṇeśa. Thus the South Indian discourse on

Gaṇeśa's celibacy is still more complex: a "marriage" is recognized, but one exclusively iconic and not indexed to any *real* divine event. M. Arunachalam retells a south Indian temple myth that exemplifies this union:

> Gaṇeśa is a confirmed bachelor. But the *devas*, out of gratitude to him for the slaying of the *asura*, gave him in marriage two celestial damsels, Siddhi and Buddhi (Siddhi is attainment of desires and Buddhi is intellect). This is only an allegorical way of saying that Gaṇeśa is the giver of all success and of all knowledge to his devotees. Similarly, he is said to have married one Vallabha, daughter of a sage. "*Vallabha*" is just power; the elephant is the biggest animal on earth and this only indicates that he is the giver of all prowness to *bhaktas*.[59]

Yet an ascetic continually flanked by women presents a contradiction, and individuals drew upon various traditional materials to structure its resolution. One common explanation was offered to me on several occasions. As a man from Mysore noted, the reason Gaṇeśa can be an ascetic and yet be imaged with two *śakti*s is that the god has several *avatāra*s; he is currently single, but in another incarnation had two consorts, Siddhi and Buddhi, and in a third only one consort, Siddhi. Thus all iconographic permutations are accounted for.

One woman in Madurai explained that Vināyaka (Gaṇeśa) created Siddhi and Buddhi for Brahmādeva, but Brahmā did not have enough strength to hold on to the *śakti*s and so appealed to Vināyaka to control them. Thus Vināyaka is partially bound to these two *śakti*s: they are too powerful for him either to destroy or to marry. Here Gaṇeśa's relationship to women is liminally structured. He can neither break free of their *śakti* nor enter into the stable and dominant position of the householder. His *brahmacarya* is here not self-imposed but occurs precisely because of the dangerous power of the *śakti*s with whom he remains ambiguously associated. The two *dasī*s bound Gaṇeśa; the triptych they form with him again suggests his mediatory position, never quite celibate, never quite married. Furthermore, their obvious duality affirms the central significatory role of the split female for Gaṇeśa. The particular splitting of the female that encompasses the division between celibacy and marriage is that which we have already seen to be central to the conceptualization of the god's *śakti*—mother versus wife.

Sarasvatī

Trudging back to our pilgrimage bus after *darśana* of one of the Aṣṭa Vināyak, the eight important shrines of Gaṇeśa near Pune, a group of older women and I were discussing the *mūrti* we had just seen, which was flanked by two small goddesses. I asked if Gaṇeśa was married. One person immediately said that he was married to Sarasvatī. Her friend corrected her: "No, he is married to Śarda." The first woman turned back to me with the revised answer: "He is married to Śarda." A third person muttered "Ṛddhi Siddhi" quietly to herself, and this set off a wave of discussion as we boarded the bus. Later, stopping for tea on the way back to Pune, the group approached me in unison. Gaṇeśa has two wives, I was told, Sarasvatī and Śarda.

The confusion among the group reflects again that the issue of Gaṇeśa's marriage is not central to his devotional persona. And yet throughout Maharashtra, Gaṇeśa heartland as it were, people associated him with Sarasvatī or Śarda. The two goddesses were identified as the same person, and thus the single wife of Gaṇeśa, by some. An elderly man sitting in the Kasbah Gaṇapati temple in Pune argued that Gaṇeśa is only married to Śarda and that Sarasvatī is a wife of Viṣṇu. Others noted the reverse, that Gaṇeśa was only married to Sarasvatī; and a few, like the women on pilgrimage, suggested that Sarasvatī and Śarda were the two consorts imaged with Gaṇeśa.

Unlike Gaṇeśa's connection with paired consorts or Lakṣmī, no mythological or ritual contexts were offered to explain the liaison with Sarasvatī or Śarda. The 1971 *Maharashtra State Gazeteer* for Nanded district describes the practice, on the day before a wedding, of women singing praises to both Gaṇeśa and Sarasvatī while preparing bundles of turmeric, wheat, and areca nut for a ceremony;[60] this pairing of the god and goddess in the context of a marriage may be tied to their being invoked as a couple.

Gaṇeśa and Sarasvatī have many parallel roles but rarely function in tandem. Both are associated with learning and music. Together with Lakṣmī, they appear on poster art; in Bengal, the three are siblings. Gaṇeśa is the divine scribe, who wrote the *Mahābhārata* with his broken tusk while Vyāsa dictated it. Like his father he is a dancer[61] and is the *mṛdangam* player of the gods. He has come to be the patron deity of *tabla* players; it is said that Gaṇeśa through his father's anger created the *tabla*. He was playing his *mṛdangam* too loudly, and ultimately Śiva in anger sundered the percussion instrument into two with his trident, giving rise to the split *tabla*. None of the parallels between Gaṇeśa and Sarasvatī, however, seem sufficient to explain their particularly close, if ambiguous, connection for Maharashtrians.

Lakṣmī

In a large house on Assi Ghat in Varanasi, a European art historian lives amidst a great assortment of collected sculpture. In a niche on one side of a stairwell sits Gaṇeśa; flanking it is the figure of a *yakṣī*. Each Diwali, the servants of this woman garland both images and offer them *pujā*, treating the *yakṣī* as Lakṣmī. Although the figure lacks any of the traditional ornaments of the goddess, her position next to Gaṇeśa clearly identifies her as Lakṣmī. Elsewhere in the city, displaced images of Gaṇeśa and a female figure, both nearly unrecognizable from years of daubing with *sindur*, lean next to one another against a tree overlooking the Ganges. For many passersby, this goddess is also Lakṣmī. Throughout Varanasi, single goddesses in close juxtaposition with Gaṇeśa may be labeled this way.

For many people with whom I spoke in Uttar Pradesh and Rajasthan, this close association between Lakṣmī and Gaṇeśa was expressed through kinship terminology: Lakṣmī was Gaṇeśa's sister or — more often — they were married. Unlike her Śaivite counterpart Pārvatī, Lakṣmī was rarely described as Gaṇeśa's mother. Her association with Gaṇeśa was rarely tied to the Tantric tradition of Lakṣmī as Gaṇeśa's *śakti* discussed above. Rather, three reasons were variously offered for the relationship: (1) their functional equivalence, (2) their joint worship on Diwali, and (3) their joint worship by the "business community."

Gaṇeśa, Lakṣmī, and Sarasvatī are often grouped together as the divinities immediately responsible for material welfare. Gaṇeśa and Sarasvatī share the control over Buddhi, but as noted above this functional equivalence does not translate into shared or even parallel ritual action. Gaṇeśa and Lakṣmī are both deities of Ṛddhi and Siddhi, Śubha and Lābha and their ritual spheres intersect and parallel one another. In a sense each is the transformation of the other: Lakṣmī, surrounded by two elephants (male, as they are "watering" her) is the opposite of Gaṇeśa, an elephant surrounded by two females. Both, as noted a man on a train in Madhya Pradesh, are unique among the gods in their role as mediators between the material and divine worlds. They occupy adjoining space inside homes and occasionally upon thresholds.

In a niche in the wall of a Jaiselmer inn is inscribed

Śri
Ṛddhi Gaṇeśay Nāma Siddhi
Mahālakṣmenam

This invocation structures the household and inn in space and time. It transforms the inn into auspicious space, and represents an attempt to secure good fortune for the establishment and its inhabitants in time. The niche is only ritually used on Diwali; images of Gaṇeśa and Lakṣmī are purchased and installed, are the objects of devotion and offerings through a special *pujā*, and are immersed at the end of the festival. As with the joint worship of the Kala Bo and Gaṇeśa or Gauri and Gaṇeśa, the recurrent juxtaposition of Gaṇeśa and Lakṣmī in rituals that invoke the auspicious is interpreted through the idiom of the epitome of the auspicious—marriage.

In the niche, Gaṇeśa is related to women on two axes; horizontally, with Ṛddhi and Siddhi, and vertically with Lakṣmī:

Ṛddhi = Gaṇeśa = Siddhi
∏
Lakṣmī

To adopt a structuralist logic,[62] Ṛddhi and Siddhi are metonymic wives, each representing a part of the total function of Gaṇeśa in a syntagmatic relationship; Lakṣmī is the metaphoric wife, functionally equivalent to Gaṇeśa and existing independently. As one man in Udaipur noted, Gaṇeśa is married in two different senses; he is of course the *mālik* of Ṛddhi and Siddhi, who each are a component of his persona, but Lakṣmī is his *dharm patnī,* his ritual or practical wife. In a sense, the joint worship of Gaṇeśa and Lakṣmī gathers its power through metaphoric redundancy. The Rajput miniature in Getty's book, described above, is the mirror image of this niche:

elephant = Lakṣmī = elephant
∏
Gaṇeśa

This joint Diwali *pujā* ensures a financially successful new year. Though in Varanasi it is observed by families of widely diverse caste and class, the ritual is specifically associated by many Banarsis with the business community. In one of several helpful conversations, Professor J. N. Tiwari of Banaras Hindu University speculated that the origins of the joint *pujā* lie with the rise of urban merchant capitalism. Others in Varanasi felt that if not the origins then the rise in prominence of this *pujā* was tied to an increasingly commercialized culture. Throughout India, business people and merchants are said to be the greatest devotees of Gaṇeśa and Lakṣmī. A cloth merchant in Varanasi told me as we sat in his shop that "Gaṇeśa and Lakṣmī are the gods of businessmen. They are married. In the morning, first Gaṇeśa *pujā* is done, and then Lakṣmī *pujā.*"

There are few temples that worship Gaṇeśa with Lakṣmī as *śakti.* One, the Dasboddhi Gaṇeśa temple, not far from the Dwarakadesh temple in Mathurā, has a *mūrti* of a ten-armed Gaṇeśa with a consort on his knee and two rats facing them. The *śakti* is Mahālakṣmī, and the Gaṇeśa is Mahāgaṇapati. According to the temple priest with whom I spoke, the two are married. Here Tantric as well as contemporary categories are drawn upon in the structuring of relations between the deities. Lakṣmī as *śakti* is placed in a dependent position; she loses her metaphoric equivalence and her power. There remains a fundamental discontinuity between the Gāṇapatya tradition of the pairing of Lakṣmī and Gaṇeśa and their modern association.

The "marriage" of Lakṣmī and Gaṇeśa each Diwali is real. Individuals structure the relation between the gods utilizing kinship metaphors to give mythic coherence to ritual praxis. The kinship is relative; it is not articulated as an alternative to Gaṇeśa's relationship to Ṛddhi and Siddhi or Lakṣmī's to Viṣṇu, but functions within a specific framework. The danger in asking the question "Is Gaṇeśa married?," and perhaps its elegance, is in forcing the comparison of what may be incommensurable frameworks. In an alley in Varanasi, a man once told me: "Gaṇeśa is married to Lakṣmī." His friend disagreed violently: "Lakṣmī is Viṣṇu's wife!" The first man was forced to acknowledge this, and thought long and hard. Finally he turned to me again and said: "Lakṣmī is married to Viṣṇu. Gaṇeśa loves her but cannot have her, so he remains *brahmacarya*. Only on Diwali can they be together." Only one day a year can the impossible love of Gaṇeśa find ritual consummation. In the person of Lakṣmī, the split female is united in metaphoric equivalence with the male, and it is in her narratively unattainable person that Gaṇeśa comes closest to achieving an unambiguous marriage.

Analyses

There are several ways, both Indian and Western, of making sense of the diverse and divisive traditions of the marriage of Gaṇeśa. The unfolding of complex and contradictory conjugal possibilities can be an expression of the god's *līla*, or divine play. The diachronic solution of *avatāra* is frequently used to explain the coexistence of different marital permutations through history: different wives for different lives. Streetcorner mythopoeisis, as we have seen, may articulate romantic triangles. A common and very contemporary apologist solution is the distinction between "true" and "mass" culture and religion; this has roots in discourses of both caste and Kaliyuga. In this solution, the masses have lost sight of the simple reality of Gaṇeśa's marriage, whatever that be. Through ignorance and illiteracy, they have transformed the basic myth into multiple differing versions.

This idea, of the corruption and transformation of one original variant, underlies a classical Western approach to cultural diversity, that of diffusionism. One can explain the multiplicity of variants of Gaṇeśa's marriage as transformations of a tradition as it was transmitted from region to region; the task is then to trace the flow and pattern of change. Other processual approachs of more recent vintage might push us to read Gaṇeśa's diverse sexualities in terms of changing local ideology—whether it be that of class (the "business community") or regionalism (the salience of north/south and other discourses of self and other).

Western interpretations of Gaṇeśa's sexuality, however, have almost exclusively focused on a Freudian reading of his mythic corpus.[63] Kakar and after him Courtright offer a more Eriksonian analysis. They stress Gaṇeśa's mediation of those powerful oppositions—mother and father, freedom and responsibility, egoism and hierarchy — that structure a young boy's passage from childhood into youth. Gaṇeśa is promoted to the verge of young manhood, and for Courtright his mediation of this transition is tied to his overall liminal function in ritual and history.[64] Yet both retain the basic father-mother-son triangle as the conflictual heart of the matter.

The tendency of psychoanalytic readings to totalize obscures as much as it reveals. R. P. Goldman's article on Oedipal conflict in the Epics is a case in point. Goldman tends to assimilate all hierarchical relations to the Oedipal triangle. By positing these "displaced Oedipal encounters," the textual field of analysis is enlarged, but critical oppositions in the text are glossed over. Men's wives come all too easily to signify their mothers through the convenient device of "unconscious reference to the oedipal crime."[65] But the opposition of wife to mother is central to many stories, and certainly critical for that of Gaṇeśa. A. K. Ramanujan demonstrates how the Oedipus in India may function in opposition to the "Greek" Oedipus—not sons displacing fathers for their mothers, but mothers displacing wives for their sons.[66] This "Indian Oedipus" is not just the crystallization of an infantile moment of crisis; the shuttling of men between their wives and mothers unfolds as the primary sexual dynamic of *male* adulthood.

Through examining narratives embedded in the regional context of their telling, we have seen that the ambiguity of Gaṇeśa resides in large part in the paradox of his relation to the split Goddess: she is never completely a mother and never completely a wife. It is in this experience of a man caught between the conflicting spheres of husband and son that the locus of ambiguity rests. As his *śakti* is split, so is Gaṇeśa: his regional identity and his role as granter of fertility depend on the duality of celibate and householder, a duality central and perhaps essential to the social construction and psychosexual maintenance of Indian masculinity.

NOTES

1. *Śiva Purāṇa* 2.5.19.15–20, 26, trans. in Paul B. Courtright, *Gaṇeśa: Lord of Obstacles, Lord of Beginnings* (New York: Oxford University Press, 1985), 123–24.

2. *Matsya Purāṇa* 260.55, ed. Jamna Das Akhtar (Delhi: Oriental Publishers, 1972), 310.

3. *Brahma Vaivarta Purāṇa, Gaṇeśa khanda* 17.12–28, trans. Rajendra Nath Sen (Allahabad: Bhuvaneshwari Ashram, 1922), 35.

4. Alice Getty, *Gaṇeśa: A Monograph on the Elephant-faced God* (Oxford: Oxford University Press, 1936), 10.

5. Balaji Mundkur, "The Enigma of Vināyakī," *Artibus Asiae* 37, no. 4 (1975):291.

6. *Ṛgveda* II.23.1; X.112.9 *Sāmaveda:* opening verse.

7. Prithvi K. Agrawala, *Goddess Vināyakī: the Female Gaṇeśa* (Varanasi: Prithivi Prakashan, 1978), 6.

8. Mundkur, "The Enigma of Vināyakī," 291.

9. Agrawala, *Goddess Vināyakī,* 6–7.

10. Mundkur, "The Enigma of Vināyakī," 291–92.

11. Agrawala, *Goddess Vināyakī,* 20.

12. *Matsya Purāṇa* 179.18, ed. Akhtar, p. 155.

13. *Liṅga Purāṇa* 2.27.9.215–16, trans. J. L. Sastri et al. (Delhi: Motilal Banarsidass, 1973), 731.

14. H. Jacobi, "Brāhmaṇism," *Encyclopedia of Religion and Ethics,* vol. 2 (New York: Scribner's, 1914), 807–8, quoted in Courtright, *Gaṇeśa,* 129.

15. *Skanda Purāṇa, Nagara khanda* 88.23, cited in Agrawala, *Goddess Vināyakī,* 7.

16. Getty, *Gaṇeśa,* fig. 40.

17. Mundkur, "The Enigma of Vināyakī," 298.

18. Agrawala, *Goddess Vināyakī,* 32.

19. Śrīkumāra, *Śilparatna* 2.25.74, trans. in Agrawala, *Goddess Vināyakī,* 11.

20. Manisha Mukhopadhyay, "Queries on Gaṇapati," *Journal of Ancient Indian History* 2 (1975):112.

21. Agrawala, *Goddess Vināyakī,* 12.

22. Ananda Coomaraswamy, *Bulletin of the Boston Museum of Fine Arts* 26, no. 153 (1928):30–31, cited in Getty, *Gaṇeśa,* 27.

23. See Courtright's summary of the literature in *Gaṇeśa,* 115–22.

24. Getty, *Gaṇeśa,* 18. She also notes the *modaka*'s possible signification of the *jambu* fruit.

25. Courtright, *Gaṇeśa,* 217–18.

26. Getty, *Gaṇeśa,* 20–21.

27. Ānandagiri, *Śaṅkaravijaya,* chap. 17, trans. in Courtright, *Gaṇeśa,* 219.

28. Courtright, *Gaṇeśa,* 219.

29. Getty, *Gaṇeśa,* 36.

30. Getty, *Gaṇeśa,* plate 12.

31. Mircea Eliade, *Yoga, Immortality, and Freedom,* 2d ed. (Princeton: Princeton University Press, 1969), 153.

32. Eliade, *Yoga, Immortality, and Freedom,* 140.

33. Eliade, *Yoga, Immortality, and Freedom,* 298.

34. Eliade, *Yoga, Immortality, and Freedom,* 307.

35. Getty, *Gaṇeśa,* 36.

36. Getty, *Gaṇeśa,* 12.

37. Aruna Sheth, "Festivals of Gujarat, *Vivekanada Kendra Patrika* 6, no. 1 (1977):227–32.

38. Courtright, *Gaṇeśa,* 103–22.

39. I adapt here Arthur Kleinman's term for the problematic reification of a culturally constructed concept as a universal category in crosscultural research; see Kleinman, "Depression, Somatization, and the New Cross-Cultural Psychiatry," *Social Science and Medicine* 11 (1977):3–10.

40. Haridas Mitra, "Gaṇapati," *Visva Bharati Annals* 8 (n.d.):246.

41. Gaṇeśa's love for bananas, well known in some parts of India, may be relevant in affirming this relationship. On the ascent to Ucchi Pillayar at the summit of the Rock Fort in Tiruchchirappalli, the path is lined with banana stalks. In Madras, Gaṇeśa is often imaged over doorways surrounded by two small *yakṣa*-like figures carrying bananas and melons.

42. B. A. Gupte, "Harvest Festivals in Honor of Gauri and Ganesh," *Indian Antiquary* 35 (1906):60–64.

43. Richard Lannoy, *The Speaking Tree* (London: Oxford University Press, 1971), 107.

44. Fred Clothey, *The Many Faces of Murukaṉ* (The Hague: Mouton, 1978).

45. Courtright, *Gaṇeśa,* 251.

46. The necessity of the duality as expression of normal adult sexuality I take from my readings of Wendy O'Flaherty, *Asceticism in the Mythology of Śiva* (London: Oxford University Press, 1973) and Veena Das, "Reflections on the Social Construction of Adulthood," in *Identity and Adulthood,* ed. Sudhir Kakar (Delhi: Oxford University Press, 1979).

47. J. A. B. van Buitenen, "Dharma and Moksha," *Philosophy East and West* 7, nos. 1–2:33–40.

48. Louis Dumont, *Homo Hierarchicus,* rev. English ed. (Chicago: Chicago University Press, 1980), 184–87.

49. Das, "Social Construction," 102.

50. Sudhir Kakar, *The Inner World: A Psycho-analytic Study of Childhood and Society in India* (Delhi: Oxford University Press, 1978), 126–32.

51. Lannoy, *The Speaking Tree,* 107.

52. Courtright, *Gaṇeśa,* 43–44.

53. Brenda Beck, "The Kin Nucleus in Tamil Folklore," in *Kinship and History in South Asia,* ed. Thomas R. Trautmann (Ann Arbor: Center for South and Southeast Asian Studies, University of Michigan, 1974):128.

54. Susan Snow Wadley, *Shakti: Power in the Conceptual Structure of Karimpur Religion* (Chicago: Department of Anthropology, University of Chicago, 1975), 136–38.

55. Stella Kramrisch, *Indian Sculpture* (London: Oxford University Press, 1933), 143.

56. Diana Eck, *Banaras: City of Light* (New York: Knopf, 1982), 52–53.

57. E. Valentine Daniel, *Fluid Signs: Being a Person the Tamil Way* (Berkeley: University of California Press, 1984), 126.

58. I am indebted to Stanley Kurtz for discussions on the role of *Gaṇeśa* in *Jai Santoshī Mā*. In my own fieldwork, there were few mentions of Santoshī Mā as part of Gaṇeśa's family, and the significance of the film in transforming the image of Gaṇeśa into that of a family man remains unclear.

59. M. Arunachalam, "Vināyaka Chaturthī," *Vivekananda Kendra Patrika* 6, no. 1 (1977):63–68.

60. *Maharashtra State Gazeteer, Nanded District* (Bombay, 1971), 122.

61. Courtright, *Gaṇeśa*, 164.

62. Claude Levi-Strauss, *The Savage Mind*, trans. George Weidenfeld (Chicago: University of Chicago Press, 1966), 24–25 passim.

63. See Paul B. Courtright, "The Beheading of Gaṇeśa," *Purana* 22 (1980):67–80 and Edmund R. Leach, "Pulleyar and the Lord Buddha: Aspects of Religious Syncretism in Ceylon," *Psychoanalysis and the Psychoanalytic Review* 49 (1962):80–102.

64. See Courtright, *Gaṇeśa*, 104–10; Kakar, *The Inner World*, 100–2.

65. R. P. Goldman, "Fathers, Sons and Gurus: Oedipal Conflict in the Sanskrit Epics," *Journal of Indian Philosophy* 6 (1978):325–92.

66. A. K. Ramanujan, "The Indian Oedipus," in *Oedipus: A Folklore Casebook*, eds. Lowell Edmunds and Alan Dundes (New York: Garland, 1983):234–265.

7

"Vātāpi Gaṇapatim": Sculptural, Poetic, and Musical Texts in a Hymn to Gaṇeśa

Amy Catlin

Introduction

The spirited musical paean to Gaṇeśa by the revered nineteenth-century "trinity"[1] composer Muttuswāmi Dīkṣitar is easily the most well known of all classical South Indian, or *karṇāṭak,* compositions. A significant percentage of the thousands of formal concerts in Madras each year open with the "inevitable Vātāpi."[2] Indeed, hardly a single procession of blaring *nāgasvaram* oboes and penetrating *tavil* drums passes by without its raucous rendition of the Sanskrit *kriti,* a classical pre-composed song form that evolved from the more popular group song forms, the *kīrtan* and *bhajan*. Students of *karṇāṭak* music learn this song in the early weeks of study, and its fame has continuously increased for nearly two hundred years: the *rāgam* and the kernel of the composition have even spread to North India.

Several factors contribute to its great popularity. It praises the elephant-headed god of beginnings, who is a favorite of many Hindus; it is set in an auspicious, novel, and relatively simple but melodious *rāgam,* or musical mode; and perhaps most of all, the bright and jaunty melody of the composition itself captures the playful quality of Gaṇeśa's personality.

Yet, far moreso than in Western music, every performance of "Vātāpi Gaṇapatim" is different, due to the importance of improvisation in *karṇāṭak* music. Thus the roles of permanence, variability, and change are central to understanding the work. How, then, can we describe the range of variability in the different texts and performances of the work? And which elements of synchronic variation have produced diachronic changes in the piece, based upon the written, oral, and recorded sources available to us?

In answering these questions, we will posit three distinct structural levels in the composition, each allowing different degrees of variability and change. The first, the core level, is a deep structure of tune and text and is the most stable; the second, middle level allows moderate variation; and the third, or surface, level supports and seems to demand a high degree of individual variation, sometimes resulting in diachronic change.

To establish these levels, we will examine here the poetic texts, musical texts, and descriptions of early performances of the piece, as well as recordings and contemporary performances. But first, we must turn to the sculptural "text," the stone image known as the "Vātāpi Gaṇapati" that is thought to have inspired Dīkṣitar.

Sculptural "Texts": The Two Vātāpi Gaṇapatis

Muttuswāmi Dīkṣitar often organized his Sanskrit compositions into sets around a single theme (e.g., the nine planets), sometimes focusing on a particular deity of a temple (e.g., Māyāvaram Abhayamba). One unique set, the "Ṣodaśa Gaṇapati Kritis," is dedicated to the sixteen Gaṇapati statues found in and around the enormous temple in his birthplace, Tiruvārūr. These included the Mahā Gaṇapati and the Pañca Mātaṅga Mukha Gaṇapati, as well as the so-called Vātāpi Gaṇapati, which the present paper addresses. The tradition associated with this particular statue is still active in Tiruvārūr today, and one version has been related in the historical novel *Śivakāmiyin Śapatam (The Vow of Śivakāmi)* by R. Krishnamurthy, the renowned Tamil writer best known by his pen name, "Kalki."[3]

Vātāpi (the name is a corrupt form of the place-name Bādāmi) is located in the present Bījāpur District. After the Pallavas under Narasimhavarma I (630 – 68) conquered Bādāmi, tradition holds that an image of Gaṇapati was brought as booty from there to the Tanjore town of Tiruccengaṭṭanguḍi. This was the home of the Pallava general Paranjyoti, a Tamilian who later changed his name to Ciruttoṇḍa and became a Śaivite saint.[4]

The oral traditions associated with the image are questionable even from the start, however, as there is no Gaṇapati listed among Paranjyoti/Ciruttoṇḍa's other war trophies.[5] According to Meister, the Gaṇeśa was later installed in a secondary shrine, where it now remains on the south wall of the *ardhamaṇḍapa* (fig. 1). It is located in the precincts of a larger temple that was formerly known as the Ciruttoṇḍa Gaṇapatīśvara. Meister considers this to be a rebuilding dating from about 988 A.D.

At some later date, the idol evidently served as an inspiration for another Gaṇapati in the Tiruvārūr temple (fig. 2). There it is also called "Vātāpi Gaṇapati," although it lacks any significant similarity to the earlier image. This "copy" is the statue that Dīkṣitar's song addresses, one of the many subsidiary deities of the temple. Both idols are still being worshiped.

Photos of these images have not previously been published, although one drawing of the Tiruvārūr idol appeared in 1946. This sketch, by the artist Chandrasekharan, was used for the cover of the weekly Tamil literary magazine, *Kalki*. It was commissioned by the journal's editor, R. Krishnamurthy, for the 23 June 1946 issue, containing his own article "Vātāpi Gaṇapati."[6]

Robert L. Brown contributes this commentary on the two images:

> The Vātāpi Gaṇapati [fig. 1] is still in worship at the Gaṇapatīśvara temple in Tiruccengaṭṭanguḍi. That it is a seventh-century Chalukyan image, the one brought back by Ciruttoṇḍa from Bādāmi, appears, however, unlikely. Judging from the photograph, the image fits best stylistically with tenth–eleventh century Chola representations of Gaṇeśa. Typical of Chola images is the enormous body with the belly resting directly on the support and with the spindly legs and arms. The lower arms are held next to the body and the hands are clenched with the large fingers clearly delineated. Very characteristic of Chola-period Gaṇeśas is the long, thin trunk that curls against the body and holds a single round *modaka* (the *om*-shaped trunk mentioned in the song).[7] Few seventh-century Chalukyan Gaṇeśas have been identified, so it is difficult to compare the Vātāpi Gaṇapati with images similar to ones we might suspect relate most closely to that brought from Bādāmi. As far as I am aware, no three-dimensional examples exist today from Bādāmi. One seventh-century example from another Chalukyan site, Alampur, shows little relationship to the Vātāpi Gaṇapati.[8] We might speculate that when the Gaṇapatīśvara temple was rebuilt at the end of the tenth century (ca. A.D. 988),[9] a Chola Gaṇapati statue of about this date was installed and called the Vātāpi Gaṇapati.
>
> The copy from Tiruvārūr [fig. 2] is even further stylistically from the supposed Chalukyan prototype, and also has little relationship to the Tiruccengaṭṭanguḍi image. It is difficult to draw very precise conclusions from the photograph, but because of such characteristics as the folded-legs posture (*vīrāsana*) and the depiction of the image in relief within the leaf-shaped stele, a date as late as the seventeenth–eighteenth century is possible. Whatever its date, we can say that the Tiruvārūr Gaṇapati is only very distantly a copy of a Chalukyan prototype, and that the Tiruccengaṭṭanguḍi Gaṇapati appears likewise to be a 'copy' of the proposed image brought from Bādāmi by Ciruttoṇḍa.

Meister's date of 988 for the rebuilding of the temple could thus be associated with the installation of a new, Chola Gaṇapati. Dr. F. L'Hernault has similarly identified the Tiruccengaṭṭanguḍi idol as Chola. Her observations are that the four hands, in clockwise order, hold the *pāśa* (noose, upper right), *modaka* (sweet), *pustaka* (manuscript), and *aṅkuṣa* (goad). It is located in the subshrine of the southwest corner of the yard of the Śiva temple, a normal location for a subshrine dedicated to Gaṇapati. Its height is 61 cm. L'Hernault cites the Tiruvārūr Gaṇapati as holding the manuscript *pustaka* (upper right hand), the second hand resting on the hip, the third not clearly holding anything, and the fourth, holding a vegetable. It is located in the gallery of the inner enclosure, also in the southwest corner (see fig. 3). Walls have been erected between two pillars of the gallery to form a small shrine.[10]

In any case, both figures resemble the Taruṇa Gaṇeśa type described by V. Ramasubramaniam. A noteworthy feature of the later icon, however, is the rare right-curving trunk, called Valamburi Gaṇeśa (Tamil: *valamburi*, turning toward the right). Specimens have been noted in Mysore, at Vallam Village in Tanjore, and at Karuppathur on the Cauvery.[11]

Thus, the sculptural "text" for Dīkṣitar's composition is actually a complex of history, oral tradition, and sculptural variations on the iconographic theme of Gaṇapati. We will now see how the poetic text of the song relates to these antecedents.

Poetic Texts

The Vātāpi Gaṇapati is praised by only one poet-singer, the Smārta Brahmin Muttuswāmi Dīkṣitar. Dīkṣitar is the author of more *kriti*s in Sanskrit than any other *karṇāṭak* composer, and his skill in the language is often praised. Frequently his songs are grouped, as in the sets of nine *kriti*s to the nine planets, five to the five *liṅga*s, and in this case, one to each of the sixteen Gaṇapatis at Tiruvārūr. Like many of his Gaṇapati compositions, this song is a doxology of attributes of the god and the icon addressed. The choice of Gaṇeśa as a subject complies with the great popularity of the deity, who must be invoked by Hindus before worshiping any deity or undertaking any important task. Gaṇeśa's association with song is revealed in no less than 140 epithets linking him to music and speech; one scholar has even cited the epithet "Gānapati" or "lord of song."[12] Only two of the more than one hundred iconographical forms of Gaṇapati, however, show a *vīṇā* in one of his hands.

The following is a transliteration, with literal and paraphrased English translations of the Sanskrit text, based on the published Telugu and Tamil script versions, said to be taken originally from Dīkṣitar's *grantha* (a

Vātāpi Gaṇapatim Bhajeham: Poetic Text of Sanskrit *Kriti* by Muttuswāmy Dīkṣitar

Pallavi:

Sanskrit	Translation
(place) lord of the gaṇas I worship vātāpi = gaṇapatim = bhajeham 1. vātāpigaṇapatimbhajeham	"I praise the Gaṇapati from Vātāpi,
elephant face boon giver (blessed . . . varaṇa = āsyam vara = pradam (śrī . . . 2. varaṇāsyam varapradam (śrī . . .	"The elephant-faced giver of boons, (the blessed . . .

Anupallavi:

Sanskrit	Translation
ghosts and others worshiped feet bhūta = ādi = saṁsevita = caraṇam 1. bhūtādisaṁsevitacaraṇam	"Whose feet are worshiped by the *bhūta*s and all others,
ghosts living beings universe support bhūta = bhautika = prapañca = bharaṇam 2. bhūtabhautikaprapañcabharaṇam	"The support of the universe of living beings and spirits,

***Vātāpi Gaṇapatim Bhajeham* (continued)**

removed passion bowed down *yogis*

vīta = rāgiṇam vinata = yoginam

3. vītarāgiṇam vinatayoginam

"Devoid of passion, To whom *yogis* bow down,

---

world creator obstacle averter

viśva = kāraṇam vighna = vāraṇam

4. viśvakāraṇam vighnavāraṇam

"Creator of the world, Averter of obstacles,

Caranam:

of old pot coming-into-being sage chosen

purā kumbha = sambhava = muni = vara = pra

1. purā kumbhasambhavamunivarapra-

"Worshiped by the sage of old, who was born of the pot [Agastya],

---

worshiped triangle middle residing in

=pūjitam trikona madhya gatam

2. -pūjitam trikonamadhyagatam

"Residing in the middle of the [Tantric] triangle,

Vātāpi Gaṇapatim Bhajeham (continued)

demon's name (epithet for Viṣṇu)
enemy of headed and others greatly worshiped
mura = āri pramukha = ādi = upāṣitam
3. murāripramukhād yupāṣitam

"Worshiped greatly by Viṣṇu and others,

---

name of Tantric cakra; also, a shrine in Tiruvārūr
residing in
4. mūlādhāra kṣētra sthitam

"Enshrined in the *mūlādhāra kṣētra*,

---

highest etc. four speech as its self
parā ādi catvāri vāk ātmakam
5. parādi catvāri vāgātmakam

"Having as its essence the embodiment of the four levels of speech, the highest and the others,

---

the mystic syllable *om* form crooked trunk
praṇava = svārūpa vakra = tuṇḍam
6. praṇavasvārūpavakratuṇḍam

"Whose trunk is curved into the form of the sacred syllable *om*,

---

***Vātāpi Gaṇapatim Bhajeham* (continued)**

without interval forehead moon portion

nir = antaram niṭila = candra = khaṇḍam

7. nirantaram niṭilacandrakhaṇḍam

"Always having the cresent moon at his forehead,

---

own left hand held sugarcane staff

nija = vāma = kara = vidhrta = ikṣu = daṇḍam

8. nijavāmakaravidhrtekṣudaṇḍam

"With the sugarcane staff held in his left hand,

---

hand lotus noose seed + full

kara = ambuja = pāśa bījā = pūram

9. karāmbujapāśa bījāpūram

"Who holds the pomegranate/citron noose-like in his lotus hand,

---

blemish far away giant shaped

kalusha = viduram bhūtā = kāram

10. kaluṣaviduram bhūtākāram

"Without blemish, shaped like a giant,

Vātāpi Gaṇapatim Bhajeham (continued)

son of Śiva   teacher   great   pleasing to   round surface
(Subrahmanya)
harādi = guru = guha = toṣita = bimbam

11. harādiguruguhatoṣitabimbam

"Whose round form is pleasing to Śiva's son [the poet's *mudrā* is *guru*]

---

swan   voice   (*rāga mudrā*)   decorated   name
haṁsa = dhvani = bhūṣita = herambam

12. haṁsadhvanibhūṣitaherambam

"Who is decorated by the *rāga* named Hamsadhvani"

Tamil script designed for writing Sanskrit) manuscript, which is no longer extant. It was prepared with the help of T. S. Parthasarathy, Sanskrit scholar and Secretary of the Madras Music Academy, and Hartmut Scharfe, Sanskritist and Professor of Linguistics, UCLA. They did not always concur, as the published versions are not without flaws; any errors resulting are mine alone.

Like most *kritis*, the song is in three sections, called *Pallavi, Anupallavi,* and *Caraṇam* (theme, aftertheme, and verse). When sung, the first line recurs as a refrain after each section, all the other lines functioning as compound adjectives modifying the noun of the first line, *Gaṇapati*. These characteristics and attributes do not describe a complete Gaṇapati, but rather they present selected physical and metaphysical qualities of the deity. Some of these attributes bear explanation here. He is called "devoid of passion," *vītarāginam* in line 3 of the *Anupallavi*, as the South Indian Gaṇeśa is typically a bachelor. The "pot-born sage" of line 1 of the *Caraṇam* refers to the sage Agastya, who was born of a water pot. Later Agastya carried a pot to Śiva for holy water during a drought, which Gaṇeśa spilled at Indra's request, and then restored in order to fulfill Agastya's wish. Hence, Agastya became a follower of Gaṇeśa.[13] Following Tantric symbolism, Gaṇapati is believed to reside in the figure of a triangle (*Caraṇam*, line 2) and in the *mūlādhāra cakra* of the human body, at the perineum; this is also a name of a shrine in Tiruvārūr and perhaps a reference to the triangular stele surrounding the image (*Caraṇam*, line 4). His *om*-shaped trunk is a reference to the curling line of the Sanskrit letter; the crescent moon comes from his father, Śiva; the noose symbolizes control of the bonds of *saṁsāra*, the restraint of passion.[14] Finally, two *mudrās* or signatures occur in the final two lines of the text. One is for the composer, *guru* being Dīkṣitar's *mudrā;* the other is the name of the *rāgam*, Haṁsadhvani, which is gracefully woven into the final line of the *Caraṇam*.

Musical Texts I: The Rāgam

The name Haṁsadhvani, the *rāgam* or musical mode Dīkṣitar chose for his song, is usually translated as "The Voice of the Swan," although the *haṁsa* is strictly speaking a ruddy goose, whose voice is traditionally believed to have a sacred character. Sarasvatī, the patroness of music, poetry, and learning, rides either the *haṁsa* or a peacock. Since ancient times, the term *haṁsa* has been used for poetic meters, as well as for one of the *devagandharvas*.[15] Thus, the *haṁsa* was associated with the arts of music and poetry long before the *rāgam* was created about two hundred years ago.

The *rāgam* is said to have been created by the composer's own father, Rāmaswāmi Dīkṣitar (1735–1817), first appearing in 1790 in the *Saṁgraha Cuḍāmaṇi,* a *cadjan*-leaf manuscript by Govinda.[16] Rāmaswāmi's two compositions in Haṁsadhvani are a *varṇam* and a *lakṣya prabandha* (composition that explains a *rāgam*) that describe the various features of the new *rāgam* in a text praising the Śiva Naṭarāja (Lord of the Dance) idol at Chidambaram.[17]

The composition sounds unusually accessible to Western listeners to whom *karṇāṭak* music often seems foreign and incomprehensible. This may be in part due to the rhythmic underlay of the text, which stresses a lively emphasis of beats 1, 4, and 7 in an eight-beat cycle. Accenting the normally weak beats 4 and 7 creates a sense of syncopation, as in the "3 + 3 + 2" rhythm often found in Indian music.

Furthermore, the *rāgam* is very compatible with Western tonality. The five tones of Haṁsadhvani — C, D, E, G, and B — occur in the Śaṅkarābharaṇa *melā,* which is roughly equivalent to our Western major scale. These five notes also comprise our tonic and dominant triads, the two fundamental chords in Western music. Western influence may indeed be at the root of this feature. Rāmaswāmi Dīkṣitar listened to considerable amounts of English band music while he was under the patronage of the zamindar Venkatakrṣṇa Muḍaliar of Manali, whose father had been a *dubhāś* (bilingual, i.e., a translating agent) for Governor Pigot and the East India Company. While in the Muḍaliar circles, Rāmaswāmi became so interested in English music that he asked his first son, Muttuswāmi, to compose Sanskrit devotional texts for at least thirty-three English band tunes, among them "God Save the Queen." His third son, Bālaswāmi, learned to play the violin. Given these enthusiasms, it is not farfetched to suppose that his *rāgam* Haṁsadhvani might have been influenced by English music. The influence, however, would have been limited to elements compatible with Indian musical sensibilities.

Although Rāmaswāmi's other two sons were also composers, Muttuswāmi was the only one to compose in this *rāgam,* and the *kriti* "Vātāpi" was his only composition in Haṁsadhvani. He otherwise preferred the more traditional—and usually more complex—*karṇāṭak rāgams*. Saint Tyāgarāja learned of the *rāgam,* probably from Govinda's work, and composed his still-popular *"Raghunāyaka Nī Pādayūgā"* in Haṁsadhvani. Other *karṇāṭak* composers since have employed the *rāgam,* and even Hindusthānī musicians have composed *khyāl* in it.[18] Today's Hindusthānī musicians continue to play Haṁsadhvani; in December 1988 alone, no fewer than three concerts of Hindusthānī classical music reviewed in the national newspapers included Haṁsadhvani. It is even something of a specialty of the sitar maestro, Ustad Imrat Khan.

According to the Tantric school of thought to which Dīkṣitar belonged, the seven musical notes are given symbolic associations. *Shadja,* the note *sā,* or the fundamental pitch, is said to be born of the *mūlādhāra cakra,* a center of energy located in the perineum, and over which Gaṇapati presides. This *cakra* in turn symbolizes the *prithvi tattva,* whose *bīja* or seed is *gandharva,* the note *gā,* or the third degree of the mode, and whose consonant note a fifth above is *nishāda,* the note *nī. Nishāda* is believed to have as its corresponding sound in nature the sound of the elephant, another link to Gaṇapati. Taking the initial consonants of the two notes *gā* and *nī* (without the retroflex position in the latter), we have the initial consonants of the first two syllables of Gaṇapati or Gaṇeśa.[19] Since the three notes, *sā, gā,* and *nī,* belong to Haṁsadhvani, the others being *pā,* the fifth degree, and its fifth, *ri,* the second degree, Muttuswāmi Dīkṣitar may well have had Tantric reasons for selecting Haṁsadhvani for worshiping Lord Gaṇeśa.

He might also have been attracted by the unique leaping contours of the *rāgam,* which somehow capture the jovial nature of Gaṇeśa. These gaps, especially the one emphasized in the composition between the lower *pā* and the middle *ri,* help create the image of a dancing, leaping Gaṇapati, and give the musician scope to make sweeping ascents into the upper registers. While these observations are subjective and cannot be proven, it seems likely that one reason for the charm and success of the composition and *rāgam* are their suitability for conjuring up the image of a very much enlivened Gaṇapati.

Musical Texts II: The Composition

According to tradition, Dīkṣitar wrote down his texts and compositions as he composed them, laboring like a true scholar of Sanskrit and music, and unlike some other composers who spontaneously composed while singing. Unfortunately, none of his autograph manuscripts are extant. Nevertheless, countless Dīkṣitar compositions are still performed today, transmitted through his descendents and eleven important students. Dīkṣitar's youngest brother, Bālaswāmi, had a daughter whose son Subbarāma he adopted.[20] Subbarāma (1839 – 1906) learned his great-uncle's compositions from his grandfather and guardian, Bālaswāmi. Upon the urging of Cinnaswāmi Muḍaliar, a remarkable publisher of hundreds of *karṇāṭak* pieces in Western notation, and Dīkṣitar's patron the Rajah of Eṭṭayapuram, Ventakeśwara Eḍḍappa III, Subbarāma published the pieces he had learned, including both texts and *svara* (syllabic) musical notations in Telugu script in the volume *Saṅgita Sampradāya Pradarṣiṇi* in 1904. The English preface to the volume describes his initial reluctance to publicize the family tradition:

> Sri Subbarāma Dīkṣitar, though unwilling at first to part with what he naturally regarded as a precious heirloom to be jealously guarded and retained in his family, yielded in the end to the wishes of his master and patron, the Rajah.[21]

It was evidently the *jajmāni* relationship between the royal and musical families that gave weight to the argument for publication, as well as the choice of the Telugu script, as the patrons were Telugus, whereas the musicians were Tamils.

The *Saṅgīta Sampradāya Pradarṣiṇi* of 1904 is a treasure of seventeen hundred pages, containing seventy-four musical biographies and assorted essays on various musical subjects, as well as detailed notations and texts for 229 *kriti*s of Muttuswāmi Dīkṣitar, and hundreds of other pieces by other composers. A new set of Telugu type was created for the project, which was one of the early printing ventures in the South, including special type for the musical ornament signs devised by the author. The following examples (figs. 4 and 5) show the title page of the work, the "Vātāpi" composition as it appears therein,[22] and a Western staff transnotation of the composition, with Roman transliteration of the text to show underlay with the melody.

With sponsorship from the national Sangeet Nāṭak Akademi, the Madras Music Academy began in 1961 to republish the 1904 Telugu volume of notations and texts in Tamil script, responding to the needs of the growing and by then predominantly Tamil-speaking community of musicians and music students of Madras. The committee of editors also sought to correct problems arising from the use of Telugu script for the Sanskrit texts, employing numerical superscripts with the Tamil letters to represent Sanskrit characters not found in the Tamil alphabet.[23]

The Tamil edition is arranged according to scale type, or *melakarta;* five volumes have been published to date. "Vātāpi Gaṇapatim" is found in volume 4.[24]

While this is the main source for the composition today, one remarkable earlier publication contains a staff notation of a fragment of "Vātāpi." Before making Subbarāma Dīkṣitar's acquaintance, Mr. Cinnaswāmi Muḍaliar published the first two sections, *Pallavi* and *Anupallavi,* of the already renowned composition in 1896, as an issue of his serial, *Oriental Music in European Notation.*[25] The "play" within is described on the title page as

Academy of the Divine Art:
A Series of Pseudo-Dramatic Musical Disputations
in 72 Divisions, Discussing in the form of a diverting
and entertaining Dialogue all the debatable and doubtful
points connected with the Divine Art, as cultivated in the
East as well as in the West, etc.

The passage on "Vātāpi" is introduced by praising the *rāgam,* Haṁsadhvani, as a unique pentatonic mode with the fourth and sixth degrees omitted. After a notation of a *kriti* in Haṁsadhvani by another trinity composer, Tyāgarāja, the dialogue proceeds between *Gāna,* "A sound scholar, fairly advanced in Music, but anxious to learn the Staff Notation," and Vainikka [i.e., a *vīṇā* player], "A Professor of Oriental Music, ignorant of the European system."

> GĀNA: "If there's anything in a name, and if the Bard of Avon be called a *Swan,* surely this RAGA deserves its name—its gait, so discerning in its selection of notes—and so true to the proverb that in sipping the milk it separates and rejects the water. [Presumably this refers to the *rāgam*'s exclusion of the non-overtone notes, the fourth and sixth degrees.]
>
> "Here's one more example—the popular melody of the great Dikshitula.—VATAPIGANAPATIM:

This notation (fig. 6) is particularly interesting because of its highly detailed depiction of ornaments, anticipations, and syncopations, usually eliminated in indigenous alphabetic notations. Very possibly, Muḍaliar transcribed it himself by ear, after hearing someone sing the piece. A violinist in his employ customarily sight-read his notations as a check for accuracy, perhaps with the performer attending to make corrections. This document departs delightfully from standard notations available today, and, incomplete though it may be, speaks eloquently of the musical liberties and style of performers at that time.

According to orally transmitted accounts of the activities of one musician of that era, the renowned Mahā Vaidyanātha Iyer sang "Vātāpi" at the beginning of virtually every performance. He repeated the lines while incorporating his own variations called *saṅgatīs*, a standard technique used by all *kriti* performers today. As he was one of the most famous musicians of his time, the composition received wide acclaim through him, and is said to have been passed down to the present day in the form he gave it.[27] Indeed, the most widely circulated recent notation for the piece is that of P. Sambamoorthy in Tamil, which contains the following acknowledgment: "All the *saṅgatīs* in this *kriti* were added later by Mahā Vaidyanātha Iyer, 1844–1893."[28] It is also probably due to Mahā Vaidyanātha Iyer's influence that "most concerts of *karṇāṭak* music open with the song *vātāpi gaṇapatim*."[29] However, in response to this tradition, and also for the sake of variety, the Madras All-India Radio adopted a policy of not broadcasting the piece.[30] Nevertheless, many performers began their radio concerts with the *rāgam* during the period of my research (1976–78), but then proceeded with a different, less familiar composition. Thus a new tradition has been established within the present century: the *rāgam* Haṁsadhvani has absorbed one of Gaṇapati's attributes and is now associated with auspicious beginnings.

Musical Performances

The purely musical elements of the *kriti* to Vātāpi Gaṇapati are perhaps the most ephemeral of all the aspects we have examined, and they differ most widely with each performance. We have seen how the two sculptural images, as well as written notations of the piece, vary, and in actual performance the renditions are even more variable. The variability, however, can be seen in three degrees, following three posited structural "levels" of the composition, which correspond to the Schenkerian background, middle ground, and foreground. In other words, the core level of the composition is the most stable, and the surface level permits the greatest degree of liberty.[31]

The core level of maximum stability was found to consist of the poetic text, its rhythmic setting within the composition, and the basic contours of the melodic setting. The middle level, permitting a medium degree of variability, consisted of such elements as tempo, pitch range, repetitions, and the structural points at which improvisation takes place. The surface level of maximum variability includes such elements as vocal or instrumental timbre of the performer, idiosyncrasies of ornamentation, expressive features, and other stylistics.[32]

The Texts in Performance

Just as an image of Gaṇeśa or any deity may be depicted in different media—bronze, stone, wood—a *kriti*'s performance medium is variable. Perhaps the most noticeable difference among the performances is the fact that half are vocal and the other half purely instrumental, employing the *vīṇā* (lute), *nāgasvaram* (oboe), violin, or clarinet. In such instrumental versions, the role of the poetic text is altered. Only the audience members who already know the poetic text can appreciate the relationships between the instrumentalist's musical expression and the poetry. But the instrumentalist may only be thinking of the poetic text intermittently; at other times, he may be completely involved in the purely musical elements of performance. Similarly, the listener may vacillate between thinking of the poetic text and concentrating on the purely musical performance, even at times enjoying its variance with other performances he might have heard of the musical text. This creates a realm of communication between artist and listener that draws upon memories of earlier renditions and a mentally pondered poetic text, either of which may be referred to only sporadically, thus defying close scrutiny. Nevertheless, it is a powerful element in any *karṇāṭak* instrumental performance. Further, the devotional realm of discourse expressed both nonverbally and within the poetic text participates in the basic foundation of all South Indian music and culture. This devotionalism forms yet another subtext to performances of all *kriti*s, including this one.

Similarly, and as for all Hindu deities, Gaṇeśa's depiction may vary in size from miniature, as found in home altars, to the larger sculptures found in temples. Likewise, a *kriti* to any deity may be performed in miniature, following the core of the composition without extensive development and variations, or on a grand scale. Thus, the dimensions of a performance are less a result of the length of the poetic and musical texts than a result of the performer's decisions concerning repetitions, variations, improvisations, and tempo. These may be mitigated by external circumstances. For example, the recording medium plays a critical role; a 78-rpm record can hold only about three minutes. Another time when brevity is normal is at the very opening of a concert, when the lord of beginnings is worshiped in song. Chitti Babu's three-minute *vīṇā* version in a swift tempo epitomizes the brief invocatory style of performing "Vātāpi" at the commencement of a recital as a tribute to the remover of obstacles. Later in a formal concert, however, the performer lengthens one or two central *kritis*, after warming up with introductory pieces and shorter renditions of other *kriti*s. The two performances cited here of "Vātāpi" in such a central position are over twenty minutes in duration and show how the piece can expand to occupy the central focus of a recital.[33] Here, far more time is given to developing the *rāgam* Haṁsadhvani before the *kriti* begins, as well as to improvised solfège passages and other elaborations. The creative as well as devotional involvement of the performer is highlighted above that of the composer of the poetic text during such "central" renditions.

There are two features that make this *kriti* to Gaṇeśa unique, however. The first is the way in which the composition parallels the deity's temporal and spatial position within Hindu ritual and cosmology. Just as he is found most often at the proper right of the entrance, where circumambulation begins, in his subsidiary shrine within a temple devoted primarily to some other Hindu deity, "Vātāpi Gaṇapatim" occurs most frequently at the opening of a concert. In both cases, Gaṇeśa's unique character as the lord of beginnings is central.[34]

But Gaṇapati also occurs as the central figure in home shrines and entire temples dedicated to him. Max Müller has referred to this context-sensitive propensity of Hindu deities to be worshiped separately, but equally, as "kathenotheism." This finds a further parallel in performances of "Vātāpi Gaṇapatim," where the *kriti* may occupy a central position of importance. Just as the image becomes the object of more elaborate rituals when worshiped as a central deity, the basic outlines of the *kriti* are highly developed and elaborate when the *kriti* is featured as a central piece in a concert. In the former case, the "work of art," the image, does not change. In the latter case, however, the "work of art," the musical and poetic text of the *kriti,* becomes refashioned by the performer's devotion and creativity. The texts then function more as blueprints or designs, to be embellished and filled out by an artist in the role of performer.

The second unique feature is the depiction of Gaṇapati's affective character in his mode of the jovial, dancing, and playful child, whose beheading and reheading created such a seriocomical problem for his parents. Dīkṣitar's delightful and rhythmic melody, which darts about in a manner quite unusual for the generally sober style of *karṇāṭak* music, embodies that essence. Elements of the same character can be seen in some visual images of Gaṇapati, as well as many dance depictions and musical expressions. Certainly the melodic and rhythmic aspects of this *kriti* epitomize that aspect of Gaṇeśa. We can safely say that, here, the musical elements of "Vātāpi Gaṇapatim" speak more eloquently of Gaṇapati's beloved nature than do either its sculptural antecedents or its poetic text. There can be little doubt that it is primarily Dīkṣitar's inspired music, more than his poetry or manipulation of iconographic allusions, that has so effectively captured the imagination and affection of South Indian musicians and listeners.

NOTES

1. The three composers belonging to South India's "trinity" of saint-singers are Dīkṣitar (1775–1835), Tyāgarāja (1767–1847), and Syāma Śāstri (1762–1827).

2. R. S., "R. K. Sūryanārāyaṇa Concert," *The Indian Express,* Madras, 13 August 1977.

3. R. Krishnamurthy, *Śivakamiyin Śapatam* (Madras: Mangala Nulagam, 1948), 932.

4. Michael W. Meister, *Encyclopedia of Indian Temple Architecture. South India. Lower Dravidadesa (200 B.C.–A.D. 1324)* (Philadelphia: University of Pennsylvania Press, 1983). See also Vincent Smith, *Oxford History of India*, 3d ed. (Oxford: Clarendon Press, 1956), 215. Compare with Kalki's account, which states that in the seventh century, a Tamilian named Paranjyoti was employed in Vātāpi as a general in the army of the Chalukya ruler Pulakesin II. During an attack on Pulakesin's fort, Paranjyoti appealed for protection to a beautifully carved Gaṇapati idol at the entrance to the fortress, vowing to carry the statue back to his home in Tiruccengaṭṭanguḍi village, Tanjore District, Tamilnadu, where he would build it a special shrine. The enemy was indeed defeated, and Paranjyoti is believed to have fulfilled his vow, bringing the present-day Gaṇapati to Tiruccengaṭṭanguḍi.

5. S. Dandapani Desikar, *Gaṇapati* (Tiruvavaduturai Adhinam, 1956), 32–33 (Tamil). Here Sekkilar's *Periyapurānam* is cited, which contains a list of all the war trophies taken by Paranjyoti/Ciruttoṇḍa. Information provided by F. L'Hernault, Institut Français d'Indologie, Pondichery.

6. *Kalki*, Tamil weekly, Madras (23 June 1946).

7. Compare the Chola Gaṇeśas in Douglas Barrett, *Early Cola Architecture and Sculpture* (London: Faber & Faber, 1974), pls. 23a, 64, 81a.

8. See Robert L. Brown, "A Note on the Recently Discovered Gaṇeśa Image from Palembang, Sumatra," *Indonesia* 43 (April 1987):fig. 3.

9. Meister, *Encyclopedia*, 227.

10. Dr. F. L'Hernault, École Française d'Extrême-Orient, Pondichery. Letter dated November 11, 1988.

11. V. Ramasubramaniam, "The Gaṇapati-Vināyaka-Gajānana Worship: Analysis of an Integrated Cult," *Bulletin of the Institute of Traditional Cultures—Madras* (January–June 1971):101–2.

12. R. Sathyanārāyaṇa, "Gaṇapati and Karṇāṭaka Music," *Journal of the Indian Musicological Society* 5, no. 2 (March–June 1974):22–26.

13. Paul B. Courtright, *Gaṇeśa: Lord of Obstacles, Lord of Beginnings* (New York: Oxford University Press, 1985), 147.

14. Ramasubramaniam, "Gaṇapati-Vināyaka-Gajānana," 148.

15. M. Monier-Williams, *A Sanskrit-English Dictionary* (Oxford: Clarendon Press, 1964; reprint of the 1899 original), 1286.

16. Pandit Subrahmanya Śāstri, ed., *Saṁgraha cuḍāmaṇi of Govinda* (Madras: Adyar Library, 1938), 173.

17. V. Rāghavan, ed., *Muttuswāmi Dīkṣitar* (Bombay: National Centre for the Performing Arts, 1975), 96.

18. Āmānalī Khān parodied the melody and text of "Vātāpi" in his *khyāl "Lagilagana Patisati,"* ("I have fallen in love with my husband"), which he composed after hearing Vina Seśaṇa perform Dīkṣitar's *kriti* in the early twentieth century. (Sathyanārāyaṇa, "Gaṇapati and Karṇāṭaka Music," 26.) Perhaps the parody of Dīkṣitar's text plays upon the concept of beginning in a romantic sense. In a culture where arranged marriage is the norm, the moment of beginning to love one's husband is worthy of note.

19. Sathyanārāyaṇa, "Gaṇapati and Karṇaṭaka Music," 25.

20. Rāghavan, *Muttuswāmi Dīkṣitar*, 34.

21. Rāghavan, *Muttuswāmi Dīkṣitar*, 30. Subbarāma's son, Ambi Dīkṣitar (1863–1936), taught many musicians in the Eṭṭayapuram palace. In his later years he moved to Madras and established a school for Dīkṣitar study, where many important artists learned from him. Ambi's son, Tiruvārūr Bālaswāmi Dīkṣitar, still lives in Madras and is said to own manuscripts of rare Dīkṣitar compositions and other family heirlooms, such as his grandfather's *vīṇā*.

22. Photocopied from a privately owned copy in Madras.

23. Śrī Subbarāma Dīkṣitar, *Saṅgīta Sampradāya Pradarṣiṇi* by the brother's grandson of the great composer, Srī Muttuswāmi Dīkṣitar, and *asthāna vidvān* of Ettayapuram. Tamil script edition sponsored by the Sangeet Nāṭak Akademi, Delhi. Written in Tamil by B. Rājam Ayyar and S. Rāmanāthan, under the supervision of T. L. Veṅkatarāma Iyer, C. Veṅkatarāma Iyer, and V. Rāghavan. Published by The Music Academy, Madras. Part I: (Melakartas 1–15), 1961; Part II (Melakartas 15–22), 1963; Part III (Melakartas 22–28), 1968; Part IV (Melakartas 28–65) (without V. Rāghavan), 1977; Part V (Melakartas 66–72) edited by T. S. Parthasārathy, 1983. 1,522 pages.

24. Śrī Subbarāma Dīkṣitar, *Saṅgīta Sampradāya Pradarṣiṇi* Part IV, 871–73.

25. A. M. Cinnaswāmi Muḍaliar, *Oriental Music in European Notation* (Madras: Ave Maria Press, 1893–96) (periodical). 1893 issue reproduced by Tamil Nadu Eyal Isai Nataka Manram, Madras, 70 pp., undated (1976?).

26. Muḍaliar, *Oriental Music*, 22.

27. Śaṅkara Iyer, V. S. Gomathi. *Isaiulagil Mahā Vaidyanātha Śivan* vol. 1 (Madras, India Music Publishing House 1974), 80 (in Tamil).

28. P. Sāmbamoorthy, *Kirtana Sāgaram*, Bk. 4, 2d ed., revised and enlarged (Madras: Indian Music Publishing House, 1967) 2.

29. Rāghavan, *Muttuswāmi Dīkṣitar*, 1.

30. During my stay in Madras from 1976 to 1978, the composition was not broadcast a single time. The Programming Officer explained to me that the policy is not to repeat any composition within one year. Similarly, any single *rāgam* is not to appear with undue frequency.

31. For further discussion of musical variation and levels, see my dissertation, *Variability and Change in Three Karṇāṭak Kritis*, Brown University, 1980.

32. These findings are based upon examination of the following ten published and/or concert recordings of the piece by prominent *karṇāṭak* vocal and instrumental musicians:

A. Commercial recordings
   1. Mysore T. Chowdiah (ca. 1900 – 1967), violin, 78-rpm disc COL GE 6539, reissued as 45-rpm SEDE 3629
   2. Thiruvengaḍu Subramania Pillai (1906–), *nāgasvaram* (oboe), 33-rpm EALP 1376 (1971)
   3. Chembai Vaidyanātha Bhagavatar (1896 – 1975), voice, 33-rpm ESX 6009 (1967)
   4. A. K. C. Nātarājan (1930 –), clarinet, 7-inch 45-rpm extended-play 7EPE 1615

5. M. Bālamurali Krishna, voice, ECLP 2376
6. Chitti Babu (1936–), vīṇā, 45-rpm SEDE 3688
7. L. Subramaniam (1947 –), violin, recorded live in concert, 4/22/78. Ravi Shankar Music Circle cassette RSMC-9

B. Concert recordings
1. Semmangudi Śrinivāsa Iyer (1908–), voice, 12/28/68
2. M. D. Rāmanāthan, voice (1923–84), 12/22/72
3. T. V. Gopālkrishnan (1948?–) voice, 6/9/77

33. In these two versions, the vocalist T. V. Gopalkrishnan spent over three minutes in *rāgam* exposition, not a very long time in the context of other *rāgam* performances; the violinist, Dr. L. Subramaniam, however, devoted over eight minutes to the exploration of the *rāgam*. Each spent seven to nine minutes in a final section of *svara kalpana* (note + imagination), in which the musician bases his improvisations on a theme selected from the composition.

34. Note that in the Tanjore temple plan, his shrine is not located near the entrance, but this is typical of South Indian temples, which often grow in unplanned stages.

Fig. 1. Gaṇeśa (Vātāpi Gaṇapati), stone, H: 61 cm. Gaṇapatīśvara Temple, Tiruccengaṭṭanguḍi. (Photo: École Française d'Extrême-Orient).

Fig. 2. Gaṇeśa (Vātāpi Gaṇapati), stone, H: 103 cm. Tiruvārūr Temple, Tiruvārūr. (Photo: École Française d'Extrême-Orient).

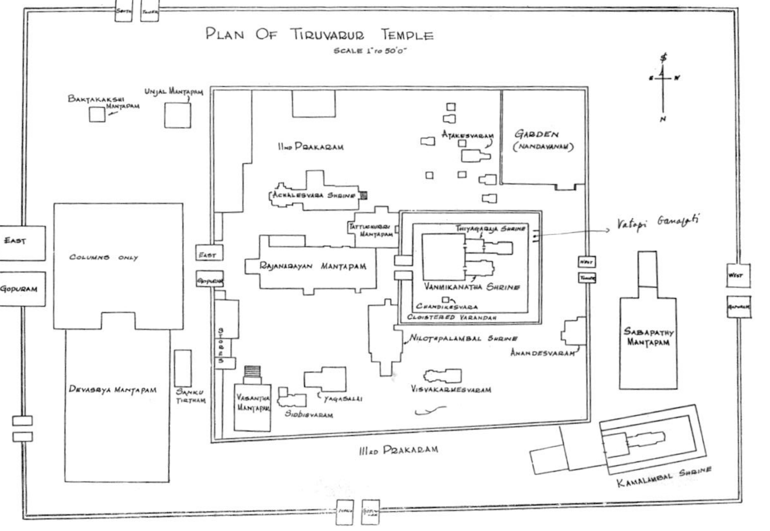

Fig. 3. Tiruvārūr Temple plan. Plan by F. L'Hernault.

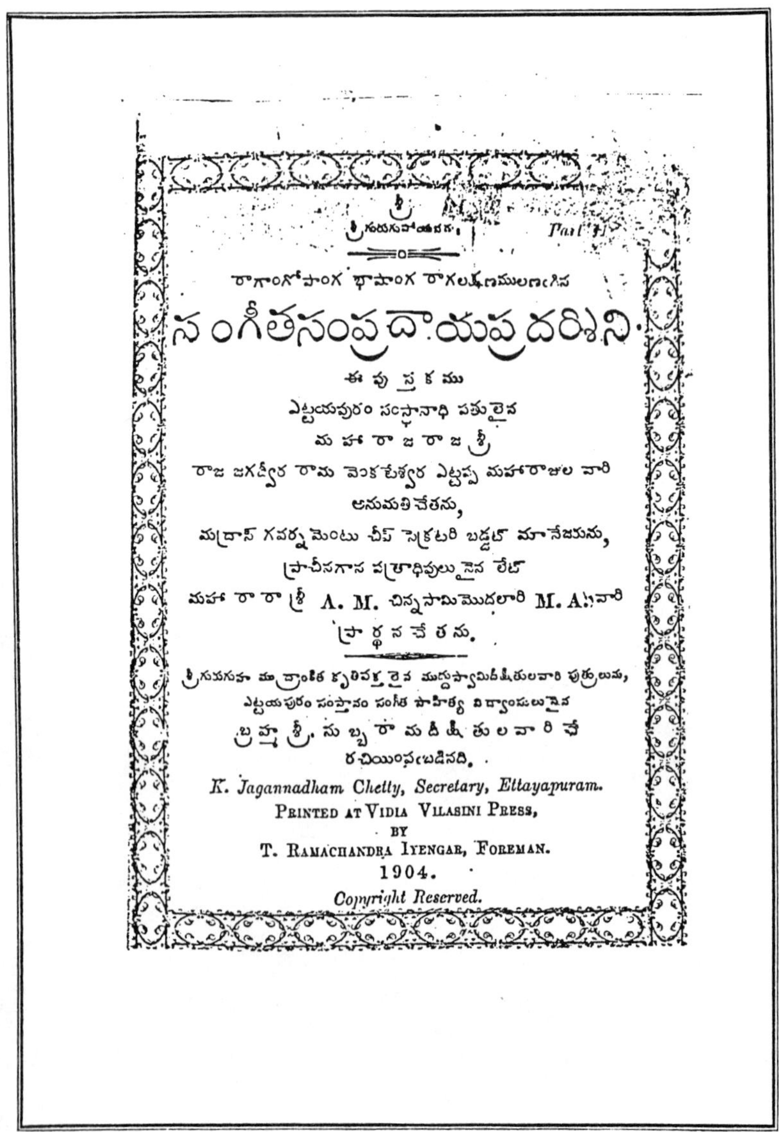

శ్రీ

శ్రీగురుగుహాయనమః | Part

రాగాంగోపాంగ భాషాంగ రాగలక్షణములఁగల

సంగీతసంప్రదాయప్రదర్శిని.

ఈ పుస్తకము

ఎట్టయపురం సంస్థానాధిపతులైన

మహారాజరాజశ్రీ

రాజ జగద్వీర రామ వెంకటేశ్వర ఎట్టప్ప మహారాజుల వారి

అనుమతిచేతను,

మద్రాస్ గవర్న్మెంటు చీఫ్ సెక్రటరి బడ్జట్ మానేజరును,

ప్రాచీనగాన పత్రాధిపులునైన లేట్

మహా రా రా శ్రీ A. M. చిన్నసామిమొదలారి M. A.వారి

ప్రార్థనచేతను.

శ్రీగురుగుహ ముద్రాంకిత కృతికర్తలైన ముద్దుస్వామిదీక్షితులవారి పుత్రులును,

ఎట్టయపురం సంస్థానం సంగీత సాహిత్య విద్వాంసులునైన

బ్రహ్మశ్రీ. సుబ్బరామదీక్షితులవారిచే

రచియింపఁబడినది.

K. Jagannadham Chetty, Secretary, Ettayapuram.

PRINTED AT VIDIA VILASINI PRESS,

BY

T. RAMACHANDRA IYENGAR, FOREMAN.

1904.

Copyright Reserved.

Fig. 4. Title page, SSP, 1904.

Fig. 5. "Vātāpi Gaṇapati," transnotated from *Saṅgīta Sampradāya Pradarṣiṇi,* 1904.

Fig. 5 (continued), page 2.

Fig. 5 (continued), page 3.

Fig. 6. "Vātāpi Gaṇapati," staff notation from *Oriental Music in European Notation,* 1896.

Fig. 6 (continued), page 2.

8

Gaṇeśa in Southeast Asian Art: Indian Connections and Indigenous Developments

*Robert L. Brown**

haraputramaśeṣagaṇādhipatiṃ
varacandrasunirmalacārungunaṃ
alicumbitagaṇḍasamākulitaṃ
varadaṃ vighnavināyakamīḍe[1]

I praise the remover of obstacles,
who grants wishes, the son of Hara,
the leader of the *śeṣa-gaṇa*, having the
perfectly pure, lovely quality of the
excellent moon, agitated from bee-kissed cheeks.

I. The Earliest Gaṇeśa Images

No one since Alice Getty has attempted a discussion of Gaṇeśa in Southeast Asian art.[2] This is understandable considering the scattered locations and relative scarcity of the images and the lack of related inscriptions, texts, and archaeological excavations. The use of a few, haphazardly available examples led Getty repeatedly to form conclusions that cannot be supported today. While much more information and material pertaining to Gaṇeśa in Southeast Asian art are available at present, the

*A number of people who helped me with this paper deserve my thanks, including Carol Bolon, Susan Buchanan, Paul Courtright, Martha Davidson, Piriya Krairiksh, Kathy Harper, Stephen Markel, Mona Meredith, Judy Mitoma, A. K. Narain, Pratapaditya Pal, and Hartmut Scharfe.

evidence remains extremely spotty; and the danger of drawing false conclusions, based upon an inadequate and nonrepresentative sampling, is still strong. The insufficient number of examples, coupled with the modest length of this essay, make any attempt here at a comprehensive survey of the Southeast Asian Gaṇeśa impossible. What I will attempt is to identify the ways in which the Gaṇeśa images from Southeast Asia are specific to the area. That is, in what ways did the Southeast Asian artists follow the Indian forms of Gaṇeśa, and what new forms did they introduce? What meaning did the Southeast Asians give to their Gaṇeśa images? I will propose from this analysis conclusions about Gaṇeśa's place and nature among the Indic gods.

Southeast Asia will include for us the mainland countries of Burma, Laos, Cambodia, Vietnam, and Malaysia, as well as the island archipelago of Indonesia. I will, however, deal with the mainland and the islands separately (beginning with the mainland), as the issues relating to Gaṇeśa tend to be different for the two areas.

The initial step in associating the Gaṇeśa images in Southeast Asia with those in India is to identify the earliest Southeast Asian images and their possible Indian prototypes. Such an undertaking, the search for the "earliest" Southeast Asian examples of an iconography or form and their Indian connections, is a slippery path and usually relatively unsuccessful. In the case of Gaṇeśa, however, the results of the search are revealing, if not without major problems of their own.

The early images of Gaṇeśa in Southeast Asia are found over a wide area of the mainland, including areas in present-day Thailand, Cambodia, and Vietnam. They form a surprisingly homogeneous group. That their style and iconography have uniformity supports what I feel is a new perception among art historians[3] that the earliest Indian-related art in mainland Southeast Asia exhibits a consistency of style and iconography. Rather than a series of different styles, each a copy of an Indian style, occurring in various areas of the mainland, a few major indigenous but Indian-influenced styles appeared suddenly and spread quickly to widely scattered areas of the mainland. These Southeast Asian objects shared more characteristics among themselves than they do with any Indian prototypes and formed the shared seed from which the later regional Southeast Asian styles grew.

Bearing this in mind, let us look first at examples of the earliest seated Gaṇeśa images from mainland Southeast Asia. We may begin by comparing the Gaṇeśa from Tuol Pheak Kin in Cambodia (fig. 1) and an image from Prasat Phnom Rung in Buri Ram Province of Northeastern Thailand (fig. 2). The two Gaṇeśas are stylistically and iconographically similar.

They share an overall naturalism and simplicity. The shapes of their heads and ears are similar, as are the ways in which their heads are attached onto their bodies without any necks, each of the awkward junctures masked by the use of a plain band, intended to represent a roll of flesh. Similar large, plain bands are used to separate the chest from the abdomen. In both cases the bodies are relatively thin, and both have two arms that, although the right arm in figure 2 is broken, are held in the same position. The list of similarities can be much expanded.

A third early seated Gaṇeśa was found in Phú-ninh in Champa (Vietnam). With only a drawing by Parmentier as evidence (figs. 3 and 4), a great deal cannot be said about this image, although it appears stylistically to fit well with the two Gaṇeśas discussed above. Jean Boisselier cautiously places it among the earliest Cham material, perhaps the second half of the seventh century.[4] For our purposes, the Phú-ninh Gaṇeśa enables us to extend the appearance of the earliest Southeast Asian type from Thailand to Vietnam.

A 650 – 700 date for the Phú-ninh Gaṇeśa agrees with the approximate dates of the other two early Southeast Asian Gaṇeśas. Piriya Krairiksh has dated the Prasat Phnom Rung Gaṇeśa (fig. 2), based on the style of the *sampot* he wears, to the Prei Khmeng style, that is, the second half of the seventh century.[5] Pierre Dupont has dated the Tuol Pheak Kin Gaṇeśa (fig. 1) to the Phnom Da style, that is, the second half of the sixth century.[6]

With parameters of 550 to 700 A.D. for some[7] of the earliest seated Gaṇeśas in Southeast Asia, we can now look to India to seek relationships. Here there is a surprise. The Indian images that compare most closely to the Southeast Asian Gaṇeśas are not Indian images of the sixth and seventh centuries but are the earlier Indian examples. It is true that these earliest Indian Gaṇeśas (figs. 5, 6, and 8) are themselves at the center of considerable debate regarding their date. They consist of a modest group of small sculptures carved from Mathurān Sikri sandstone.[8] The images are either standing (fig. 8) or seated (figs. 5 and 6), and share a number of characteristics, such as being small, two-armed, dwarf-like, relatively unadorned, and frequently nude. Getty published one example that she felt "may be the most ancient representation of the god in stone as yet discovered."[9] While she does not date it specifically, she states that "Gaṇeśa is not to be found in sculpture before the Gupta period," by which she means that "no images . . . have been discovered which could be placed unquestionably earlier than the fifth century."[10]

As more examples of this type of Gaṇeśa have been recognized, however, some scholars have considered an earlier dating, either Kuṣāṇa (first to third centuries A.D.) or Gupta-Kuṣāṇa transitional (ca. fourth century

A.D.).[11] I feel there is nothing to argue against a Kuṣāṇa-period date for some of these images, but whether the earliest Indian Gaṇeśa sculptures are of the Kuṣāṇa period, are Kuṣāṇa-Gupta transition, or are early Gupta need not be resolved here. If the type began in the Kuṣāṇa period, it certainly continued into the fourth century, and we will accept an uncontroversial fifth-century or earlier date for these images.

We are fortunate to have a seated Gaṇeśa carved in relief at Cave 6 at Udayagiri in Madhya Pradesh, where there is a dedicatory inscription dated to 401–2 A.D. (fig. 7).[12] The Gaṇeśa can probably be dated in relation to this inscription.[13] The image follows closely the early Mathurān type, with the additional interesting iconographical detail of being ithyphallic (*ūrdhvaretas*). Therefore, with a ca. 400 A.D. date for the image, we can compare it to the Tuol Pheak Kin Gaṇeśa (fig. 1) of 150 to 200 years later. The similarities are striking. The two share such general likenesses as body proportions and the relation of the head to body, as well as such specific characteristics as the shape of the ears with the fold of skin along the top and the plain band at the throat. If we allow a comparison among all six of the early seated Gaṇeśas (three Indian: figs 5, 6, and 7, and three Southeast Asian: figs. 1, 2, 3, and 4), we can derive a convincing list of concordances, with such details as the plain headbands found on the Udayagiri and Mathurā Gaṇeśas (figs. 7 and 6) and the band on the Prasat Phnom Rung Gaṇeśa (fig. 2).

While this list can be much expanded, there are general characteristics that the two groups, Indian and Southeast Asian, do not share. The Indian Gaṇeśas, for example, hold a bowl piled high with rounded cakes (*modaka*), while the Southeast Asian images hold what appear to be empty bowls. Likewise, the three Indian Gaṇeśas are apparently naked, as frequently are the early Indian Gaṇeśas (cf. fig. 8), but the three Southeast Asian examples are clothed; and on the two where the clothing is clearly depicted, they wear Southeast Asian dress. These types of differences are perhaps not unexpected. The *modaka*, while taking a variety of forms in India,[14] would supposedly be an unknown food and symbol to the Southeast Asian and thus be susceptible to elimination in the art. The unabashed revealing nature of Indian sculpture, particularly the exposure of the genitals, was generally rejected by the Southeast Asians, who clothed Gaṇeśa as they did most of their gods. In other words, the changes in the Southeast Asian Gaṇeśas are the result of seeing or reading Indian models through an indigenous Southeast Asian perspective. The important point here is that the three early Southeast Asian examples from areas separated by over one thousand kilometers share a stylistic and iconographic unity that already can be defined as Southeast Asian.

I have thus far considered only seated examples of Gaṇeśa, but equally early standing images occur in India (Mathurā, see fig. 8) and in Southeast Asia (although to my knowledge only in Cambodia; see fig. 9). The Indian Gaṇeśa we may date to the fifth century or earlier, while the Cambodian Gaṇeśa is, to judge by the *sampot,* an example of Dupont's "prolongements du style du Phnom Da"[15] and would date to the seventh century. I need not belabor the many similarities these standing Gaṇeśas share with the seated images, nor that we are again matching the Southeast Asian object to the proper Indian prototype, although they are separated by perhaps two centuries. There are, however, two major changes in the standing Cambodian Gaṇeśa: he is not naked but wears the Khmer *sampot,* and his legs and body, while stocky, are naturally proportioned. These two characteristics will be consistently found on later Cambodian Gaṇeśas, and they relate to a point I will return to, which is that the Gaṇeśa in mainland Southeast Asia largely shed his *yakṣa* and *gaṇa* form, including his dwarf-like proportions, while retaining his early *yakṣa* function.

By the sixth century Gaṇeśa images are prevalent in many areas of India. The earliest form of Gaṇeśa seen at Mathurā and Udayagiri has now by and large changed, the deity taking the fully developed form he will essentially maintain up until the present. A sixth-century example from Śāmalājī in Gujarat (fig. 10) shows, when compared to the standing Cambodian Gaṇeśa, the lack of correspondence of which I am thinking. The sixth-century Indian image has now the presence, the girth and proportion, the flexion of the body (*bhaṅga*), that we recognize as typical of the Indian Gaṇeśa.[16]

Not all sixth-century Indian Gaṇeśas are necessarily as elaborate as the Śāmalājī Gaṇeśa; some are simpler and tend to suggest the earlier Mathurān type. Nevertheless, such details as the sunken heads of the Southeast Asian Gaṇeśas point rather precisely to the earliest Indian images.

The earliest Southeast Asian Gaṇeśas (second half of the sixth to the seventh century) appear therefore not to be modeled on the contemporaneous Indian Gaṇeśas but on types that date to the fifth century at the latest. There is thus a possibly 150–200 year gap between the Indian models and the resulting Southeast Asian images. The gap is not easy to explain. One explanation, that there could be a time lag of this length for Indian models to reach Southeast Asia, is in my opinion highly unlikely. Evidence supports that Indian art and ideas reached Southeast Asia, on the whole, very rapidly.[17] That sixth- to seventh-century Indian models, such as that from Śāmalājī (fig. 10) were somehow unavailable to the Southeast Asians, while the earlier Mathurān types were introduced at this late date, is equally unlikely. It is probably not that the later Indian models were not available, but that, however haphazardly introduced, they were not generally adopted by the Southeast Asians.

The time lag is perhaps less problematic if we assume that the Indians and Southeast Asians shared the Mathurān type as their earliest model. The four early Southeast Asian Gaṇeśas illustrated here (figs. 1, 2, 3, 4, and 9) are not "copies" of the Indian Gaṇeśas, but are developments of the earliest Indian type, just as are the sixth-century and later Indian Gaṇeśas. The later Indian Gaṇeśas, as I mentioned above, vary as to how closely they follow the early Mathurān type. While the Śāmalājī Gaṇeśa (fig. 10) is quite divergent from the Mathurān type (fig. 8), an even later seventh-century seated Gaṇeśa from Benisāgar in Singhbhūmi District of Bihar (fig. 11) can be used as an example that in many ways retains more characteristics of the early Mathurān type while evincing a later style. The sharply turned trunk, the raised left hand with the *modaka* bowl, and the simple bands between the breasts and stomach and at the throat, are particularly archaic features. Yet we cannot argue that the Benisāgar Gaṇeśa type could have served as a model for the earliest Southeast Asian Gaṇeśas. The Gaṇeśa from Bihar reveals its seventh-century date in such characteristics as the head raised above the shoulders and the flattened and more stylized face, aspects not reflected in the early Southeast Asian images. In other words, the Benisāgar and contemporaneous early Southeast Asian images correspond in certain ways not because they are model and copy but because they have developed from a shared prototype.

II. Eighth-Century Gaṇeśa Images

We are, nevertheless, left with many unanswered questions. How, when, and where were the early Mathurān Gaṇeśas introduced into Southeast Asia? Were there earlier Southeast Asian Gaṇeśas (made in wood and now lost, or in stone or metal and as yet undiscovered) that are closer to the Indian model? Is the Southeast Asian style we find characterizing the earliest examples due to the dominance of one Southeast Asian center or to a similar interpretation of the model due to a shared indigenous aesthetic? The attempt to answer these and similar questions would involve comparisons with other early Southeast Asian art and take us far from our immediate topic. One point raised in the last question, however, that the sixth- to seventh-century Gaṇeśas partake of a Southeast Asian style, leads us to ask if eighth-century Southeast Asian Gaṇeśas that follow relate in a similar way.

By the eighth century Gaṇeśa is fully implanted in Southeast Asia, and his popularity is attested by numerous artistic remains. One of the most remarkable eighth-century examples is the Cambodian Gaṇeśa from Triton (figs. 12 and 13). This standing, two-armed image would be over two meters high if complete and is unusual in several respects. The attributes he holds, a water jar (*kalaśa*) in his left hand and a rosary (*akṣamālā*) in his right, identify an ascetic's nature. While the rosary is a common attribute of Gaṇeśa, the ascetic's jar is very rarely held by the god in either Indian or Southeast Asian art.[18] A second unusual, perhaps sculpturally unique, characteristic is that his trunk is kept tightly rolled up.[19]

The Triton Gaṇeśa can be compared quite closely to another large (H: 80 cm) Gaṇeśa of about the same date, the Mī-so'n E.5 Gaṇeśa from Vietnam (figs. 14 and 15).[20] It is similar to the Triton Gaṇeśa not only in frontality and stance, but also in such details as the peculiar three-braided belt that these two Gaṇeśas alone share. The E.5 image has its own idiosyncrasies, such as the tiger's skin worn around his hips, the only known instance of this in Southeast Asian art. Also peculiar to this example is the attribute held in the lower right hand. It is known only through Parmentier's drawing (our fig. 14), the hand and attribute being lost today.[21] Parmentier describes it as "une sorte de bouquet pendant, dont le bout audessus de la main est brisé."[22] Jean Boisselier discusses two possible identifications, that it is a tusk with its "roots" or a radish (*mūlaka*), but is skeptical of both.[23] The more likely of the two, that it is a radish, he doubts based on Getty's opinion that the radish is an attribute confined to Nepal, Tibet, and Japan and is "almost unknown in India."[24] Getty suggests that the radish may have arisen from "a misinterpretation of a badly executed broken tusk."[25] In actuality, however, the radish is quite popular in early Indian Gaṇeśa iconography. One need only look at the seventh-century Gaṇeśa from Benisāgar (fig. 11) to see a radish held in the right hand with the leaves, divided into three, pointing downward. The presence of this attribute can be pushed back at least to the sixth century with such examples as the Āmjhara Gaṇeśa that Sara Schastok dates to ca. 530 A.D.[26] One may be tempted to ask, in fact, if the broken tusk may not have evolved from a misunderstanding of the radish.[27]

The "radish" that comes closest in form, with the long fall of foliage, to that of the E.5 Gaṇeśa (that I have found) is held by the Gaṇeśa in the mid sixth–century Rāvaṇa Phadi Cave at Aihole (fig. 16). The comparison between the two images does not stop there. The Aihole Gaṇeśa's heavy *yajñopavīta* of twisted strands of beads may help to explain the unusual thick and similarily granulated (indicated by the cross-hatching in Parmentier's drawing) cord that falls over the E.5 Gaṇeśa's left shoulder and rests on top of his belt. The depiction of the E.5 image's *sampot* in strong horizontal bands may relate to the similar, although narrower, bands on the Rāvaṇa Phadi Gaṇeśa's loin cloth, especially as this treatment is highly unique in the art of both cultures. Furthermore, the ambiguously placed side panels of the E.5 Gaṇeśa (again rare in Cham art of this period) may be compared to the side falls of cloth on the Aihole Gaṇeśa.

Nevertheless, the Indian sources possible for the Cham Gaṇeśa are not restricted to this Chalukyan site, for the presence of the tiger's pelt (*vyāghracarma*) leads us in just the opposite direction, to the northern part of the subcontinent. As R. C. Agrawala has written: "The lion-skin [sic] is usually not to be found in early Indian Gaṇeśa statues other than those from Mathurā, Kabul, and Brahnmor (Chambā). . . ."[28] The extant Indian examples are few, but the Gardez (Afghanistan) Gaṇeśa's tiger pelt is very similar to that of the E.5 Gaṇeśa, both having frontal, flattened faces (see Dhavalikar, fig. 1); the skins on both images are similarly tied over a cloth skirt that falls to a point between the legs.[29] Do relations from Aihole to Afghanistan make sense for the E.5 Gaṇeśa? Boisselier says

> le Gaṇeśa de Mi-so'n E.5, comme tant d'oeuvres chames, semble ainsi bénéficier d'apports très divers tant dans le domaine de la technique que de l'iconographie mais il est dommage que les sources de cette dernière restent encore, dans ce cas particulier, impossibles à préciser.[30]

We now can at least propose certain specific Indian sources, however imperfectly understood the actual relationships may be. The sources show, as stated by Boisselier, a complicated diversity.

Yet a third large Gaṇeśa that can be compared to those from Triton (figs. 12 and 13) and Mī-so'n (figs. 14 and 15) was recently discovered in Thailand (figs. 17 and 18). When found at Muang Pra Roth, Dong Si Mahapot (Prachinburi) in 1972, the Gaṇeśa was broken into pieces. As restored in the National Museum in Bangkok it is 1.70 meters high. The two-armed image wears a lower garment, indicated by the belt at the back, but no jewelry. M. C. Subhadradis Diskul relates the Muang Pra Roth Gaṇeśa, not unreasonably, to the Tuol Pheak Kin image (fig. 1), saying the two images should date to about the same time (he says sixth to seventh century).[31] I find a much closer relationship, however, between the Muang Pra Roth Gaṇeśa and that from Mī-so'n: a comparison of the shape of the head and remaining arm with those of the Mī-so'n Gaṇeśa shows a very close similarity (figs. 15 and 18), and a late-seventh- to eighth-century date for the Muang Pra Roth Gaṇeśa appears most reasonable to me.

There is yet another interesting connection between these two images: each was placed on a stone slab with grooves on top (*somasūtra*) to drain off liquids used during worship (a *snānadroṇī*). Again we must rely on Parmentier, who clearly depicted the *snānadroṇī* in his drawing (our fig. 14). Unfortunately his comment in the text is not particularly helpful: "le piédestal que portrait le dieu est simple; il est creux, et les morceaux en sont assemblés d'une façon curieuse."[32] Boisselier does not mention the pedestal in *La Statuaire du Champa*, and his illustration (our fig. 15) shows the sculpture without the *snānadroṇī*. The Muang Pra Roth Gaṇeśa, unlike the E.5, is a seated figure, but he is sculpted with a small attached base that in turn sets into a *snānadroṇī*. Diskul writes that "he [Gaṇeśa] sits on a large stone base which has a groove for holy water in the front (*yoni*)."[33] That these two Gaṇeśas were placed on *snānadroṇī*s is not in itself surprising. The placement of Hindu deities, usually individual images of Viṣṇu and Śiva, on pedestals with *snānadroṇī*s is well documented in Vietnam, Cambodia, and parts of Thailand.[34] Specific evidence for this practice with Gaṇeśa images is, however, rare.

We have seen Gaṇeśa images, this time dating to the eighth century, appearing from distinct cultures and in several widely spaced areas of Southeast Asia, that reveal an unexpected mutual influence. It is reasonable to suggest, given these images' size, elaborateness, and, in two examples, placement on a *snānadroṇī*, that Gaṇeśa at this time was considered an important deity in his own right, assuming, perhaps, an independent status that he had not yet achieved in India.

III. Gaṇeśa as a Major Deity

There is additional evidence that supports this assessment. All the Southeast Asian Gaṇeśas we have seen thus far are independent images. They maintain a frontality; they lack subsidiary figures and a narrative context; and they have no vehicles, that is, no rat *vāhana*s. They share these characteristics with the earliest Indian Gaṇeśas. Unlike in Indian art, however, these characteristics will continue with few exceptions in the art of Cambodia, Champa, and Thailand. The mainland Southeast Asian Gaṇeśas are thus essentially icons.

It is not always easy to tell how the Gaṇeśa icons were placed and used, as most images have been loose finds. Nevertheless, archaeological and epigraphical evidence indicates that some Gaṇeśa images had sanctuaries of their own. The Triton Gaṇeśa (figs. 12 and 13) was, according to Malleret, probably installed in a now-ruined brick temple.[35] Likewise the Muang Pra Roth Gaṇeśa (figs. 17 and 18) was found associated with a rectangular temple, only the laterite base of which remains.[36] One later (tenth century) Cambodian Gaṇeśa was found by Parmentier in a small temple. This Gaṇeśa appears to have been the only image housed in the temple, and, although the sculpture is broken, Parmentier could reconstruct its placement as at the center of the sanctuary. The importance of this image is apparent from its size, being, at 2.30 meters including the base, the largest Cambodian Gaṇeśa known.[37] In Champa the Mī-so'n E.5 Gaṇeśa (figs. 14 and 15) apparently had his own sanctuary, as did another Mī-so'n Gaṇeśa and one from Nha Trang.[38]

Inscriptional evidence for Gaṇeśa images having their own temples includes an inscription at Angkor Borei dated 611 A.D. that dedicates a sanctuary to "Mahāgaṇapati"[39] and one dated to the reign of Jayavarman I (r. 656–81) that dedicates a sanctuary to "Śrī-Gaṇapati."[40] Two monasteries ("*āśramas*") were dedicated to Gaṇeśa (called "candanādrigaṇeśa" or Gaṇeśa of Sandal Mountain) by Yasovarman I (r. 889 – 900).[41] Likewise a Cham inscription dated 817 states that a temple was raised for Śrī Vināyaka at Po Nagar.[42]

None of the Gaṇeśa images referred to in these inscriptions, nor in any of the other Cham and Cambodian inscriptions that mention the god, can be identified today. Only one intriguing seventh-century inscription from Prasat Prei Kuk in Cambodia refers to a specific seated image in a sanctuary niche. Unfortunately, we must again rely on drawings by Parmentier (see our fig. 19). These, along with his textual description, convey an odd arrangement indeed. On the inside back wall of a now mostly ruined brick sanctuary was a large niche in which sat a Gaṇeśa image: "Elle en a les jambes pliès á l'indienne, la taille fine et le ventre gros, la tête large attachée au fond."[43] The Gaṇeśa is placed on a *snānadroṇī,* which in turn, along with the entire niche, is supported by what Parmentier identifies as "un garuda posé en atlante."[44] Equally curious is that the central Gaṇeśa is flanked by what appears in the drawing to be two other Gaṇeśas, although Parmentier calls them crouching elephants that project but halfway out of the wall ("elephants accroupis sortant à mi-corps du mur"[45]). Above each of these elephants is an inscription, only one of which is readable.

When Coedès published this inscription he said its meaning was not clear and the translation he proposed was to be considered tentative.[46] The Sanskrit text is as follows:

(1) ya + kaś cid dānavendra paraviṣayaharo nirjjito nyena śaktyā
(2) vaddho vai śṛnkhalābhiś ciram iha patito yaṃ stuvañ chailaruddhaḥ

(3) tan dṛṣtvā kinnarābhiś śatagaṇasahitas svapnaśoṣe himādrer
(4) āyāto mokṣaṇārthañ jayati gaṇapatis tvaddhitāyeva so yam

Coedès's translation is this:

> La victoire est à ce Gaṇapati qui, ayant vu dans son sommeil le roi des Dānava, le ravisseur des territoires d'autrui, vaincu par son ennemi, puissamment enchaîné, tombé ici depuis longtemps, retenu par la montagne, chantant ses louanges, est venu, à son réveil, de l'Himādri avec les Kinnarā, en compagnie de cent Gaṇa, ayant en vue la délivrance, comme si c'était pour ton bien.

My own translation, which follows, considerably modifies that of Coedès but is offered with equal reservation:

> This Gaṇapati, who, for your welfare, conquers for the purpose of liberating, has come from the Mountain of Snow accompanied by one hundred *gaṇa*s and *kinnarā*s, having seen [there] upon awakening the Chief of the Dānavas, who, ravishing other's territory, was conquered by another with might [and] bound with chains, praising him [the conqueror] after having fallen here for a long time [and] shut up in the mountain.

The reference may be to Rāvaṇa[47] shaking Mt. Kailāsa. As told in the *Rāmāyaṇa,* the demon Rāvaṇa, after defeating Kubera ("ravishing other's territory"?), attempted to lift Mt. Kailāsa on which Śiva and Pārvatī were making love. Śiva merely pressed his toe on the shaking ground, which trapped Rāvaṇa within the mountain. The demon king was allowed his freedom from the mountain prison after singing Śiva's praises ("praising him [the conqueror]") for one thousand years.

Scenes of Rāvaṇa shaking Mt. Kailāsa are very popular in Indian art. B. N. Sharma has traced the theme back to the Gupta period.[48] Gaṇeśa is present in many of the scenes, which is not surprising considering that Kailāsa, located in the Himalayas (the snow mountain *"himādri"*), is home to Śiva's family.[49] The presence of Gaṇeśa in Rāvaṇa shaking Mt. Kailāsa scenes is also found in Cambodian art. One of the finest, dating to 967, is on a pediment of a library at Banteay Srei. The pyramidical Kailāsa has Śiva and Pārvatī seated on top, while other denizens of the mountain are lined up on each level.[50] Gaṇeśa appears on the second level from the top.

Whatever the interpretation of the inscription, the Prasat Prei Kuk evidence confirms that Gaṇeśa was the focus of worship with his own temples as early as the seventh century in Cambodia. The phrase in the Prasat

Prei Kuk inscription, *mokṣaṇārthañ jayati* (conquers for the purpose of liberating), suggests that Gaṇeśa was regarded as able to lead a worshiper to *mokṣa*, a role reserved for the major deities and not assumed by Gaṇeśa in India until the seventh century at the earliest, but to any significant degree only considerably later.[51]

IV. Roles and Innovations of Gaṇeśa

While Gaṇeśa may thus have been considered a major deity in the seventh and eighth centuries in Thailand, Cambodia, and Vietnam, it was Gaṇeśa in his role as remover of obstacles that was primarily accepted in mainland Southeast Asia. Even today in Buddhist Thailand Gaṇeśa is regarded as remover of obstacles and thus god of success.[52] Ancient evidence for this role includes inscriptions. The Po Nagar inscription mentioned above refers to Gaṇeśa as Vināyaka, literally "removing" in the sense of removing obstacles. The same name for Gaṇeśa is used in a Cambodian inscription dating to the reign of Jayavarman V (r. 968 – 1001).[53] It is from Vināyaka that the Old Burmese name for Gaṇeśa, Mahāpinay purhā, is derived.[54] Other names with a similar meaning occur frequently in Cambodian inscriptions, such as Vighnesá and Vighneśvara, both of which mean "Lord of Obstacles."[55] Yet another name with an identical meaning, Vighnapati, occurs in an inscription from Prah Phnom dating to 930 A.D., but with the added interest of the text referring specifically to the purpose of the Vighnapati image as being "to remove obstacles" (*avighnakāriṇi*).[56] Other evidence for this role in Cambodia includes the frequent use of Gaṇeśa images on dedicatory and territorial markers where his function as remover of obstacles is paramount.[57]

Gaṇeśa's role as lord of obstacles is very popular in India as well. It is also probably the role associated with his earliest Indian forms,[58] and presumably came to Southeast Asia along with them. As noted in part 1, the Indian Gaṇeśa is a *gaṇa* or *yakṣa* type with a large belly, dwarf-like proportions, and informal postures. The Southeast Asian tended to reject these characteristics, transforming Gaṇeśa into a more naturally proportioned and formalized deity, while, however, accepting his propitiatory function.

Thus far two uses of Gaṇeśa in mainland Southeast Asia have been outlined: as a major deity, with his own temples and monumental images, and as a popular but subordinate lord of obstacles. In both cases Gaṇeśa is represented by individual, icon-like images.

In Indian art, Gaṇeśa has numerous other roles. While these were certainly introduced into mainland Southeast Asia, they were hardly depicted at all in the art. Some of the largely neglected roles of which I am thinking are that with his *śakti;* that in his female form, Vaināyakī; that of a dancer; and that in a family scene, as in the familiar Indian Umā-Maheśvaramūrti. There are no mainland Southeast Asian examples, of which I am aware, of the first three types. While the absence of Gaṇeśa with his *śakti* and in a female form can perhaps be understood in light of their relative scarcity in India, the lack of a dancing Gaṇeśa, a very popular form in India, is surprising. One possible reason for the absence of the dancing Gaṇeśa in Southeast Asian art is the rejection, as already noted, of his *gaṇa* nature; *gaṇa*s love to dance and are frequently shown in Indian art playing and dancing to music. Gaṇeśa also, however, danced to mimic his father, Śiva. It is perhaps the late sixth-century relief in Bādāmi Cave 1 where Gaṇeśa, his feet still firmly planted on the ground, first attempts to mimic his father's dance by extending his right arm.[59] This relief is of particular interest as its type was the model for two seventh- to eighth-century Cham reliefs,[60] one of which, from Mī-so'n A'.1, includes a Gaṇeśa. The Mī-so'n A'.1 Gaṇeśa, placed in a relationship to Śiva similar to that of his Bādāmi counterpart, gains some animation by extending his trunk in the air toward his father, but cannot be considered dancing.[61] In Cambodian reliefs of Śiva dancing, Gaṇeśa is also sometimes present, but he apparently never dances himself.[62]

Yet another early form of the dancing Gaṇeśa in Indian art is that associated with the *matṛka*s.[63] The mothers, however, are not often found in the art of Southeast Asia. Both the Cambodian examples of which I know have Gaṇeśa present, but he is seated.[64]

Gaṇeśa is even more frequently depicted in Indian sculpture as dancing alone than with other figures, yet no independent images exist in Southeast Asia (there are very late, nineteenth- and twentieth-century, exceptions in Thailand). The absence is understandable due in part to the relatively late popularity in India; examples before the eighth century are very rare.[65] It is again, however, not the lateness of its probable introduction into Southeast Asia that is significant, but that by the eighth century the Southeast Asian Gaṇeśa has the two primary roles discussed above and was hesitant to adopt others.

The final neglected role, Gaṇeśa in a family context, is also one that occurs with any frequency only after the seventh century in Indian art. Gaṇeśa's familial role, as son to Śiva and Pārvatī and brother to Skanda (Kumāra), is the one elaborated upon in the Purāṇic literature. The Purāṇas defy precise chronological ordering, but the more detailed narratives of Gaṇeśa's life are in the late texts (ca. 600–1300 A.D.). Artistic representations of Gaṇeśa in a familial context tend to increase in popularity over time as well, culminating in the often tender scenes of Śiva with his family at home in the cremation grounds depicted in eighteenth- and nineteenth-century Pahari paintings. On the whole, this role of Gaṇeśa as family member was not stressed in Southeast Asian art. It is not that Gaṇeśa was not frequently associated with Śiva. He was, and with Skanda and Pārvatī as well. The Prah Phnom inscription mentioned above (see the text given in note 56) dedicates images of Śiva, Umā, a *liṅga*, and the *graha*s, along with Gaṇeśa. The Hoá-quê stele of the Cham king Bhadravarman III, dated 909 A.D., says the king's mother dedicated images of Devī, Gaṇapati, and Kumāra.[66] But it is clear that Gaṇeśa is always being invoked as an independent deity and an independent image.

Gaṇeśa's relation to Śiva as a separate deity, rather than as son to father, is stressed in what may be a unique Cambodian arrangement. Before introducing this innovation, however, I want to address generally the extent of Gaṇeśa's iconographical and iconological novelty in the art of mainland Southeast Asia. While there are dozens of regional modifications, Gaṇeśa's iconographic changes have been on the whole minor. I mean by this the visible changes, such as Gaṇeśa in Cambodian art holding the conch and the discus, Viṣṇu's attributes. Unfortunately, we have no means (that is, no texts) to know what the precise iconological impress (the level of symbol and meaning) may have been for this modification, as well as for most others. Perhaps it indicated a radical shift from Indian perceptions of Gaṇeśa. The "explanation" on which scholars have relied for the attributes is either Dupont's "contamination de l'iconographie vishnoüite"[67] or Bhattacharya's "un syncrétisme religieux,"[68] both of which amount to almost the same thing and tell us very little.

Furthermore, as Getty has pointed out, these attributes as related to Gaṇeśa are not unknown in Indian texts.[69] In this regard, many of Bhattacharya's and Getty's own suggested innovations need to be reconsidered as Indian examples are found. One, for example, is Bhattacharya's publication of a three-headed Cambodian Gaṇeśa as "unique in Brahmanical iconography,"[70] and which Boisselier calls "une énigme iconographique."[71] In actuality, the three-headed Gaṇeśa is not unknown in medieval Indian art,[72] and the antique shops in Delhi are today filled with wooden, South Indian three-headed Gaṇeśas. There is even a twelfth-century three-headed Gaṇeśa from Pagan in Burma.[73]

One unpublished Southeast Asian innovation, however, is as radical as any change Gaṇeśa underwent. The stone Cambodian stele in figure 20 shows Śiva riding on a lion at the center, flanked by his two sons, Skanda on the peacock on his left and Gaṇeśa on an elephant on his right. This triad is unusual in itself; it is never found, to my knowledge, in India. In

Cambodian art it is also rare,[74] and I have not found it mentioned in the scholarly literature.

The source for the arrangement and form of the deities and their vehicles on the stele appear to be the depictions of the *navagraha*s in Cambodia. The example from Kuk Roka (fig. 21) dates to 1001 A.D. As is standard in these reliefs, Ketu is the ninth deity and rides on a lion; Indra is the central deity and rides on an elephant; Skanda appears infrequently as a *graha* and in various positions on the reliefs, but here he is the fourth deity and rides a peacock. It appears that the sculptor of the Los Angeles sculpture used the familiar form of the *graha*s when depicting his Śivaite triad. The adoption of an elephant as the vehicle of Gaṇeśa (used for Indra on the *graha* reliefs) must have seemed the most logical. Please remember that the rat vehicle was not adopted in Cambodia.[75]

The next step that this iconography took was even more innovative. Illustrated here are two tiny bronze triads, one from Cambodia (fig. 22) and one probably from Thailand, but in the Khmer or Lopburi style (fig. 23). Dating to the twelve and thirteenth century respectively, the deities and vehicles are the same as those on the stone relief, but an amazing transformation has taken place. Gaṇeśa has become fully human. I am not unaware of the irony and appropriateness in this change, considering that the earliest literary references to Gaṇapati/Gaṇeśa make no mention of an elephant head and that Gaṇeśa was probably initially an anthropomorphic deity. It remains to be seen whether there are other such examples of Gaṇeśa in Southeast Asian art that have gone unidentified because of their fully human form.

V. Gaṇeśa in Indonesian Art

Gaṇeśa was extremely popular in the art of the islands of what is today Indonesia, and nowhere in Southeast Asia did he adopt more novel and interesting forms. The island material is largely unpublished and unexplored, however, and I can here only note very briefly some of the peaks of what remains a vast uncharted area of study. The earliest Gaṇeśa images in Indonesia may be those from the Dieng Plateau (fig. 24). These sculptures deserve a careful study, but they do not, in my opinion, date much before the eighth century and can be compared with such eighth-century Indian examples as the Gaṇeśa in Cave 17 at Ellora.[76] The Dieng Gaṇeśas already have, as did the earliest mainland images, a style and iconography of their own, as for example the "empty" *modaka* bowl and the seated posture in which the soles of the feet press together before the body. The first, the empty *modaka* bowl, connects the Dieng Gaṇeśas to other Southeast Asian images, raising again the question of a Southeast Asian aesthetic and its possible sources. The second example, the seated posture, is almost always said to be found only in the Archipelago.[77] However, in the 1930s H. G. Quaritch Wales and his wife found at Kedah in Malaysia a Gaṇeśa seated in this posture. Wales wrote that "the soles of the feet are represented as touching. This attitude seems to have been considered hitherto as found exclusively in Javanese Gaṇeśas; but the present discovery suggests that the attitude is of Indian origin."[78] The posture does indeed occur in Indian art, although I have found only one example, a terra-cotta image in the collection of the Bharat Kala Bhavan.[79]

The posture and other characteristics of the Dieng Gaṇeśas[80] continued to be popular for centuries in Indonesian art. There were, however, particularly when compared to the mainland Gaṇeśas, several major Indonesian innovations. In Bali, for example, a Gaṇeśa image was used as a water spout at an important sacred bathing place, Goa-Gajah. The apparent central location of the Gaṇeśa between groups of human-figure spouts suggests that the Gaṇeśa was the focus at the bath. The exact significance of this tenth-century Gaṇeśa, however, has defied even the most thorough and careful research.[81]

On the other hand, a second unique Indonesian Gaṇeśa has recently been subjected to a sensitive analysis by Stanley O'Connor that helps to explicate a hitherto enigmatic image.[82] At Candi Sukuh in central Java a remarkable fifteenth-century relief shows three figures, an iron smith squatting on the proper right, a dancing Gaṇeśa in the center, and a bellows operator on the left (fig. 25).[83] The scene is interpreted by O'Connor as representing Bhīma, the focus "of a cult of deliverance of souls during the fifteenth century,"[84] as the smith who is miraculously forging iron, "iron working . . . [being] a metaphor for spiritual transmutation in ancient Java."[85] O'Connor continues that

> within the framework of Tantric thought, it is possible to discover the meaning of the dancing elephant man who is the central figure of the relief. He wears a crown and is Gaṇeśa, the guardian of thresholds, the remover of obstacles, and his presence here, in my view, embodies the process of crossing over from one state to another through the transformative power of the metallurgist's art.[86]

It is thus Gaṇeśa's typical liminal character that enables him to play a role in the metaphysical meaning of the relief. But it is Gaṇeśa in a demonic guise: he is dancing on one leg, the other drawn up; he is nude with his genitals exposed; and he holds in one hand a rosary of bones and in the other an animal, probably (according to O'Connor) a dog, the most unclean of animals and a scavenger of burial grounds.

The Sukuh artist's choice of a Tantric form of Gaṇeśa can be understood first of all because the matrix of fifteenth-century Javanese religion is largely Tantric, and demonic Gaṇeśa images, as we shall see, abound. O'Connor, however, has suggested that "in our relief it is the darkly energetic dance of Gaṇeśa, the guardian of thresholds, who breaks open a path for the soul."[87] In other words, Gaṇeśa's unconventional form and actions are necessary, in the context of this relief, literally to dislodge the soul from the dead person.

Before turning to other Tantric forms of Gaṇeśa, I want only to add one observation. The Sukuh Gaṇeśa is, O'Connor assumes, dancing. The dance is appropriate considering the supposed Tantric nature of the relief, as esoteric rituals frequently involve dancing. O'Connor suggests a possible connection between Gaṇeśa's dance posture and a 1932 account by W. F. Sutterheim of a Javanese court dance, which includes such Tantric characteristics as liquor and sex, in which a performer dances by hopping from one foot to another.[88] While this reference is helpful, another may be suggested. Gaṇeśa's actual leg positions, with the right stiffly upright, the other raised with the heel of the foot near the buttocks, is an Indian dance pose;[89] it is, however, a pose that is not common in Javanese dance, if we may judge from contemporary practices.[90] In Indian dance the pose is associated with Śiva in his destructive manifestation, particularly as Kālārimūrti (the enemy of time, or death) and as Gajāsurasaṃhāramūrti (destroyer of the elephant demon). In South Indian art, the pose is most frequently used in depictions of Śiva as the destroyer of the elephant demon. As in this thirteenth-century example from the Nāṭāraja Temple at Cidambaram (fig. 26), Śiva in this dance posture is usually shown with his legs in profile, buttocks in three-quarter view, and torso and head *en face*. The profile depiction of the Sukuh Gaṇeśa, while not identical, is worth noting in this connection. It is also noteworthy that in some Indian myths it is the destroyed elephant demon (Gajāsara) that supplies Gaṇeśa with his elephant head. There are, in fact, myths in which Gaṇeśa fights the elephant demon himself, and Courtright discusses what he calls the "Śiva-Gajāsura-Gaṇeśa cycle of myths."[91] I do not wish to make more of these connections than is warranted, but assuming the Tantric practices associated with Gaṇeśa came from India, as with the *Gaṇacakra* mentioned below, would not the adoption of this destructive dance position of his father have been appropriate for the demonic Gaṇeśa? In other words, might we be seeing in the Sukuh Gaṇeśa's dance a reflection of an esoteric ritual dance performed by Gaṇeśa and his followers in India?

The Sukuh dancing Gaṇeśa shares his Tantric character with a number of other Javanese Gaṇeśa images. The example I am illustrating (fig. 27) comes from Singasari in Eastern Java but is today in the National Museum in Bangkok, having been taken to Thailand, along with other Javanese sculpture, by King Chulalongkorn at the end of the nineteenth century.[92] It is an image of enormous power, and at 1.72 meters in height is even larger than the much more frequently illustrated monumental Singasari Gaṇeśa now in Leiden.[93] The two Singasari images are very similar, however, and share characteristics with many other Tantric Gaṇeśas.[94] Among these are their attributes: the upper hands hold an axe (*paraśu*) and rosary (*akṣamālā*), while both lower hands hold bowls depicted as skulls. The Tantric nature of these images in fact rests entirely on this one motif, the skull. As in the Bangkok Singasari Gaṇeśa, skulls are used as adornment (in Gaṇeśa's crown and earrings), as the bowls he holds, and as decoration around the base (to suggest the cemetery?). The removal of the skulls for most of these Gaṇeśas, including that in Bangkok, would eliminate their Tantric identification. The association of the skull with horrific Indian deities and the skull cup with Tantric rituals is well known. The skull is not, however, seen with any frequency on Indian Gaṇeśas (Getty says it is "a purely Javanese conception"[95]) although instances among the numerous late (seventeenth century on), predominantly folk, and largely Tantric Indian metal Gaṇeśas would hardly be surprising; Mrs. J. LeRoy Davidson, for example, owns a late (eighteenth century?) metal Gaṇeśa who holds a severed head in one hand.

In Indonesian art, however, the skull, placed at the center of the *jaṭa* above a crescent moon, was a standard motif seen on central Javanese period Gaṇeśas (that is, eighth to tenth centuries). The source for this was images of Śiva, where this motif was frequently placed in the hair. The twelfth- and fourteenth-century Javanese artists created their Tantric Gaṇeśas merely by multiplying this single skull.

The Bangkok Singasari Gaṇeśa, as with many of the other Tantric Gaṇeśas, is carved against a stele and was intended to be placed in a temple niche. The original location of the Leiden Singasari Gaṇeśa has been proposed for a niche of a reconstructed temple at the site, the funerary shrine of King Kṛtanagara, whose death in 1292 may have been due to a Tantric ritual.[96] Gaṇeśa would have been placed in the temple's rear or east niche, with Durgā (as Mahiṣāsuramardinī) in the north and Agastya in the south.[97] This is precisely the arrangement found in Javanese temples during the central Javanese period as well, so the Tantric nature of the eastern Javanese Gaṇeśa did not change his iconographic placement in the temples.

It is difficult, however, to know exactly what role Gaṇeśa may have played in his Tantric guise in Java. We do know from the fourteenth-century Javanese text *Nāgara-Kĕrtagāma* that the Singasari king mentioned above, Kṛtanagara, "in His somewhat old age . . . held to the esoteric (sense) of all *kriyās* (rites)."[98] The poem goes on to mention specifically the *Gaṇacakra* and *Prayogakriyā*.[99] Elsewhere in the text Prayoga appears to refer to Gaṇeśa, as he is said to remove obstacles.[100] The *Gaṇacakra* (Gaṇa = Gaṇeśa) is referred to in Tāranātha's history as a nocturnal rite performed on a burial ground.[101] Pigeaud comments that "evidently in Javanese esoteric religious thinking the elephant-god had the function of a guide, a preparer of the Way."[102] This is, of course, the role O'Connor suggests for the Sukuh Gaṇeśa, and it is consistent with the god's most characteristic function as remover of obstacles on a worshiper's path toward enlightenment. It may be that no matter how complex and esoteric the Tantric rites and their desired ends were, Gaṇeśa's basic role, his reason for being, remained essentially the same as before.

One last innovation that substantiates the Indonesian Gaṇeśa's continuing function as creator and remover of obstacles is the addition to many of a face of glory (*kīrttimukha*) or face of time (*kālamukha*). The well-known Gaṇeśa from Bara dated 1239 is a good example (figs. 28 and 29). The *kāla* face is sculpted on the back of Gaṇeśa's own, and Gaṇeśa's upper arms have the hands turned toward the rear, functioning simultaneously as those of Gaṇeśa and of *kāla*. The *kālamukha* is placed over temple doorways and windows throughout Java, in order to keep out the unworthy but allow the prepared to enter.[103] In other words, the *kālamukha* is a threshold guardian, a creator and remover of obstacles, as is Gaṇeśa, and their juxtaposition (or amalgamation) is conceptually appropriate. The Bara Gaṇeśa (figs. 28 and 29) was intended to be seen in the round, unlike the Singasari Gaṇeśas, and perhaps the addition of the *kālamukha* was a device to allow Gaṇeśa's protective power to emanate in all directions on images intended to be placed in the open.

The presence of a *kālamukha* on a Gaṇeśa does not mean that the image is Tantric. P. H. Pott has argued that the Bara Gaṇeśa was recut when skulls were added to what was assumedly a nondemonic image.[104] I have also seen in a private collection a large central Javanese-period Gaṇeśa with a *kālamukha*. Nevertheless, the amalgamation became more popular in later Indonesian art.

VI. Conclusions

Let me now make some final conclusions, including some drawn from the brief discussion of Indonesian Gaṇeśas. For mainland Southeast Asia, the earliest Gaṇeśa images date to the second half of the sixth century through the seventh and cover an area from Thailand to Vietnam. They appear to relate most closely to the earliest (that is, fifth century or earlier) Indian examples. These earliest Southeast Asian Gaṇeśas do not relate as closely to their contemporaneous sixth- and seventh-century Indian Gaṇeśas. There is, therefore, an unexplained time lag of one to two or more centuries between the Indian model and the Southeast Asian related image.

Even with the earliest Southeast Asian Gaṇeśas, however, there is a homogeneity of style, a Southeast Asian aesthetic, and not a direct copying of Indian forms. This Southeast Asian interrelation is seen as well in the eighth century, in this instance among three monumental images from Thailand, Cambodia, and Vietnam. These images had their own temples in which they were the focus of worship. Their size and placement indicate that Gaṇeśa was a god of importance. The seventh-century Gaṇeśa from Prasat Prei Kuk with its inscription supports the possibility that Gaṇeśa was regarded as a supreme deity.

Gaṇeśa's most popular role in mainland Southeast Asian art, however, is as remover of obstacles, a function thoroughly documented in Cham and Cambodian inscriptions. Other roles Indian Gaṇeśas assumed were on the whole rejected by the Southeast Asians.

In adopting Gaṇeśa, the Southeast Asians made some consistent modifications. For example, the god's *yakṣa* form was usually not accepted. He was given more human proportions and a more formal, iconic stance. Nevertheless, major iconographic innovations were slight.

In Indonesia, the earliest Gaṇeśa images are later than on the mainland, dating perhaps to the eighth century. They do not reflect the earliest Indian Gaṇeśa type but that of the contemporaneous (that is, eighth century) Indian Gaṇeśas. But, like the early mainland Gaṇeśas, the early Indonesian images have their own style and iconography that define them as separate from the Indian Gaṇeśas but connect them to those of the mainland.

Gaṇeśa was extremely popular in Indonesia, and he took a number of innovative forms. He adopted a demonic form as Tantric practices became important. His function as threshold guardian and obstacle remover, however, appears to have remained his primary role.

It is, in fact, this role that best explains Gaṇeśa's ready adaptability throughout Southeast Asia. Gaṇeśa is the god whose aid is enlisted before any task is undertaken, including the worship of other deities. In this capacity, Gaṇeśa must be worshiped frequently and is largely nonsectarian. He therefore could be adopted by various sects, classes, and castes of Hindus and even by Buddhists in Southeast Asia.[105] His use by various sects was facilitated by his being usually depicted as an independent icon in Southeast Asian art and thus free of exclusive Śivaite associations inherent in many narrative contexts. The Southeast Asian Gaṇeśa's nonsectarian character is apparent in his adoption, as noted above, of Viṣṇu's attributes, the conch and the wheel. A metal plaque in the collection of the Los Angeles County Museum of Art (fig. 30) exemplifies the independence that, I think, helped Gaṇeśa win broad popularity. The plaque shows a two-armed Śiva standing between Viṣṇu on his left and Gaṇeśa on his right. Both Viṣṇu and Gaṇeśa hold in their upper hands the conch and wheel and, in their identical size, demonstrate that they are considered of equal importance and in a similar relationship to Śiva.[106]

While Gaṇeśa was used by the Buddhists in Southeast Asia as well as the Hindus, he never became an important Buddhist deity as he did, for example, in Nepal and Tibet. The only exception would be such eastern Javanese Gaṇeśas as those from Singasari, if, participating as they do in the idiosyncratic Buddhist/Śivaite religion of the time, they can be considered to be Buddhist. Otherwise, we can cite the small Gaṇeśa plaques and figures from Pagan in Burma that Luce published.[107] Of interest here are the examples that sit in *padmāsana* and, although four-armed, place one right hand, holding a rosary, in the earth-touching gesture (*bhūmisparśa-mudrā*).[108] While the exact meaning is not known, the Buddhist context is clear. In Cambodian art, Gaṇeśa appears on bells with Buddha images (figs. 31, 32, and 33). These bells were used in religious rituals by the priests, and Gaṇeśa's role as remover of obstacles again makes his appearance here appropriate.[109] Such relatively minor uses of Gaṇeśa as these by the Buddhists at Pagan and in Cambodia occur within what appears to be the limited iconological parameters for the Southeast Asian Gaṇeśa sketched above.

If then, our final summation is that the Southeast Asian Gaṇeśa tended to rely predominantly on his role as Vināyaka, remover of obstacles, for his popularity, he nevertheless took such numerous and inventive forms as to place him among the major artistic and intellectual accomplishments of the area.

NOTES

1. The quotation is from a manuscript, written in Tamil *grantha* script, kept in the National Library in Bangkok. It has been published by Neelakanta Sarma, *Textes Sanskirts et Tamouls de Thailande* (Pondichery: Institut Française d'Indologie, 1972), 86.

2. Alice Getty, *Gaṇeśa: A Monograph on the Elephant-faced God* (Oxford: Clarendon Press, 1936).

3. See Robert L. Brown, "The Buddha Image in Sri Lanka and Southeast Asia," in *Light of Asia: Buddha Sakyamuni in Asian Art* (Los Angeles: Los Angeles County Museum of Art, 1984), 160.

4. Jean Boisselier, *La Statuaire du Champa, Recerches sur les Cultes et l'Iconographie* (Paris: École Française d'Extrême-Orient, 1963), 29.

5. Piriya Krairiksh, *Art Styles in Thailand: A Selection from National Provincial Museums, and An Essay in Conceptualization* (Bangkok: Department of Fine Art, Ministry of Education, 1977), 70 (text in Thai and English).

6. Pierre Dupont, *La Statuaire Préangkorienne* (Ascona: Artibus Asiae, 1965), 60–61.

7. I do not propose that these three images are the only Southeast Asian Gaṇeśas that fit into this time period. Some images that have been proposed by other scholars, however, appear to me to be later. One is the Sathing Phra Gaṇeśa (Songkhla Province in Southern Thailand) that Krairiksh dates to the late sixth century. [Piriya Krairiksh, *Art in Peninsular Thailand Prior to the Fourteenth Century* A.D. (Bangkok: The Fine Arts Department, 1980), 110 and pl. 16.] Krairiksh has, however, in a personal letter suggested that his date should be revised to the tenth century. I feel an eighth, or possibly ninth, century date is most probable. A second image just published for the first time in an article by Chirasa Khochachiwa entitled "The Oldest Gaṇeśa Sculpture in Thailand" is given a sixth- to seventh-century date. [Chirasa Khochachiwa, "Pratimakamphraphikhanesawarkaothisutnaiprathetthai" (The Oldest Gaṇeśa Sculpture in Thailand), *The Journal of Silpakorn University* (1986):78–82 (text in Thai).] This image is today in the Brahmin Temple in Bangkok but is reported (apparently from an interview with the local Brahmin priest) to have come from Southern Thailand (Nakon Si Thammarat). Khochachiwa bases the image's early date on relations she finds with Gupta-period Indian art, stressing such points as Gaṇeśa having only two arms, his lack of adornment, and the figure's naturalism. I do not agree, however, with the author's analysis. Her opinion that the ears are naturalistic, which she mentions several times, is quite contrary to their highly stylized renderings. Nor can two arms and unadornment be used, in India or in Southeast Asia, as a necessary indicator of an early date. There are simply too many exceptions. Two-armed and simply adorned Gaṇeśas were popular in both Cambodia and Champa through the eleventh and twelfth centuries. In fact, it is to Cham images of the eighth to tenth centuries that this image relates. Compare it, for example, to the Cham Gaṇeśa recently acquired by the Musée Guimet and given a tenth-century date ["Activités du musée Guimet," *Arts Asiatiques* 40 (1985):fig. 7 on p. 120].

8. A. K. Narain has suggested that the earliest representation of Gaṇeśa may be on an Indo-Greek coin of ca. first century B.C. See A. K. Narain, "On the Earliest Gaṇeśa," in *Senart Paranavitana Commemoration Volume* (Leiden: E. J. Brill, 1978): 141–44. Also see his article in this volume. There are candidates, other than the Mathurān examples, for pre–Gupta period sculptural Gaṇeśas. Illustrated in *Indian Archaeology 1959–60—A Review* (New Delhi: Department of Archaeology, Government of India, 1960) is an extremely interesting terra-cotta from Chandraketugarh now in the Asutosh Museum in Calcutta (pl. 65, e). It is identified as "attributable to the Kushan period, . . . a unique figure of an elephant-god, holding

on his lap a dwarf woman" (77). A similar Chandraketugarh terra-cotta, but without the woman, is illustrated in *Indian Archaeology 1961–62—A Review,* this time being identified as "an elephant toy-cart" (106, pls. 155, 5). From the illustrations, it appears that the figurines probably had wheels, but both have what look like arms and torsos, and stylistically a Kuṣāṇa-period date is probable.

A second group of possible early Gaṇeśa images has been found at Nāgārjunakoṇḍa. These images are, as far as I know, unpublished, and have A.S.I. negative numbers: 245/63, 246/63, 247/63, 248/63, and 249/63. They are all stone, two armed, and, except for 247/63, crudely carved. One (246/63) appears to be nude. A second (249/63) is only about 8 cm. high. While a date for these images is, at this point, a guess, the third century A.D. would not be impossible.

9. Getty, *Gaṇeśa,* 10.

10. Getty, *Gaṇeśa,* 11.

11. A Kuṣāṇa date is proposed by M. K. Dhavalikar in this volume. See also Prithvi K. Agrawala, "Some Varanasi Images of Gaṇapati and their Iconographic Problem," *Artibus Asiae* 39, no. 2 (1977):139, where he says that the "Ganesa [sic] figure . . . begins to occur only from the fourth century A.D. at Mathura." These references can be expanded.

12. John Faithfull Fleet, "Inscriptions of the Early Gupta Kings and their Successors," *Corpus Inscriptionun Indicarum* vol. 3 (repr. Varanasi: Indological Book House, 1963):21–25.

13. See Joanna Gottfried Williams, *The Art of Gupta India: Empire and Province* (Princeton: Princeton University Press, 1982), 42.

14. V. Ramasubramaniam has given several interesting ideas as to the association of the *modaka* with Gaṇeśa, the relationship coming "from the Vidūshaka-Vikata of the classical Indian stage, the Vināyakas of the Srauta-sūtra, the driṣṭi-dosha, and the Omkāra philosophy of the Upanishad." (V. Ramasubramaniam, "Gaṇapati-Vināyaka-Gajānana Worship: Analysis of an Integrated Cult," *Bulletin of the Institute of Traditional Cultures—Madras* (January–June 1971):132–33.

15. Pierre Dupont, *La Statuaire Préangkorienne,* 51–70.

16. For sixth-century seated examples see Getty, *Gaṇeśa,* pls. 3a, 3b.

17. It makes prima facie sense that Indian culture did not move in tiny slow hops toward Southeast Asia but with the rapidity of a ship crossing the Bay of Bengal, and that the art and ideas the people carried were of their own time. Kamaleswar Bhattacharya has shown, for example, that the time span between religious developments in India and their appearance in Cambodia is frequently slight [Kamaleswar Bhattacharya, *Les Religions Brahmaniques dans l'Ancien Cambodge, d'après l'Épigraphie et l'Iconographie* (Paris: École Française d'Extrême-Orient, 1961), 45 and passim]; and in one instance, that of the South Indian goddess Kāraikkālammaiyār, the earliest extant representation occurs in Cambodia rather than India. [See Mireille Bénisti, "Notes d'Iconographie Khmère: VII. Kāraikkālammaiyār," *Bulletin de l'École Française d'Extrême-Orient* 55 (1969):159–61.]

18. Getty, *Gaṇeśa,* 18–35.

19. Louis Malleret discusses the rolled-up trunk at some length in "La Statue de Gaṇeça de Rochefort-sur-Mer," *Arts Asiatiques* 3 (1956):218–19. His suggestion that this indicates, on analogy to actual elephant behavior, that Gaṇeśa is in a state of agitation and thus is revealing his malefic side, seems highly unlikely.

20. Jean Boisselier dates it to the style of Mī-so'n E.1 (629–757 A.D.). Boisselier, *La statuaire du Champa*, 47–48.

21. A related image of Gaṇeśa has recently been acquired by the Cleveland Museum of Art. It compares quite closely to the Triton Gaṇeśa yet holds in its right hand an object very much in appearance like the leafy attribute of the Mī-so'n E.5 Gaṇeśa. The museum has attributed it to Cambodia and dated it to the seventh century. See *The Bulletin of the Cleveland Museum* 75, no. 2 (1987):fig. 202.

22. Henri Parmentier, *Inventaire Descriptif des Monuments Chams de l'Annam*, vol. 1 (Paris: Imprimerie Nationale, 1909), 416.

23. Boisselier, *La Statuaire du Champa*, 47.

24. Getty, *Gaṇeśa*, 18.

25. Getty, *Gaṇeśa*, 18.

26. Sara L. Schastok, *The Śāmalājī Sculptures and 6th Century Art in Western India* (Leiden: E. J. Brill, 1985), 80 and fig. 69.

27. The attributes held in the lower right hands of early (Gupta period and earlier) Indian Gaṇeśas vary considerably and often are unidentifiable. The earliest Mathurān Gaṇeśas sometimes hold no attributes. [See Stella Kramrisch, *Manifestations of Shiva* (Philadelphia Museum of Art, 1981), no. 61.] In any regard, the broken tusk does not appear to be a common early attribute. Scholars tend, in my opinion, uncritically to identify all elongated attributes as tusks. Aschwin Lippe, for example, identifies the object in the right hand of the Bādāmi Cave 1 Gaṇeśa as a tusk [Aschwin Lippe, "Early Chalukya Icons," *Artibus Asiae* 34, no. 4 (1972):275 and fig. 2]. This object, due to its rounded top, small size, and pliable form, is more likely to be a vegetable. Getty makes an interesting comment in her text (*Gaṇeśa*, 62) to a reference for Gaṇeśa holding a radish in the fifth-century text, the *Bṛhat Saṃhitā*. R. C. Hazra notes that the radish is one of the offerings appropriate to Vināyaka mentioned in the 300 A.D. or earlier *Yājñavalkyasmṛti* [R. C. Hazra, "Gaṇapati-Worship, and the Upapurāṇas Dealing with It," *Journal Ganganatha Jha Research Institute* 5, part 4 (August 1948):269]. The radish is also mentioned as an offering in the *Gṛhyasūtra*. I suspect a careful analysis of the texts could expand such early references.

28. R. C. Agrawala, "Ūrdhvaretas Gaṇeśa from Afghanistan," *East and West* n.s. 18, nos. 1–2 (March–June 1968):168. Agrawala uses the words *tiger* and *lion* interchangeably in this article, even switching them within the same sentence (166). In the *Viṣṇudharmottara* references that Agrawala cites, Gaṇeśa is described as "having a tiger skin garment" (*vyāghra-carmāmbaradharah*) (166). The lion and tiger have been associated in Indian thought since the Vedas [Monier Monier-Williams, *A Sanskrit-English Dictionary* (Oxford: Oxford University Press, 1974), 1036] and are frequently interchanged in artistic iconography.

29. Agrawala, "Ūrdhvaretas Gaṇeśa from Afghanistan," fig. 1. The Gardez Gaṇeśa has an inscription that paleographically is dated by various authorities from the fifth to seventh centuries (see *ibid*, 166). A date in the later part of this time frame is stylistically more appropriate.

30. Boisselier, *La Statuaire du Champa*, 48.

31. M. C. Subhadradis Diskul, "pratimakam 4 rupsungphoengkhonphopmai phainaiprathetthai" (Four Images Recently Discovered in Thailand), *boranakhadi (Archaeology)* 5, no. 1 (July 1973):7 (text in Thai).

32. Parmentier, *Inventaire Descriptif*, 416.

33. Diskul, "pratimakam 4," 7 (translated from the Thai).

34. For detailed discussions of the pedestal in Cambodian art see Jean Boisselier, *Le Cambodge* (Paris: Éditions A. et J. Picard et Cie, 1966), 210–17, and Mireille Bénisti, "Recherches sur le Premier Art Khmer: IV — Piedestaux Décorés," *Arts Asiatiques* 26 (1973):191–224.

35. Malleret, "La Statue de Ganeça," 211–12.

36. Diskul, "pratimakam 4," 7–8 (in Thai).

37. Henri Parmentier, *L'Art Khmer Classique. Monuments du Quadrant Nord-Est* (Paris: École Française d'Extrême-Orient, 1939), 73–75, fig. 15 and ph. 29.

38. Henri Parmentier, *Inventaire Descriptif des Monuments Chams de l'Annam*, vol. 2 (Paris: Éditions Ernest Leroux, 1918), 415.

39. Georges Coedès, *Inscriptions du Cambodge*, vol. 2 (Hanoi: Imprimerie d'Extrême-Orient, 1942), 21–23.

40. Coedès, *Inscriptions du Cambodge*, vol. 2, 45–56.

41. A. Bergaigne, *Inscriptions Sanscrites de Campā et du Cambodge* (Paris: Imprimerie Nationale, 1893), 355–76.

42. Bergaigne, *Inscriptions Sanscrites*, 263–70.

43. H. Parmentier, "Complément a l'Art Khmer Primitif," *Bulletin de l'École Française d'Extrême-Orient* 35 (1936):79.

44. Parmentier, "Complément," 79.

45. Parmentier, "Complément," 80.

46. Georges Coedès, *Inscriptions du Cambodge*, vol. 5 (Paris: E. de Boccard, 1953), 63.

47. Rāvaṇa is referred to in the inscription as chief of the *dānavas* (*dānavendra*), the *dānavas* being a class of demons.

48. Brijendra Nath Sharma, "Rāvaṇa Lifting Mount Kailāsa in Indian Art," *East and West* n.s. 23 (September–December 1973):328–29.

49. Sharma, "Rāvaṇa Lifting Mount Kailāsa," figs. 2, 3, 7, 8, 9, 10, 11, etc.

50. Henri Parmentier, Victor Goloubew, and Louis Finot, *Le Temple d'Içvarapura (Bantāy Srĕi, Cambodge)* (Paris: G. Vanoest, 1926), pls. 25–27.

51. Paul B. Courtright, *Gaṇeśa: Lord of Obstacles, Lord of Beginnings* (New York: Oxford University Press, 1985), 217ff.

52. Monwibha Chaiyabhand and Kulsaph Kesmankit, "duangtraphrakhnesr" (Seal of Phra Ganesh), *Silpakon* 13, no. 5 (January 1970):47–65 (text in Thai).

53. Louis Finot, "Nouvelle Inscription du Cambodge," *Bulletin de l'École Française d'Extrême-Orient* 28 (1929):58–75.

54. Gordon H. Luce, *Old Burma — Early Pagan*, vol. 1 (Locust Valley, NY: J. J. Augustin, 1969), 205.

55. For references see Bhattacharya, *Les Religions Brahmaniques*, 133–34.

56. The text reads:

bhaktisthirīkarttun avighnakāriṇi
dvipañcamurtto śivasomanāmā
candīśvaravighnapatiñ ca liṅgam
grahais saha stāpitavān subhaktyā

Coedès's translation is:

> Pour affermir la dévotion, le nommé Śivasoma,
> écartant les obstacles, dans (l'année marquée par les)
> (8) formes (de Śiva)—cinq—deux, a pieusement
> érigé Caṇḍī (Umā), Īśvara (Śiva), Vighnapati (Gaṇeśa),
> un liṅga, avec les images des planètes.

(G. Coedès, *Inscriptions du Cambodge,* vol. 3 (Paris: E. de Boccard, 1951), 120.) In reference to this inscription K. Bhattacharya writes: "Notre fondateur visait tout à la fois, si l'on en croit ses propres terms, à 'affermir la dévotion' (*bhaktisthirīkartum*) et à 'écarter les obstacles' (*avighnakārī*). Il semble donc que, si l'érection des images Śiva et de Caṇḍi, jointe à celle du liṅga, repondait à la première préoccupation, l'érection de Gaṇeśa et des *graha* répondait a la second." (*Les Religions Brahmaniques,* 133.)

57. Bhattacharya, "Les Religions Brahmaniques," 134. For examples, see J. Boulbet and B. Dagens, "Les Sites Archéologiques de la Région du Bhnaṃ Gūlen (Phnom Kulen)," *Arts Asiatiques* 27 (1973), phs. 39, 64.

58. The development, in part, of Gaṇeśa from malevolent demons (usually called *vināyakas*) who create obstacles that can be removed only through offerings and praise is convincingly argued by several scholars. See, for example, Hazra, "Gaṇapati-Worship," 263–76.

59. C. Sivaramamurti, *Nataraja in Art, Thought and Literature* (New Delhi: National Museum, 1974), fig. 17. Most fifth- and sixth-century reliefs of Śiva dancing that include Gaṇeśa show him rather ambiguously hanging in the air, probably because while the other deities could be depicted arriving by flying through the air on their vehicles, Gaṇeśa at this early point had no *vāhana.* Examples occur at Ellora, Elephanta, Sirpur, etc. See *ibid.,* figs. 9, 10, 11, 12.

60. Boisselier, *La Statuaire du Champa,* figs. 17, 18.

61. Sivaramamurti has published a tenth-century (Sivaramamurti dates it eighth-century) Cham relief of a dancing Śiva, identifying a very abraded subsidiary figure as a dancing Gaṇeśa (fig. 22). He may be correct. As I said in my introduction, absolute categorical statements are extremely dangerous. Boisselier in his discussion of the same relief hazards no identification of this figure (*La Statuaire du Champa,* 189). A very similar relief, however, illustrated in Parmentier, *Inventaire Descriptif,* vol. 2, fig. 113, has both small dancing figures present, and both are human figures.

62. See Sivaramamurti, *Nataraja,* fig. 15. Sivaramamurti says on p. 357 that Coedès "has described . . . at Angkor Wat . . . an elaborate carving of Naṭarāja accompanied by Brahmā, Vishṇu, Gaṇeśa, and other celestials . . . all joining his dance in great glea [sic]." Sivaramamurti unfortunately gives no reference, but it may be to an obscure article in the *Bulletin de la Commission Archéologique de l'Indochine* for 1913 entitled "Trois piédroits d'Aṅkor-Vat," 105–9, in which Coedès published a relief of some sixty figures each within a circle of foliage (his pl. 10). One of them is a dancing Śiva, flanked by seated figures of Viṣṇu and Brahmā; Gaṇeśa is kneeling. This appears to be Sivaramamurti's reference, as he says the naṭarāja is "a small medallion."

63. See, for example, Schastok, *The Śāmalājī Sculptures,* fig. 51.

64. See Boisselier, *Le Cambodge*, 295 and pls. 51, 1; E. Lunet de Lajonquière, *Inventaire Descriptif des Monuments du Cambodge*, vol. 3 (Paris: Ernest Leroux, 1911), 127–28; and Bhattacharya, *Les Religions Brahmaniques*, 143–44.

65. Devangana Desai, "Dancing Ganesa," *Pushpanjali* (1980):30–38.

66. H. Huber, "Études Indochinoises, XII, L'Épigraphie de la Dynastie de Dông-du'o'ng, 6, La stèle de Hoá-quê," *Bulletin de l'École Française d'Extrême-Orient* 11 (1912):285–86.

67. Dupont, *La Statuaire Preangkorienne*, 121.

68. Bhattacharya, *Les Religions Brahmaniques*, 135.

69. Getty, *Gaṇeśa*, 50.

70. Kamaleswar Bhattacharya, "An Unpublished Gaṇeśa Image from Cambodia," *Artibus Asiae* 21, nos. 3/4 (1958):270.

71. Boisselier, *Le Cambodge*, 291.

72. See, for example, Prithvi K. Agrawala, "Some Varanasi Images of Gaṇapati and their Iconographic Problem," *Artibus Asiae* 39, no. 2 (1977):fig. 17.

73. Luce, *Old Burma—Early Pagan*, vol. 3, pl. 236d.

74. The triad occurs in the relief at Boeṅ Gaṃnūr at Phnom Kulen. See Boulbet and Dagens, "Les Sites Archéologiques de la Région du Bhnaṃ Gūlen (Phnom Kulen)," ph. 53 (on the right side above the lion). This grouping is incorrectly identified by Lunet de Lajonquière as Brahmā, "un personnage sur un lion," and Gaṇeśa (*Inventaire Descriptif*, vol. 1, 319).

75. The use of an elephant for Gaṇeśa's vehicle is unique in art, although Gaṇeśa riding on an elephant is mentioned in the *Skanda Purāṇa*. I want to thank Prof. Ludo Rocher for first mentioning this textual reference to me. It is also cited in Courtright, *Gaṇeśa*, 79.

76. See Lippe, "Early Chalukyan Icons," fig. 3.

77. Getty, *Gaṇeśa*, 19, 56.

78. H. G. Quaritch Wales, "Archaeological Researches on Ancient Indian Colonization in Malaya," *Journal of the Malayan Branch of the Royal Asiatic Society* 18, part 1 (February 1940):14, pl. 20 (left side).

79. *Chhavi: Golden Jubilee Volume*, ed. Anand Krishna (Banaras: Bharat Kala Bhavan, 1971):fig. 540.

80. The placement of Gaṇeśa on a lotus would be another Dieng characteristic that, unusual in the Indian context, continued in Indonesian art.

81. See the discussion in Judith Ann Patt, *The Use and Symbolism of Water in Ancient Indonesian Art and Architecture*, Ph.D. dissertation, University of California, Berkeley, 1979, 298–304.

82. Stanley J. O'Connor, "Metallurgy and Immortality at Candi Sukuh, Central Java," *Indonesia* 39 (April 1985):53–70.

83. The relief is in situ and open to the elements. Both my photograph (taken in 1985) and those illustrated in O'Connor's article show the relief much deteriorated as compared to earlier taken photographs. An excellent illustration can be found in A. J. Bernet Kempers, *Ancient Indonesian Art* (Amsterdam: C. P. J. Van der Peet, 1959), pl. 334.

84. O'Connor, "Metallurgy and Immortality," 57.

85. O'Connor, "Metallurgy and Immortality," 54.

86. O'Connor, "Metallurgy and Immortality," 60.

87. O'Connor, "Metallurgy and Immortality," 63.

88. O'Connor, "Metallurgy and Immortality," 62.

89. The pose is classified as Type C.II by Anne-Marie Gaston in her *Śiva in Dance, Myth and Iconography* (Delhi: Oxford University Press, 1982). Illustrations of a dancer in this pose are her pls. 8r, 71a, 71b, and 78c.

90. I wish to thank Prof. Judy Mitoma of UCLA's dance department for this information.

91. Courtright, *Gaṇeśa,* 34–37, 80–82.

92. See Th. van Erp, "Hindu-Javaansche Beelden thans te Bangkok," *Bijdragen tot de taal-, land- en Volkenkunde* 79 (1923):419–518, and Th. van Erp, "Nog eens de Hindu-Javaansche Beelden te Bangkok," *Bijdragen tot de Taal-, Land- en Volkenkunde* 83 (1927):503–13.

93. See Getty, *Gaṇeśa,* pl. 31a.

94. Getty, *Gaṇeśa,* pls. 31b, c, d.

95. Getty, *Gaṇeśa,* 57.

96. Kempers, *Ancient Indonesian Art,* 78.

97. Kempers, *Ancient Indonesian Art,* pls. 237, 238.

98. Theodore G. Th. Pigeaud, *Java in the 14th Century: A Study in Cultural History,* vol. 3 (The Hague: Martinus Nijhoff, 1960), 49.

99. Pigeaud, *Java in the 14th Century,* vol. 3, 49.

100. Pigeaud, *Java in the 14th Century,* vol. 3, 3 and Pigeaud's discussion in vol. 4, 131.

101. Pigeaud, *Java in the 14th Century,* vol. 4, 131.

102. Pigeaud, *Java in the 14th Century,* vol. 4, 131.

103. See Adrian Snodgrass, *The Symbolism of the Stupa* (Ithaca: Cornell Southeast Asian Program, 1985), 305–17.

104. P. H. Pott, "Four Demonic Gaṇeśas from East Java," *The Wonders of Man's Ingenuity* (Leiden: E. J. Brill, 1962), 125, 131.

105. These characteristics, of course, help to explain Gaṇeśa's great popularity in India as well, even up until today. They are, for example, why the Maharashtrian activist Bal Gangadhar Tilak chose Gaṇeśa around which to organize his resistance to the British at the end of the nineteenth century. See Courtright, *Gaṇeśa,* 226–47.

106. For a second possible arrangement of these three gods see Henri Parmentier, "Catalogue de Musée Khmer de Phnoṃ-Peñ," *Bulletin de l'École Française d'Extrême-Orient* 12, no. 3 (1912):fig. 2 on p. 11 (although Parmentier identifies the Viṣṇu as Umā).

107. Luce, *Old Burma—Early Pagan,* vol. 3, pls. 88, 89.

108. Luce, *Old Burma—Early Pagan,* pls. 88a–f. Discussion vol. 1, 205–6.

109. The bells, and other ritual equipment, were not restricted to the Buddhists, and Gaṇeśa appears on examples with Hindu iconography as well. A. Zig-

mund-Cerbu published what he believes is a *vajra* decorated with Gaṇeśa and Viṣṇuite deities. ["À Propos d'un Vajra Khmer," *Artibus Asiae: Felicitation Volume Presented to Professor Georges Coedès on the Occasion of his Seventy-fifth Birthday* 24, nos. 3/4 (1961):phs. A, B.] I find, however, his argument that Gaṇeśa here is the elephant/serpent Vāmanairavata unnecessarily complex and strained. Gaṇeśa's presence on this ritual equipment needs no such complicated justification. See also F. D. K. Bosch's comment in his *The Golden Germ: An Introduction to Indian Symbolism* (The Hague: Mouton & Co., 1960), 234–35.

Fig. 1. Gaṇeśa. Tuol Pheak Kin, Cambodia. Sixth to seventh century. Stone. H: 75 cm. (Photo: after Getty, *Gaṇeśa,* Pl. 25a)

Fig. 2. Gaṇeśa. Prasat Phnom Rung, Buri Ram, Thailand. Seventh century. Stone. H: 24 cm. Maha Wirawong National Museum, Nakhon Ratchasima, Mus. No. Ph. R. 131. (Photo: Piriya Krairiksh)

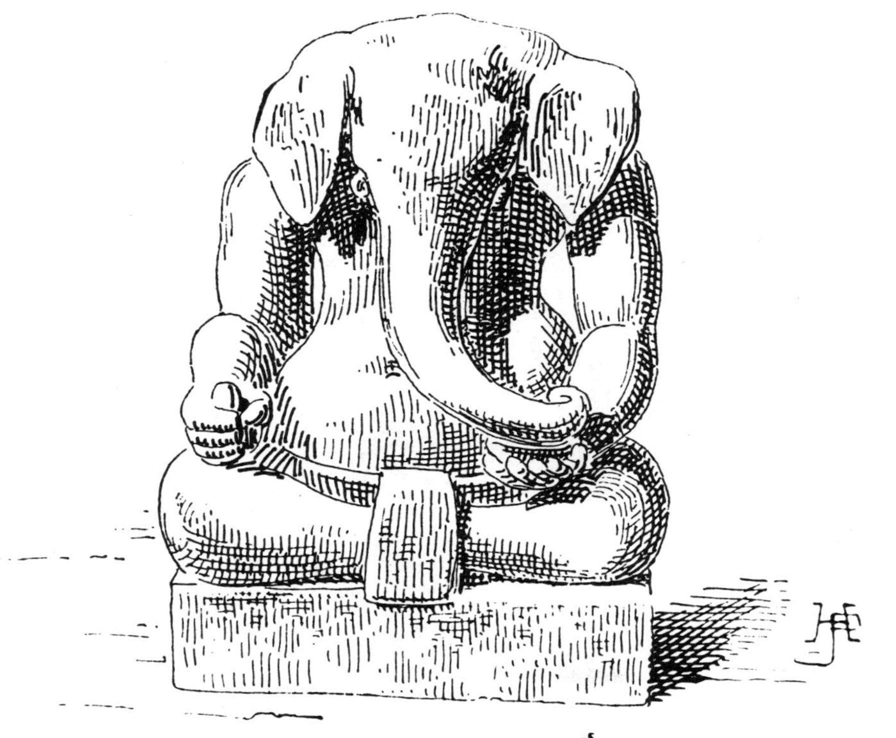

Fig. 3. Gaṇeśa. Phú Ninh, Vietnam. Seventh century. Stone H: ca. 80 cm. (Photo: after Parmentier, *Inventaire Descriptif des Monuments Chams de l'Annam*, vol. 3, Fig. 117)

Fig. 4. Gaṇeśa. Phú Ninh, Vietnam. Seventh century. Stone. H: ca. 80 cm. (Photo: after Parmentier, *Inventaire Descriptif des Monuments Chams de l'Annam*, vol. 3, Fig. 118)

Fig. 5. Gaṇeśa. Mathurā, India. Fifth century or earlier. Stone. Government Museum, Mathurā, Mus. No. 964. (Photo: Government Museum, Mathurā)

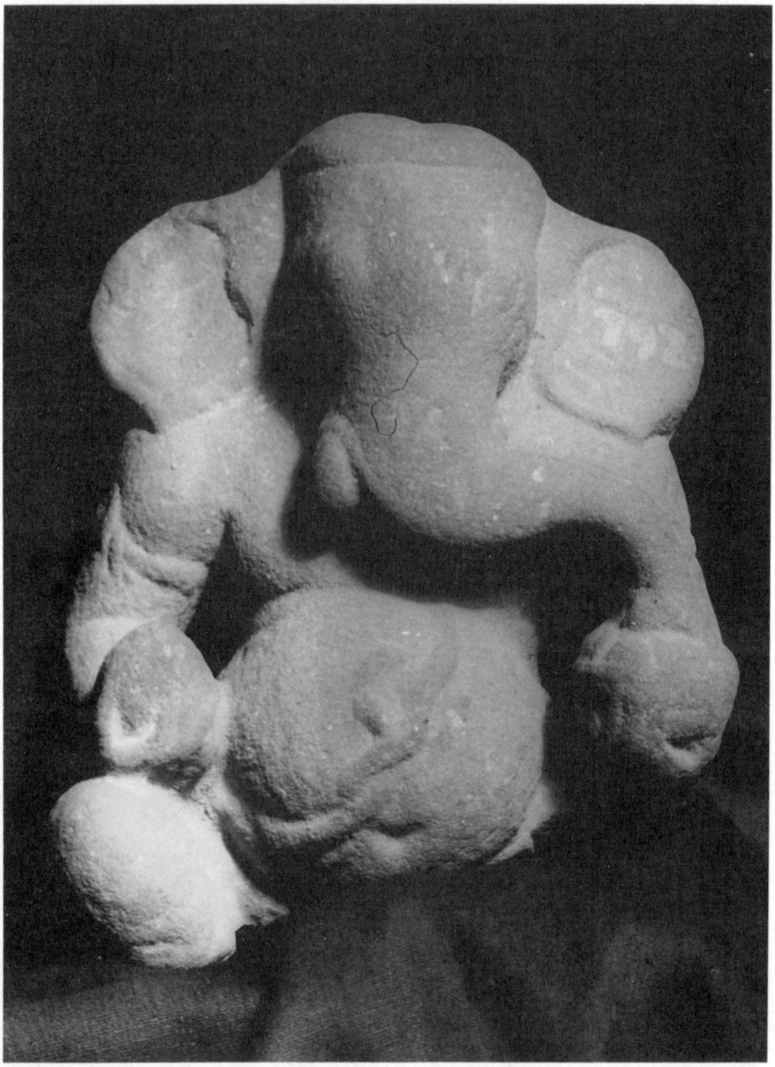

Fig. 6. Gaṇeśa. Mathurā, India. Fifth century or earlier. Stone. Government Museum, Mathurā, Mus., No. 792. (Photo: Government Museum, Mathurā)

Fig. 7. Gaṇeśa. Cave 6, Udayagiri, India. ca. 400 A.D. Stone. (Photo: Robert L. Brown)

Fig. 8. Gaṇeśa. Mathurā, India. Fifth century or earlier. Stone. H: ca. 20 cm. Government Museum, Mathurā, Mus. No. 758. (Photo: Robert L. Brown)

Fig. 9. Gaṇeśa. Cambodia. Seventh century. Stone. H: 44 cm. Metropolitan Museum of Art. (Photo: Los Angeles County Museum of Art)

Fig. 10. Gaṇeśa. Śāmalājī, India. Sixth century. Stone. H: 87 cm. Baroda Museum and Picture Gallery, Mus No. Ac2.537. (Photo: AIIS)

Fig. 11. Gaṇeśa. Benisāgar, Singhbhūmi, India. Seventh century. Stone. H: 55 cm. Patna Museum. (Photo: Robert L. Brown)

Fig. 12. Gaṇeśa. Triton, Cambodia. Eighth century. Stone. H: 140 cm. Musée de Rochefort-sur-Mer. (Photo: after Malleret, "La Statue de Ganeça de Rochefort-sur-Mer," Fig. 2)

Fig. 13. Gaṇeśa. Triton, Cambodia. Eighth century. Stone. H: 140 cm. Musée de Rochefort-sur-Mer. (Photo: after Malleret, "La Statue de Ganeça de Rochefort-sur-Mer," Fig. 3)

Fig. 14. Gaṇeśa. Mī-so'n E.5, Vietnam. Eighth century. Stone. H: 80 cm. (Photo: after Parmentier, *Inventaire Descriptif de Monuments Chams de l'Annam* Vol. 1. Fig. 94)

Fig. 15. Gaṇeśa. Mī-so'n E.5, Vietnam. Eighth century. Stone. H: 80 cm. (Photo: after Boisselier, *La Statuaire du Champa,* Fig. 14)

Fig. 16. Gaṇeśa. Rāvaṇa Phadi Cave, Aihole, India. Sixth century. Stone. (Photo: Robert L. Brown)

Fig. 17. Gaṇeśa. Muang Pra Roth, Dong Si Mahapot, Prachinburi, Thailand. Eighth century. Stone. H: 170 cm. National Museum, Bangkok. (Photo: Robert L. Brown)

Fig. 18. Gaṇeśa. Muang Pra Roth, Dong Si Mahapot, Prachinburi, Thailand. Eighth century. Stone. H: 170 cm. National Museum, Bangkok. (Photo: Robert L. Brown)

Fig. 19. Gaṇeśa in a Wall Niche. Prasat Prei Kuk, Cambodia. Seventh century. Stone (?). (Photo: after Parmentier, "Complément à l'Art Khmèr Primitif," Pl. XIII)

Fig. 20. Gaṇeśa on an Elephant, Śiva on a Lion, and Skanda on a Peacock (from viewer's left). Cambodia. Tenth century. Stone. H: 56 cm. Los Angeles County Museum of Art, Museum Acquisition Fund. (Photo: Los Angeles County Museum of Art)

Fig. 21. The Nine Deities (*navagrahas*). Kuk Roka, Cambodia. 1001 A.D. Stone. [Photo: after Bhattacharya, "Notes d'Iconographie khmère. II.—Les 'Neuf Deva,' " *Arts Asiatiques* 3, no. 3 (1956):Fig. 2]

Fig. 22. Gaṇeśa on an Elephant, Śiva on a Lion, and Skanda on a Peacock (from viewer's left). Cambodia. Twelfth century. Bronze. H: 9 cm. Collection of Natasha Eilenberg. (Photo: Otto E. Nelson)

Fig. 23. Gaṇeśa on an Elephant, Śiva on a Lion, and Skanda on a Peacock (from viewer's left). Thailand. Thirteenth century. Bronze. H: 9 cm. Los Angeles County Museum of Art, Gift of Dr. and Mrs. Pratapaditya Pal. (Photo: Spink & Son Ltd.)

Fig. 24. Gaṇeśa. Dieng, Java, Indonesia. Eighth century. Stone. (Photo: after Getty, *Gaṇeśa*, Pl. 30d)

Fig. 25. Dancing Gaṇeśa (at center), Bhīma on viewer's left, Bellows Operator on right. Sukuh, Java, Indonesia. Fifteenth century. H: ca. 165 cm. (Photo: Robert L. Brown)

Fig. 26. Śiva. Nataraja Temple, Cidambaram, India. Thirteenth century. Stone. (Photo: Robert L. Brown)

Fig. 27. Gaṇeśa. Singasari, Java, Indonesia. ca. 1300 A.D. Stone. H: ca. 170 cm. National Museum, Bangkok. (Photo: Robert L. Brown)

Fig. 28. Gaṇeśa. Bara, Java, Indonesia. 1239 A.D. Stone. H: 150 cm. (Photo: after Getty, *Gaṇeśa,* Pl. 30a)

Fig. 29. Gaṇeśa. Bara, Java, Indonesia. 1239 A.D. Stone. H: 150 cm. (Photo: after Getty, *Gaṇeśa,* Pl. 30b)

Fig. 30. Gaṇeśa, Śiva, Viṣṇu (from viewer's left). Eighth century. Bronze. H: 19.6 cm. Los Angeles County Museum of Art. (Photo: Adrian Maynard)

Fig. 31. Bell. Cambodia. Thirteenth century. Bronze. H: 20 cm. Collection of Margot and Hans Ries. (Photo: Los Angeles County Museum of Art)

Fig. 32. Detail of 31 showing Gaṇeśa. (Photo: Los Angeles County Museum of Art)

Fig. 33. Detail of 31 showing reverse side with Buddha. (Photo: Los Angeles County Museum of Art)

9

The Tantric Gaṇeśa: Texts Preserved in the Tibetan Canon

Christopher Wilkinson

I. Introduction and the Texts

Gaṇeśa is a deity who began his career in India and subsequently spread his influence throughout Asia, including Tibet. There are thirty texts in the Tibetan Buddhist canon of direct interest for the study of Gaṇeśa. All of these texts were composed in "Indian" languages, presumably Sanskrit or some Prakrit, and it is perhaps only in their Tibetan translations that these texts survive today. There is also a significant postcanonical development of Gaṇeśa in the schools of Tibetan Buddhism, and the practices associated with Gaṇeśa as a Buddhist Tantric deity survive up to this day.

The intention of this article is to present a representative sampling of the canonical literature related to Gaṇeśa in English translation. Fifteen of the thirty texts concerned with Gaṇeśa are translated below. Time and space prevent the translation of all the texts, and the same restrictions prevent a study of the postcanonical development of Gaṇeśa. Furthermore, I have foregone any extensive critical discussion. The historical section (section II) on the authors and translators has been added by Robert L. Brown, primarily from information supplied by Tim Shaw. Otherwise, the translations stand on their own. Hopefully, they will provide a major new source for scholars working on Gaṇeśa.

All thirty of the canonical texts relating to Gaṇeśa present him in a Tantric character. There is, however, no attempt in any of the texts to make claim to any particular class of Tantra. Gaṇeśa is presented as a deity from whom food, wealth, sex, and supernatural attainments may be received by the practitioner. Gaṇeśa's relationship with Mahādeva, better known as

Śiva, is admitted in some of the texts, yet the predominant tendency is to identify Gaṇeśa as an emanation of the Bodhisattva Avalokiteśvara. This may suggest that an attempt was made to strip Gaṇeśa of his non-Buddhist heritage and incorporate him fully into the Buddhist pantheon. It also perhaps reflects the tendency to associate Avalokiteśvara and Śiva in later Buddhism. It may, finally, and as evidenced by a number of essays in this book, indicate that Gaṇeśa was originally not a Buddhist, Hindu, or Jaina deity, but rather an Indian deity who was incorporated equally into all major Indian religions.

The following bibliography presents the texts thematically, in the order they are to be presented in translation, rather than chronologically. Text numbers refer to the Peking Edition of the Tibetan canon. The marker ">" indicates that the text is one of the fifteen translated in this article.

A. Text from the *bKa 'gyur*
   1. >*Ārya gaṇapati hṛdaya, 'Phags pa Tshogs kyi bDag po'i sNying po*. (Peking #338).
   2. >*Mahāgaṇapati tantra, Tshogs kyi bDag po'i rGyud*. (Peking #337).

B. Iconographical text
   3. >*Mahāvināyaka rūpopadeśa cintāratna, bGegs bdag Chen po'i sKu bri ba'i Man rgag Yid bzhin nor bu*. (Peking #4978). Author, Nag po pa. Translators, Gāyadhara and Zla ba'i 'Od zer.

C. The *Bali* ceremony
   4. >*Ārya gaṇapati bali vidhi, 'Phags pa Tshogs kyi bDag po'i gTor ma'i Cho ga*. (Peking #4979). Au. Nag -po zhabs. Trans. Gāyadhara, Zla ba'i 'Od zer.

D. The fire ceremonies (S. *homa*)
   5. [*Vināyaka*] *homa vidhi* [*prabhāsana*], *bGegs bdag gi sByin sreg gi Cho ga Rab tu bShad pa*. (Peking #4980).
   6. *Ārya gaṇapati homa vidhi, 'Phags pa Tshogs kyi bDag po'i sByin sreg gi Cho ga*. (Peking #4988).

E. Vināyaka as an evil demon
   7. >*Vināyaka graha nirmocana, Log 'dren gyi gDon las Nges par Thar pa*. (Peking #3812). Au. Ye shes rDo rje (Jñānavajra).

F. Practice methods (*Sādhana*)
   8. *Mahāgaṇeśa sādhana, Tshogs kyi dBang ldan Chen po sGrub pa'i thabs*. (Peking #5176).
   9. >[*Gaṇapati sādhana daridra nidhiprada nāma*]. *Tshogs bdag gi*

bsGrub pa dbul ba'i gTer sByin Shes bya ba. (Peking #3855). Au. dPal Mar me mdzad bzang po (Śrī Dīpaṁkarabhadra).

10. *Gaṇapati guhya sādhana, Tshogs kyi bDag po gSang ba'i sGrub thabs.* (Peking #4560). Au. Amoghavajra. Trans. Dīpaṁkaraśrījñāna, Nag tsho Tshul khrims rGyal ba.
11. *Meghāloka gaṇapati sādhana, sPrin kyi sGron ma Tshogs kyi bDag po sGrub thabs.* (Peking #4562). Au. Rin chen rDo rje (Ratnavajra). Trans. Dīpaṁkaraśrījñāna, Nag tsho Tshul khrims rgyal ba.
12. >*Śrī ājñā vinivarta gaṇapati sādhana, dPal Tshogs kyi bDag po 'Jur gegs Sel ba Shes bya ba'i sGrub thabs.* (Peking #4563). Au. Indrabhuti. Trans. Dīpaṁkaraśrījñāna, rGya brTson 'grus Seng ge.
13. *Gaṇapati sādhana mahācakra nāma, Tshogs kyi bDag po'i sGrub thabs 'khor lo Chen po Shes bya ba.* (Peking #4972). Au. Avadhūti-pā (Avadhūtapāda). Trans. Dīpaṁkaraśrījñāna, Tshul khrims rGyal ba.
14. >*Vināyakarāja sādhana, bGegs kyi rgyal po'i sGrub thabs.* (Peking #4973). Au. Nag-po sPyod pa pa. Trans. Gāyadhara, Zla ba'i 'Od zer.
15. *Vināyakarāja sādhana, bGegs kyi rGyal po bsGrub pa'i thabs.* (Peking #4976). Au. Nag po pa. Trans. Gāyadhara, Zla ba'i 'Od zer. [Readings differ from Peking #4973.]
16. *Sunipuṇa mahādeva vignarāja sādhana, Shin to Myur ba'i Lha Chen po bGegs kyi rGyal po'i sGrub thabs.* (Peking #4981). Au. Dīpaṁkara.
17. *Subudha devamahāvighna vighnarāja sādhana, Shin tu Myur ba'i Lha bGegs Chen po bGegs kyi rGyal po bsGrub pa'i thabs.* (Peking #4982). Trans. Vairocana of Kośala.
18. *Śrī gaṇapati cakra sūrya, dPal Tshogs kyi bDag po'i 'Khor lo'i gSal byed.* (Peking #4983). Au. Ḍombhiheruka.
19. >*Śrī gaṇapati śānti sādhana, dPal Tshogs kyi bDag po Shi ba'i sGrub thabs.* (Peking #4986). Au. Jo bo.
20. *Ārya gaṇapati cintāratna* [*sādhana*], *'Phags pa Tshogs kyi bDag po Yid bzhin Nor bu'i sGrub thabs.* (Peking #4987). Au. Nag po pa.
21. *Gaṇapati guhya sādhana, Tshogs kyi bDag po'i gSang ba'i sGrub thabs.* (Peking #4990). Au. Dīpaṁkarajñāna.
22. *Mahāgaṇapati dhātutrika rakta vaśikara sādhana, Tshogs kyi bDag po Chen po Khams gsum dbAng sDud dMar po'i sGrub thabs.* (Peking #4992). Au. Canṭapa. Trans. dPal Vairocana of India, Chos kyi Grags pa.

23. *Krodha gaṇapati sādhana, Tshogs kyi bDag po Khro bo'i sGrub thabs.* (Peking #4994). Au. gSer gling pa (Suvarṇadvīpa).
24. >*Ghaṇapati samaya guhya sādhana, Tshogs kyi bDag po Dam Tshig gSang ba'i bsGrub thabs.* (Peking #4995). Au. Canakīrti. Trans. Vairocana, Chos kyi Grags pa.

G. Praises (*stotra, stuti*)

25. >*Ārya gaṇapati rāgavajra samaya stotra, 'Phags pa Tshogs kyi bDag po Chags pa rDo rje'i Dam tshig gi bsTod pa.* (Peking #4561). Au. Dīpaṁkaraśrījñāna. Trans. Dīpaṁkaraśrījñāna, Tshul khrims rGyal ba.
26. >*Ārya gaṇapati stuti, 'Phags pa Tshogs kyi bDag po la bsTod pa.* (Peking #4977). Au. Nag po Zhabs.
27. >*Ārya gaṇapati stuti, 'Phags pa Tshogs kyi bDag po la bsTod pa.* (Peking #4989). Au. Nag po Zhabs. [Identical to Peking #4977.]
28. >*Gaṇapati stotra, Tshogs kyi bDag po la bsTod pa.* (Peking #4991). Au. Amoghavajra.
29. >*Kameśvara stotra, 'Dod pa'i dbAng phyug gi bsTod pa.* (Peking #4993). Au. Candapa.

H. The precious elephant text

30. >*Hasti ratna dhana deyopadeśa, gLang po Rin po che la Nor bLang ba'i Man Ngag.* (Peking #4971). Au. kLu grub (Nāgārjuna).

II. A Note on the Authors and Translators of the Gaṇeśa Texts

Most of the authors and translators of the thirty Tibetan texts that deal with Gaṇeśa and that are listed above can be identified. The earliest among the authors appear to have lived in the eighth and ninth centuries A.D. These include such writers as Śrī Dīpaṁkarabhadra (dPal Mar me mdzad bazng po) (author of *Gaṇapati sādhana daridra nidhiprada nāma,* our no. 9), an Indian monk who wrote some thirty-nine tāntrika treatises and was active in the Bengal and Bihar area of India in the late eighth and early ninth centuries.[1] A second eighth-century monk, Amoghavajra, who wrote the *Gaṇapati stotra* translated below (no. 28), is one of the most famous Indian Tantric teachers. He, along with his equally famous teacher, Vajrabodhi, translated many important Tantric texts into Chinese; Amoghavajra is particularly known for his Chinese translation of the *Tattvasaṁgraha.*[2] Another monk on our list with a well-known name, Nāgārjuna, author of the precious elephant text translated below (no. 30), is probably Ārya Nāgārjuna rather than the earlier and even more famous Nāgārjuna who founded the Mādyamika school. Ārya Nāgārjuna lived in the seventh or eighth centuries and was a student of Saraha, who taught at Nālandā. It appears that Nāgārjuna's own student, Nāgābodhi, was the teacher of Vajrabodhi and thus of Amoghavajra, mentioned above.[3] It is also possible that with this text, and perhaps others, we are dealing with a later text that was legitimized with the name of an earlier famous author.

The latest dates for the authors of these texts corresponds to the dates they were translated and introduced into Tibet, the tenth and eleventh centuries. Here again we have authors who are well known and who often are related as teacher–pupil. Jñānavajra (Ye shes rDo rje), for example, author of *Vināyaka graha nirmocana* (no. 7 translated below), was from East Bengal and lived in the late tenth and eleventh century. He has numerous names, as did many of the Tantric monks, a practice due to their receiving new names with each mastering of a set of teachings or doctrines, usually under different teachers.[4] Jñānavajra's other names include Advaya-jñānavajra, Advayavajra, Maitrīpa, Maitrīgupta, and Avadūtī-pā.[5] Avadūtī-pā is listed as the author of no. 13 on our list, the *Gaṇapati sādhana mahācakra nāma*, and thus both treatises on Gaṇeśa (nos. 7 and 13) are probably by the same person. Avadhūtī-pā is associated specifically with the important Vikramaśīla Monastery in Bihar and was a teacher of Atīśa.[6]

It is Atīśa's name that appears most frequently on our list, both as an author and a translator. Atīśa, under his name Dīpaṁkaraśrījñāna, is listed as the author of text number 21, as both the author and translator of text number 25, *Ārya gaṇapati rāgavajra samaya stotra* (translated below), and as the translator of four other texts (nos. 10, 11, 12 [translated below], and 13).[7] Jo-bo (no. 19) is another name for him. He is also mentioned as bringing with him to Tibet the longest of our translated texts, the *Mahāgaṇapati Tantra*, which, being spoken by the Buddha, is not given an author's name. Atīśa's life is well documented, although the sources do not agree in many details. He was born at the end of the tenth century to a royal family, probably in Bengal,[8] and from boyhood proceeded to study with a series of teachers, ultimately mastering teachings of various schools and most areas of Buddhist knowledge. His constant movement and search for new teachers and doctrines is typical of the monks who wrote the Gaṇeśa texts; perhaps of most interest was that Atīśa's search took him to Southeast Asia to study with *ācārya* Dharmakīrti (Dharmapāla) of Suvarṇadvīpa. It is thought that Suvarṇadvīpa, literally "Land or Island of Gold," a name used for a variety of Southeast Asian locations over a very long period of time, was in the eleventh century a reference to the maritime kingdom of Śrīvijaya, located somewhere in Sumatra, Malaysia, and peninsular Thailand. Atīśa studied with Dharmakīrti for over a decade before returning to India around 1025 when he became the head (*mahāsthavira*) of the Vikramaśīla Monastery. Atīśa's fame continued to grow, and he was asked by King 'Od-lde of Tibet (the kingdom of mNa'ris in western Tibet) to come to his country and teach. Arriving in 1042, Atīśa worked on translating—in collaboration with his Tibetan disciple Nag tsho Tshul khrims rGyal ba, who is listed as cotranslator of four of the Gaṇeśa texts—Sanskrit texts into Tibetan.[9]

We know Atīśa translated works of his teacher, Dharmakīrti,[10] who, under his name Suvarṇadvīpa (gSer ling pa)—an obvious reference to his Southeast Asian location—is given as writing text number 23 on our list, *Krodaḥ gaṇapati sādhana*.

Atīśa was involved in translating five of the twelve Gaṇeśa texts for which we have translators named. A second Indian teacher, Gāyadhara, along with his Tibetan colleague, Zla ba'i 'Od zer, are responsible for another four of the twelve (nos. 3, 4, 14, and 15—all translated here except 15). Gāyadhara, a contemporary of Atīśa, was active in the first half of the eleventh century and visited Tibet several times. His collaborator, Zla ba'i 'Od zer, is well known as the first translator of the *Kālacakra Tantra*. The four works they have translated all have authors whose names are variations of Kṛṣṇa: Nag po pa, Nag po zhabs, and Nag po sPyod pa pa. The authors of texts numbers 20, 26, and 27 on our list have Kṛṣṇa names as well; thus, there are seven Gaṇeśa texts by authors with names that are variants of Kṛṣṇa. Some of these writers are probably the same person. Unfortunately, however, Kṛṣṇa is a common Tibetan name for tāntrikas and siddhas. One likely candidate would be Kṛṣṇa the Elder, an expert on the Hevajra Tantra and author of the *Yogaratnamālā* who lived in the ninth century.[11] Another would be Kṛṣṇapāda, one of Atīśa's teachers (and thus living in the eleventh century) who, along with Atīśa's Tibetan pupil, Tshul khrims rGyal ba, translated Candrakīrti's *Madhyamakāvatāra*.[12]

The final two translators, Vairocana and Chos kyi Grags pa, are listed as translating together two works (nos. 22 and 24, the later translated below), while Vairocana is listed as sole translator of text number 17. Here, based on the identification of the translator of text number 17 as Vairocana of Kośala, and assuming the other two Vairocanas are the same person, we can probably identify him as Vairocanarakṣita, another contemporary of Atīśa, whose career parallels Atīśa's in many ways. He was constantly moving, studying with new teachers, and conquering new doctrines. Only a partial review shows him moving from his home in southern India to western India, then to Magadha, to Vārāṇasī, to Nālandā, and to Vikramaśīla. His teachers include most of the famous pandits of his time; he even is said to have gone to China.[13]

I have not mentioned all of the authors and translators of the Gaṇeśa texts, but we now can draw certain conclusions. One point is that there was a small number of monks and adepts who introduced the Gaṇeśa literature to Tibet. In addition, these translators and teachers were among the most famous and important practitioners of Tantric Buddhism in Tibet. The worship of Gaṇeśa was clearly an accepted aspect of Buddhist teaching and doctrine of the time, and reflects practices at such important Indian monasteries as Nālandā and Vikramaśīla,[14] as well as Tantric teachings outside of India, as in China and Southeast Asia.

A second point that relates to the small number of authors and translators is that they were often connected, either in a teacher–pupil lineage or in a parallel process studying with the same teachers. Their desire to study with famous teachers kept them in constant peregrination, epitomized by Atīśa's trip to Southeast Asia to study with Dharmakīrti. We should probably see here a desire to meet, to actually be in the presence of, the honored teacher. We can assume that these authors knew one another's writings, and those on which they were based, regardless of the doctrine or school they professed. Again, Gaṇeśa's acceptance among this most highly learned and sophisticated group of preeminent Buddhist teachers helps us to understand that he was not a god of the periphery, but, by the eighth century, was a Buddhist deity of importance.

III. The Translations

A. *Texts from the* bKa 'gyur

There are two texts in the *Translations of the Pronouncements (bKa 'gyur)*. The first presented here, the *Gaṇapatihṛdaya*, is in the format of a traditional Mahāyāna sūtra. The role Gaṇapati plays in this text is that of a mediator between Buddhist and non-Buddhist traditions, for by using the *mantra* contained in the text, non-Buddhist ceremonies can be transformed into Buddhist ones. The second text presented, the *Mahāgaṇapati Tantra*, is clearly a collection of various rites and descriptions of Gaṇapati and must be a compilation. The text does not present itself in the format of a traditional Buddhist Tantra, and it leaves out such characteristic features as the "Thus have I once heard" at the beginning. Being contained in the *bKa' 'gyur*, the presumed author of both texts is the Buddha himself, and no translators are mentioned.

In the Indian language:
Āryagaṇapatihṛdaya
In the Tibetan language:
'Phags pa Tshogs kyi bDag po'i sNying po
[In the English language:
***The Essence of Gaṇapati*]**

Homage to all the Buddhas and Bodhisattvas!

Thus have I once heard:

The Blessed One was dwelling in Rājagṛiha together with a great community of 1,250 monks and of Bodhisattva-Mahāsattvas. At that time the Blessed One spoke to the venerable Ānanda: "O Ānanda, the tasks of anyone who comprehends the *Essence of Gaṇapati-Gaṇeśvara* will all be accomplished. One's wishes are fulfilled by comprehending it; and every *mantra* will bring attainment: *"Tadyathā/ Namo stutemahāgaṇapataye svāhā/ Oṃ kaṭa kaṭa/ Maṭa maṭa/ Dara dara/ Vidara vidara/ Hana hana/ Grihna grihna/ Dhāva dhāva/ Bhaṃja bhaṃja/ Staṃbha staṃbha/ Jaṃbha jaṃbha/ Moha moha/ Dehi dehi/ Dāpaya dāpaya/ Dhāna dhānya siddhi me prayaccha samayamanusmara mahārudra vacanīye svāhā/ Oṃ kuru kuru svāhā/ Oṃ turu turu/ Oṃ muru muru svāhā/ Oṃ bāva saṃti vasu puṣṭiṃ kuru svāhā/ Adguta bindu kṣyabhita mahāvidāra/ Samagacchati mahābaya/ Mahābala/ Mahāvarakra/ Mahāhasti/ Mahādakṣiṇiya pracidayami svāhā/ Oṃ kuru kuru/ Curu curu/ Muru muru/ Oṃ ga ga ga ga ga ga ga ga/ Oṃ namo nama svāhā/*

"O Ānanda, when any son of noble family, daughter of noble family, monk, nun, lay man or lay woman goes to a place of worship other than where the Three Jewels [are worshiped] or enters the palace retinue of a king and practices the *mantra*s [recited in that place] and begins with this *Essence of Gaṇapati-Gaṇeśa,* he pays homage to the Blessed Buddhas [as if] with flowers and incense. Upon hearing this *Essence of Gaṇapati* all one's tasks will be accomplished. Have no doubts about it. If one is mindful [of this *mantra*] in fights, arguments, confusions, and wars, they will all be pacified. If you get up early each morning and recite it, you will attain learnedness. *Yakṣas*, *rākṣasas* and *ḍākinīs* will not rob your health but will promise to stay far away."

After the Blessed One proclaimed these things, the gathering and everyone in it, along with the world and its gods, men, demigods, and *gandharvas*, rejoiced and praised the Blessed One's teaching.

This completes the *Essence of the Noble Gaṇapati.*

In the Indian language:
Mahāgaṇapatitantra

In the Tibetan language:
Tshogs kyi bDag po Chen po'i rGyud
[In the English language:
***The Tantra of the Great Gaṇapati*]**

Homage to the Lord of the World!
Chapter One: Attaining Accomplishments (siddhi)

Homage to the great, glorious Gaṇapati! Place an image of the delightful, glory-endowed Gaṇapati in a four-cornered *maṇḍala*. You must worship it for six months. Your fortune in this life will equal the universal monarch (*cakravartin*) of the gods, and you will acquire great merit. Your pleasures will equal the gods', and your life will be most long. You will be a lord of men and other beings. The sons of gods will be like your slaves. Your orders will be heeded, and even *nāga*s will follow them, doing the various works like slaves. You will have the pleasures of the gods, and any pleasing things you desire will come to you [p. 200b]. An apparition (*nirmāṇa*) by the great god Mahāgaṇapati is brought about by the force of a disciple with the fortune to attain accomplishments. Upon attaining the supreme accomplishment, you will obtain magical powers, and your pleasures will increase according to your desires. He is the world-benefitting god of gods whose worship brings accomplishment.

Chapter Two: The Mantra *of Divine Accomplishment*

Now make a four-cornered clean *maṇḍala* in a secluded place. Smear it well with cow dung. When it is smooth and soft place an image of Gaṇapati on the raised-up middle. Sprinkle it with white flowers. Denude yourself and worship it [while visualizing] yourself in the form of Vināyaka. Recite eighteen hundred *mantra*s three times daily for a six-month *varataka* [retreat]. All your mind's hopes will be realized.

Oṃ is a glorious will-being; it must be put at the beginning of a *mantra*. The accomplishment-granting letter that is like a wish-fulfilling jewel must be put after it in the row. The sun-like letter must be read after that. The first sign of the Tathāgata, the supreme letter, must be taken up next. Then the first consonant must be uttered. One who desires accomplishment recites the *mantra* with the jewel syllable *Svā* and the action syllable *hā*.

Chapter Three: Gaṇapati's Description

Gaṇapati is white. He has the head of an elephant. The tusk on one side is broken. His right hand holds a radish. He rides a rat vehicle (*vā-*

hana). His body is bedecked with precious jewels. His head is ornamented with the full moon. He glows with rays of clear light. His complexion and color are good. He is fat-bellied and bedecked with jewels [p. 201a].

Chapter Four: Propitiation of Gaṇapati with One Face and Four Arms

Now an expert, holding white flowers, should draw an image of Gaṇapati on the day of *Puṣya,* white with the head of an elephant. His right hand holds a radish. His left holds a precious jewel. He is fat-bellied, ornamented with every sort of jewelry, seated atop a moon and a rat. Sit with your face toward the center of the *maṇḍala* and worship, [visualizing] yourself in the image of Vināyaka.

Chapter Five: The Mudrā *of Gaṇapati*

Now in the proximity of Indra, there is the white Gaṇapati with an elephant's head. He rides a rat. His third eye holds a crescent moon. His right [hands] hold a radish and a knife. His left hold a trident and a skull. To make the *mudrā* of Gaṇapati you must clench the left hand with the thumb and middle finger extended then seize the joint of the middle finger with the bent thumb.

Chapter Six: The Mantra *of Mahāgaṇapati*

Now to explain the *mantra*. The glorious *Oṃ* is placed at the beginning. Then inscribe the wish-fulfilling jewel, the letter of gems. The first section of consonants should be written after that. Then the first sign of the Tathāgata must be unified with the eight vowels. Imagine the letter of the first consonant, and inscribe it with your mind. The third of the third section should be conjoined with the fourth of the first. The third of the seventh section should be subjoined to the first of the third. Put the fifth of the fourth as a companion to the wish-fulfilling jewel letter. This must be ornamented with the third vowel. Then recite it with the third of the fourth. The syllable of realized accomplishment must be recited at the end. The Lord of the World himself gives the accomplishment of this *mantra*. All your wishes will be fulfilled [p. 201b].

Chapter Seven: The Mantra *of the Name*

Now, furthermore, the speech that is the essence of attaining accomplishments, called "the *mantra* of the name that attains every accomplishment," is made by putting *Oṃ,* the letter of glory, and *Yaṃ,* at the beginning. Subjoin the syllable of the sun to the wish-fulfilling jewel letter.

Subjoin this to the sixth vowel. This must be ornamented with the *bindu nada*. The letter of the first sign should be spoken next. Then the fifth of the fourth should be attached. The first of the fifth should be written. Then write the first sign of the Tathāgata. The syllable of the wind element must then be ornamented with the eighth vowel. The second letter of peace should be announced at the end of it all. "The *mantra* of the name" is the fulfiller of every desire.

Chapter Eight: Worshiping Gaṇapati

Now this must be explained as well: Extract the perfume of white flowers. Make an image of Gaṇapati about the size of a thumb out of white sandalwood, fat-bellied with four arms. Do it carefully and do it well. When the Great White One [the sun] is brilliant, lustrate the image with morning dew. Wash it with a vase that is clean, bright, attractive, and fragrant, and with perfume with the scent of white flowers. Then immediately offer white flowers to invite [Gaṇapati] to the center of the *maṇḍala*. Then offer a large *bali* made of radishes and pastries. Make offerings of incense, scent, lamps, and eatables. Offer the *bali* of radishes, pastries, water, and the three whites with the [above mentioned] *mantra*. Offer incense and flowers as well. If done in this way, Obstacles will be evermore incapacitated [p. 202a].

Chapter Nine: The Food for Attaining Accomplishments

Now a "radish" is a turnip that has eight flavors. It is the most excellent of all foods as well. It is endowed with the eight [sic] supreme flavors: bitterness, sourness, astringency, sweetness, hotness, and saltiness. It is mild and has the greatest relish. It is the remedy for the eight sorts of illness. It benefits the bile, phlegm, and fever; the blood, pus, and indigestion; the nerves and contagious diseases. There is no food grown like it! The lips of the gods quiver for it! It is the food for attaining accomplishments! It should be offered to the Lord of Hosts. The food called "pastry" (*modaka*) is made from the three sweets and the three grains. It, too, enslaves one with its delicious smell.

Make little balls of wheat paste. Churn milk into butter, and make a large *bali* for the hosts. Make offerings to Gaṇapati with butter, pastry flour, the three sweets, and various suitable foods [Verse ends].

[Make offerings] to Gaṇapati like this: Put Gaṇapati's image in the palm of your right hand; recite out loud one hundred thousand recitations [of the *mantra*], not thinking of anything else. If you offer a radish after blessing it with the *mantra*, your merit in this very life will equal that of a universal monarch. If you offer white flowers, you will not be defeated by kings or others. Royalty, etc., will be attained [by you]. Kings, ministers, and others will come under your control [Prose ends].

Chapter Ten: Achieving Kingship, etc.

Now I will explain the ceremony. Make a large image of Gaṇapati out of the precious substance "silver." It must hold a valuable gem in its hand. The large *maṇḍala* measures a full cubit. Scatter it with jewels and white flowers. Recite one hundred thousand *mantras*. Sickness and suffering will thereby be pacified.

As a wise man procures an image of Gaṇapati made from crystal and silver, all his worldly suffering will be cleared away [p. 202b]. An image of Gaṇapati made from crystal should be about the size of a thumb. Recite the *vidyāmantra* called *"senapra"* one hundred thousand times; lustrate the crystal image; and on the day of *Puṣya* point yourself to the east, put on white clothes, wash yourself, put your palms together, and solicit [Gaṇapati] with your hopes.

"What is the Obstacle that harms me? I lustrate the crystal image which remains unmoving, unwavering atop the mirror and look to the east. Let any *Jarapa* or thieves there may be appear in the mirror, then become their identities." Worship and consecrate this crystal image of Gaṇapati as is fitting and recite one hundred thousand of the *vidyās* called *"nagakuru."* If you merely show this image to a person afflicted with sickness or suffering, any disease will be healed. The person will also be liberated from suffering. This is the ritual of great peace.

Make an image of Mahāgaṇapati out of the precious substance "gold." Reveal it on the day of *Puṣya*. Make offerings and consecrate it. Recite one hundred thousand *mantras* called *"vara."* Every sort of wealth will increase in the house where the image rests. All Obstacles will offer jewels upon seeing a golden Gaṇapati. Unable to work the woes of Obstacles, they will worship you like a king. A rain of jewels falls upon the land where a golden Gaṇapati resides. A golden Gaṇapati receives every sort of wealth from all the kings of Obstacles. You will be transformed into a gracious, glorious, and wealthy individual. The *yakṣas* open their treasury to the good qualities of the one who makes the finest image of Gaṇapati. In this life and the next his possessions will continually increase. The Lord of Wealth, Vaiśravaṇa, will serve and honor him like a king [p. 213a].

Now put the image of Gaṇapati on a four-cornered *maṇḍala*. Recite the *mantra* called *"bhaga"* one hundred thousand times. Whatever accomplishment is desired will be granted thereby in this very life. The propitiator will be given the might of the king of the gods.

The great compassionate Gaṇapati, being a most compassionate individual (*atman*), protects the poor with great compassion.

Draw this great God of Wealth on silk or cotton. Reveal it on the day of *Puṣya*. His estate whose house it resides in will be fortunate.

Carefully craft an image of Mahāgaṇapati in copper. Put it atop a *maṇḍala* upon earth anointed with red sandalwood. Honor it with *banduka* flowers (*pantapates phoenicea*), rubies, and red flowers. Recite the *vidyāmantra* called "bruṃ." A king's daughter will come under your power. Divine maidens, *nāga* girls, humans — any kind of girl you want — daughters of Brahmins, women as they should be, those with the best of bodies, will [all] adore you. They will follow your orders like slave girls. This and limitless other wonderful things.

Realize these things by depending on images. Merely worshiping them will fulfill [your wishes].

Or make an image of Gaṇapati out of precious jewels. Let it rest upon a *maṇḍala*. You must recite the *vidyā* called *"ratnasiddhi"* one hundred thousand times. Treasure mines beneath the earth will be revealed. Anything you wish for, you will enjoy.

Chapter Eleven: The Maṇḍala *of Mahāgaṇapati*

Now the great glorious Gaṇapati is the great wrathful one, the fierce one, him having the heart of a Buddha and the head of an animal. He is ornamented with a young elephant's head, has three eyes, four tusks, four arms, and four legs. He sits enthroned on a large *nāga*. His first left [hand] holds a white tusk. [In the hand] beneath it there is a noose. [On the right] he holds an axe and a trident. His stomach and tusks are dark blue. Make this kind of Gaṇapati image of bell metal (*kaṃsa*) and molten bronze (*sarakam*). Consecrate it on the day of *Puṣya*.

Now seek out a spot for erecting the *maṇḍala* to do contemplation and propitiation. Draw out the *maṇḍala* described in the ninth chapter. It should have doors and portals. In the center, on an eight-petaled lotus, Gaṇapati stands upon the object desired. [The image] must be placed atop a moon seat, not being separate from the consort. Her name is Arcikari, the adamantine pig-faced woman (*rdo rje phag gdong ma*). She carries in her hands an axe and a *banda* full of blood, which she feeds to the principal deity (Gaṇapati) [Verse ends].

In the yellow eastern section [of the *maṇḍala*] sits the Lord of the Three Realms holding a radish and a knife. In the blue southern section sits the great black *yakṣa* Adamantine Lips (*rdo rje mchu*) with the face of Mahādeva, holding a staff and hammer. In the red western section sits the red *yakṣa* king named Lord of Clouds (*sprin gyi bdag*) holding a water-filled cloud bank and a noose. In the green northern section sits the green *yakṣa* lord called Abode of Wealth (*nor gnas*) carrying a club and a jeweled staff. In the white northeastern section sits the black Vināyaka with an elephant's head, carrying a trident and a radish. In the red southeastern section is the black Lord of Hungry Ghosts (*yi dags kyi bdag po*) called Wrath (*drag po*) carrying an axe and an entire skull. In the black southwestern section Illuminatress of Clouds (*sprin gyi sgron ma*) holds in both hands a cloud bank with lightning bolts in it. In the black northwestern section is the king of Obstacles called Remover of Obstacles – Twisted Trunk (*Log-'dren sna yon, Vakratuṇḍavināyaka*) with an elephant's trunk, carrying a trident and a dry skull filled with radishes and meat. The deities are served by the eight nāga kings: The nāga kings Avala, Varuna, Śamkhapala (*dung-skyong*), Takṣaka (*'jog po*), Kulika (*rigs ldan*), Śeṣa (*mtha' yas*), Padma, and Mahāpadma. At the eastern door is the great king Dhṛtarāṣṭa (*yul 'khor srung*); at the southern door Virūḍaka (*'phags skyes po*); at the western door Virūpākṣa (*sprin me bzang*); at the northern door Vaiśravaṇa (*rnam thos sras*). You must know their respective colors: white, blue, red, and green. Each carries in his hands a precious jewel and a sword. Their consorts are not portrayed [p. 204a].

Make a three-cornered secret *maṇḍala* in the northeast of the drawing. Draw inside it an image of your enemy out of monkey fat. Make it lengthy, black, and with disheveled hair. Smear it with sesame butter. Write his name and family at the heart. Tie a rope made from a corpse's hair to its neck. Then set out a *bali* of pastries and radishes for each of the eight great *yakṣas* and a red *bali* made from the discordant mixture of fish meat and garlic for each of the eight great *yakṣas*, a large *bali* for the eight great *nāgas*, and one each for the four great kings. If [this many] are not possible, make one big one. Delicious food must [nonetheless] be offered up to each [member of the *maṇḍala*].

The ritual implements for a wrathful [deity] must be set out: the skull of a wolf, a black spike, black mustard seed of two kinds (*ske tshe* and *yungs nag*), and white mustard seed [Prose ends].

Chapter Twelve: The Stages of Practice

This must be explained as well: The stages of contemplation must be carried out in [the following] way, or they will not be carried out at all. You must practice with great secrecy.

Out of emptiness, whose nature is *Ya*, there arises the seed syllable *Huṃ* with a nature of light and a group of eight *Ya*s. The emanations of the wrathful one are born from the *mantra* of the name and fill the triple universe. They melt into light and are absorbed into the original *Huṃ*. Mahāgaṇapati arises [from the *Huṃ*] for the sake of living beings. He is a great terror whose form is fear. His consort and retinue emerge as well. From the letter *Bhe* and their [respective] names the eight kings and eight *nāgas* arise like bodhisattvas. The kings arise looking like the wrathful one. Conjure them forth with light: [The light] emanates out and gathers [the deities] with a *Dza* and a *Dza;* they are drawn down with vast hooks, and the *mantra Huṃ* and *Huṃ,* thus endowing them with efficaciousness. Then worship and offer a *bali,* which must be augmented with the heart mantra *bāligṛihanaka*.

Chapter Thirteen: The Mantras *of the Great* Yakṣas

Now the king of *mantras* is counted [by first reciting] the vowels and consonants. The first of the fourth is written after that. The fifth of the fourth is put in the row. Then contemplate the wish-fulfilling gem letter. Recite the first mark of the Tathāgata. Ornament it with the eight vowels [p. 204b]. Put together the syllables of conjuration and the syllables of the wind element with the second vowel, and it is known as "The King of Victorious Ones."

The second vowel should be conjoined to the wish-fulfilling gem syllable. Then write the syllable of the sun and the fifth of the fourth. Ornament the letter that is the fourth of the second with the fourth vowel. Conjoin the letter that is the fifth of the third to the fourth of the fifth. Ornament the letter that is the first of the fourth with the fourth vowel. Subjoin the syllable of the wind element. Recite the precious gem letter and the action letter at the end. This basic *mantra* of Mahāgaṇapati is the realizer of every wish.

The *mantras* of the eight *Yakṣas,* "*Ya,*" etc.; "*Ya Ya,*" etc.; "*Baṃ,*" etc.; "*Vināyaka,*" etc.; "*Baira,*" etc.; "*Huṃ*" and "*Tri,*" the eighth being "*Hu,*" are grounded at the end with "*Phaṭ,*" which is the essence of life. The *mantras* for the *nāgas* come from their names. They should have *Oṃ* [at the beginning] and *Huṃ Phaṭ* [at the end]. The *mantras* of the great kings are the *mantra* called "*Bhai,*" the one called "*Bhi,*" and the one called "*Bha.*"

Chapter Fourteen: The Wrathful Mantra

The *mantra* that conjures up the object of propitiation is *Ya* and *kṣa* and *ka* and *ma* and *hā* and *bairabhai; tri* and *rā* and *ca* with *śetrūṃ nṛijaniya*. It must be recited many times.

Take hold of the enemy's effigy with the *mantras* of the eight *yakṣas*. Then burn the effigy. Then leave the effigy.

The king of hidden *mantras* is *Ya* and *kṣa* and *ka* and *la; ma*, and *ha* and *bherabhe, deva yakṣa yama* and *nāga nāga*, all [recited] together. The entire mass of enemies, whoever they are, must be admonished by saying *"Ya Ya Ya."*

Now the secret of secret *mantras* is *Ma* and *hā* and *bherabhe, yakṣa*, etc., as above. Then recite the following: *Ṣaya curṇa curṇa tralaya, nāgayakatramaraya, hanacakra* twice; then say "You, O so and so, *māraya phaṭ phaṭ*."

Chapter Fifteen: Praising Gaṇapati

Now for another wrathful *mantra: Oṃ vighna phibabhya sarva vidya viṣaya hṛidametaya, hum cidu patu, ḍamarutaya, hanahana, gṛigana gṛihana, vaca vaca, bhrahma bhrahma, bhrahmaya bhrahmaya, hum hum phaṭ phaṭ.*

Make an image of Mahāvināyaka out of bell metal or copper. Consecrate it and worship it. Put an image of your enemy beneath it; make him the foot mat of Gaṇapati. There is no doubt this enemy will die. These yogic techniques are mentioned on account of great necessity.

Make an image of Gaṇapati out of sandalwood or precious jewels. Perform a consecration and offer up worship [Verse ends]. If you desire to stop hail, make images of the lords of hail, the wind god, and the water god; make an image of a cloud and an image of a dragon. Then place them beneath Gaṇapati as a seat. Imagine they are beneath yourself as well. When you recite *mantras* like the one called *"hikacandra,"* the hail will be stopped. Scatter white mustard seed all around.

If you want to send down hail, draw out a *maṇḍala* of water and clouds. Meditate on Mahāgaṇapati riding a dragon. Imagine him to be your servant. For the secret ritual implements use iron filings, gold filings, and copper filings. Knead them with rain water and rice flour. Make it into shapes just the size of the hail you want. Smear them with blood. Make seven [of these] and many [bunches of] seven. Pour them into the skull of a crow. It must be covered with clouds. The *mantra* must be written on the crow's skull three times. The ritual implements for the image must also be set out. When you recite one hundred thousand *mantras* like the one called *"bruṃ bruṃ bhariṣaya"* and there actually appear inside the crow's skull three or seven or eight hail stones, then carry it to your enemy's land and recite the *mantra;* [the hail] will fall.

If it doesn't fall, turn the image of Gaṇapati upside down. Hide it in the center of your enemy's locale with its feet up. It is absolutely certain the hail will fall. It will approximate the size of a *kalantaka* bird's egg. the red-colored testicles of a deer, or a fruit; and it will fall for a long time. The crop-destroying *mantra* is called *"Bruṃ."* If you want to stop [the hail], you must remove the image and crow['s skull], for hail will fall every day as long as they remain. You must offer worship to the image of Gaṇapati and recite 108 rosaries of the *mantra* perfectly from its beginning to its end on a rosary made from precious gems. Lustrate the image and beseech it to remain in the center of its *maṇḍala* [prose ends].

These and limitless other excellent things are the works of Gaṇapati.

Homage, O delightful, glorious Gaṇapati! Homage, great, glorious, peaceful, and wrathful one!

The *Gaṇapatitantra* called "The Arising of Attainments" is finished.

The Indian sage Dīpaṃkarasrījñāna came [to Tibet] carrying [this text] from India for the sake of worldly attainments. It was entrusted to rGyal ba'i 'byung gnas.

This *Tantra* fulfills one's wishes.

B. Iconographical Text

The *Mahāvināyaka rūpopadeśa cintāratna* includes not only an iconographical account of Gaṇeśa, but a mantric practice to go with it.

In the Indian language:
Mahāvinayaka Rūpa Upadeśa Ratna
In the Tibetan language:
bGegs bdag Chen po'i sKu bri ba'i Man ngag Yid bzhin Nor bu
[In the English language:
***The Jewel of Instructions on the Form of The Great Lord of Obstacles*]**

Homage to the glorious Vajraḍākinī!

Bowing to Cakrasaṃvara, draw an icon
Of the great Lord of Obstacles!
The *maṇḍala* of the elemental spirits must be attained
By putting the eight of fourteen black things
On such special surfaces as
Cotton from the earth of Playful Cover (T. *rol gyogs*)
Cotton that has been pierced by weapons,
Cotton whose meat has been destroyed by insects,
Or the skin of an ox.
The one who makes the picture
Possesses the commitments.
It must be drawn by practitioners.
It has four corners and four doors.
It is well endowed with door protectors.

The good qualities of all attainments abide in it.
It is full of the five good qualities of desire.
Thinkers must draw the *maṇḍala* ornamenting it with the five offerings.
The center of all *maṇḍala*s is encircled with a line
And is most beautiful.
Draw an eight-petaled lotus.
Worship it with red flowers.
Fill it with *bali* that are suitable for worshiping,
Such as special kinds of perfume and incense, [vessels] filled with the five ambrosias, fish, meat, and beer.
The great Wrathful One in the center of this
Has one face and four arms.
The tusks on his face are a bit sharp.
His wrathful mouth is smiling.
His supreme body is blue and is a great fright.
He is well ornamented with a rosary of skulls.
He rides a hungry ghost (S. *preta,* T. *yi dags*)
And sits upon a sun.
He brings fear to [the heaven of] the Thirty Three, Tuṣita.
He holds a garment made from the skin of a tiger.
He has three eyes and has a fine form.
He holds three banners, a flaming *vajra,*
A skull, and a *mudrā.*
Likewise he holds in his right and left hands
A bow and an arrow.
Oṃ vajra krota ḍaki huṃ phaṭ.
This is recited.
In front of this is the great Lord of Obstacles.
His light blazes in great splendor.
Draw him with twelve hands and being most fearful.
On eight petals there are eight *yakṣa*s.
Draw the great Lord of Obstacles just as he is.
First make the proper sort of cotton.
Then make an artist of divinities who has the proper happy character
So that he will draw it attractively.
Then an expert at consecration endowed with blessings
Must perform the ceremony of consecration in the proper way,
Using any required offering substances that are possible.
Facing a vast space
Fiercely generate benevolence, compassion, and *bodhicitta.*

Worship and dedication must be performed extensively.
This is a wish-fulfilling jewel.
If you continually worship,
Your needs and desires will come forth.
This is the instruction of the icon.
The *maṇḍala* of the elemental spirits is to be attained,
And when you do one hundred thousand recitations,
[Gaṇapati] will come before you in actuality.
Set up an image and worship it.
It is proclaimed that then your needs and desires will all come forth.

The Jewel of Instructions on the Form of the Great Lord of Obstacles composed by the great master Nag-po-pa is finished.

It was translated by the great Pandita Gāyadhara and the translator Gyi jo Zla ba'i 'Od zer.

C. *The* Bali *Ceremony*

The *Ārya gaṇapati bali vidhi* describes the making and use of a *bali* (T. *gtor ma*). This form of offering is essential to every Tantric practice of Gaṇeśa. Its importance is demonstrated not only by the frequent reference to *bali* offerings in the texts dealing with Gaṇeśa but also in the occurrence of an entire text devoted to this offering.

In the Indian language:
Āryagaṇapatibalividhi
In the Tibetan language:
'Phags pa Tshogs kyi bDag po'i gTor ma'i Cho ga
[In the English language:
***The Bali Ceremony of the Noble Gaṇapati*]**

Homage to the glorious Vajraḍākinī!

It is desirable to offer *bali*, for one must perfectly please the noble Gaṇapati. First, fill a perfect vessel made of precious jewels with such eatables and drinkables of perfect color, taste, and scent as husked rice, dandelion, the three whites, the three sweets, white pastries, radishes, beef, and grapes, then place it before you.

Sit on a comfortable mat, and then contemplate the four abodes of Brahma, go for refuge to the three [jewels], and generate the supreme *Bodhicitta*. Then meditate on the selflessness of all *dharmas*.

Think that from a *Bhuṃ* [appears] a spacious and vast vessel made of precious jewels, inside of which [there appears] a *Khaṃ* from which [appears] food of a hundred flavors which fills [the vessel] to overflowing.

Bless it with the three thusnesses (T. *de nyid gsum*) and *"Oṃ Ā karomukhaṃ sarvadharmānāṃ adyanutpananatuat Oṃ Ā Huṃ Phaṭ Svāhā."*

Then concentrate on the seed syllable in your own heart. The light of this summons the noble Gaṇapati of Wisdom. Then visualize him in front [of you]. Then show the *mudrā*.

Make offerings with *"Oṃ nama tute/ Namaḥ gaḥnasataye/ Idaṃ bali kha kha khāhi khāhi svāhā,"* and think that by this he enjoys [the offering] unto satisfaction and then is pleased.

Then say these words:

I offer without any grasping
Such attractions of the ten directions' gods and men
As fruits, medicine, jewels,
Pastries, radishes, beef,
Grapes, wine, husked rice, and dandelions.
You, O Protector, eat these things
Through your total love of me!
For I beg you to be pleased!
And make it so that all my works come to fruition!
Make it so that obstructions are well pacified!

Then praise him perfectly with words of praise. Then recite as many rosaries of root *mantras* and spells as you are able. Then you must pray for the object of your desire.

Then request the Wisdom One (T. *ye shes pa*) to depart. Thoroughly dedicate the roots of merit that have been accumulated and recite the one hundred syllable [*mantra*].

The Bali Ceremony of the Noble Gaṇapati [by which] the great master found supreme attainment, composed by Nag-po zhabs (Kṛṣṇapāda), is finished.

Translated by the Paṇḍita Gāyadhara and the translator Gyi Jo Zla ba'i 'Od zer.

D. The Fire Ceremonies

The *Vināyaka homa vidhi prabhāsana* and the *Ārya gaṇapati homa vidhi* are highly cryptic texts related to the use of Gaṇeśa for fire offerings (S. *homa*, T. *spyan sreg*). There are no available commentaries on the texts to assist in their interpretation and translation. A study of Gaṇeśa in this role using these texts is certainly necessary, but must await future attention.

E. Gaṇeśa as an Evil Demon

The *Vināyaka graha nirmocana* describes how the practitioner can escape the sorrows caused by the evil demon Vināyaka. No iconographical description of the demon is present in the text, and it is not possible to be completely certain that the demon in question is truly Gaṇeśa; yet the name he shares with Gaṇeśa is of sufficient value to warrant inclusion of the text in this article. If it is Gaṇeśa that is being referred to here, the detailed description of the harm he causes is highly interesting for an insight into Gaṇeśa's role as a demonic lord.

In the Indian language:
Vināyaka graha nirmocana
In the Tibetan language:
Log 'dren gyi gDon las Nges par Thar pa
[In the English language:
***Freedom from Vināyaka*]**

Homage to the glorious Vajrapaṇi!

One who desires freedom from the Vināyaka demon (T. *gdon*) of the world must, to begin with, know the signs. If smells come out of a body of common family, when one is wearing bad clothing, when one has for food the leftovers of others, when one is a woman or a child, when one is excreting or urinating, when one is abiding nakedly, or on the fifth and fourteenth days of the waning moon or on the new moon it starts. The signs of it starting are groaning, smoke, one's wealth being squandered, one is not attractive to others, if one is a man one does not find a woman, if one is a woman one does not find a man, if one does business one fails, one is not born in a good land, or even if one finds a woman her mind changes, so one is devoured by the Vināyaka demon.

The practice of the means to reach freedom from these things is to offer to the west a *bali* made of four demon-vessels (T. *gdon ma'i bum pa*), parched grains, cooked meat, raw meat, dandelion, perfume, a garland of white flowers, porridge, and various kinds of incense.

Then illuminate and throw in the fire medicinal incense (T. *gu gul*), white mustard, melted *'gi wang*, horn, and horse hooves. Put in sandalwood, black aloewood, and saffron in equal parts with cow urine and goat urine. Then do as [was mentioned] before by covering [the fire] with butter, etc. Do such things as anointing and rubbing [the *bali*].

You will certainly be freed from the Vināyaka demon.

This composition of the Master Jñānavajra (T. Ye shes rDo rje) is finished.

F. Practice Methods (Sādhana)

There are seventeen texts devoted to ceremonies of practice for Gaṇeśa in the Tibetan Buddhist canon. While it is not possible to present translations of all of the texts, representative samples have been selected to provide a general insight into how Gaṇeśa manifests in these texts. Five

Sādhanas are here translated: (1) the *Gaṇapati sādhana daridra nidhiprada,* (2) the *Śrī ājñā vinivarta gaṇapati sādhana,* (3) the *Vināyaka-rāja sādhana,* (4) the *Śrī gaṇapati śānti sādhana,* and (5) the *Gaṇapati samaya guhya sādhana.*

In the Indian language:
Gaṇapati sādhana daridira nidhiprada nāma
In the Tibetan language:
Tshogs bdag gi bsGrub pa dbul ba'i gTer sByin Shes bya ba
[In the English language:
The Propitiation of Gaṇapati that Gives the Treasure of the Poor]

The practitioner possessing the commitments (S. *Samaya,* T. *dam tshig*) who desires to attain the enjoyment of the full gift of all desired purposes through the works of Gaṇapati makes a round *maṇḍala* that is very even, like the face of a mirror, in a mentally satisfying building. Make it of blue color, just two cubits in size, and in the blue diagram inside it [put] the main syllables in a circle, and inside them write the *Essence of Gaṇapati* with gold. Then draw the image of Gaṇapati on blue cotton and consecrate it. Then roll up a variety of silks and put them inside.

Inside the heart of a monkey [put] gold — which comes from the earth, as many precious jewels as you find, and as many kinds of meat as you find; and place it on top of the *maṇḍala.* Fasten a rope made of wrapped-up elephant hair and monkey hair. Clearly meditate that the body color and *mudrā* of Gaṇapati are upon [this *maṇḍala*].

Establish yourself in the pride of being Vidāraṇa, then recite *"Namo ratnatrayāya/ Oṃ Ga Svāhā/"* a thousand thousands [times] without being distracted by others, and think that Gaṇapati gives you enjoyments according to your desire.

On the eighth of the waxing [moon] or the eighth of the waning [moon] offer an extremely fine Gaṇapati *bali* that has various kinds of meat, butter, dandelion, and various wonderful tastes; and pray for the object of your desire. It is not proper that others see this.

The Propitiation of Gaṇapati that Gives the Treasure of the Poor, composed by Dīpaṃkarabhadra (T. Mar me mDzad bZang po) and advice for those who desire wealth and food, is finished.

In the Indian language:
Śrī Ājñā Vinivarta Gaṇapati Sādhanaṃ
In the Tibetan language:
dPal Tshogs kyi bDag po 'Jur bgegs Sel ba Shes bya ba'i sGrub thabs
[In the English language:
Clearing the Obstacles of Entanglement: The Method of Practice for the Glorious Gaṇapati]

Homage to the Great Compassionate One!

Paying reverent homage to the manifestation
Of he who continually holds
All sentient beings with equanimous compassion,
Gaṇapati,
I will explain the secret method of practice.

First set up an image of Gaṇapati.
[Draw] the Noble One on a horsehide or fine cotton
With a body color that is white like snow.
He has three faces, six arms, and four legs.
The faces are an elephant's, a rat's, and a monkey's.
In his right hands are a radish, a jewel, and a sword.
His left [holds] a pastry, a skull full of beer, and an axe.
His right leg is stretched out, his left drawn in.
The other two [legs] are crossed in a good bent-knee position.
Beneath him the goddess Pleasure Woman (*dGar mo*),
Who has the face of a monkey,
Must sink in about half of the Noble One's secret.
As foot supports she has two goddesses.
Jewels fall from this consort's mouth.
They fall into vessels
To remove the practitioner's poverty and fulfill his hopes.
This must be drawn under the great stars.
[Draw] with *'gi wang* on the four sides of it
Tadyathā/ Namaḥ stute gaṇapati/ Katta katta/ Madda madda/
Radda radda/ Daha daha/ Grihna grihna/ Bhañja bhañja/ Namaḥ stute/
Gaṇapati rurucanaya svāhā/ Oṃ A bhuṃ travinabukhanānce dhara
bhrama gacchati/ Hahaya/ Mahūhatikṣitananapraye mayemi/ Kuru
kuru/ Curu curu/ Muru muru/ Namo nama svāhā/.
Write it many times and increase it.
Behind it you must write the long spell.
For the consecration, put before [the drawing]
A white *maṇḍala* with eight petals.
Then on sandalwood that has been anointed with water
Arrange white flowers in separate bunches.
Worship the Noble One with beer, radish, pastry, husked grain, dandelion, etc.
Then make yourself [into] a tutelary deity
And recite this *mantra:*
Oṃ Gaṃ Gaṇapati māma ratna siddhi/
Ga ga ga ga ga ga ga ga Gaṇapati svāhā/.

Apply this to the sign of the number.
You will gain attainment in one month.
Then, to worship the image,
Wrap a human leg in the middle of a piece of silk,
And inserting it [into the vessel] with your hand in the early morning,
Offer a *bali:*
Oṃ Gaṃ Gaṇapati ratna siddhi/ Ga ga ga ga ga ga ga ga/
Gaṇapati svāhā/ Oṃ Gaṃ Gaṇapati baliṃ takhāhi khāhi/.
You must offer this with the *mantra* of seven [syllables].
Then make praises using this *mantra:*
Oṃ Gaṇapati ratna ratna ratna siddhi māma rodha rodha/
Gaṇapati/ Ga ga ga ga ga ga ga ga kaṭa kaṭa svāhā/ Gaṇapati
ratna puṣṭikāra maṭa maṭa svāhā/ Gaṇapati siddhi vaśiṃ kuru
raṭa raṭa svāhā/ Gaṇapati ratana bauṣaṭa grihna grihna
svāhā/.
Your mental aspirations will be completed
By reciting this 108 times.
After reaching the state of a universal monarch
You will find wealth without effort.
You will attain this without the necessity of making a profit.
For this reason you must strive to [offer] *bali.*
By the merit of composing this method of practice
Of the Noble One who clears away all the obstacles of entanglement
May I have power over the wealth of the world
And obtain the unexcelled result.

The method of practicing the Noble Gaṇapati called *Clearing the Obstacles of Entanglement* composed by the great master Indrabodhi is finished.

It was translated by the great *pandita* Dīpaṃkaraśrījñāna and the translator rGya brTson 'grus Seng ge at Yam bu Gar ta ri.

In the Indian language:
Vīnayakana Rāja Sadhànaṃ
In the Tibetan language:
bGegs kyi rGyal po'i sGrub thabs
[In the English language:
***The Method of Practice of the King of Obstacles*]**

Homage to the glorious Vajraḍākinī!

The meditator strives to make good in a witch's (S. *mātṛkā,* T. *ma mo*) house or a delightful place by concentrating on an icon. The intelligent one begins by making offerings so that the dancer (T. *gar mkhan*) will always remain bound.

The glorious Gaṇapati abides with his right leg stretched forth. His red body color flames with red light and trembles in redness. He has one face. He has three eyes. His elephant head holds the crown ornament of braided hair (T. *ral pa*). His tusks are sharp. He is short in stature, but fat and bulky. His stomach is twisting and large. He is extremely fearsome. He is ornamented with every ornament. He has twelve hands. The first on the right holds an axe, the second a staff, the third a bow, the fourth a *khatvaṃka,* the fifth an iron hook, and the sixth a skull full of blood. The first on the left holds a *vajra,* the second a sword, the third a skull full of great things, the fourth a small radish, the fifth a trident, and the sixth a roped spear. He sits on the throne of a sun and red lotus.

Oṃ gaḥ gaḥ siddhi siddhi sarva artha me prasādha huṃ huṃ jah jah svāhā. This is the invoking *mantra.*

Oṃ Āḥ Gaḥ Huṃ Svāhā. This is the reciting *mantra.*

You will gain attainment by one hundred thousand [recitations], and thereafter works will be perfectly initiated.

Make a circle, reciting the whole [*mantra*] at one time. If fortunate *mantra* practitioners see it, they will delight. You will receive great homage at the door of the king, and all your enemies will be frightened. All Obstacles will be exorcised. The fruition of all your desires will be granted. This will come to pass without any doubt at all.

This ceremony is true practice. Witches are the supreme gainers of attainment!

The Method of Practice of the Glorious King of Obstacles composed by the master Nag po sPyod pa, who found the austerities of attainment, is finished.

This was translated by the Pandita Gāyadhara and the translator Gyi jo Zla ba'i 'Od zer.

Mangālaṃ.

In the Indian language:
Śrī Gaṇapati Śāntana Sādhanaṃ
In the Tibetan language:
dPal Tshogs kyi bDag po Ṣhi ba'i sGrub thabs
[In the English language:
***The Practice Method of the Peaceful, Glorious Gaṇapati*]**

Homage to the Lord of the World Avalokiteśvara!

First anoint a four-cornered *maṇḍala* with the five things from a cow in a secluded and attractive place. Sprinkle it with medicine and good-smelling water. Make a circle with perfume from white sandalwood. Set out a bunch of white flowers. Arrange butter lamps, perfume, incense, and food offerings. The *bali* is a food made of mash and barley flour kneaded together and having the three whites and three sweets. Each [*bali*] has a radish and a piece of pastry. If you have a traditional image or a painted image, request it to abide there.

When everything is set up in this way, begin by making offerings to the three jewels, generate yourself as your tutelary deity (S. *iṣṭadevatā*, T. *yi dam*), then think that from an Ā that is before you comes a moon, on top of which is a white letter *Huṃ*. Clearly meditate that from this [*Huṃ* there appears] the glorious Gaṇapati. His body color is white. He has an elephant's head. In his two right hands he holds a radish and an axe. In his left two he holds a skull filled with jewels and a *Khatvaṃkha*. He is ornamented with precious jewels and divine flowers. He sits on the throne of a blue rat.

Then light emanates forth from your own heart and invites the glorious Gaṇapati from the Abode of True Nature (T. *rang bzhin kyi gnas*). Then he melts into that [image] before you.

Show the *mudrā* of the commitment. Lustrate the image. Make offerings by means of *mantra*s. Then you must recite this: *Oṃ varataka svāhā* [Peaceful]/ *Oṃ bagavate ekadaṃṣṭavanidha siddhi huṃ* [Productive]/ *Oṃ bruṃ gaṇapatiye svāhā* [Powerful]/.

If you recite one hundred thousand of the peaceful seven-syllable [*mantra*], you will be given any attainment you desire. Your thoughts will be accomplished. Your enjoyments will be great, and your possessions will increase. All the wealth of the three realms will come to you, and you will become a rich man. If you do offerings and recitations for a six-month quintessential *Bhagavati* [retreat], then even if you are an ordinary person your merit will be equal to a universal monarch. If you do offerings and recitations for a six-month Essence of the Name of Gaṇapati [retreat], everyone will come under your power, including kings, ministers, men, and women.

After making the recitations, recite *mantra*s over the *bali* and offer it.

The commitment is that you must abide in the *dharma*.

The *bali* is a food that has a hundred tastes in even a small bit and is meditated to fill the sky. Think that you are praying to it [as follows]:

> Homage, O delightful glory-endowed Gaṇapati!
> Homage, O great glory-endowed Peaceful One!
> Homage, O great glory-endowed Wrathful One!
> Grant me whatever attainments I desire
> In this very life!

Give the practitioner the rulership of the King of Gods!
From that individual of extreme compassion
Comes the greatly compassionate great Gaṇapati!
Protect the poor with great compassion!
I myself, through faith, praise in homage
You, great God of Wealth!
The glory-endowed great Gaṇapati
Has white body-color and the head of an elephant.
In his right hand he holds a radish.
In his left he holds a wish-fulfilling gem.
In his lower [hands] he holds an axe and a *Khatvaṃka*.
His fat belly is ornamented with every kind of ornament.
He sits on the throne of a moon and rat.
Homage to the glory-endowed Gaṇapati!
Eat this *bali* of radish!
Increase my life and enjoyments!
Pacify sickness and elemental spirits!
May humans, gods, *nāga*s, and *yakṣa*s become my servants!
May the good qualities of the many enjoyments of the gods that I desire come forth!
May the Mighty One who is able to grant attainments
Manifest his form by the power of the disciple!
May the great great Lord Gaṇapati also
Protect the world and grant attainments!
Be a friend for my future attainment of enlightenment!

Immediately upon finishing the recitation, you must recite *mantra*s over the *bali* and offer it.

Then the Wisdom Being (S. *jñānasattva,* T. *ye shes sems dpa'*) departs.

You must practice in conjunction with the commitments.

Show this to individuals who delight in brevity.

This was composed by the Lord based on the *Tantra of the Arising of Attainments (dngos grub 'byung ba'i rgyud).* He gave it in the presence of 'Brom.

Mangālaṃ.

In the Indian language:
Ghaṇapati Samayanusmara Guhya Sādhanaṃ
In the Tibetan language:
Tshogs kyi bDag po Dam tshig gSang ba'i bsGrub thabs
[In the English language:
*The Practice Method of the Secret Commitment of Gaṇapati***]**

Homage to the glorious Gaṇapati!

As you, O noble Avalokiteśvara,
God who looks with compassion on others throughout the three times,
Have manifested him in your heart,
I will write the great and supreme method of practice
Of Gaṇapati, just as I have found it.

One who desires to propitiate Gaṇapati, the supreme king of all elemental spirits, who is truly loving to practitioners, should first, for his propitiation of the *yakṣa,* be devoted to the glorious guru, for this increases his great compassion and sedulous faith. Before [anything else] the guru must be pleased.

One who has the transmission and teachings sets up a besprinkled *maṇḍala* and offerings in a delightful place. To begin with, generate *bodhicitta.* Then worship the guru, the Buddha, etc. Then pray for refuge and present a *bali.* Dedicate the merit. Then you must pacify all the passions with the Four Immeasurables, which begin with benevolence toward sentient beings in all the three worlds. After that contemplate all the inner and outer *dharmas* as emptiness. *Oṃ svabhava viśuddho sarva dharma svabhava viśuddho haṃ.* Then think that immeasurable wisdom abides in the state of compassion. *Oṃ śujñanata jñana vajra svabhava atmako haṃ.* Thus must one contemplate purity.

From the sphere of emptiness the yogi visualizes [himself] clearly as some tutelary deity. In front of him [appears] Gaṇapati atop a moon and a rat. He is white, with one face and four arms. He stands with one leg drawn in and one stretched forth. Divine garments are his upper clothing. He is ornamented beautifully with precious jewelry. In his right hands he holds a radish and an axe. In the left he holds a trident and a skull. He has three eyes. The third is very wide. Upon his head on a full moon there sits Amitābha. Think of the three syllables that conjure the Wisdom [deity] into your own place. Worship him and present a *bali.* Then the *mantra* arises either from the awareness of the image or the heart, goes out of the mouth, enters Gaṇapati's mouth, and melts into his heart. Praise him, and from the [visualized] image's navel [the *mantra*] comes forth and enters your own navel. Contemplate worshiping him and serving him.

Thus I present the *mantra* to be recited: It comes from the path of the guru and is presented according to the instructions of the Tantras. *Oṃ* is first, with the syllable of fire placed on the throne upon the wish-fulfilling gem that increases one's thoughts. The six vowels are subjoined. This must be ornamented with the *bindu nada*. The first sign must be taken up. Then the fifth of the fourth should be attached. Then write the first of the fifth. The first sign of the Tathāgata should be shown after that. Then give the seed [syllable] of wind. This must be ornamented with the eighth vowel. The two concluding tastes (T. *dro ba*) should be shown with the two vowels. This is the secret *mantra* of the name. It grants the results one desires.

Oṃ is glory-endowed prosperity. The syllable of jewels that grants one's mental [desire] and accomplishes one's intent must be thought of after that. Then write the seed [syllable] of the sun. Then the first sign of the Tathāgata must be taken up by the mind. Then recite the first consonant. Then give it the seed [syllable] of jewels. Then recite the syllable of action. Presenting this for a long [time] accomplishes one's desires.

Oṃ is the first purity. Then place the jewel of desiring wealth. Then show the first consonant. Then the first sign of the Tathāgata. Ornament it on top with the eighth vowel. Then there is the first consonant. Then the fifth of the first must be joined to the fourth of the third class. The first of the fifth class is shown by the first of the third. The syllable that fulfills desires is subdued by the fifth of the fourth. Put the third of the fourth after that. By applying wrathful action like the great seed [syllable] of anger, one will meet with the god one desires.

In this way one who desires supreme attainments must fully exert himself at the *mantra* until the face of the great god is shown. This is the holy *mantra*.

If you want to undertake a work, you must make offerings to the Noble Ones with beer, radishes, pastries, and milk. Praise [Gaṇapati], and any tasks you contemplate will be realized. This is the delight of Mahādeva. Or make an image out of copper or bell metal, place it atop a *maṇḍala*, and make it happy by worshiping it. It will give you attainments. Or skillfully draw [an image] on a clean piece of cotton, worship and praise the Victorious One, and whatever you contemplate is realized. Or recite *mantras* over red flowers and throw them atop [the image]. All your wishes will be fulfilled. Or make [an image of] the Noble One out of silver or crystal, worship and praise it, then put it on top of your head and recite the *mantra* of men. When you enter the center of a city the people will gather. Or make a drawing [of Gaṇapati] on cotton with mixed-together secretions from an elephant's temples (S. *Gajamada*), blood, and maddening semen. Prostrate, worship, praise, and make prayers to it. Recite the proper *mantra* and admonish him. You will become equal to a Noble One. You must not show this image to everyone. Offer your prayers with radishes and *mantras*. Lustrate the image with sandalwood water. If this [water] is drunk or rubbed in, there will be freedom from all diseases.

Make a copper Gaṇapati the size of a thumb. Put it in your left hand. Take some milk from the king's woman and pierce it with the elephant's trunk. Think "She truly loves me" and recite the *vidya* of the name. Then she will certainly come. This is believed to be the result of the *mantra*. Tie twenty-one knots in a thread of a young [woman's] lower skirt. Imagine one god for each *mantra*. Tie it to your left shoulder, and that thing will quickly come to pass.

Draw Gaṇapati in [a combination of] ghi, *hangkara*, brown sugar, honey, and your own semen. Concentrate on it and recite the hundred-syllable [*mantra*]. Then concentrate on the object of your desire. It will be realized by reciting [the *mantra*] 108 times. Then roll up the image with silk and hide it in your left armpit. By this all desires are realized. Make balls of milk, beef, and parched grain. Pile sandalwood atop the *maṇḍala* of Gaṇapati and burn them. As [the fire] swallows them and rises, all your purposes will be realized. By doing it for seven days, a poor man will become perfectly endowed.

Draw an image on the meatless shoulder blade of an elephant. Encircle it with the *mantra*. Show it to the sky, and hail will stop. Draw an image of Gaṇapati on smooth cotton. Encircle it with the *mantra*. Tie it to the end of a long piece of wood. Thus the opposing armies are turned back. All these various sorts of works without exception delight the gurus and delight the gods. This [worship of Gaṇapati] is supreme among the methods of attainment.

May my composition of this practice method of Gaṇapati bring to pass the fruition of my desired ends and absorb my thoughts in the supreme *bodhicitta*.

The practice method that is called "The Supreme Secret Commitment of Gaṇapati" was composed by the guru who had gained attainments, Canakīrti. *The Requirement of Pleasing the Glorious Gaṇapati* is finished.

The great Indian yogi Vairocana and the translator Dhare Bandhe Dharmakīrti (T. Chos kyi Grags pa) translated this at Nyar smad rma lung.

From the Southern king Ghunasosprava to pandita Nag po dPal 'dzin. From him to yogi Kanacanara. From him to guru Canakīrti. From him to guru Tathāgatarakṣita. From him to guru Janakaśīla. From him to guru Dhorocana. It was composed based on the *Arising of Attainments Tantra*, the *Replies to Vajrasattva Tantra*, and the teachings of guru Kanacinira.

This is the great practice method. There are many others that are smaller than this. It is called "profound." There are no mistaken readings in this text. The guru has said that if you have the transmission, the very best thing is to practice.

Prosperity!

G. *Praises*

There are five texts in the Tibetan canon devoted to the praise of Gaṇeśa, two of which are identical. All four dissimilar texts are here presented.

In the Indian language:
Ārya Gaṇapati Rāgavajra Samaya Stotra
In the Tibetan language:
'Phags pa Tshogs kyi bDag po Chags pa rDo rje'i Dam tshig gi bsTod pa
[In the English language:
***The Praise of Commitment of the Noble Gaṇapati Vajra of Desire*]**

Homage to the venerable Avalokiteśvara!
Homage, O glorious Gaṇapati, the delightful!
Homage, O glorious generator of peace!
Homage, O glorious great wrathful one!
You grant any attainment desired in this very life!
You grant the power of the king of gods to the practitioner!

The Great Compassionate Gaṇapati,
Being a most compassionate individual,
Protects the poor with great compassion!

I bow down to you and praise you,
Great God of Wealth, with reverence.

The glorious great Gaṇapati is
Three headed, six eyed, and four armed.
His faces are an elephant's, a rat's, and a monkey's.
He holds a radish, a sword, a jewel,
A vessel of beer, a pastry, and an axe.
He stands with bent legs, one in, one out,
Above the consort.
A rain of jewels falls from her mouth,
Removing the practitioner's poverty.
His fat belly is ornamented with jewelry of every kind.
Homage to glorious Gaṇapati!

Eat this *bali* of butter, pastry,
Radish, and boiled porridge!

Increase my life and my pleasures!
Pacify sickness and demons!

May all men, demons, *yakṣas*, and *māras* become my slaves!
May the good things I desire
From amongst the gods' many pleasant things
Come to me.
O Great God Gaṇapati, with the power to grant attainments,
Whose body emanates from the strength of discipline,
Protect this world and be a helpful friend
For my attainment of enlightenment!

You should make your requests while reciting this praise, and offer a *bali* when the moon rises.

The Praise of Commitment of the Noble Gaṇapati Vajra of Desire, composed by the *pandita* Dīpaṃkaraśrījñāna, is finished.

It was translated by that great pandita himself and the translator Tshul khrims rGyal ba.

In the Indian language:
Gaṇapati Stotra
In the Tibetan language:
Tshogs kyi bDag po la bsTod pa
[In the English language:
***Praise of Gaṇapati*]**

Homage to the Noble Avalokiteśvara!

The chief of the gods, Gaṇapati,
Lives in the divine land of the Thirty-Three Gods, Tuṣita.
Born the son of Mahādeva by amassing the accumulations
[Of merit and wisdom],
And by the strength of his aspiration,
He became master of the four continents by the blessing of Great Compassion (S. *mahākaruṇa*).

I praise you, O Emanation of the Most Noble Avalokiteśvara!

Your four arms, the four modes of action, enact the purposes of living beings.
Youthful, you sit with half-crossed legs.
Bedecked with jewelry made from wish-granting gems,
You send down every desire as rain.
With great wrath, might, and discipline you drive back the battalions of demons.

I praise you who are arrogantly wrathful and greatest of the proud!

You hold the sun, the moon, a radish, a rosary, an axe, and a bowl.
You adorn your body with the divine clothing *pañcalika*.
There is no other supreme god like you in the world.
I salute and praise your glowing image,
Most Noble One of perfect qualities!

Your body is without the darkness of the three poisons, [bright] like a conch.
Bedecked with beautiful ornaments,
Goddesses gather upon merely a glance.
Standing amidst the divine troops your whistle strikes down the trilocosm.
The light rays emanated from your hideous screams
Defeat the Obstacles.
Your furious roar singes the *nāga*s of the sea.
Homage and praise to you, Mighty One Without Rival!

You manifest in a monkey's body to generate coarse awareness (S. *sthūlavijñāna*).
Your monkey-face, with its upturned eyes,
Is somewhat terrifying.
Your red body is lustily powerful like a rat.
Two of your hands' palms are joined.
The smell of your infatuating incense gathers the gods.
With the Grandfather at your right,
You take control of the race of women.
With Ranu's symbol at your left, you take in men as workers.
Sending forth rays of light from your heart, you enslave the three realms.
You wander freely throughout the sky
Like the cold north wind.
Your body's hooked-shaped light rays gather into one
All the wealth in the world,
And a rain of wealth falls upon me as well!
Desires, needs, and all the objects of delight melt into ambrosia.
Descending from the paths of the channels (T. *rtsa*),
It is gathered from the secret *vajra*.
The stream is churned, and—from the penetration of the *karavati*—is thrown down.
I take refuge in the liberating stream of ambrosia!
Before the Great of Hosts, the Glorious of Hosts,

The Mighty of Hosts, the Lord of Hosts,
The queen Hari bows and offers homage,
As do I to your image, O Great God!
Will you please bring about all the things that I desire?

The pandita Amoghavajra who was attained in the glorious Yamāntaka's attainments praised Gaṇapati [with these words] after having a vision of him in the cemetery *Kaṃkaru sPungs* (S. *skandha*).

In the Indian language:
Āryagaṇapati Stuti
In the Tibetan language:
'Phags pa Tshogs kyi bDag po la bsTod pa
[In the English language:
***The Praise of the Noble Gaṇapati*]**

Homage to all the Buddhas and Bodhisattvas!

Homage and praise to Gaṇapati,
The Protector of the World, Creator of Appearance,
Maker of Glory, and Enactor of Benefits,
The Unequaled and Unparalleled!

Homage and praise to Gaṇapati,
Master of Secret *Mantra,* King of *Vidyā Mantra,*
Matrix of Enjoyments, Supreme Treasure,
Shower of the Result of True Realization!

Homage to the chief of elephant-trunked ones,
Great Hero, Victorious over Demons (S. *māra,* T. *bdud*),
Great Power, Defeater of Obstacles
Who defeats the battalions of emotional defilements (S. *kleśa,* T. *nyon mongs*),
Pacifier of Suffering!

Homage to You, O Possessor of an Elephant's Trunk,
King of Jewels,
You whose jewel body brings forth the jewel of great jewels,
Protector of the Jewel Doctrine!

Homage to the chief of elephant-trunked ones,
Gaṇapati, Great Miracle,
The One who takes the breath of the white armies of gods,
The One who turns back the battalions of black demigods (S. *asura*)!

Homage to the chief of elephant-trunked ones,
Whose body is the jewel of good qualities,
Whose speech is the true essence of good qualities,
Whose mind has the identity of good qualities!

The Praise of Gaṇapati composed by the master Nag po Zhabs is finished.

Mangālaṁ. Prosperity. Subhaṁ.

In the Indian language:
Kameśvara Stotra
In the Tibetan language:
'Dod pa'i dbAng phyug gi bsTod pa
[In the English language:
***The Praise of the Lord of Desire*]**

Hri!
Protector Gaṇapati, born from Speech,
Has the countenance of the newly risen sun.
He has an elephant's head
And is bejeweled with the wealth of the gods.
His three eyes are beautiful like the anthers of a blue lotus.
Looking far and wide he protects the poor among living beings.
His white tusks have the luster of precious jewels.
His right hands, in the wealth-bestowing *mudrā,*
Hold a rosary and a bowl of many foods and pastry.
His left hold a red axe, remover of every difficulty,
And the food of evil spirits, a radish.
He has jewelry and costume finer than the gods'.
His spiraling crown of plaited hair emanates forth like an angry cloud.
The roar of his voice screaming out "Hri"
Brings the three realms under control.
It fulfills one's heart's desire.
Blue-black robes beautifully cover his body's lower part.
On his throne, a white lotus and the light of the moon.
He sits upon a vessel of pleasing things
That is blue, the color of lapis,
And grants the fruition of one's desires.

I praise you, O Great God Lord of Desire (S. *Kameśvara*, T. *'Dod pa'i dbAng phyug*)!

I praise you, O Protector of the Victorious One's Doctrine!
I praise you, O Controller of the Heterodox!
I praise you, O Inexhaustible Sky-Treasury of Pleasing Things!

Keep your promise and grant me every attainment!
The great guru Canṭapa's praise is completed.

H. The Precious Elephant Text

The *Hasti ratna dhana deyopadeśa* is devoted not to Gaṇeśa, but rather to the elephant itself as a granter of wishes. Its close association with Gaṇeśa is evident not only by the content of the text but also by its location in the canon, grouped together with the largest body of texts on Gaṇeśa. The text claims to be written by the great Buddhist author Nagarjuna. This claim can easily be contested on account of its references to yaks and crosses between yaks and cows — neither of which existed in India — as well as on account of its specific mentioning of Indian ink, Indian paper, and so forth, which would not be necessary if the text were written in India. This text will nonetheless be useful for gaining insights into the close connection between Gaṇeśa as an elephant-headed deity and the elephant itself, despite its questionable authorship.

In the Indian language:
Hasti Ratna Dhanaṃyeti Upadeśa
In the Tibetan language:
gLang po Rin po che la Nor bLang ba'i Man Ngag
[In the English language:
***The Instructions for Acquiring Wealth through the Precious Elephant*]**

Homage to you, O Precious One
Who satisfies all needs and desires,
Most noble among the seven jewels (T. *Rin chen*, S. *ratna*),
Treasury of treasures!

One who desires to remove the suffering of poverty
And desires to acquire the stuff of wealth
Must exert himself in this treasury of treasures.
An expert who desires to attain the wealth
Known as the "Elephant-Treasure-Treasury"
Must grind the five kinds of jewels
Into [a mixture of] fine substances that are able to burn,
And make it into the form of an Indian elephant
With many strengths and virtues, and beautiful to look upon.
[It should have] short legs, a fat belly,

And a head ornamented with a wish-fulfilling jewel.
This is to be ripened by fire.
One must know that placed inside of it are *mantra*s and substances.
First the character of the *mantra* must be written,
In gold if possible.
If not possible, it must be written with Indian ink
On a white piece of Indian paper.
One must apply sandalwood with the five good smells.

This is the *mantra:*
Oṃ mahahatiratna sarva siddhi phala huṃ/ ratna pune siddhi siddhi huṃ.
May I gain the great attainment of a treasure of precious things!
Dhanaṃ medhihisiddhi huṃ.
May I gain the great attainment of wealth, food, and enjoyment!
Nanakheddhi siddhi siddhi huṃ.
May I gain the attainment of all supreme and great foods!
Dhala sasvo siddhi siddhi huṃ ja ja.
May I gain the great attainment of a retinue and enjoyments!
May there be prosperity!
Satya thēdan vijaye vijaye ugge ugge svasti trapati akhume/
Prasaradha/ Svadhi/ Prahakhe/ Mune mune gurane gurane/
Akhemu akhemu rage murage/ Svaste guranayā/ Sarva vasti bruṃ
bruṃ bruṃ/ Svisti svisti/ Mule mule/ Keśe keśe/ Curna/
Curna/ Bhimale svāhā/ Oṃ kaṃ kara/ Kaṃ kara/ Niragatcatani/
Nirgatcatasvasti/
May this house, which is known as *Chegemo,* become a precious palace filled with treasures!
May a rain of grains and enjoyments fall!
May a retinue and enjoyments be gathered like clouds!
May my sons and all my lineage expand and prosper!
May my fame and renown be equal to the sky!
May conditions (T. *rkyen,* S. *pratyaya*) and obstructions be well pacified!
May I have a long life free from sickness, with perfect bliss and happiness!
May my life force (T. *tshe srog*) be hard as a rock!
May the manifestation of my enjoyments become equal to that of the delighted gods!
May all my food and wealth grow and increase!
May my deposit of men, wealth, and food become full!
May all my storehouses of grain become full and increase like a box of sesame!

May all that is scattered be gathered!
May all that has failed be restored!
May all that has declined be augmented!
May all that is low become high!
May all the haughty be deceived!
May the day of *dMu yad* come down!
May perfect bliss and well-being come forth!

Then draw the seven precious things on a white piece of Indian paper,
And write this *mantra* on your own back:
Oṃ cakra ratna phala/ Siddhi hūṃ/ The precious wheel/
Oṃ mahāratna phala svati hūṃ/ The precious jewel/
Oṃ bhihi ratna phala sviti hūṃ/ The precious queen/
Oṃ mahāratna phala siti hūṃ/ The precious minister/
Oṃ hati ratna/ Phala siti hūṃ/ The precious elephant/
Oṃ dhana ragamaśa ratna siti phala hūṃ/ The precious horse/
Oṃ ghati ratna phala siti phala hūṃ/ The precious general/

Furthermore, draw all eight of the substances of prosperity on a white piece of Indian paper
And put it in the inside of the elephant.

Secondly, the stages of substances are:
Exactly nine *srang* measures of earth from the fields and earth from the houses of nine rich people,
Earth from the fields and earth from the houses of nine poor people,
Gold, silver, copper, iron, smoke, crystal, coral, pearl,
The five kinds of grain, fine silk, many kinds of food, the three whites, the three sweets,
The hair of nine domestic animals belonging to a rich woman
With the exception of crossbreeds between a yak and a cow (T. *mdzo*) and mules,
The hair of good-quality horses, goats, and sheep,
The hair of both male and female yaks,
The six kinds of good medicine, flowers,
The barley of seven rich people,
And expensive substances that bring prosperity.
Put all of these inside the elephant.
Recite the *Essence of Dependent Origination* (T. *rTen 'brel snying po*) one hundred eight times
Over the above-mentioned substances.

Then you must tie the legs up well.
Invite the precious elephant who brings forth all needs and desires
From the divine realm of the Thirty-Three (S. *tuṣita*).
He melts in nonduality into the [effigy].
The clay elephant he dissolves into
Becomes an elephant of jewels.
Think that by this transformation all your desires come forth from the elephant.

All needs and desires come forth,
And that which comes forth enters your treasury or safe.
The method for placing them in the silo or treasury is as follows:
Attach five kinds of silk to the trunk.
Praise the precious elephant
And place it on a three-bladed knife (S. *kīla*, T. *Phur-ba*)
Made of Acacia Catechu
That is four finger-widths [in size].
You must consecrate it according to the above [account].
Make round-shaped offerings (T. *'brang-rgyas*)
And request prosperity.
If a treasure of wealth substances comes to you on that very day and time,
It is an extremely good omen,
And thus is a sign that attainments will come forth.
Then one must not allow people to see this clay elephant.
You must have great prosperity,
And must not hasten to pass it around.
You must not distribute it into people's hands.
The good qualities of acting in this way are
That you will become most mighty
And will be equal to the gods who delight in miracles (T. *'phru ga' lha*).
Whatever you think of will come about spontaneously.
You will become the aspiration of all sentient beings.
Wealth and food will be gathered like clouds.
Your lineage will grow like a forest.
You will be liberated from disease and demons.
Your bliss and well-being will be perfect.
In brief, the precious elephant amounts to each and every good quality.
Therefore you must strive at this.
All needs and desires come forth from this.

That which is called "The Falling Rain of Jewels of the Precious Elephant" is an instruction that brings together all food, wealth, enjoyments, long life, and merit like clouds. It is an elaborated teaching that grants possessions and *sMu yad*. The supreme *mantra* that is most profound is *Oṃ mahāhāstiratna sarva siddhi phala paśang kuru hūṃ hūṃ*. Write this on paper many times. Put it inside the elephant.

May I, the author, increase all my wealth and possessions!
Ārya Nāgārjuna wrote this.
Mangālaṃ.

It is clearly evident from the materials here presented that a major study of Gaṇeśa's role in Indian Buddhism, as well as his impact on Tibet and Tibetan Buddhism, remains to be made. It is hoped that the small contribution here offered provides a beginning to this research and will encourage scholars to devote attention to this subject.

NOTES

1. See Alaka Chattopadhyaya, *Atīśa and Tibet* (Delhi: Motilal Banarsidass, 1981), 37–55; George N. Roerich, trans., *The Blue Annals,* 2d ed. (Delhi: Motilal Banarsidass, 1976), 371–73.

2. See Yukei Matsunaga, "A History of Tantric Buddhism in India with Reference to Chinese Translations," in *Buddhist Thought and Asian Civilization, Essays in Honor of Herbert V. Guenther on His Sixtieth Birthday,* eds. Leslie S. Kawamura and Keith Schott (Emeryville: Dharma, 1977), 177–78, and J. W. DeJong, "A New History of Tantric Literature of India," review of Yukei Matsunaga, in *Studies of Mysticism in Honor of the 1150th Anniversary of Kobo-Daishi's Nirvāṇam, Acta Indologica,* 6 (1984):101–2.

3. D. S. Ruegg, *The Literature of the Madhyamaka School of Philosophy in India* (Wiesbaden: Otto Harrossowitz, 1981), 104–5.

4. Giuseppe Tucci, "Animadversiones Indicae," *Journal of the Royal Asiatic Society of Bengal* 26 (1930):139–40.

5. Tucci, "Animadvesiones Indicae," 139–40. Also see Ruegg, *The Literature of the Madhyamaka School,* 107, and Keith Dowman, *Masters of Mahāmudrā* (Albany: State University of New York Press, 1985), 282.

6. Rahula Sankrityayana, "Acārya Dīpaṁkara Śrijñāna," in P. V. Bapat, gen. ed., *Twenty-Five Hundred Years of Buddhism* (New Delhi: Govt. of India Publications Division, 1976), 201, 203.

7. It is not possible to know if the Dīpaṁkara listed as the author of no. 16 is Atīśa or Dīpaṁkarabhadra, or in fact another pandit.

8. As with most facts having to do with Atīśa's life, the date of his birth, as well as where he was born and the names of his parents, vary with the sources. They

tend to place the birth in the 980s and agree that his parents were of royal blood. See, for example, Roerich, *The Blue Annals*, 241, 247, and Chattopadhyaya, *Atīśa and Tibet*, 57–59.

9. For discussions of Atīśa's life, see Chattopadhyaya, *Atīśa and Tibet;* Ruegg, *The Literature of the Madhyamaka School*, 111 – 12; S. C. Das, ed., dPag-bsam-ljon-bzang of Sum pa mkhan po ye shes dpal 'byor (Calcutta: 1908); Roerich, *Blue Annals;* 241ff.

10. Ruegg, *The Literature of the Madhyamaka School*, 111. See also Alex Wayman, "Reflections on the Theory of Barabuḍur as a *Maṇḍala*," in *Barabudur: History and Significance of a Buddhist Monument*, eds. Luis Gomez and Hiram W. Woodward, Jr. (Berkeley: Berkeley Buddhist Studies Series, 1981), 140–41.

11. David Snellgrove, *Hevajra Tantra*, vol. 1 (London: Oxford University Press, 1959), 13–14.

12. Ruegg, *The Literature of the Madhyamaka School*, 107 and n. 343.

13. Roerich, *Blue Annals*, 844–46.

14. Several of the other authors of the Gaṇeśa texts I have not mentioned were associated with Vikramaśīla. For example, Ratnavajra (Rin chen rDo rje), author of *Meghāloka gaṇapati sādhana* (no. 11) that was translated by Atīśa and Tshul khrims rgyal ba, was a contemporary of Atīśa and a gatekeeper at the Vikramaśīla monastery. See Roerich, *Blue Annals*, 205–6.

10

Gaṇeśa in China: Methods of Transforming the Demonic

Lewis R. Lancaster

There are three sources for a study of Gaṇeśa in China: the extant images and paintings, the Japanese Shingon cultic practice centering on Gaṇeśa with texts and rituals that can be traced back to China, and the textual references to Gaṇeśa found in the Chinese Buddhist canon. The first of these three, the art that still survives, has been described in the pioneer work of Alice Getty.[1] The number of pieces of art devoted to Gaṇeśa in China is quite limited. One painting of the elephant-headed deity is found in Cave 285 at Tun-huang, a chamber that was excavated in the Northern Wei dynasty, although some of the decorations in it date to the T'ang dynasty. Pelliott suggests a date of the first part of the sixth century for this representation of Gaṇeśa.[2] A stone sculpture of the deity is to be found at Kung-hsien, and this image carries an inscription dating it to the year 531 A.D.[3] Both of these are of special interest because they predate any image of this figure in India.[4] A third piece of Chinese art depicting Gaṇeśa is in the Cleveland Museum; it is a seated figure with arms outstretched, one leg resting on the pedestal, and an earth deity holding up the throne. Professor Getty was aware of this image and included it in her plates[5] but did not attempt to date it and was not certain of its Chinese origin. Munsterberg in his study of Chinese Buddhist bronzes identified it as Chinese and on the basis of style placed it within the T'ang dynasty.[6] These few pieces of artwork in China indicate that Gaṇeśa has been a part of the religious tradition but has not had a sustained base of support.

The Japanese situation offers much more information with which to research the Chinese approach to the cult of Gaṇeśa. We see reflected in the oral and textual traditions of the Shingon sect a preservation of the ancient teachings that were being passed on to Japanese monks in the ninth century. This material focuses on the dual form of Gaṇeśa, the two elephant-headed figures embracing.[7] Since the dual Gaṇeśa plays such an important role in Japan, most scholars there have concentrated on the particular texts that discuss this aspect of the deity, and they have tended to ignore the other major description of Gaṇeśa as Vināyaka, the Hinderer.

There is a great deal of material in the Chinese Buddhist canon that focuses on Vināyaka, and that material is the focus of this study. In most of these texts, Vināyaka is considered to be the one who keeps the practitioners from progressing and is thus a negative force that must be overcome. There was also a revulsion expressed toward the fact that this spirit was shown in the form of being a human with an elephant head. One of the earliest descriptions of this feature came in the *Dharmaguptavinaya* translated by Dharmakṣema in the fifth century. In this text the Chinese were to find that the punishment for breaking the rules of conduct as outlined in the *vinaya* were severe, and those who failed to fulfill their obligations to those rules of conduct could expect to be born with limbs missing, with two heads or even three, or with the head of an animal, either horse or elephant.[8] Paramārtha, in the sixth-century rendering of the *Lokaprajñaptyabhidharma,* provided the Chinese with the frightening notion that there are those whose *karma* is so bad that they will be born into one of the hells, and in that hell with all its tortures and fires, they will have the further punishment of possessing the awful feature of having the body of a man with the head of an elephant.[9] This aversion to the elephant head continued to appear in texts. The famous Korean disciple of Hsüan-tsang (Xuanzang), Wŏnchuk, in his commentary to the *Jen wang pan jo po lo mi ching* (The Perfection of Wisdom of the Benevolent King) speaks of the elephant-headed spirit that hinders all vows.[10] Dānapāla in his 983 translation of the *Mahāsāhasrapramardanasūtra* lists the elephant-headed one as a *yakṣa*.[11] Paramārtha in 558–59, provided a translation of the *Li shih a pi'i t'an lun* (The Abhidharma of the Natural Laws), a text concerning astronomy and cosmological features, where we find a description of the hell in which there are creatures with bodies of men and heads of elephants.[12] The same idea of the elephant-headed ones in hell was echoed by the translation team of Jih-ch'eng and Dharmarakṣa in the *Fu kai cheng hsing so chi ching*.[13] Thus long before any of the cultic aspects of Gaṇeśa appear in the extant texts, the Chinese had an idea that elephant-headed creatures were the result of bad *karma* and were the symbols of evil actions.

This negative view of the elephant-headed creatures was to be reinforced by much of the literature that resulted from the translation bureaus in China. Under the name of Vināyaka, the Hinderer, Gaṇeśa became an important part of the pantheon of demonic beings described in the canonic literature of the seventh and eighth centuries. The Chinese were introduced to a new spirit, one that had no counterpart in their own culture, a spirit with a grotesque form that could hinder the process of moving toward enlightenment. But if the Buddhists presented a new and heretofore unknown problem, they were also ready with a solution. The texts we identify as belonging to the Tantric tradition present a wealth of references to Vināyaka along with the spells, *dhāraṇī, mudrā,* and other rituals that could keep this malevolent spirit under control. As early as the middle of the seventh century, a Chinese monk was translating a text about the rituals used to control Vināyaka. Chih-t'ung, in the *Kuan tzo tsai p'u sa sui hsin chou ching,* provided an account of a simple ritual procedure for dealing with this bothersome deity. There we read that it was not always necessary to make an elaborate altar, but one could take a small tree branch and *ayali* flowers with fragrant oils and conduct a ritual that would cause Vināyaka to be sent far away.[14] In a translation entitled *Pu k'ung chüan so t'o lo ni ching,* Li Wu-ch'an in 700 provided a description of a ritual for dealing with hindrances to practice. The recitation of the spell, done 108 times, followed by a fasting period of one day and night or three days, will result in the destruction of the barriers such as the fears produced by hearing strange sounds in the night, and having driven away Vināyaka, the mind will be concentrated.[15] The same idea was given in a text ascribed to Amoghavajra, a text similar to the *Amoghapāśakalparāja,*[16] where the ritual at the altar with the use of white mustard seeds is said to cause great difficulties for all malevolent *deva*s, *yakṣa*s, enemies, and Vināyaka, and thus make them move far away.

Atigupta in 654, in his translation of the *Dhāraṇīsamuccaya,* gives a classic description of the positive view of the intertwining elephant-headed creatures. The text provides the information that, in order to achieve the desired results, one should make an image, using white solder and copper, wood and other material, to make either cast images or carved wooden ones. The image should be in the shape of a man and wife in embrace, with the bodies of humans and the heads of elephants. The image should be made without regard to its cost. Having made the construction, on the first day of the full moon in a place that has been ritually purified, a circle made of cow dung is to be used as the area for the placement of the image. Pure sesame oil is to be heated and after reciting the spell 108 times, the oil is sprinkled over the head of the image 108 times. If this procedure is followed correctly, good things will occur in accordance with the wishes of the one performing the ritual, and all calamity and misfortune will disappear.[17] It is this account that gives us an indication of the way in which the dual Gaṇeśa is treated in Japan. Later in this same text of Atigupta's we have an account of dream interpretation. A dream of a predator bird attacking or frightening domesticated fowl is an indication that Vināyaka has been offended.[18] While Atigupta could give a positive account of the dual figures, he also has a negative view of Vināyaka, for his translation says that when the spell is chanted the entire cosmic realm will shake and Vināyaka and all of the evil spirits will be fearful. The unbelievers feeling the trembling of the earth will want to run away to the mountains or to the sea, but they will be unable to do so.[19] This mixed message about the elephant-headed creatures gives the suggestion that in the Tantric tradition represented by Chinese translations, there are a variety of these creatures, and while the dual ones are helpers, the demonic ones are to be controlled.

The Buddhist literature in China takes on a new form with the arrival of such Tantric masters as Vajrabodhi, Bodhiruci, Ratnacinta, and Śubhakarasiṁha. These teachers came one after the other by sea and the ancient central Asian trade routes. Bodhiruci reached Ch'ang-an in 693,[20] and in the same year Ratnacinta is reported to be in Lo-yang.[21] Vajrabodhi, one of the senior monks of the Tantric school, travelled around the Malayana peninsula and started his work at present-day Guangzhou in 719.[22] The work of these monks constitutes the major part of the textual references to Gaṇeśa in his Vināyaka form.

Bodhiruci undertook the task of translating the *Amoghapāśakalparājasūtra* and completed the work in 707 at Hsi ch'ung fu Monastery.[23] In this text we find the description of spells that can be used to control Vināyaka. One of these spells when recited seven times will cause blood to gush forth from all of Vināyaka's facial orifices. The same source also relates the spells for the control of Vināyaka in terms of lunar cycles, such as the eighth day of the full moon down to the evening of the fifteenth day. As a part of the ritual process, the practitioner should spend one day and night without speaking.[24] In a smaller work, the *Fo shin ching*, Bodhiruci provided the Chinese with a passage that promises, as part of the reward for this chanting of the spells, the attainment of the enlightened state and the perfection of the wisdom of the Bodhisattva and the ability to keep the spell constantly in mind for seven days. When this occurs all those who have fallen into the path of Māra and all the Vināyakas will seek to come near and give homage.[25] The *Padmacintāmaṇidhāraṇī* translated in 709 gives even more glowing reports of the rewards and powers that are to be achieved through the use of the spells. Enlightenment will come to Vināyakas and others who have accumulated terrible *karma*. Even those who are in hell, if they recite the spell, can themselves open up the gates and escape. All beings will be able to attain liberation and exhaust all birth in the lesser realms and be born into a heavenly sphere where they will experience bliss and joy.[26] By 706, Bodhiruci had produced a number of translations at his center, among them the *dhāraṇī* text that says, on the one hand, that the Vināyakas hearing the spell will attain full enlightenment, and on the other, that the right use of the spell will destroy them. The reciter will be able to crush all Vināyakas and will be able to attain the state of being invisible to all *yakṣas*. In this state of invisibility, one is protected from those who hate them and wish to do harm.[27] A later translation of 709, *I tzu fo ting lun wang ching*, says that if Vināyaka produces barriers and defilements, then a ritual using rice mixed with black oil put into the fire and followed by the recitation of the spell 1,008 times over a period of thirty days will remove all hindrances. In this text, we again see dream divination where creatures such as demons, wild boars, dogs, deformed beings and dead men appear to frighten the dreamer. However, by reciting the spell, one can make these types of unlucky dreams fade away, and in their place pure spiritual dreams will occur; the practitioner will have a comprehension of the true nature of the body and, with the power resulting from this insight, can remove his body from any place where Vināyaka holds forth, even in the dream state.[28]

Śubhakarasiṁha provides us with another selection of texts that deal with Gaṇeśa. The message regarding Vināyaka in these translations is similar to that found in Bodhiruci's corpus of texts. Vināyaka is defined as a Hinderer, but if one makes use of the ritual power of the spells, then Vināyaka will become fearful and take flight.[29] One who fully comprehends the spell cannot be defiled by demons such as Vināyaka.[30] There is a great focus on the magical quality of the spells, a power that is great enough to cause flags to flutter when there is no wind or incense to burn spontaneously.[31] By use of the spells the reciter can have the magical power of bringing disasters to the malevolent spirits — floods, great windstorms, day and night without any light, thunder and lightning causing injury — and finally the *vajra* scepter can be used to crush evil demons until they are ground into powder and dust. Vināyaka will in this way be mortally wounded, and there will be no necessity of fearing him.[32]

The next missionary to take up the theme among the Tantric schools was Vajrabodhi. He was a contemporary of Śubhakarasiṁha, and the works that occupied him had themes similar to those already discussed. In one of his *dhāraṇī* texts, he provided a description of the iconographic details of the Vināyaka image. The image could be made by drawing on a piece of white cloth or carving either white or purple sandlewood. The wood should have a pleasing scent and be hardwood, described as being difficult to polish. The body of Vināyaka is made in an upright position with the trunk curved to the right. In his upper arm he holds a sword and in the other arms, knives, circles, rope, and so on. Above his head are five colored clouds in which are seen *deva*s scattering flowers. Along side of Vināyaka, are four *yakṣa*s, each with a different head, one a cow-headed creature, the others either boar, elephant, or horse headed.[33] Here is an example of a situation where Vināyaka with his elephant head is the central figure in the ritual painting or the altar, while a separate being, with the body of a *yakṣa* rather than a human one, is surmounted with an elephant's head. While Vināyaka has been described in one aspect as a *yakṣa,* in this text we see him as being a special being with a body that is human in form, and thus he is not always to be seen as one of the *yakṣa* genre of deities. As we follow the other texts translated by Vajrabodhi, we can perhaps see something more of the reason behind and procedures followed in the rituals related to such images. We are informed, in a text devoted to the Buddha Vairocana, that Vināyaka and all of the evil *yakṣa*s will be seized with fear and run away when they hear the spell being recited.[34] More specifically, all those who obstruct or destroy the *dharma* of the Buddha will, by the power of the spell, be instantly transported seven leagues away from the practitioner and no longer cause trouble. These who obstruct are Vināyaka, evil spirits, ghosts, and the like.[35]

At the end of the seventh century, Ratnacinta arrived at Lo-yang coming from Kashmir. In two of his translations, we find evidence of Vināyaka, who is described in terms similar to those often used for Māra. He is the one who causes fear that is a barrier to practice and can destroy the concentration of the meditator. In the *Amoghapāśakalparājasūtra,* we find that the method for chasing away Vināyaka is to scatter white mustard seeds in the area of practice.[36] In the 705 translation of the *Ekāksarabuddhoṣṇīṣacakra,* there is a firm promise that for those who follow the subtle teaching there is protection from all evil spirits who are under the control of Vināyaka, and the demonic forces cannot evade the power of the spell that will scatter them by means of this teaching and use of spells.[37]

Later in the eighth century, the most famous of all the Tantric teachers in China began to translate texts that contained, among other things, information about Vināyaka. Amoghavajara was a unique teacher because even though he had been born in Ceylon, he was brought to China by his uncle at an early age. While in China, he met and became a disciple of Vajrabodhi and traveled back to India after he had reached adulthood. With his background it is little wonder that the Chinese looked upon him as a very special person, an Indian who was Chinese in many respects. After his 741 – 746 trip to India, he was able to provide the Chinese Buddhists with the newest information on Tantric developments in the southern regions.[38] It is not surprising to find that the texts associated with

Amoghavajra echo the themes found in those of his teacher Vajrabodhi. The practitioners are told that if one recites the spell 108 times, all those who obstruct and hinder progress, such as Vināyaka, will be banished.[39] In addition, the incantations and ritual use of sesame oil will provide the meditator with power over this demon, by virtue of the fact that the Tantric teaching will be fulfilled[40] and one can crush him.[41] The *Mahāmaṇivipulavimānaviśvasuparatiṣṭhitaguhyaparamarahasyakalparājadhāraṇī* provides us with at least one explanation for making an image of Vināyaka. If one wishes to control him, the oil of white mustard seed should be poured on the head of his image while reciting the spell 108 times. This is followed by washing the image in milk so as to achieve liberation.[42] Another text recounts that when Avalokiteśvara pronounces the *mantra*, the earth shakes in six ways and from the sky flowers fall down, the cold hells warm up, the hot ones cool off, and a glow is created that can be seen all the way to Akaniṣṭha Heaven. As these wondrous events occur, all of Māra's hosts, Vināyaka and his gang, are vanquished, and they howl and rage in despair. As a contrast to the wailing of the demonic, the *deva*s with melodious voices chant in unison the verses of the Sūtras.[43] In the *Vajrakumāratantra*, the process of taming Vināyaka takes place when the spell is recited and the world systems shake in the six directions. Vināyaka and his hosts of demons feel their palaces being severely rocked by the quakes, and they become frightened and uneasy. After thirty days of this ritual and continual shaking, these once-mighty beings are all cowed and can be easily conquered.[44]

Perhaps one of the most complete descriptions of the Vināyaka ritual occurs in the *Mārīcīdhāraṇīsūtra* done by Amoghavajra sometime between 746 and 774.[45] An image of Vināyaka, here called the "King of the Demons," is to be made from mud that is taken from the soil of the two banks of a river. Using this mud, the image of the king is made as well as one hundred images of his demon gang. Vināyaka is to have the head of an elephant and the body of a man. The other spirits are depicted with the heads of animals, some of short stature, others tall. They have four or eight arms. After the figures have been made, they should be put on a platform made of wood that has been soaked in the river water. On the platform are placed six thrones, made of five-colored soil, two to the north, two to the south, two to the east, with one in the center. The master of the ritual sits in the western "gate" of the circular altar and faces east. The image of Vināyaka is placed on the central throne. Using incense, flowers, and other ritual items as part of the ritual, the master recites the spell 108 times. After this, he takes seven-colored string and binds up the images of the demons, and with the feces of a young calf he draws 108 circles around the images.

This traps the demons, and they can do no harm for a long time. For the one who constructs such a temporary altar beside the river, even if he be near death with a sickness that is the result of bad *karma*, health returns. The spirits who have for eons been caught in the life of a malevolent ghostly presence will be set free from this existence that has brought so much distress and fear to others. When the spell is recited over the images thus bound up in the thread, they will all achieve liberation. They will give a reward to the one who can exorcise them; that reward will be prosperity. In this we see a glimpse of the process by which Vināyaka within the ritual setting has become a bestower of prosperity, as he moves from bondage in a state that causes hindrance and fear to others, to liberation through the power of the ritual.

The theme of aiding the demonic spirits in order to control them and to stop the hindrances they create is continued in the works of a mid–eighth century Chinese disciple of Amoghavajara. Han-kuang pointed out that Vināyaka had many forms, the embracing figures, Gaṇapati, and the elephant-headed king. This Chinese Tantric master taught that the elephant-headed king is a symbol of the great power Vināyaka possesses, but just as an elephant can be tamed by the keeper, so Vināyaka can be tamed by certain rituals. Thus, when a meditator finds that there are obstacles to success in his practice, he should anoint the image of Avalokiteśvara 108 times and then anoint the image of Vināyaka. When this is done, Vināyaka will be like an elephant that is fully tamed, and all the hindrances will spontaneously disappear.[46]

After looking at all of these texts and seeing the way in which Vināyaka was viewed as being a spirit who causes distress, fear, and obstacles to spiritual progress, it is understandable that a proscription went out from the Chinese court regarding the making of his image. While the Amoghavajra text suggested that the freeing of the demons from their terrible state of existence could result in great rewards, the Chinese canonic literature was dominated by a negative image of Vināyaka. When we see the high esteem within the Shingon group in Japan for the dual Gaṇeśa, it leads us to the conclusion that Japanese models for practice do not always work for China. In a situation such as the one surrounding Gaṇeśa in China, we find that the canon provides us with the source for making a study of what was being taught during the T'ang times. The negative view of this deity dominated the Tantric tradition in China, and it is understandable that the cult of Gaṇeśa did not thrive. On the other hand, inadvertently, the Chinese translations of those early Tantric texts from India give us a glimpse of the history of Gaṇeśa and an older aspect of how he was seen by Indians. His identification as a giver of prosperity is seen in these

Buddhist texts as the result of his appreciation for the services rendered him by the Tantric practitioners in helping to free him from the terrible state of being an elephant-headed spirit. Using all of the resources, we can perhaps begin to reconstruct the shifts that have occurred over the centuries regarding the conceptions associated with Gaṇeśa.

NOTES

1. Alice Getty, *Gaṇeśa, A Monograph on the Elephant-faced God* (1936; reprint ed., Delhi: Munshiram Manoharlal, 1971).
2. Getty, *Gaṇeśa*, 67.
3. Getty, *Gaṇeśa*, 68.
4. Getty, *Gaṇeśa*, 69. But see the essays in this volume by Brown and Dhavalikar.
5. Getty, *Gaṇeśa*, pl. 34b.
6. H. Munsterberg, *Chinese Buddhist Bronzes* (Tokyo: Tuttle, 1967), pl. 125.
7. See Getty, *Gaṇeśa*, and references given in James Sanford's paper, this volume.
8. *Taishō Shinshū Daizōkyō: The Tripiṭaka in Chinese*, J. Takakusu and K. Watanabe, eds., 85 vols. (Tokyo: Taishō Issaikyō Kankōkai, 1924–32), 1428–814b (hereafter *T*).
9. *T.* 1644–208c.
10. *T.* 1708–408b.
11. *T.* 999–582a.
12. *T.* 1644–208c.
13. *T.* 1671–739b.
14. *T.* 1103–462b.
15. *T.* 1096–412c.
16. *T.* 1098–439c.
17. *T.* 901–884c.
18. *T.* 901–885a.
19. *T.* 901–851c.
20. See biographies: *Hsu ku chin i ching t'u chi* by Chih-sheng (*T.* 2152–371a); also his *Kai yüan shih chiao lu* (*T.* 2154–570a) and Yuan Chao's *Chen yuan hsin ting shih chiao mu lu* (*T.* 2157–872c).
21. See biographies above: *T.* 2152–369b; *T.* 2154–567a; *T.* 2157–867b.
22. See biographies above: *T.* 2154–571b: *T.* 2157–875a, and Ming–chuan's *Ta chou k'an tung chung ching mu lu* (*T.* 2153–372b).
23. *T.* 1092–258a.
24. *T.* 1092–267c.
25. *T.* 920–3b.

26. *T.* 1080–189a.
27. *T.* 1006–656b.
28. *T.* 951–235c.
29. *T.* 893–629c.
30. *T.* 895–720b.
31. *T.* 973–379c.
32. *T.* 1239–198c.
33. *T.* 1269–303a–b.
34. *T.* 849–57a.
35. *T.* 923–24a.
36. *T.* 1097–424c.
37. *T.* 956–316a.
38. See biographies above. *T.* 2156–754a; *T.* 2157–889c.
39. *T.* 1005–625a.
40. *T.* 1005–629a.
41. *T.* 1005–629a.
42. *T.* 1005–625a.
43. *T.* 1032–9c.
44. *T.* 1222–120b.
45. *T.* 1254–257b–c.
46. *T.* 1273–322a.

11

Literary Aspects of Japan's Dual-Gaṇeśa Cult

James H. Sanford

Preliminary Considerations

The history of Gaṇeśa in Japan is commonly thought to have begun with Kūkai (774–835), the transmitter—perhaps better, the founder—of the Shingon sect of Japanese Buddhism.[1] However, the dating of the Chinese version of the synoptic *T'o-lo-ni chi-ching* (Compiled *Dhāraṇīs*) of Atikūṭa[2] at 653–54 and the existence of ritual texts on Gaṇeśa attributed to such major figures as Bodhiruci (trad. 572–727), Śubhakarasiṃha (637–735), Vajrabodhi (671–741), and Amoghvajra (705–44) makes an earlier, Nara period (710–94), familiarity with Gaṇeśa not unlikely. The inclusion of several iconic forms of Gaṇeśa in each of the two major Shingon *maṇḍalas* and Kūkai's authorship of the brief ritual text, the *Kangiten shidai,* (Kangiten Procedural)[3] simply allow us to posit the early ninth century as a secure, not necessarily a conclusive, date for the arrival of this divinity in Japan.

In general, and perhaps even in the case of the ritual and textual transmissions of Kūkai, we can speak of two separate provenances for the appearance of Gaṇeśa within the Shingon tradition. The first of these is as a constituent deity, repeated in several variants, of the two great *maṇḍalas*. Six such forms of Gaṇeśa are found in the various courts of the Vajra-dhātu (Kongō-kai) *maṇḍala* and one more in the Garbhakoṣa-dhātu (Taizō-kai) *maṇḍala* (fig. 1).[4] Gaṇeśa is, in this regard, but one of a number of Hindu divinities who, having "converted" to Buddhism, came to serve in minor roles as outer guardians of the courts of the twin *maṇḍalas*.

It is in the second Shingon provenance—as a *besson* or "separated divinity" broken loose from the pleromatic wholeness of the twin *maṇḍalas* and become an individual cultic figure, a divinity more nearly resident in the worldly realm and concerned most directly with its needs and values — that we see the Gaṇeśa most typical of Japan, the so-called *Sōshin* Kangiten or "Dual-bodied Gaṇeśa."[5] The term *besson,* like its synonym *isson,* "singular object of worship," signals the existence within Shingon of a private, largely praxis-oriented wing alongside the more normative, philosophical-doctrinal wing. The primary aim of the cultic worship of single deities was the attainment through specific ritual procedures of equally specific material or spiritual (usually the former) ends.

A number of issues are raised by the existence of any *besson* cult. These include, along with historical questions of origin and development, consideration of the iconic forms of the divinity, the specific rituals used in worship, their mythological associations or rationale, and the individual and communal aims and attitudes of the worshipers. The venue of this paper cannot provide space for a complete treatment of the manifold complexities inherent in any one of these issues with regard to the dual Gaṇeśa, but I hope, nonetheless, to provide at least a useful initial survey of the written texts associated with the dual-Gaṇeśa image and the, perhaps at first glance somewhat unexpectedly intense and persistent, worship devoted to it in Japan.

Much of our access to the rituals, iconography, and historical development of the dual-Gaṇeśa cult, from its Chinese "origins" in the seventh and eighth centuries up to the Tokugawa era (1603 – 1867), is textual. It is also typically fragmentary and scattered. Although some of the specific fragments are of considerable length, never for the early periods do we have a very broad range of materials to look at. Repetition of stereotyped patterns and verbatim quotation of standard passages is the norm. It is only from 1600 on, following the development of a powerful cultic center of Gaṇeśa worship at Hōzanji temple on Mount Ikoma near the ancient Japanese capital of Nara, that materials become a good deal richer and include biographies, accounts of visions of Gaṇeśa, certificates of initiation, guidebooks for pilgrims, apologetic tracts, and so on. However, before moving into the textual arena we first need a brief introduction to the most obvious element of the cult, its *honzon* or "principal object of worship," the dual-Gaṇeśa image itself.

The Dual Icon

Altogether, if minor variations in attributes and the like are taken into account, there may be thirty or more distinguishable forms of Gaṇeśa in the Japanese iconographic tradition. For most of these we find associated rituals in the manuals, and we can suppose that all of these rituals were performed at least occasionally. Only the dual form, however, shows a long history of ritual appropriation and the eventual crystallization around it of a full-blown cult; it clearly occupies a special place in the overall history of Japanese religion.

There are a number of variants of the dual form of Gaṇeśa. Of these four stand out as worthy of immediate notice. The Embracing Kangi is the most typical dual form. Its iconic characteristics, described in some detail in numerous sources, are as follows. Two figures, elephant headed and human bodied, male and female, stand in embrace. The female wears a jeweled crown, a patched monk's robe, and a red surplice. Her tusks and trunk are short. Her eyes are narrowed. Her body is whitish. The male wears neither a monk's robe nor a crown, though he may have a black cloth over his shoulders. His body is reddish-brown.[6] His trunk is long. His eyes are wide open. His countenance is not compassionate, but loving. His head rests on the female's shoulder. The feet of the female may rest atop those of the male.

The Embracing Kangi icon has two close variants. In the first of these, the Shōten Fondly Smiling form (fig. 2), the two divinities look into each other's eyes, and both smile happily. According to textual descriptions, the male should have tight-fitting clothes and the female loose clothes, though in some illustrations they are, in fact, wrapped up in a single garment. The second variant, Embracing Shōten Looking Over the Shoulder (fig. 3), is closer to the standard embracing form than the Shōten Fondly Smiling, differing basically only in posture. Here each figure is supposed to look across the back of its counterpart.

Orthodox Shingon makes much of the details of all three of these images, interpreting them as sophisticated allegorical symbols. Their most obvious common feature, the bifurcation into a pair of almost wholly separated, sexually differentiated figures, is taken to mark a preliminary duality of opposites. But the fact that these two figures are locked in an embrace that unites them back into one is taken to signal the further, more profound, nondual *coincidentia oppositorum* mode of being. That this is a nondual rather than simply a monistic mode is further indicated by such subtle, but sexually explicit, clues as the feet-on-feet attribute of the Embracing Kangi form and the single garment of the Fondly Smiling version. Similar interpretative clues are provided in the textual tradition by the fact that the two halves of the icon, male and female, share a single name and further by the fact that that the most common form of that name is the epithet Kangiten, "the Deva of Bliss." These orthodox Shingon interpretations, of considerable eventual importance in the worship of Gaṇeśa, probably represent a Heian period attempt to upgrade and legitimize Gaṇeśa. Interestingly, these forms seem clearly to be connected to the "four attitudes" of Indian and Tibetan Tantra. Tsong-kha-pa, for instance, allows that the ritual classification of Tantric texts as Kriyā-tantra, Carya-tantra, Yoga-tantra, and Anuttara-yoga-tantra is dependent on whether the central divinities smile at one another, look at one another, embrace one another, or are sexually united. David Snellgrove locates the origin of these variations in Indian commentaries on the *Hevajra-tantra*'s Four Consecrations and the attendant Four Joys as follows: Smile = Master Consecration = Joy; Gaze = Secret Consecration = Perfect Joy; Embrace = Wisdom Consecration = Joy of Cessation; and Union = The Fourth Consecration = Innate Joy (Sahaja or Mahāsukha).[7] Since the *Hevajra* is itself usually classed as an Anuttara-yoga-tantra (or a Yoginī-tantra), the explicitly sexual symbols in the Sino-Japanese Gaṇeśa corpus should best be seen as an inherent constituent of the materials rather than as little tradition accretions. (The Embracing and the United forms of the *Hevajra* tradition appear to have been conflated, and somewhat bowdlerized, in China and Japan into a single Embracing form.)

The Elephant and Boar Shōten dual form is perhaps even more provocative. In this case we have not a figure with two elephant heads, but one with an elephant's head and a boar's head. This seems the most uncompromisingly Tantric of all the variations, since the nonduality of the mundane and the Absolute is symbolized not only by sexuality but also in such a way as to emphasize the bestial side of creation. Some texts allow that this is the form to use if it is desired to represent Buddha and *bodhi* separately. It is also clear that this form has an organic connection with the "Vajra-faced" Kongōmen-ten form in the Kongō-kai *maṇḍala*. It is probably not connected with the *Hevajra* tradition (although the boar head does perhaps distantly recall Vajravārāhī, the "Diamond Sow" of the *Hevajra*). It may, rather, have become part of Shingon's set in order to keep the number of images at four once the *Hevajra*'s Embracing and United had been conflated into one in the Sino-Japanese texts (or their prototypes).

Dual Gaṇeśa According to the Early Chen-yen Masters

Generally speaking, the iconographic, historical, and popular sources relating to the Japanese worship of Gaṇeśa can be considered in terms of four sequential groups. The earliest, and in many ways most important, layer comprises the Sino-Japanese ritual texts on Gaṇeśa collected in the Chinese Tripitaka. Most of these are gathered together in a solid block of texts attributed to the famous names of the brief period of Tantric efflorescence in the Chen-yen (the Chinese reading of Shingon) school of eighth-century China. These often quite short texts detail the iconography of Gaṇeśa and the *mudrās*, *mantras*, and various special-purpose rituals associated with the image. Some of them also give brief folktale-like myths that purport to explain the origins of the dual form. All of these works are similar in style and structure. In fact, their brevity and formulaic format suggest that they are summary digests of longer original versions from a still earlier textual tradition that is perhaps now wholly lost to us.

Though it is not the earliest text in this group, the most widely quoted and most nearly normative of the entire group is the *Ta Sheng T'ien Huan-hsi shuang-shen p'i-na-yeh-chia fa (Daishōten Kangi sōshin binayaka hō,* "Rite of the Dual-bodied Vināyaka, Daishōten Kangi") attributed to Amoghavajra (705 – 74).[8] This piece is sufficiently crucial, yet also sufficiently brief, to warrant translation in full.

i

The body *mantra:* "Nōba binōyokkyasha kashitchibokyasha taniyata on nōyokkya nōyokkya binōyokkya binōyokkya tarayokkya haritarayokkya shōkyakashitchi shōkyakashita (senji kyara) sowaka." [Namo vināyakasya hastimukhasya tadyathā oṃ nayaka nayaka vināyaka vināyaka trāyaka pritrayaka ca mukhasti ca mukha kacita (?) svāhā].[9]

The heart *mantra:* "On kiri gyaku (un sōka)." [Oṃ hrīh gaḥ (huṃ svāhā).]

The heart-of-hearts *mantra:* "On gyaku gyaku un sowaka." [Oṃ gaḥ gaḥ huṃ svāhā.]

ii

If you wish to perform the ritual of this *deva,* you must first depict his image. This can be done using pewter, brass, [ordinary] wood, or the wood of fragrant trees. Whether one casts the image or carves it, it should be in the form of two figures standing in embrace. These should be about five *ts'un* or seven *ts'un* [about seven or eight inches] high and have human bodies and elephant heads. One should not begrudge the cost of the image.

Once the image has been completed, one goes into a purified chamber on the first day of the first half of the lunar month and there molds a more or less round altar from pure cow dung. This can be any size one likes. Next pour a *sheng* [about two quarts] of clear sesame oil in a clean brass vessel. Recite the previously noted *mantras* over this oil 108 times. Then heat the oil and place the image in it. Install the image on the altar [compare figs. 4 and

5]. Then, using a brass spoon or dipper, pour the oil over the two figures in equal amounts 108 times to annoint them. Each day thereafter the oil is poured over the figures in seven sessions of 108 pourings each—four times at dawn and three times at noon, seven times in all. This ritual should be performed for seven days. If you always keep in mind what you are making a vow for, your desire will be answered. As the oil is poured you should make repeated vows.

Afterward make offerings of buns made from curds, honey, and parched flour [compare fig. 6]; of radishes; and a cup of wine.[10] These bliss buns should be offered with fruits of the season; each day everything must be freshly made. Thus you will in return obtain all the good things you wish for and avoid all calamities. The practitioner must himself eat all the offerings presented in this ritual; only thus can he obtain their vitality.[11]

iii

For the calling-in *mudrā* [compare fig. 7], hook ring fingers and little fingers together and turn them inward. The two middle fingers should be held upright but apart. Each index finger should stand up beside its middle finger. The thumbs should be held up near the index finger. They should wag back and forth.[12] The *mantra* is "On hakyara shudateihataya." [Oṃ bhagata cudatipātya.] Chant this *mantra* seven times.

The *mantra* of praise: "On gyanahachi senchi sowa shitchi makagyanahachi sowaka."

The dismissing *mantra:* "On hakyara shudaya sowaka." Chant this *mantra* seven times.

Mantra used to empower water to protect the body: When you wish to perform this ritual, first chant the previous *mantra* over the water seven times. First use it to rinse out your mouth; then take the water and chant over it seven times. Then scatter the water over your body with willow branches. This *mantra* is for protection. Afterward go to the ritual place in the room of the *mantra.*

Ablution *mantra:* "On adahajiriparuidaka (soka)." [Oṃ atha vajri paryānaḥ (svāhā).] This is the *mantra* used to empower the water and for the ablution.

To disperse *vināyaka*s and call in all *deva*s use the Tejorāśyauṣṇīṣa *mudrā.*[13] The little fingers and ring fingers are linked and turned into the palm. Middle fingers are held erect. The fingertips are twisted together. The index fingers are placed behind the middle fingers halfway down the first joint. The thumbs wag back and forth. The *mantra* is "On shatoro haramadaniyui sowaka" [Oṃ catru pranadane svāhā]. Chant it seven times.

If someone who chants this *mantra* has frightful dreams, the beasts and evils he sees in those dreams indicate the anger of King Vināyaka.[14] If you want to stop such dreams you must humbly beg, "Let there be no anger," and the next day make fervent offerings of food and drink. Smear water on the earth to make a round altar about two cubits in breadth. As big as a plate will also do. For this, roast five kinds of cake and three kinds of radish. Light fragrant incenses such as liquidambar and frankincense at the altar. The person doing the chanting should sit at the west end of the altar and facing the east chant the Maheśvara *mantra* 108 times. When this is finished you should confess your errors and leave. Taking the various items from the altar, place them on a tray and leave the room. Face the west as you go out. Or northwest will also do. You must then intone the *mantra* "Saraba yayasha aranja ayui shaka sawa jyakyasha." After you have recited this and departed, all will be well. The *mantra* of Maheśvara is "On bitara sani hara maridani shindani shindani shindani hindani hindani sowaka." If you chant this *mantra* 108 times, joy (*kangi*) will fill your heart—except perhaps in your dreams. But if you recall the magic of the previous ritual, even that will turn out fine.

iv

Method of making the image. The image must be elephant headed and human bodied. The left tusk is missing, and the right one broken short. The head is inclined slightly to the left, and the trunk is bent outward. The image has six arms. The left upper hand holds a knife, the middle one a fruit bowl, and the lower hand a wheel. The upper right hand holds a cudgel, the middle one a noose, and the lower hand a tusk. You must not grudge the cost when making the image. Supply whatever it takes. It can be cast, carved, or painted.

v

These great secret rituals of Daishōten are known to very few. In truth, you must not disperse them freely. Take heed of this warning.

This short work contains, in a nutshell, almost all of the key features of the early Gaṇeśa texts. Its overall structure is a perfectly typical example of the genre. Analytically it can be divided into five discrete segments (unmarked in the original). The first of these is the introductory statement of three major, and progressively esoteric, *mantra*s associated with Gaṇeśa (fig. 8).[15] This is followed by a *locus classicus* statement of the iconography and ritual of the dual form. The third segment begins with three general controlling *mantras* used to invoke, flatter, and dismiss the divinity, then details three subrituals: a ritual used to protect oneself from harm, a ritual used to get rid of *vināyakas* (including apparently even Gaṇeśa himself), and a ritual used to end the bad dreams that are likely to follow use of the second, dismissal, ritual. The fourth segment is a brief, apparently tacked-on, section that describes the iconography of the six-armed form of the *deva*. The fifth and final section is a stern admonition to keep the teachings in the text inviolate. None of these elements, not even the obviously stitched-together nature of the constituent segments, is in the least irregular for this body of texts.

With Amoghavajra's *Ta Sheng T'ien Huan-hsi shuang-shen p'i-na-yeh-chia fa* in mind as contextually most typical and historically most important, we can proceed to summarize briefly the other texts of the early Chen-yen group and thus provide a more complete sense of the range of their contents. The earliest of all of these texts would seem to be the *Shih chou fa-ching* (*Shiju hokyō*, "Scripture of the *Mantras* and Rituals of the Gaṇa") attributed to Bodhiruci (P'u-t'i Liu-chih; trad. 572 – 727) and its longer variant, the *Ta* (Greater) *shih chou fa-ching (Dai shiju hokyō)*, both of which were probably written between 693 and 713.[16] The shorter version of the work begins with a very *sūtra*-like opening, "At that time on Mt. Keira, Vināyaka and a gathering that included Brahmā, Śiva, Indra, and a host of lesser gods and demons. . . ."[17] It then relates how Vināyaka (almost certainly the word is intended as a proper rather than a common noun) asks Śiva for permission to teach the "one-syllable" *mantra* "On gyaku kiri on ka un hattsu" for the weal of all sentient beings. Then follows a passage on the ritual to the dual Gaṇeśa that is virtually identical to passage 2 in Amoghavajra's *Ta Sheng T'ien Huan-hsi p'i-na-yeh-chia fa*.

In the next segment of the text, Vināyaka advises 9,800 demon kings to make a vow to support Buddhism, to have compassion, and to bring profit to all sentient beings. He then recites a long *gāthā*. The demons, moved by this recitation, agree to answer the needs of all who utter the one-syllable *mantra* (though they also stipulate 100,000 to 200,000 repetitions as a desirable *quid pro quo*). A long final *mantra* to Gaṇeśa closes the text.

The *Ta shih chou fa-ching* is a longer version of the same basic text, a fact that suggests that both texts are redactions of an earlier non-Chinese original. The longer version includes a number of elements omitted in the shorter variant. It begins with the same opening and introduces the same "one-syllable" *mantra*. This *mantra* is then fragmented and each of its elements associated with a part of the body. Next follows a fairly complex description of the iconography and ritual of the four-armed form of Gaṇeśa.

This passage also includes a number of subrituals to be used for such special purposes as attracting love, warding off wild animals, attacking enemies, becoming wise, and so on. The next section lists eight "*vināyaka*s" including one that has a goat's head, a human body, and ox hooves.

Then follows a segment on the dual Gaṇeśa icon and ritual that, again, is nearly identical to that of Amoghavajra (and possibly the model for that more familiar text). This is followed by a further Amoghavajra-like section on bad dreams as an expression of Gaṇeśa's anger. Next come the 9,800 demon kings, a *gāthā,* and a vow-of-protection motif, which is immediately followed by a second, detailed but new, version of the dual Gaṇeśa icon and ritual. Finally there is a long expository segment that is almost surely the annotation of a later hand.

The *Ta Sheng Huan-hsi shuang-shen Ta-tzu-tsai T'ien p'i-na-yeh-chia wang kuei-yi nien-sung kung-yang fa* (*Daishōten Kangi sōshin Daijizaiten binayaka-ō kie nenzu kuyō hō* "Ritual of the *Mantra*s and Offerings that Converted the Vināyaka-king Daishōten Kangi, the Dual-bodied Maheśvara"), composed about 723–36 and attributed to Śubhakarasiṃha, contains two important new elements.[18] The first of these is the identification of Shōten and Śiva.[19] Secondly, it includes an origin story (translated below) that links the "Hindu" Vināyaka king with the Buddhist Avalokiteśvara (Kannon). Both of these features seem intended to legitimize the dual Gaṇeśa, the link to Śiva giving added general prestige and the link to Avalokiteśvara certifying the Buddhist nature of the ritual. Otherwise, the text is a self-proclaimed summary of the standard icon, altar, *mantras, mudrās,* main ritual, and subrituals of the dual Gaṇeśa. Most of these come in bare list form.

There is, in fact, a second Gaṇeśa text attributed to Amoghvajra. This rather short piece with a quite long title is the *Mo-ho P'i-lu-che-na Ju-lai ting-hui chün-teng ju Fo san-mei-yeh shen Ta Sheng Huan-hsi P'u-sa hsiu-hsing pi-mi fa yi-kuei* (*Makabiroshana Nyorai jōei kintō nyū samaya-shin sōshin Daishō Kangiten Bosatsu shugyō himitsu hō giki,* ("Tantra on the Practice of the Secret Ritual of the Dual-bodied Daishō Kangiten Bodhisattva, the Samaya-Body Copenetrated by Meditation and Wisdom of the Tathāgata Mahāvairocana").[20] Stylistically and in terms of content, this work is somewhat unlike Amoghavajra's *Ta Sheng T'ien Huan-hsi shuang-shen p'i-na-yeh-chia fa.* It is framed in categories that though quite familiar in the developed Chen-yen/Shingon tradition are a good deal more sophisticated than those of the works we have examined so far. For example, it describes the ritual of the dual Gaṇeśa as a procedure for obtaining four kinds of *siddhi: siddhi* of protection, of gain, of love, and of subjugation. (The classification follows that of the four kinds of *homa* ritual). These benefits, all quite material in nature, come in three grades.[21] The upper grade gives one the majesty of a king; the second grade brings fabulous wealth; the third grade provides adequate food and clothing. In parallel to the material results, there are three levels of initiatory attainment. The highest class of adept can know the inner secrets; the middling class can read this *tantra;* the bottom class may not even pour their own oil during the ritual but must sit to one side and let a more developed practitioner conduct the ritual for them.[22] An interesting sidelight to this text is the amount of space it devotes to justifying the offering of wine to Gaṇeśa. It calls this "like using poison as a medicine," refers to wine as *Kangi-sui* or "Water of Bliss," and asserts that what is medicine to a good man is poison to an evil-doer. This, like the text's use of sophisticated vocabulary, suggests that the dual-Gaṇeśa ritual is being incorporated—with some effort—into a more orthodox context.[23]

One final, though somewhat anomalous, early text that needs mention is the *Sheng Huan-hsi T'ien shih-fa* (*Shō Kangiten shikihō,* "Ritual of Shō Kangiten") dated at 861 and attributed to one Po-jo-je Chieh-lo.[24] This quite brief text describes a mandalic visualization of the dual Gaṇeśa aimed at obtaining magico-religious powers. A number of secondary divinities including Indra, Agni, Yama, and Vaiśravaṇa[25] (fig. 9) are involved in the visualizations. Interestingly from a historical perspective are the two Taoist-type amulets depicted in this text.[26] It concludes with a long list of special visualizations such as those that will bring wealth, love, and the sudden death of an enemy.

There are two primary points to take note of with regard to these early texts.[27] The first is simply their content—what they tell us about the iconography and ritual of Gaṇeśa. The second is, to repeat a point, that these texts indicate earlier, and perhaps forever lost, prototypes of unknown provenance. Though some of them copy and repeat each other, even the earliest seem to be translations or summaries of still earlier, possibly fuller, texts that stand behind them.

Japanese Besson Manuals and Their Origin Myths

There is in the Buddhist canon a second series of documents relating to Gaṇeśa that comprise a single group or genre. These are found in the encyclopedic *besson* guides that emerged in Japan at the end of the Heian period (794–1185). These works are systematic and comprehensive rationalizations of numerous "single-divinity" texts. They are usually arranged divinity by divinity and then by iconic subforms. They include massive amounts of iconographic and ritual detail—often expressed in direct quotation and showing considerable internal repetition.[28] In the case of the Gaṇeśa entries, much, though not all, of the material is quoted from the early sources outlined above. One important new element in the *besson* compilations is the inclusion of a number of "origin myths." These appear to have served two primary purposes. One was to further legitimate the dual Gaṇeśa's place in a Buddhist context. The second was to make more coherent the relationship of the peculiar icon of the dual form to the ritual in which it was used. These origin myths—of wholly unclear provenance—are of sufficient centrality from Heian times on to warrant some considerable attention. Below I translate four of them, beginning with the earliest, which is in point of fact *not* from a *besson* encyclopedia, but is the introductory segment of Śubhakarasiṃha's *Ta Sheng T'ien Huan-hsi shuang-shen Ta-tzu-tsai p'i-na-yeh-chia wang kuei-yi nien-sung kung-yang fa.*

Myth One: Vināyaka and Senayaka[29]

> Jizai-ten is the *deva*-king, Maheśvara Daijizai. Umā is his wife. These two had three thousand children. King Vināyaka was the foremost of the 1,500 on the left. He practiced every sort of evil deed and commanded a host of 107,000 *vināyaka*s. Senayaka, a *deva* who held to the good, was first among the children on the right side. He practiced every profitable action and was the leader of a group of 178,000 followers who fostered fortune, skill, and good. This King Senayaka was actually a transformation body of Avalokiteśvara, who, in order to subdue the bad actions of King Vināyaka, took simultaneous birth with Vināyaka so that they would be younger and elder brother, husband and wife. The iconic shape is that of two bodies united in embrace. [Text continues with a description of icon and ritual.]

The most salient feature of this origin story is its clear separation of Śiva and Gaṇeśa/Vināyaka. "Vināyaka" here seems to have only its most basic sense of demon of obstruction. Good intrudes as a separate divinity, Senayaka (probably a reference to Skanda,[30] identified here with Avalokiteśvara), whose relationship to Vināyaka is one of subjugation of evil by good. Since the passage is followed by the standard description of the dual-Gaṇeśa icon and ritual, it is clearly intended as an introduction to them, but the fit seems very forced. Indeed, quite possibly the odd conjunction of "elder brother and younger brother, husband and wife" marks the juncture between earlier "Hindu" materials and later concern with a Tantric Buddhist context for the ritual.

Myth Two: The Cannibal King of Marakeira[31]

> Marakeira, again, had a king who ate nothing but the flesh of cows and radishes. With time, these gradually became rare throughout the land, so they offered him the flesh of dead people instead and then, when corpses too

became scarce, the bodies of living people. At this point the great ministers and the populace raised four armies to punish the king. But he became the great demon-king, Vināyaka, and with a host of *vināyaka*s flew into the air and departed.

After that, the country of the king suffered epidemic illness, and the ministers and the people prayed for aid through the vow of the eleven-headed Avalokiteśvara. Avalokiteśvara took on the form of a female *vināyaka* and enticed the king's evil heart. His heart was thus filled with joy [*kangi*], and the sickness left his land and the people were at peace.

The initial paragraph of this myth seems entirely unconnected with the origin story of Śubhakarasiṃha's *Ta Sheng T'ien Huan-hsi shuang-shen Ta-tzu-tsai p'i-na-yeh-chia wang kuei-yi nien-sung kung-yang fa*, save that again Vināyaka/*vināyaka* is a demonic figure (but apparently the living transformation of a human being). The second paragraph, as in Śubhakarasiṃha's piece, identifies the female half of the dual icon with Avalokiteśvara (here specifically the eleven-headed manifestation). It also gives a rationale for the epithet, Kangi (Great Bliss), and hints at a motif of conversion through seduction. Mentioned, but not really explained, is the link between Vināyaka and the radish. The interchangeability of the radish with bovine and human flesh probably reflects the Indian sense that the radish, like some other roots, is an impure vegetable, and thus a fit offering for certain marginal deities.

Myth Three: The King's Minister[32]

In ancient times there was a high minister at court who came to be on intimate terms with the queen. As soon as he heard of this, the king wanted to kill his minister. He laid out a great feast and, as was his custom, called his many officers in to eat it. The king served only elephant meat. He called the minister into his private quarters to insist that he eat some too.

The queen secretly worried for the man and told him, "Sir, you must go to Mt. Keira. There is a lake of oil there. Enter it and wash your body. Then dig some radishes and eat them. If you do not do this, your life will not last long, because what you have eaten was elephant's flesh. You must quickly take this cure."

The minister listened to her words and immediately went to that mountain, where he cured himself according to her instructions and soon felt bright and well again. But, as his heart was now full of resentment, he made a vow to the spirit of the mountain to become a demon. His head turned into an elephant's head; he grew a long trunk; he became very strong. In the dark of the night he presented himself to the queen and confessed his lust for her. Thereupon, the queen, by the force of karmic attraction, left the palace and, standing in his arms, vowed to be his consort. Her body became as his in form. From that time they have always stood thus, in embrace.

This story seems to be a conflation of myth 2 and an etiological rationale for the radish offerings and oil ablutions of the dual-Ganesa ritual. It is interesting that the radish is here a prophylactic to the dangers involved in eating elephant flesh—a pattern that suggests almost a totem-and-taboo relationship. Further, in spite of his lust, the minister is, unlike the Vināyaka figure in the first two myths, basically a sympathetic character.[33]

Myth Four: Avalokiteśvara and the Vināyaka King[34]

There was a mountain called Mt. Vināyaka. This means "Elephant-head Mountain." Another name for it was Mountain of Obstacles. A number of *vināyaka*s lived there. Their king was called "Kangi." Although he was head of a limitless host, he received an order from Maheśvara [Daijizai-ten] to go into the world of mortal creatures to steal their vitality and block their paths with obstacles, for at that time Maheśvara was not yet a convert to the Buddhist *dharma.* As a result, the Bodhisattva Avalokiteśvara, heart fragrant with the sweet sympathy that comes from the power of well-planted roots of compassion, took on the form of a female *vināyaka* and went to the palace of King Kangi. When he saw her, the king's heart burst into flames; he wanted to touch the *vināyaka* woman, to embrace her. But she, in spite of having taken on the form of a Mother of Obstacles, refused to receive his attentions.

The king became very despondent and approached her with [more] respect. Whereupon she told him, "Although I appear to be an obstacle-making female, I have from ages past been a follower of the Buddhist teachings. I wear the saffron robes. If you truly wish to touch my body, you must follow the same teachings. Can you, like me, be a protector of Buddhism until the most distant day has come? Can you, like me, protect those who come before you and foresake setting up obstacles in their way? Can you follow me forever and foresake all evil thoughts? If you will practice these teachings, then be my dear friend."

The king responded, "By great, good fortune I now value your way. Hereafter I will take your advice and protect the *dharma.*"

Then with a melodious laugh the *vināyaka* lady embraced the king, and he achieved Great Bliss [*kangi*].

> "Wonderful!" he exclaimed. "From now on I, and my kind, will follow your command and protect Buddhism forever. No more will we set up obstacles."
>
> Thus did he come to know that the *vināyaka* woman was the bodhisattva Avalokiteśvara.

This, the fullest version of the origin of Kangiten and the dual-Gaṇeśa ritual, is also the most "Buddhist" of the four stories. It is as well probably the most Tantric in the sense that the Great Bliss that converts the Vināyaka king to Buddhism is clearly of a sexual nature and is of such potency that it even gives him his name.

The ultimate source of these rather folktale-like origin stories is not certain, nor is it clear when and how they were connected to the dual ritual and its texts. The setting for the action of these tales seems to be the extreme northwest corner of the Indian cultural orbit. This is suggestive, but it does not in and of itself prove their emergence in that region. Once in place in the Japanese *besson* materials, these stories became a normative part of the dual-Gaṇeśa complex.

Kakuban's Kangiten Kōshiki

The late Heian *besson* texts, though fuller in all their details, represent nonetheless a fairly direct continuity of intent with the earlier Chinese texts; their main purpose is still to facilitate ritual concerns. There is one important Heian text that carries the concern with Gaṇeśa a step further. This is the *Kangiten kōshiki* (Ritual of Kangiten) of Kakuban (1095 – 1143). Kakuban was the founder of the Shingi branch of Shingon and the most important Shingon prelate after Kūkai. In terms of impact on the popular wing of Shingon and the fusion of folk and "great tradition" values, he is the paramount figure. In this regard it is not too surprising that in his *Kangiten kōshiki* Kakuban elevates the elephant-headed *deva* to new heights of eminence and respectability. His text is too long to translate in full, but an excerpt or two will illustrate the direction it takes.[35]

> The merits of King Daishō Kangiten reach higher than the heavens; the profit [he extends to others] is broader than the earth is wide. He defends the *dharma* in every direction. His Original Ground is as Lord of Universal and Wondrous Enlightenment, a rank [the nature of which is concealed] as if it were hidden in a spotless moon. The Manifest Trace takes on the form of a male and female *deva*.[36] This transformation form drifts down like a cloud into this world. It holds the unfailing power of a vow of Great Compassion

> that profits all creatures. Wealth and wisdom, courage and love can all be drawn from that vow. With it you can subjugate demons, dispel sickness, and extend life, just as you wish. . . .
>
> King Daishō Kangiten is the root source of *yin* and *yang*. From him the ten thousand images are born.[37] He is the teaching king of the Womb and Vajra *maṇḍala*s from which all Buddhas are born. In the Mitsugon Paradise he appears as Vairocana. . . .
>
> [In the dual form] the male *deva* is a transformation body of Maheśvara. He drives off both celestial and earthly demons and distributes profit in this world and the next. The female figure is a transformation of Avalokiteśvara's eleven-headed form, the most potent of her thirty-three forms. These two standing in conjugal embrace represent the union of *yin* and *yang*. That they have elephant heads and human bodies is to show the copenetration of all ten realms.[38]

In this text we see the equation of Kangi not only with Śiva but also with the central Buddha of Shingon, Mahāvairocana (Japanese: Dainichi). Even if this is seen more as an instance of henotheism than as apotheosis pure and simple, the elevation is striking, as is the inflation of language seen throughout the text. Kakuban's words are much quoted by later devotees of Gaṇeśa; indeed, they eventually reach an importance on a par with those of Amoghavajra.

Tankai Shōnin, The Shaman-Saint of Mt. Ikoma

Between Kakuban's *Kangiten kōshiki* and the seventeenth century, mentions of Gaṇeśa, other than those found in a few Shingon texts that are little more than repetitions of earlier works, are quite scattered. The lack of new materials does not, of course, tell us anything about the popularity of the dual ritual. It may well have had a number of regular adherents all along.[39] This paucity of documentary evidence changes radically with the emergence in the Tokugawa period of Hōzanji temple near Nara. Since its founding early in that era, Hōzanji has been the center of Japanese Gaṇeśa worship. It has long maintained, and in recent years published in readable transcription, a sizable collection of primary documents on the popular cult of Kangiten.[40] Chief among these are the various biographical accounts of Tankai Shōnin (1629–1716), the founder/revitalizer of the temple. There also appear to have been a number of popular tracts about the miracles of Kangiten produced in the Tokugawa period, but I have not myself seen any of these and know of them only from a few snippets in quotation. A variety of pilgrim guides and tracts were also written at or for Hōzanji. These continue to be produced even today.

The life and legacy of Tankai (1629–1716), also known as Hōzan Oshō or Hōzan the Monk, is of sufficient interest to invite a full-length treatment on several counts—and enough materials survive to allow such a study to be done with relative ease. Here, however, I would like only to sketch out the life of this unusual monk with enough detail to cast some light on three issues: the nature of Gaṇeśa as he is perceived in this fully developed Japanese cult devoted to him; the historical origins of the cult; and the style of the biographical materials associated with this movement and its founding figure.

The following account largely consists of paraphrase summary or direct translation of some key passages in the *Hōzan Oshō gyōjō* (Acts of the Monk Hōzan) written in 1697 by Tankai's disciple, Rentai (1663–1726), while Tankai, though aged, was still alive.[41] Though its tone may seem to us fictive and legendary, these impressions are more the result of the hagiographical conventions used than of the author's distance from the basic events of Tankai's biography. I have for the most part, even in summary paraphrase, tried to echo the hagiographic tone of the original text. Where I make analytic comments, the shift is clearly signaled.

The monk Tankai, also known as Hōzan, was born in a small hamlet in Ise province. He was artistically precocious, and because of this his parents initially refused to let him enter Buddhist orders. Nevertheless, in 1646 at age eighteen, Tankai left home and went to Edo (modern Tokyo), where he became a lay ascetic and eventually received several esoteric initiations.[42] He also made extended journeys to Mount Kōya and Kyoto, where his studies included both the Buddhist tradition and the Confucian classics. Throughout this period, as befit his ascetic nature, he also maintained a rigid program of fasting, chanting, and repeated pilgrimages to Mt. Atago.

Doubtless as a result of his constant practice, Tankai, though still a youth, soon began to experience a series of potent dreams in which he encountered and was advised by such Buddhist deities as Śākyamuni, Jizō (Kṣitigarbha), Avalokiteśvara, and Maitreya and such major Shinto *kami* as the sun-goddess Amaterasu, Hachiman Gongen, and the god of Kasuga. In one of these visions Amaterasu predicted that Tankai's austerities could not fail to bring him the *siddhi* he was so ardently seeking but also warned him of the dangers that would surely come to him through the envy of his great gifts by the worldly.

Among the divinities that Tankai had honored "from the beginning" was Kangiten, the *deva* of bliss, and he too soon appeared in the lay monk's dreams. Indeed, he appeared in such diverse forms (though, significantly, not initially in the dual form) that Tankai at first doubted his dreams. But subsequent omens soon convinced him of their spiritual authenticity, and, as a result, he made a thousand-dipper water offering to Kangi. This brought him a dream encounter in which the *deva* sent him to Kyoto to establish a small hall devoted solely to the worship of Kangi.

After Tankai had spent two years at the Kangi Hall his old master in Edo, Shūkō, summoned him back to take charge of a project to build a shrine to Hachiman. At first Tankai was loathe to leave Kyoto, but a dream from Kangiten authorized his departure, and the *deva* even promised divine aid in completing the project. But after an early good start the venture began to falter. At this unexpected turn of events Shūkō was filled with sorrow

> but Tankai was angry. "Kangi told me it would be sure to be completed in 1666 or 1667; has the divinity now sold me out?" he demanded. And he went before the altar intending to perform an oil ablution himself and had others prepare a bun offering. Suddenly Tankai developed severe stomach pains that rent him both physically and mentally. His followers said to him, "This illness came on with extreme suddenness. How is it that the ritual brings no attainments? You had better take some rest." Tankai paid no attention to this advice, but made the firm vow, "Whether seven days, or a hundred days, or a thousand, I'm not going to rest until either I get a response or die first."[43] Then he took a purifying bath, changed his clothes, and crawled to the sacred precincts.
>
> On the night of the fourth day an old man appeared [in a dream] from the southeast. When Tankai looked closely, he saw it was Hachibei of the Minoya, though there was no indication of the meaning of this. At dawn on the fifth day, Tankai dreamed that a young boy came by and placed the sum of two hundred *ryō* on the altar. He had a wondrous voice that left Tankai filled with joy. When on the seventh day Tankai left the altar to report to Shūkō, Shūkō stood up in surprise and asked, "After all this time was there still nothing accomplished?"[44] Tankai laughed and replied, "The *deva* has accepted the offering; the attainment will follow shortly." Shūkō, full of joy, was thanking Tankai for his efforts when suddenly there was a knock at the door. When Shūkō asked who it was, the response came, "Hachibei of the Minoya." Just as had been predicted, he came with two hundred *ryō* tucked up in his bosom. A bit later Watanabe Osumi no Kami added his strength to the project. Unasked, he had on his own gathered a great treasure so that in no time at all it was possible to complete the shrine.

This key passage requires us to step back a bit and look at the text with an eye to some submerged meanings. On the surface we seem to have, after a rather unexpected hitch or two, an eventually successful collaboration by Tankai and Kangiten. But just beneath that smooth surface we can sense currents that indicate a surprisingly strained relationship between the monk and his tutelary guardian. Kangi is, it appears, given to jealousy and fickleness. He claims to support Tankai's religious goals, but actually wants all the attention himself. Further, he is ready to punish any perceived unfaithfulness in a very direct manner. Only increasingly elaborate rituals, it turns out, will keep him happy.

In response to Kangi's growing demands, Tankai increased his ritual observances by performing several one-thousand- or two-thousand-day oil-ablution ceremonies. It was, indeed, in the middle of one of these—on the five-hundredth day of a one-thousand-day ceremony — that Tankai was finally rewarded with a vision of Kangi's true form.

> On the five-hundredth day, the *deva* appeared in its true form. The female *deva* had the aspect of a beautiful goddess, with a human torso and an elephant's trunk. She was seven feet tall, with her long trunk hanging between her breasts and an unopened lotus flower standing in adornment on her head. The male divinity was imposing and stern, like a hero. He had an elephant head, and the rest of his body was human. Both his trunk and his tusks were extraordinarily long. But Kangi knew innumerable other divine transformations as well. When Tankai asked if his hopes would meet success or not, the *deva* gave him a host of signs. For example, Tankai always sat in lotus posture on a rope bed in order to keep from sleeping, but when he happened to doze off Kangiten would rub his head to make him wake up. Tankai sketched out the form of the divinity that he had seen, then cast a sculpture of it.[45]

The gift of this vision was bestowed only with some expectations attached. Their nature was soon made clear to Tankai.

> One night Tankai had a dream. He had cut some clothes for himself that were exactly like those worn by the *deva.* Kangiten came before him and said, "Promise to become my follower. I will quickly give you your heart's desire." Tankai answered, "I left my home to take up a life of austerities in order to attain Buddhahood. Grant me entry among the ranks of the Buddhas." But the *deva* replied, "That is not my *samādhi*. I will give you whatever you want in this life, and sovereignty in the next. Is that not enough?"[46] Tankai asked, "Can I, then, attain the Lordship of a major divinity like yourself?" The *deva* answered, "To obtain the divine power of sovereignty, as I have, required me to perform a thousand years of meditation atop Chōkō

> mountain." "The life of a human," responded Tankai, "does not reach one hundred. How can I hope for a thousand years?" "These thousand years will pass like a night's sleep," promised the divinity. Tankai thought to himself, "I took Shōten to be the Soverign Lord, Maheśvara, but if he is a *vināyaka* and I now become his devotee, how will I fulfill my goal of becoming a monk?" When Tankai voiced these doubts to Kangi, the *deva* scowled and said to him, "Your idea that I was Maheśvara Vināyaka was a great mistake. I am a transformation of a *vināyaka* whose name is Daishō Kangiten. I am called "Great Lord" because the other *vināyaka*s all follow me. My name shows that I am unlike the other *vināyaka*s. I distribute joy to the people of the world; I am the *avatāra* who brings their deepest wishes to profitable fruition. If you do not know this, look into the ancient books of the Mandala Temple of the Ono lineage."[47]
>
> Tankai still had his doubts. He told no one about all of this, but then one day as he happened to be passing by one of the halls of Tōji [in Kyoto], he saw on a desk there a one-volume text labeled "Bibliography of the Ono Mandara-ji Temple." When he asked further about this, he learned that it belonged to the Ono [lineage's] Zuishin-in Hall. This led him to look at the *Kakuzen-shō*, in which he found a secret commentary on Shōten that said, "In the *Records of Chishō Daishi*, the rituals to this *deva* are included in the section headed 'Maheśvara,' but this is a great error.[48] This divinity's special characteristic is that of lord of *siddhis*, thus he is called 'Jizaiten.' He ought not to be confused with any other *jizai ten*." All of Tankai's doubts were melted away by this text, but he still had no desire to become a devotee of Kangiten. As his hesitation extended into days, the divinity continued to importune him.

By this time in his life Tankai's devotion had become increasingly directed toward the higher goal of spiritual liberation and toward specific reverence of the Bright King, Fudō Myōō (Acalanātha Vidyārāja). Finally Tankai became determined to transfer the Gaṇeśa hall in Kyoto, and its ritual obligations, to his disciple Shūhan.

> Thereafter Tankai took the monk Ennin as master, received the Bodhisattva vows, and became a fully ordained monk. The Kangi hall he transferred to Shūhan. Shūhan told him, "I want to continue in your footsteps and likewise be a master of this powerful *dharma*. I would be most grateful if you would aid me in an offering ceremony to Kangi to seal the transmission." Tankai could not refuse, but during the oil ceremony he told the *deva*, "This ceremony will mark the beginning of a long farewell between us. Pray give your support to Shūhan hereafter." The angered Kangiten responded, "I

cannot say what will happen if you abandon me, but you, at least, will see a lifetime with no tranquility." And every hair on the *deva*'s arm stood on end as he scowled at Tankai with eyes that seemed full of blood. Later . . . just as might have been expected, Tankai contracted an illness that no treatment could cure. "This affliction is all because I angered the *deva*," he realized. "Perhaps I had better show some remorse." And he prayed, "I am thinking that I should practice your *dharma* every day as I used to do. I seek forgiveness." That evening Kangiten came to him in a dream and in a gentle voice told him, "You think that all the troubles you have encountered were due to me, but that is quite wrong. Although I was angry at first, my feelings have mellowed since then. Do not imagine I could hate one who has stirred his *bodhicitta* and taken the precepts. What is there to be angry at in that? I would not interfere with the workings of *karma*."

However, in spite of the pious claims made in this passage, when somewhat later Tankai entered a period of deep meditation, Kangiten sent in hordes of his followers to harass the monk.

Sometimes his whole body was shaken. At other times he was attacked by disturbances in his chest. The *vināyaka*s appeared in horrible forms; they came before him as beautiful women, naked and with silky skins; they came before him in the beastly form of a herd of *vināyaka*s. Tankai paid no attention to any of it. He relied on the rite of Mañjuśrī's "One-line Samādhi"[49] and sat cross-legged for two hundred days, never speaking, never sleeping, rising only to eat or to go to the latrine. Meditation and yoga brought him ease until suddenly he attained the realization that all *dharma*s are of one quality, that the passions are themselves enlightenment.[50]

In 1678 Fudō Myōō revealed the existence of Mt. Hōzan, "a miraculous place that is neither a dream nor a reality," to Tankai and bade him move there and reestablish a temple on a site that had long gone to ruin. In order to mollify Kangiten, Tankai promised to make a statue of the elephant-headed *deva*, to install him as a guardian of the mountain, and to continue to perform oil ablutions to him. In return Tankai asked of Kangi, ". . . only that you will protect me and aid me to attain *siddhi*."

By 1680 Tankai had gathered numerous followers on Mt. Hōzan and had been able to build a temple complex, which he called "Hōzanji." The chief deity of the temple was Fudō, but in accord with his promise Tankai also erected a special Kangi hall as well. But when Tankai attempted to withdraw into silence and perpetual meditation, Kangi became angered once more.

> One day Tankai encountered obstacle after obstacle, until finally he took a three-pronged *vajra* in his hand, entered the *samādhi* of Kuṇḍalī, and began to intone the *mantras*.[51] Kangiten appeared then and told him, "These obstacles have been my doing. Stop these prayers and listen to me. When you need something, you worship me, but when you don't need anything you cast me aside hatefully. But though you cast me aside, I have never abandoned you. And even though I gave you good omens from the outset, you still haven't attained enlightenment. . . . When you were in Kyoto you vowed to observe my ritual for twenty years. Next year the term will be complete. But even if you then abandon me, I will not turn away from you. Still, it would be best if you were to continue to worship me as you did long ago. What profits have your bitter efforts in the search for the Inner Buddha brought you? The statue you and your disciples have built of Fudō will not satisfy your needs. I am the transformation body of Vairocana. I am the secret deity within the Buddhist *dharma* who brings the attainment of *siddhi*. If you propitiate me, all the vows you have made will be accomplished."

The tug of war between Fudō and Kangiten for the attentions of Tankai was not concluded until around 1688, when Tankai's spiritual resolve finally became so firm that even Kangi was forced to give in.

> Tankai considered further, "Although the great *deva* has remonstrated with me several times, a heart set along the Way is not easy to turn back, and I cannot accept his command. I have practiced the cereal and salt abstentions and foresaken worldly wealth. To me, profit and fame are like drifting clouds. Therefore, although I do not take the worship of Kangiten lightly, it cannot be like it was in the old days. Thus I have been afflicted by the *deva*'s reproaches and received bad omens. But, the *deva* is Daishō Gongen, the great saintly *avatāra,* and I am a mere mortal. Even if I carry out the oil ceremony for him, how can such a crude offering affect his pleasure? Yet I will see that my disciples daily make such offerings and pray that the *deva* will grant me his compassion and mercy and be my protector." Kangiten replied with a laugh, "I must let you off. Hereafter, there will be no more obstacles. You may practice your austerities in peace."

The rest of Rentai's biography is but a paean of praise to Tankai's (thereafter unobstructed) success in expanding Hōzanji. The final paragraphs of the biography show the now sixty-nine-year-old Tankai to be a virtual living Buddha.

> Hōzan is now sixty-nine, but due to his having taken the spiritual medicine of Maitreya's *tantra*, his face is not aged. And though he eats but once in every ten days—and even then without enthusiasm—his vigor is undiminished. Day and night he intones the incantation of compassionate salvation, one-hundred, perhaps two-hundred thousand times. A mirror moon resides in his lotus heart, where the fires of wisdom exhaust the tinder of illusion. Due to the yoga of nonobstruction of the Six Elements, he has attained the state of *nyūga ga'nyū*. Due to the power of his prayers, he has gone beyond the many and into the Singularity, "A." The Buddha state is proven in his own body.[52] His glance sees everything; his slightest thought produces everything. For if any activity is participant in all activities, what cannot be accomplished? If each accomplishment is participant in all accomplishments, who will not rejoice?

In the excerpts given above we have primarily looked at the relationship of Tankai and Gaṇeśa. Much more could be gleaned from this and the other hagiographical accounts of Tankai, and still more from the massive collection of other documents preserved at Hōzanji. But at this juncture I want to press the discussion of the history of the Gaṇeśa cult at Hōzanji on one point only. This is the continued tension between two cultural levels—popular and elite. We have already seen this issue within the biography in at least two ways. One is the disparity made between Fudō as representative of normative, "high culture," enlightenment-oriented Shingon, and Gaṇeśa/Kangiten as a powerful, but somewhat untrustworthy provider of worldly benefits whose basic appeal is to the vulgar needs of the vulgar masses. This division is echoed, unconsciously perhaps, in the biographer's depiction of the dual nature of Tankai himself, since Tankai begins his career as a lay ascetic, a shamanic holy man of the sort ordinarily associated with popular culture, and only quite late in his life is fully accepted and fully ordained and thus fit to fill the standard hagiographic role assigned to orthodox temple founders.

This intriguing, perhaps dialectically creative, tension of levels persists at Hōzanji even to the present day. For although it is clear that pilgrimage to the Kangi hall in order to ask for performance of rituals to Gaṇeśa provides the bulk of the temple's impressive wealth, Kangiten himself is still relegated to a place of marginal importance in comparison to that of the central deity of the complex, Fudō.[53] This can be seen in a number of ways, of which I will single out only two. In spite of his economic importance to the contemporary temple and in spite of Tankai's own lasting, if ambivalent, connection to him, there is at Hōzanji only one hall to Kangi, a hall marked simply, almost halfheartedly, by a single signboard. By contrast, Fudō is celebrated in numerous statues that, in a psychological sense at least, surround Gaṇeśa and indeed seem intended to tuck him entirely out of sight.

Even more telling is the parallel arrangement of the official pilgrim-oriented souvenir guidebook of 1978, *Hōzanji*.[54] This work begins with sixty-seven pages of glorious color plates of the many halls of Hōzanji, of its major statues and paintings (including fourteen of Fudō), and of the important art treasures owned by the temple. There is in this official presentation, however, not one plate of the Kangi hall, nor any representation at all of Gaṇeśa.[55] The text is arranged in somewhat similar fashion. It begins with a twenty-five-page history of the temple and its environs. It then moves into a second chapter of about the same length and in rather easy Japanese, the primary goal of which seems to be to persuade the reader that, contrary to popular belief, Kangi is more interested in bringing spiritual solace than in providing worldly benefits. Finally it closes with an appendix of one of the classical Japanese biographies of Tankai, a text that must present considerable difficulty to the vast majority of its readers.

The generally tendentious nature of the guidebook's selective presentation in and of itself makes it perfectly clear that the ordinary pilgrim to Hōzanji is indeed interested first and foremost, not in the enlightenment values associated with Fudō, but instead in the worldly benefits available through the Kangi rituals. It is also almost certain that that same pilgrim will carry off the mountain not only the official guidebook but also one of the small under-the-counter dual-Gaṇeśa statues sold for home worship in religious-goods shops outside the precincts of the temple proper.[56]

The brief outline of Tankai's life given above brings to a substantial end our summary foray into the primary documents associated with the Japanese worship of the dual Gaṇeśa. A full, sociologically sound study of the living Japanese cult of Kangiten would, of course, be an added valuable contribution. One might, for example, be able therein to trace the historical development of an early analogue to the quasi-shamanic and nativist-millenarian movements of the nineteenth and twentieth centuries that go in Japan by the general rubric *shinkō shūkyō* or "New Religions." A full study would, however, constitute not simply a chapter but a whole volume. In the present, more limited, and primarily documentary summary we cannot delve very deeply into such issues. I do, however, want before concluding this essay to touch, even if a bit unsystematically, on three issues that are not documentary per se. Firstly, I want to provide the reader with *some* picture of the worship of the dual Gaṇeśa in contemporary Japan. Then I would like to pose a speculation or two about the underlying meaning of the unusual but ritually specified items offered during the oil ablution. Finally, I want to provide suggestions regarding the possible origins of the twin-bodied icon.

Contemporary Praxis in the Gaṇeśa Cult

As suggested above, a complete treatment of the contemporary practices as Hōzanji and related temples would require extensive, multidisciplinary investigations.[57] What follows is not such primary work. Rather it is a survey of a limited number of secondary sources and is particularly indebted to two works written by Muraoka Kū in Japanese and the one substantial English language article pertaining to these matters that I know of, D. C. Holtom's half-century-old "Japanese Votive Pictures (The Ikoma Ema)."[58] Let me, borrowing rather heavily from these sources, outline a typical pattern of devotional involvement in the Kangi cult at Ikoma.

Gaṇeśa is in Japan (as elsewhere) one of those numinosities whose importance lies in his control of the dangerous aspects of life, aspects that he can either inflict or withhold at will. In the case of Gaṇeśa the commodity in question is "obstacles." However, since the question of having problems is a relative one, it takes only a moment's thought to realize that to have obstacles withheld from oneself is tantamount to being blessed. Thus, though Gaṇeśa's innate character may be negative, his actual utility can be positive. From this it follows quite naturally that devotion to Kangi often takes on the pattern of a crisis cult.

According to Matsumoto Jitsudō, the Abbot of Hōzanji at the time of Muraoka's visit there in the early 1970s, conversion to the cult typically occurs in several stages. Initially someone is brought to the temple by a friend who is already a member of a Kangi-oriented confraternity (*kō*). If attracted to the cult, the newcomer may go through a long period that involves no more than monthly pilgrimages to Ikoma with this group. But at some time or other, given the normal ups and downs of life, some business or personal problem that needs immediate help is bound to occur. At this juncture the previously casual follower will be moved to arrange for a full-scale oil ritual.[59] If the problem is not resolved by this, the newcomer can either leave the cult or find reason to try some further petitioning. If the petitions (initial or continued) seem to work, the follower has, of course, good cause for a strengthened association with the temple, at least on an occasional basis, and should dramatic improvement in a situation be effected at some point, he or she is likely to become an ardent supporter and a proselytizer of his or her friends.[60]

A central feature of the modern practice that does not seem to figure in the classical texts is the offering of *ema* votive placards at the outer margins of the temple. These are presented as an indication of a vow of *tachimono,* the sacrificial abstention from some pleasure in exchange for increased benefits in some other arena or at some later time. In the case of Ikoma, such placards typically contain the word *kokoro,* "heart," written in blue on a yellow background. Through this character is painted an old-fashioned Japanese lock to "fasten the heart up." Above the locked heart is a symbolic representation of a particular abstention to be undertaken—a die for gambling, a pipe for smoking, and the like. Often there is a short text that further specifies this. I quote five of these directly from Holtom's article.

1. A man of forty-five vows to abstain from betting on Mah Jong for a period of three years, beginning May 25, 1935.
2. A man born in November of 1897, the year of the cock, vows to abstain from stock speculation and deceptive practices connected with stock selling for a period of three years.
3. A man of thirty, born in the year of the rat, vows to abstain from women, with the exception of his wife, for a period beginning May 1, 1929, and ending May 1, 1934.
4. A woman of twenty-nine, born in the year of the horse, vows to sever relations with men for the rest of her life, with the exception of her present man, forty years of age. Accompanied by a prayer for health and long life, for prosperity in shelter and sustenance, and for success in the vow.
5. A man of twenty-eight, born in the year of the dragon, vows to abstain from meat and women for a period of one year, excepting relations with a woman of twenty-seven, born in the year of the hare.[61]

Muraoka and Holtom's reports of specific attitudes and ideas held by devotees at Ikoma help to clarify several features of the ritual. As can be seen from the inscriptions on a number of the *ema,* it is possible to ask Kangi for favors that are of a fundamentally immoral nature, for he will "grant boons that other Buddhas and bodhisattvas would turn away from." This, in turn, legitimates the expense one must be willing to bear in sponsoring the ritual. For if one hopes to see unworthy, virtually immoral, aims effected, he or she cannot, in exchange for such special favors, expect to get by with less than expensive rites and serious sacrifices. Week-long oil rituals, complex food-offering rites, and subsidiary gifts of substantial amounts of money (to a degree in lieu of the costly images specified in the earliest Chinese texts) are simply part of the price one must gladly pay. Further, since the benefits of the cult are preeminently more worldly than spiritual, the insistence that devotees eat the offerings themselves underscores and legitimates the underlying goal of selfish satisfaction. (An alternative explanation of this "anamoly" is discussed below.) Finally, we must note that the erotic imagery of the Kangi statues mirrors, and probably encourages, the sexual nature of many of the vows (including numerous petitions for revitalized sexual powers that both male and female followers present). While few modern devotees would perhaps want to follow the early texts' prescriptions for invoking Kangi to provide the death of an enemy,[62] the general amorality and this-worldly instrumentality of the cult are, in point of fact, of a piece not with the spiritualized representations of Kakuban's *Kangi kōshiki* or the modern Hōzanji prelates' official guidebooks, but with the basic goals of the oldest strata of literature associated with the cult. That such "archaic" values have maintained themselves for over fifteen hundred years—and in spite of repeated efforts to modify them—is a compelling testimony to human nature.

Radish, Buns, and Wine

One of the most intriguing features of the Japanese worship of Gaṇeśa is the nature of the three standard offerings made to Kangi: wine, radishes and *kangi-dan* or "bliss buns" (fig. 6)—particularly the latter two, since they are not only Kangi's "favorite foods" but also serve as his specific iconographic attributes.

That the radish is phallic and the bliss bun emblematic of female sexuality is, I think, unarguable. Since everyone knows what radishes and carrots look like, we need spend little time on these save to note that simply as a locution the Japanese word for radish, *daikon* ("big root"), is especially susceptible to a sexual interpretation and is, further, quite similar to the common word for penis, *dankon* ("male root"). Like Gaṇeśa's broken tusk, and trunk, the radish has fairly obvious sexual connotations.[63]

The *kangi-dan* bliss buns are a bit more curious, primarily in that they are a manufactured item rather than an object of nature, like the radish. This "made" quality in fact opens them to wider ritual uses than those available for the radish. Ingredients can be varied in accordance with the particular boon one is seeking from Kangiten. It is true that Japanese *kangi-dan* are clearly descendants of the round *modaka* confections that the Indian Gaṇeśa loves to excess, but the womb-like shape given them in Japan underscores their transformation into a sexual symbol—though a good deal of room would be left for metaphors of consumption and insatiability by any sweetmeat form. Together, of course, these two offerings parallel the two halves, male and female, of the dual icon. But whereas that duality can be taken to represent a philosophical unity, the radish and bliss bun show quite directly Kangiten's primary connections with worldly profit, the acquisition of the lower *siddhi.*[64] In like fashion, the forbidden nature of wine underscores the radically selfish, at times antinomian, nature of the cult, and this is surely the original reason for its use in the ritual.[65]

Possible Sources of the Dual-Gaṇeśa Icon

Iconography can be of particular value in tracing the history of a divinity, for certain iconic forms are limited to, or at least typical of, certain regions and not others. Regarding the dual-Gaṇeśa image, this is particularly true of its duality—two figures that are to be construed as one—and the erotic posture of the image. Erotic images of Gaṇeśa are by no means unique to Japan. There are, first of all, some *yab-yum* forms found in Tibet and Nepal. Indeed, one speculation might be that the dual Kangi of Japan is basically a bowdlerized version of a *yab-yum* form borrowed from central Asian or Tibetan Buddhism.[66] I am unconvinced of this, however. It is my suspicion that the female half of the dual Kangi represents, not a borrowing of a Buddhist form of Gaṇeśa, but a fairly direct amplification of or adaptation of the attendant *devī* of the boon-giving Ucchiṣṭa Gaṇapati form of Hinduism.

The Ucchiṣṭa Gāṇapatya school is one of six major forms of Gaṇeśa worship catalogued in classical Indian sources. According to Ānandagiri's work of about the tenth century, the *Śaṅkaravijaya,* this was a left-handed Tantric cult led by one Herambasuta. The name of the group derives from the term *ucchiṣṭa,* "leftovers," possibly in reference to the foods left over at the end of a ritual offering to the deity or, more likely in a Tantric context, to foods deliberately left in the mouth in order to render them ritually impure.[67]

According to Ānandagiri, Herambasuta held several unorthodox views.

> I have become content that there is no other view [*mata*] that can compare with this one. According to the teaching of the left-hand path, Gaṇapati and Devī are part of one another: just as, though the self [*jīva*] is smaller than the lord [*īśa*], even so they are one. This is my view. Having taken up both ways of thinking [the orthodox and the Tantric] I have put the marks of this sect on my forehead and left off all other marks . . . I have drunk from the well of highest knowledge. So I am born into bliss and acquired the knowledge of the three worlds.[68]

The object of meditative visualization prescribed by Herambasuta is described in Ānandagiri as follows:

> They meditate on Gaṇapati as follows: four-armed, three-eyed, each hand holding a noose, axe, and a gesture relieving fear, with the tip of his trunk he sucks up wine.

Except for the wine, this form seems rather far from the dual-Gaṇeśa image. However, Herambasuta also speaks of a second image used in worship.

> The image the Hairamba Gaṇapatis worship is one who is seated on a great throne, in whose left lap sits the goddess (Devī) whom he embraces while the tip of his trunk touches her sexual organ [*bhaga*].

This iconic form, which moves us a bit nearer the Japanese dual image, is also listed by T. A. Gopinatha Rao as one of six Śakti-Gaṇeśa forms.[69] Rao notes especially that the icon is supposed to consist of a large figure of the elephant-headed god who is flanked by a reduced figure of a human female attendant. Further,

> [Gaṇapati] should be reddish in color; he should be seated upon the *padmāsana*, with a nude Dēvī, and should be shown as if he is making attempts for coition . . . [and/or] . . . the fourth hand should be touching the private parts of the naked figure of the associated Dēvī. This god should have three eyes and be of dark colour. He should wear on the head a *ratna-makuṭa*. The nude Dēvī should be sitting on his lap; she should be decked with all ornaments and have only two hands. The name of the goddess is Vighnēśvarī, and it is particularly stated that she should be sculpted beautifully.

Rao goes on to note that actual sculptures often do not follow this textual form. For example, in the case of the four-armed Ucchiṣṭa Gaṇapati statue of the Nāgēśvarasvāmin Temple at Kumbhakōṇam, Rao tells us that Gaṇeśa

> has four hands, and carries in three of them the *paraśu*, the *pāśa*, and a *mōdaka*, while the fourth is employed in embracing the goddess. The proboscis of the image is touching the private parts of the goddess, who is herself carrying a flower in her left hand and is touching with her right hand the private parts of Ganapati.[70]

Rao neglects to mention that Gaṇeśa's "private parts" are fully and blatently erect in this statue. One might also note that the sitting posture of the Devī, due to the scale difference between herself and Gaṇeśa, is hard to discern; only close examination shows that she is not a standing figure. (This seems, in fact, to be a feature common to the attendant *devīs* in all of the Śakti-Gaṇeśa figures illustrated by Rao.)

It is, however, in the Khotan region that we come even closer to the Japanese dual forms. Consider for example the following passage from M. K. Dhavalikar's "Gaṇeśa Beyond the Indian Frontiers."

> Another figure [at Khalik] shows Gaṇeśa seated on a cushion with *prabhāvalaya* at the back. He wears a crown and jewelry on his person. The trunk is turned toward the right and he appears to be looking at the female attendant on his left. He has four arms, each holding a radish, a *modaka,* an indistinct object and one hand is seen resting on the thigh. He wears a bluish lower garment.[71]

Though the figure has four limbs, is blue instead of red, and is seated, the crown and jewelry, the set of the trunk and head, and the attributes of this image all recall elements of the Japanese dual forms. The move from these Ucchiṣṭa Gaṇeśa forms to the Japanese dual-Gaṇeśa icon, though not enormous, would, however, require that the female attendant grow to equal size with her consort, take on his elephant head in place of her own human visage, and shift from a side-by-side posture to one of a face-to-face embrace. Such a process might well have been hastened if this image were to become conflated with elements of another unusual iconic form, that of the "female Gaṇeśa," the goddess Vināyakī.

This "freestanding" goddess has very old and apparently complex roots. Agrawala insists, on quite defensible grounds, that this figure is not to be confused with Gaṇeśa's regular human-headed consorts, Buddhi and Siddhi. For although she is an offshoot of Gaṇeśa, she very early on became a separate, if minor, divinity in her own right, across Hindu, Buddhist, and Jain contexts.[72] The earliest textual reference to an icon of Vināyakī is the second-century Buddhist text, the *Āryamañjuśrīmūlakalpa,* but a richer description is that given by the sixteenth century author Śrīkumāra in his *Śilparatna.* According to this source Vināyakī is

> from the neck upwards an elephant and whose lower body is of a youthful female, has vermilion-red colour of the evening, a corpulent belly, the breasts which make the bodily frame bow down owing to their weight, and beautiful

> hips; is shining with two proboscises which are (like) two great chains of molten gold.[73]

Agrawala, noting especially the twin trunks of this figure, believes that Vināyakī derives from the vertically split Ardhanārīśvara form of Śiva combined with his *śakti,* Ambikā. Śrīkumāra's description, though late chronologically, would represent a fairly early stage of the logical development of Vināyakī in which (as Ambikā) she was still fused with her consort. Eventually the two halves of the figure would have divided and Vināyakī become an independent deity.[74] To this reasonable, though not proven, supposition I would like to add one more possibility. If the Ardhanārīśvara, or some similar semidual form, were the source of the independent Vināyakī image and divinity, it might equally have helped to inspire a twinned form along the lines of the Sino-Japanese dual type as well. The parallel development of such a dual form might, in fact, have been even easier in a fairly early Buddhist, and central Asian, context, where any emerging orthodox Hindu conceptions about Gaṇeśa or Vināyakī would carry relatively little compelling authority.[75] Indeed, the nonorthodox Hairambas (or their precursors) could well have effected, emerged from, or simply shared common ground with the Buddhist (possibly proto-Buddhist) devotees of such a dual, male-female Gaṇapati.

At this point I would surmise that whatever the direction and source of the lines of transmission of the Gaṇeśa literary corpus that eventually made its way to Japan in the 800s, the iconography would seem to have old roots in India followed by some particular refinements in central Asia and that, further, the original Indian roots were part of, or prototype to, the Ucchiṣṭa school of the Gāṇapatya tradition.[76] But these issues have already taken us well beyond the reach of my own training and competence and I can, thus, offer them only in the most preliminary and tentative fashion.

NOTES

1. This view is found alike in works as old as Alice Getty's *Gaṇeśa: A Monograph on the Elephant-faced God* (Oxford: Oxford University Press, 1936), 78, and as recent as Dwijendra Nath Bakshi's *Hindu Divinities in the Japanese Buddhist Pantheon* (Calcutta: Benten Publishers, 1979), 94.

2. *Darani jikkyō* in Japanese. *T*901; 18:785–897 (Gaṇeśa entry at 884–85). *T* refers to the modern Japanese "Taishō Tripitaka" edition of the Buddhist canon, *Taishō shinshū daizōkyō* (Great Scriptural Collection Newly Edited in the Taishō Era), ed. by Daizōkyō Kankōkai (Taipei: Hsin-wen Feng, 1975). References to *T* in these

notes are formulaic. In the present example 901 is the serial text number, 18 the bound volume in which this text is found, and 785–897 its pages within that volume.

3. This text is not found in *T*, but is included in *Kōbō Daishi zenshū* (Collected Works of Kōbō Daishi [Kūkai]), 82(2).

4. A fundamental feature of the Shingon school is its twin Vajra-dhātu (*Vajra*-realm) and Garbhakoṣa-dhātu (Womb-store) *maṇḍalas*. These sexually-toned psychocosmograms depict the nondual identity of the Mind and the Body of the Cosmic Buddha, Dainichi (Vairocana), as manifested simultaneously in noumenal *nirvāṇa* and phenomenal *saṃsāra*. For the fundamentally phallic meaning of *vajra* see Ananda K. Coomaraswamy, "Angel and Titan: An Essay in Vedic Ontology," *Journal of the American Oriental Society* 55, no. 4 (December 1935):374–75.

The outer court of the Vajra-dhātu *maṇḍala* contains six forms of Gaṇeśa. Four of these are directional guardians: (1) In the east is Kongōsai-ten, "the Vajra-Parasol Deva," whose attribute is a parasol; (2) in the south is Kongōonjiki-ten, "the *Vajra* Food and Drink Deva," whose attribute is a garland of flowers; (3) in the west is Kongōe-ten, "the *Vajra*-Garbed Deva," also known as Kyūsen Binayaka, "*Vināyaka* of the Bow," whose attribute is a bow and arrow; (4) in the north is Kongōchōbuku-ten, "*Vajra*-Victory Deva," whose main attribute is a sword and whose secondary attributes are *kangi-dan* buns and the three-pronged *vajra*. The other two forms stand outside the directional scheme. One of these is (5) Binayaka-ten, "the Vināyaka-Deva." This is a very general form of Gaṇeśa, the varying attributes of which include radish, *modaka*, axe, and winnowing fan. Since it is very close to the form of the Garbhakoṣa-dhātu *maṇḍala*, we may suspect that it is to a degree a kind of visual cross-reference that links and marks the ultimate oneness of the two *maṇḍalas*. The other "extra" form is (6) the Kongōmen-ten or "*Vajra*-faced Deva," whose formal attribute is a three-pronged *vajra*, but whose most notable feature is a pig's head in place of the usual elephant head. This curious substitution may have begun as one of confusion. M. K. Dhavalikar, "Gaṇeśa Beyond the Indian Frontiers," in Lokesh Chandra, et al., eds. *India's Contribution to World Thought and Culture: Vivekananda Commemorative Volume* (Madras: Vivekananda Memorial Committee, 1970), 5–6, notes a Gaṇeśa image at Bezeklik for which "the elephant face does not follow the usual representation of the god because the trunk somewhat resembles the snout of a wild boar. However, the god being in the company of Śiva and Kārtikeya, there should be little doubt about his identity as Gaṇeśa." In other instances, confusion cannot be the issue. The *Newsletter of the Royal Anthropological Institute* 36 (February 1980):10, illustrates, for example, a seventeenth- or eighteenth-century Himalayan bronze Gaṇapati with three heads: on the left an ape, in the center an elephant, and on the right a boar.

The sole form of Gaṇeśa seen in the Garbhakoṣa *maṇḍala* is, as already noted, quite similar to the general, Binayaka, form of the Vajra-dhātu save that its attributes are regularly an axe in one hand and a radish in the other. All seven of the forms above are seated on lotus thrones; none is shown in a standing posture.

5. Gaṇeśa is known by a number of names in Japanese. Many of these are transliterations (through Chinese) of Sanskrit names and epithets. They include Ganabachi (Gaṇapati) and Ganisha (Gaṇeśa), Binayaka (Vināyaka), Shōten (Saintly Deva), Daishōten (Great Saintly Deva), and Tenson (Honored Deva). Most common perhaps is Kangiten (Deva of Bliss), whose name seems to be a transla-

tion of the erotically toned Tantric term, *Mahāsukha,* "Great Bliss." Gaṇeśa is also often denominated by the epithets Jizaiten and Daijizaiten, which are translation equivalents of Īśvara and Maheśvara.

6. The white and red of the bodies of the dual figures are doubtless an indirect expression of the common Tantric association of these two colors whereby white symbolizes semen and red menstrual blood, the twin essences of procreative power.

7. See David Snellgrove, *Indo-Tibetan Buddhism: Indian Buddhists and Their Successors,* vol. 1 (Boston: Shambhala, 1987), 235, 249–53; D. L. Snellgrove, *The Hevajra Tantra Part 1: Introduction and Translation* (London: Oxford University Press, 1959), 95–96, 138–39; and Per Kvaerne, *An Anthology of Buddhist Tantric Songs: A Study of the Caryāgīti* (Bangkok: White Orchid Press, 1986), 32–36, 61–64.

8. *T* 1266; 21:296–97.

9. In the original texts the Sanskrit *mantras* are transliterated syllable by syllable into character equivalents. Accurate reconstruction of these is very difficult. Here I have given only what I feel are good readings (in their Japanese rendition) and trustworthy Sanskrit reconstructions. Most of these are based on Ōyama Kōjun, *Himitsu Bukkyō Kōya-san Chūin-ryū no kenkyū* (Studies on the Esoteric Buddhism of the Chūin School of Mt. Kōya) (Mt. Kōya: Kōya-san University, 1965), 438–39.

10. The meaning of the unusual nature of these offerings is discussed in more detail in the section "Radish, Buns, and Wine," below.

11. Though the Sino-Japanese texts are insistent in their assertion of the oddity of eating the offerings, they seem unable to make any great sense as to just why such a practice should be so odd. For more on this feature, see note 67, below.

12. The wagging thumbs presumably mimic Gaṇeśa's elephantine ears.

13. Tejorāśyauṣnīṣa, "Gathered Brilliance," is one of a set of five bodhisattvas who are emblematic of the Five Wisdoms of Shingon.

14. The connection between Gaṇeśa and dreams is consistent throughout the Chinese and Japanese literature, as for instance in the dream visions of the monk Tankai described later in this paper. But Hindu views of the elephant-headed god also connect him with dreams. See, for example, the possession-by-nightmares motif of the *vināyakakalpa* of the *Mānava Gṛhyasūtra* quoted in Paul B. Courtright, *Gaṇeśa: Lord of Obstacles, Lord of Beginnings* (New York: Oxford University Press, 1985), 132.

15. A single utterance of *Gaḥ,* the seed syllable of Gaṇeśa, brings his presence and power into play. Reduplicated as "Gaḥ, gaḥ," it becomes the deeper, more esoteric, and still more powerful "Heart of Hearts" seed syllable of Gaṇeśa's nondual, dual-bodied form. Written out in *shittan* (a Japanese form of *siddham* script), *Gaḥ* and *Gaḥ gaḥ* become visual as well as verbal vessels of power (fig. 8).

16. *T* 1267, 21:297–98; and *T* 1268, 21:298–303.

17. At first glance *Keira* might seem to be a transcription of Kailāsa, Śiva's mountain abode. Miyasaka Yūshō, *Kōgyō Daishi senjutsu shū* (A Selected Anthology of the Works of Kōgyō Daishi [Kakuban]), vol. 2 (Tokyo: Sankibo Busshorin, 1977), 319, however, states that it is a transcription of Hila, the name of a mountain in the Bunir valley in Swat (north of modern Peshawar).

18. *T* 1270; 21:303–5.

19. This confusion or conflation, like that eventually made between Gaṇeśa and Mahāvairocana, the central Buddha of Shingon, is motivated primarily by the wide range of usage allowed the terms Īśvara and Maheśvara and their Japanese equivalents, Jizai and Daijizai.

20. *T* 1271; 21:303–5.

21. Shingon ritual is usually directed toward one of two or three kinds of *siddhi*. In the two-level schema these are outer *laukikasiddhi* aimed at effecting worldly transformations and inner *lokottarasiddhi* aimed at the achievement of enlightenment. The three-level schema speaks of superior, middling, and lower *siddhi* that lead respectively to transcendent intuitions, to the heavenly realms, or to command over the world of illusion. *Goma (homa)* rites are also regularly classified according to desired goals: (1) *sokusai,* avoidance of calamity; (2) *zōyaku,* increase of profit; (3) *kyōai,* attracting love and respect; and (4) *chōbuku,* conquest. In some cases a fifth rubric, *kōshō,* or enticement, is added, though this is in reality but a variant of *kyōai*. Offerings, altar shape, and *mantra*s can all be varied to support the attainment of specific ends.

22. This is the probable precedent for the Japanese Gaṇeśa cult's restriction of ritual performance to trained priests, a monopoly of considerable importance in the economic well-being of the temples associated with this divinity.

23. Kūkai, or his immediate predecessors in China, took a number of disparate lines of Tantric materials and rationalized them into a formal and generally "right-handed" system. This the Japanese call *junmitsu* or "pure esotericism." Items left out of this "canon" were called, by contrast, *zōmitsu* ("miscellaneous esotericism"). In the Japanese mind, *zōmitsu* was both older and less civilized than the pure Shingon teachings. Nonetheless, with the passage of time many "impure" notions filtered back into the orthodox stratum.

24. *T* 1275; 21:324–25.

25. Vaiśravaṇa or Kubera (Bishamonten in Japanese) is the only other Buddhist figure with a dual form fully comparable to that of the dual Gaṇeśa, and like Kangi he too is served with an oil-ablution ceremony, wine, radish, and sweet cakes. The dual icon of Viaśravaṇa presents him as two armored warriors joined at the back and facing outward in opposite directions. It is probable that both this image and its attendant oil ritual are adaptations by the Tendai school of the more erotic Kangi rite of Shingon. (It is worth noting in this connection that Sir Charles Eliot, *Japanese Buddhism* [London: Routledge & Kegan Paul, 1935), 356, tells of a photograph he was shown of a dual Gaṇeśa image in which the two figures stood not face to face but back to back.]

Also involved may be some kind of systematic parallel between Kangi and Avalokiteśvara on the one hand and Vaiśravaṇa and Lakṣmī (Kichijōten) on the other. The Tendai monk Shōchō (1205–82) in his *Asaba-shō* (Compendium of the Three Sections), *T* Supplemental Volume 9; 427–28, makes the dual Gaṇeśa a conflation of Vaiśravaṇa and Lakṣmī. This would accord with certain Indian conventions. In the *Skanda Purāṇa,* for example, Lakṣmī is forced to take on an elephant-headed guise. See Prithvi Kumar Agrawala, *Goddess Vināyakī the Female Ganesa* (Varanasi: Prithivi Prakashan, 1978), 9. Courtright notes both the similarity of Gaṇeśa and Kubera and the link commonly made in contemporary popular Hinduism between

Gaṇeśa and Lakṣmī (*Gaṇeśa,* 130–31, 22, pl. 4). T. A. Gopinatha Rao, *Elements of Hindu Iconography,* vol. 1 (New York: Paragon Book Reprint, 1968), 53–57, 64–65, discusses five Śakti-Gaṇeśa iconic forms of which two have Lakṣmī as the specific consort of Gaṇeśa.

With regard to Shingon Buddhism's linkage of Gaṇeśa and the Eleven-headed Avalokiteśvara (Juichimen Kannon), Getty, *Gaṇeśa,* 81, 83, notes that it was probably Amoghavajra who first brought an image of this form (possibly already feminized) to China in 746. Getty (81–82) also notes the close similarity of the set pair Fudō (Acalanātha) and Aizen (Rāgarāja) to the Gaṇeśa and Avalokiteśvara of Shingon iconography in images as far west as a cave temple at Bezeklik, and even in India at a Gaṇeśa temple at Unakoti where the Acalanātha/Rāgarāja pair are even given elephant-headed bodies. In Japan the dual Aizen-Fudō ritual texts have some erotic overtones, but the standard image has a quite normal body from which emerge two heads.

26. *T* 1275; 21:324. One of these amulets is an almost mathematical-looking diagram of twelve small squares joined by a latticework. It is labeled, "Amulet Carried in Secret." The second, whose label *may* mean "Offering of the Dead," takes a form that could be likened to that of an elephant's ear. Both diagrams are inserted into the text without further explanation.

27. Several other texts are also included in the same section of the Taishō edition of the Buddhist canon. The *Fo shuo chin se chia-na-po-ti t'o-lo-ni ching* (*Bussetsu konjiki Ganahattei darani kyō* or Buddha-Spoken *Sūtra* of the *Dhāraṇī* of the Golden Gaṇapati; *T* 1269; 21:303) attributed to Vajrabodhi (Chin Kang Chih, 671–741) falls within the same period but, in fact, belongs to a separate cycle of Gaṇeśa texts. It is short, and outlines the benefits derived from and ritual connected to the worship of a six-armed form of Gaṇeśa. The *P'i-na-yeh-chia Yi-na-po-ti yü-chia hsi-ti p'in pi-yao* (*Binayaka Ganahatei yuga shittei hin hiyō* or Secret Essence of the *Yoga-siddhi* of the Vināyaka Gaṇapati: *T* 1273; 21:321–23) of Amoghavajra's disciple, Han-kuang, and the *Ta Sheng Huan-hsi shuang-shen p'i-na-yeh-chia t'ien hsing-hsiang p'in yi-kuei* (*Daishō Kangi sōshin binayakaten keizō hin giki* or *Tantra* on the Image of the Dual-bodied Vināyaka-deva: *T* 1274; 21:323) written by Han-kuang's follower, Ching-seng, both fall outside of the category of truly early, formative texts (as perhaps do the second "Amoghavajra" text and Po-jo-je Chieh-lo's *Sheng Huan-hsi T'ien shih-fa*). The last text of this group, the *Chin-kang Sa-t'o shuo p'in-na-yeh-chia t'ien cheng-chiu yi-kuei fa* (*Kongosatta setsu binnayakaten jōju giki kyō* or *Tantra* Spoken by Vajrasattva on the Vināyaka King: *T* 1272; 21:306–321) of Dharmabhadra (?–1001) is later still. Dharmabhadra, also known as Fa-hsien, studied at Nālandā and came to China in 973. He was a prolific author of Buddhist texts. His piece on Gaṇeśa is similar in many respects to those of the Japanese *besson* genre.

28. Among the more important of these *besson* texts we may note the *Besson zakki* (Miscellany of Separate Deities) of Shinkaku (1117–80), *T* Supp. Vol. 3:1–618 (Gaṇeśa entry: 476–87); the *Byaku hokkushō* (The White Jewel Oral Commentary) of Ryōzen (1258–1341), *T* Supp. Vol. 6:1–516, 7:1–383 (Gaṇeśa entry: 7:171–98); the *Kakuzen-shō* (Commentary of Kakuzen) of Kakuzen (1143–1213), *T* Supp. Vol. 4:1–546, 5:1–651 (Gaṇeśa entry: 5:436–56); and the *Zuzō shō* (Compendium of Icons), *T* Supp. Vol. 3:1–55 (Gaṇeśa entry: 42–44, written prior to 1247).

29. *T* 1270; 21:303.

30. Bakshi, *Hindu Divinities,* 101, makes this connection. Senayaka would presumably derive from Senānī, Mahāsena, or some similar epithet.

31. From the *Byaku hokkushō, T* Supp. Vol. 7:181. Marakeira would seem to be an expanded form of Keira. (See note 17, above).

32. *Byaku hokkushō, T* Supp. Vol. 7:181.

33. A slightly fuller, and probably later, variant of this story adds the following specifics. The minister is named Isoka or else "Minister Long-nose." The poison in his food is elephant tusk. The mountain with the lake of oil is unnamed but located in the foothills of the Himalayas. Further, after the minister becomes a god of illness, he demands the queen as a sacrifice and only later falls in love with her and is thus converted to goodness.

34. From the *Besson zakki, T* Supp. Vol. 3:476.

35. Miyasaka, *Kōgyō Daishi senjutsu shū,* vol. 2, 27–31.

36. "Universal" and "Wondrous" enlightenment are the fifty-first and fifty-second steps of Mahāyāna's fifty-two stage schema of enlightenment. "Original Ground" and "Manifest Traces" translate *honji* and *suijaku.* These terms initially referred to the two segments of the *Lotus Sūtra,* but in Japan they took on a specialized, secondary meaning. *Honji* were original Buddhas, and *suijaku* were their *avatāra*s in the form of Shinto divinities (*kami*). Here, and even more clearly in some of the literature from Hōzanji, Gaṇeśa is seen more as a folk or Shinto deity than an orthodox Buddhist figure.

37. A set-phrase for "the phenomenal universe."

38. The six lower states of rebirth: hell dwellers, *preta*s, animals, *asura*s, *deva*s, and men, plus the four higher states of *śrāvaka*s, *pratyeka-Buddha*s, bodhisattvas, and Buddhas.

39. Bakshi, *Hindu Divinities,* 103, following personal correspondence with the Hōzanji prelate, G. Nitta, allows that the great Japanese hero, Sugawara Michizane (845–903) was already an earnest worshiper of Kangiten in the late ninth century, and that by the thirteenth century an annual oil-ablution ceremony was a regular feature of the calendar of the Imperial Palace.

Evidence for the Ashikaga period (1333 – 1600) seems even more fugitive, although one poem by the Zen eccentric Ikkyū Sōjun (1394 – 1481) seems to show clear familiarity with the the ritual. See James H. Sanford, *Zen-man Ikkyū* (Chico, CA: Scholars Press, 1981), 187.

40. The three-volume set *Hōzan Tankai denki shiryō shūsei* (Compiled Documents Concerning the Legend of Hōzan Tankai), ed. Kobayashi Takeshi (Ikoma: Hōzanji, 1966) includes photographs, and transcriptions practically down to the level of grocery lists.

41. Aoyama Shigeru, et al., eds., *Hōzanji* (Ikoma: Hōzanji, 1978), 48–60.

42. Unordained, shamanic holy men or *hijiri* constitute a vitally important aspect of Japanese religious history. The most useful English introductions to the variety and importance of these figures are Ichiro Hori, "On the Concept of Hijiri (Holy-Man)," *Numen* 5, no. 2 (April 1958):138 – 60, and vol. 5, no. 3 (September 1958):199 – 232; Carmen Blacker, *The Catalpa Bow: A Study of Shamanic Practices in Japan* (London: George Allen & Unwin, 1975); and H. Byron Earhart, *A Religious Study of the Mount Haguro Sect of Shugendō* (Tokyo: Sophia University, 1970).

43. Tankai's vow here is doubtless intended to recall that made by the Buddha just prior to his final drive to enlightenment.

44. The Japanese text is much concerned with "success" and "accomplishments." These are plain-language equivalents of the more technical term *siddhi.*

45. The hagiography's claim that Tankai was artistically precocious is hardly an exaggeration. A number of his statues and paintings survive, and the statues in particular are of the highest quality.

46. "Sovereignty" here translates *jizai,* a term that once again promotes the conflation of Gaṇeśa and Śiva.

47. Mandaraji, "the Mandala Temple," is a common nickname for the Zuishin-in Hall in Kyoto.

48. Chishō Daishi or Enchin (814–891) was a key figure in the ninth-century process that greatly "Shingonized" the Tendai sect.

49. The connection, if any, between this one-line *samādhi* and the one-line *mantra* of Gaṇeśa described in the *Shih chou fa-ching* and *Ta shih chou fa-ching* is unclear. This passage recalls the legend of Māra's attack on the Buddha, but it is also a standard depiction of Gaṇeśa-sent nightmares. See Courtright, *Gaṇeśa,* 132.

50. Though enlightenment based on the intuition of the unity of passions and *nirvāṇa* is perfectly natural in a Shingon framework, the use of this motif in a passage that is intended to contrast the spirituality of Tankai with the this-worldliness of Gaṇeśa seems a bit odd.

51. A number of texts prescribe the worship of the goddess Kuṇḍalī (Gundari Myōō) as a specific counteragent to the importunities of Gaṇeśa.

52. This concluding passage of the hagiography is packed with orthodox Shingon stock phrases, but probably only three of these need brief explanation. *Nyūga ga'nyū* is the fusing into one of the aspirant and the deity during ritual/meditation; "A" is a meditative focus that symbolizes the nonduality of all things; "proven in the body" translates the central Shingon byword *sokushin jōbutsu* (literally, "Buddhahood in this very body"), a term very close in meaning to Indian Tantra's *jīvan mukti.*

53. The contribution of very large sums of money to Kangi in expectation of or in thanks for his boons is apparently not uncommon. Muraoka Kū, *Ai no shinbutsu* (Gods and Buddhas of Love) (Tokyo: Daizo Shinsho, 1975), 201, mentions one man who left a paper bag stuffed with five million *yen* on the doorstep at Hōzanji in honor of Kangi, and Prof. Minor Rogers of Washington and Lee University (personal communication, May 1980) was told by the proprietess of a religious goods store on the edge of the Hōzanji precincts that she had not long before contributed two million *yen* to the temple in response to the material blessings brought her by Kangi. Such open handedness, which doubtless accounts for the richness of Hōzanji, may also help explain why its officers are willing to live, albeit in less than happy compromise, with the fact that while their formal central divinity is Fudō, the functional center of the multitudes of visiting pilgrims is the Kangi hall.

54. See note 41. An earlier, and in some ways fuller, counterpart of the current guidebook is Yamashita Jōshō, *Kangi tenson no goyurai to saishiki* (The Origins and Ceremonies of Kangi Tenson) (Ikoma: Tsujimoto Shoten, 1932).

55. Even so, the first plate in the book, of the main gate, cannot hide the large stone pillar there on which the inscription, "Sacred Headquarters of Kangiten:

Hōzanji," is engraved. The standard souvenir postcard collections at Ikoma also ignore Kangiten and his hall.

56. Pilgrims to Hōzanji can buy quite crude and fairly cheap versions of the dual icon at stalls just outside the temple. My colleague, Minor Rogers, bought me one of these statuettes in 1980. It cost ¥ 1,500. To simply look at it would, he was told, cost exactly the same amount, so he bought it sight unseen in a plain brown wrapper, literally from under the counter. The fact that the primary Kangi image at Hōzanji is a secret image seen only by the priests probably encourages pilgrims' efforts to circumvent the clerical monopoly surrounding these mysteries, but even these popular statuettes are provided with a small brocade cover that is equivalent to the *liṅga-koṣa* covers used to protect temple images of Kangi whenever they are not in ritual use. The intensity of the feeling of tabooed sacrality directed toward the main Kangi image at Hōzanji is such that even official documentary photographs "of" it show only the pedestal and a whited-out outline of the statue itself.

Other items sold from the religious goods stalls included an inexpensive booklet, Matsumoto Jitsudō, *Kangiten shinkō e no michi* (The Way of the Kangiten Faith) (Ikoma: Orientaru Sangyo, 1967), the text of which is virtually identical to the middle section of the *Hōzanji* guidebook, and a small accordion-style chapbook, Oyagi Minoru, *Daishō Kangiten hairei kōshiki* (Rituals of Worship of Daishō Kangiten) (Tokyo: Oyagi Kyobundo, 1964), which contains *mantra*s, hymns, and *sūtra* selections suitable for individual worship of Gaṇeśa.

57. In point of fact, although Ikoma has been the most important center of Kangi worship since the seventeenth century, it is not the only locus of such activity. The prelates of Hōzanji can list over two hundred temples with Kangi images. Even if this is, for the contemporary situation at least, a greatly exaggerated figure, it is true that several other temples have been important centers and that several of them still possess superb images of the dual Kangi. It is also notable that not all of these temples were associated with the Shingon sect.

We ought also to note in this context that the worship of Gaṇeśa in Japan has not been limited to the selfish masses' greedy search for personal gain. The Tokugawa political reformer Matsudaira Sadanobu, for instance, was a serious devotee of Kangi who in 1788 paid a private visit to the Kitsushō in Reiganjima (Edo) where he pledged before Kangiten that he would bring his economic reforms to a successful end, "to make rice again available at a normal price and to bring about financial solvency; to this purpose he offered his own life and that of his wife and children." Herman Ooms, *Charismatic Bureaucrat: A Political Biography of Matsudaira Sadanobu 1758–1829* (Chicago: University of Chicago Press, 1974), 85–86.

58. Muraoka, *Ai no shimbutsu*, 188–204; Muraoka Kū, "*Mikkyō to minzoku*" (The Esoteric Tradition and Folk Culture) in Miyasaka Yūshō, et al., eds., *Gendai mikkyō kōza* (Modern Esoteric Studies), vol. 7 (Tokyo: Daito Shuppansha, 1977), 363–67; and D. C. Holtom, "Japanese Votive Pictures (The Ikoma Ema)," *Monumenta Nipponica* 1, no. 1 (January 1938):154–64. Some old, brief, but still informative notes can also be found in Eliot, *Japanese Buddhism*, 138–39, 355–57.

59. Though the oil annointment is the chief ritual, it is not the only kind of worship addressed to Gaṇeśa. Even the early texts mention a *kesuiki* or "flower-water consecration." Basically this amounts to annointing Kangiten with perfumed water. Some texts specify this ritual for use after noon because "*deva*s do not eat after this time." A second differentiation between the oil and water rituals is the icon

used. Normally two statues are used in the flower offering, the usual dual-bodied Kangi of the oil ritual and a separate image of the eleven-headed Avalokiteśvara. These can be annointed either together or at separate altars—in which case Kangi's consecration follows that of Avalokiteśvara.

As far as the modern cult goes, Muraoka, *Ai no Shimbutsu,* 195–96, found that along with the central oil ablution, three other rites were commonly performed. The first of these was the *kesuiki,* which Muraoka likens to an evening supper or formal tea for the divinity. Then there is the *Daihanya-gyō tendoku,* the symbolic reading — by rippling through its pages — of the *Mahāprajñāpāramitā Sūtra* for Kangi, and the *hyakumi kuyō* offering of a hundred delicacies to the image, a ritual that Muraoka was told was usually sponsored by a whole group of devotees or else done in a truncated form of twenty-one, fifteen, or seven delicacies. Neither the *tendoku* nor the *hyakumi* are rituals unique to Kangi.

60. It is interesting to note in this context that while Muraoka stresses the number of women he saw offering prayers and circumambulation in the outer precincts of Hōzanji, Abbot Muramoto, in interviews given at the same time, stressed the number of small-businessman adherents. Holtom's 1938 article implies that the cult was at that time heavily male-supported.

61. Holtom, "Japanese Votive Pictures," 161–63. In 1980 Minor Rogers saw, on racks near the main gate of Hōzanji, several thousand *ema,* many with inscriptions virtually identical to those copied by Holtom in 1938. One poignant example was that of a mother who petitioned Kangi to arrange for her daughter to separate from her husband and get a divorce.

62. Even in modern times some worshipers may come close to this. Muraoka, *Ai no shimbutsu,* 203–4 notes a case in which both a wife and a mistress of the same man petitioned Kangi "to get rid of" the rival. Unfortunately, he fails to tell us who won or how.

63. According to M. K. Dhavalikar, "Gaṇeśa Beyond the Indian Frontiers," 4, Nepalese sculptures regularly "replace" the broken tusk with a radish, a transformation that also sees an early textual occurrence in Varahamihira's sixth-century work, the *Bṛhat Saṁhitā.*

The sexual meanings implicit in Gaṇeśa's tusk, trunk, and head are commonly recognized, as are the richly Oedipal overtones of his mythology. Nor is explicit sexuality uncommon. Dhavalikar, "Gaṇeśa Beyond the Indian Frontiers," 2–3, fig. 1, describes a four-armed, ithyphallic, sixth-century statue of Gaṇeśa from Gardez, Afghanistan, and another early (possibly sixth century) statue from Sakar Dhar, north of Kabul, that is also ithyphallic and, in addition, carries its trunk high on the left shoulder in a fashion reminiscent of some Japanese dual images.

The somewhat attenuated sexuality of the dual male-female image of Gaṇeśa is, in fact, not the only erotically toned form found in Japan. Occasionally more explicit images are also encountered, such as that seen by Genchi Kato on a small "Shōten" island in a pond near Tokyo's Ueno park. This image was a fairly ordinary image of Gaṇeśa from the front, but its back and head were rendered as an erect phallus when seen from the rear. Genchi Kato, *A Study of Shinto* (repr. New York: Barnes and Noble, 1971), 172. Kato also notes the existence at the Tozen-in in Tōtōmi Province of a "Dōraku jizō or the pleasure-seeking Jizō, a divine couple in a posture of coition."

64. A number of other Japanese religious practices deal primarily with worldly benefits. Indeed, the theme is so pervasive that there is a technical term, *genze riyaku*, "profits in this life," to describe it.

65. It is very tempting to seek links, or at least taxonomic parallels, between the wine, buns, and radish offerings of the dual Gaṇeśa cult and the infamous *pañcamakāra* of Hindu left-handed Tantra, the ritual consumption of five things forbidden to ordinary men, namely: *mada*, wine; *matsya*, fish; *māṃsa*, meat; *mudrā*, parched kidney bean (or other reputed "aphrodisiac"); and *maithuna*, ritual sex. Since early Indian texts such as *Mānava Gṛhyasūtra* list meat, fish, and cakes as proper propitiatory offerings for demonic *vināyaka*s, perhaps we should consider the Gaṇeśa rituals as "proto-Tantric." Possibly even the use of hot oil in the Gaṇeśa cult is antinomian in intent. Professor Phyllis Granoff of McMaster University informs me that in some Hindu ritual texts, oil is restricted virtually without exception to rites of black magic.

66. Getty, *Gaṇeśa*, 71–72; Bakshi, *Hindu Divinities*, 97; and Agrawala, *Goddess Vināyakī*, 18, all give some weight to this possibility. However, Agrawala's further contention that Tantric Buddhist *yab-yum* forms in which both Gaṇeśa and his consort have elephant heads are "very late," a judgment apparently based wholly on Tibetan and Nepalese examples, is belied by the early Sino-Japanese textual materials.

67. Here at last we might find a logical reason for the constant refrain of the Sino-Japanese texts about the oddity of the aspirant rather than the divinity eating the offerings. In the Tantric inversion of normal practices (the Japanese Buddhist texts show no sign of familiarity with anything like the regular Hindu practice of *prasād*), the leftovers—otherwise the archetype of impurity—become a central locus of sacral power. (See Courtright, *Gaṇeśa*, 218–19, for this motif among the Hairambas.) Leftovers would, of course, be a doubly appropriate symbol in the case of Gaṇeśa, since it was from the leftover residue of Pārvatī's bath and body that he was himself created.

68. This and the two following quotations are from Courtright, *Gaṇeśa*, 219.

69. Rao, *Elements of Hindu Iconography*, 53–57, discusses the Ucchiṣṭa form as one of five subtypes of the Śakti-Gaṇeśa image: (1) Lakshmī-Gaṇapati images in which a four-armed Lakṣmī and a four-armed Gaṇeśa, either white or golden in color, stand in side-by-side embrace; (2) Uchchhiṣṭa-Gaṇapati images, red in color, of Gaṇeśa and his naked consort, Vighnēśvarī—a form used especially in seeking boons from Gaṇeśa; (3) Mahā-Gaṇapati images that show a red, ten-armed Gaṇeśa with a white Śakti on his lap; (4) Ūrddhva-Gaṇapati images of a six-armed golden Gaṇeśa in side-by-side embrace with a "lightning colored" Śakti; and (5) Pingaḷa-Gaṇapati images of a six-armed Gaṇeśa with Lakṣmī at his side. I have for the names of these types followed Rao's own highly idiosyncratic transliteration.

70. Rao, *Elements of Hindu Iconography*, 65, pl. 11, fig. 2.

71. Dhavalikar, "Gaṇeśa Beyond the Indian Frontiers," 6.

72. Agrawala, *Goddess Vināyakī*, 4. Brijendra Nath Sharma, *Iconography of Vaināyakī* (New Delhi: Abhinav Publications, 1979), 25–26, notes that the female forms of Gaṇeśa can be found associated with the *mātṛkā*s or mother goddesses, as a member of the sixty-four *yoginī*s (in both Hindu and Jain contexts), and as an in-

dependent deity. He, like Agrawala, distinguishes the independent Gaṇeśanī-Vaināyakī from the Śakti-Gaṇapati Ardhanārīśvara composite.

Discussion of the images of Vināyakī (or Vaināyakī) can be found in several recent sources: B. N. Sharma, "Vaināyikī in Medieval Indian Art," *Oriental Art* 16 (1970):169–72; Mary C. Lanius, "An Image of Vaināyikī from Harshagira (Sirkar) Rajasthan," *Oriental Art* 17 (1971):38; B. N. Sharma, "A Note on Vainayiki Images," *Oriental Art* 18 (1972). Most of these images date between the seventh and eleventh centuries A.D., but one (Sharma, "Vināyakī in Medieval Indian Art," fig. 1) may be as early as the first century B.C.

Dhavalikar, "Gaṇeśa Beyond Indian Frontiers," 5–6, mentions "extremely rare" female forms of Gaṇeśanī in India and Tibet. This is most probably the Gaṇaptihṛdayā form illustrated in Sharma, *Iconography of Vaināyakī,* pl. 34. On p. 48 of the same volume, Sharma notes that Gaṇapatihṛdayā's name occurs in the *Hevajra Tantra*. Historically, Gaṇapatihṛdayā seems to be the personification of a *mantra* used in the worship of a male form of Gaṇeśa.

Finally, we may note that if female divinities can be engendered by attendant figures or even *mantras* of Gaṇeśa, these female figures can, in turn, spawn their own minor male subsidiaries. Agrawala, *Goddess Vināyakī,* 32, quotes K. K. Pillay's *The Sūcindram Temple* (Aydar: 1953), 266–67, which describes a four-armed Vināyakī with the additional element "that, beneath the seat of Gaṇeśanī there appears a masculine figure with the face of an elephant."

73. Agrawala, *Goddess Vināyakī,* 11.

74. Agrawala, *Goddess Vināyakī,* 15–16.

75. Getty, *Gaṇeśa,* 84–86, describes a sort of vertical *ardhanārī* of Gaṇeśa with four arms and four legs. Though no Japanese versions are known, she cites examples at both Endere and Tun-huang.

76. The identification of "Mt. Keira" with a location in Swat would, if taken seriously, also suggest the early importance of the Greco-Buddhist region of central Asia in the development of Gaṇeśa worship. So too might the assertion of Roy Andrew Miller, *The Japanese Language* (Chicago: University of Chicago, 1967), 256, that the Japanese term for radish, *daikon,* is probably an ancient loanword from the Greek d'az'koz, "wild carrot."

Fig. 1. "Standard" Vināyaka of the Garbhakoṣa *maṇḍala*.

Fig. 2. Shōten Fondly Smiling.

Fig. 3. Embracing Shōten Looking over the Shoulder.

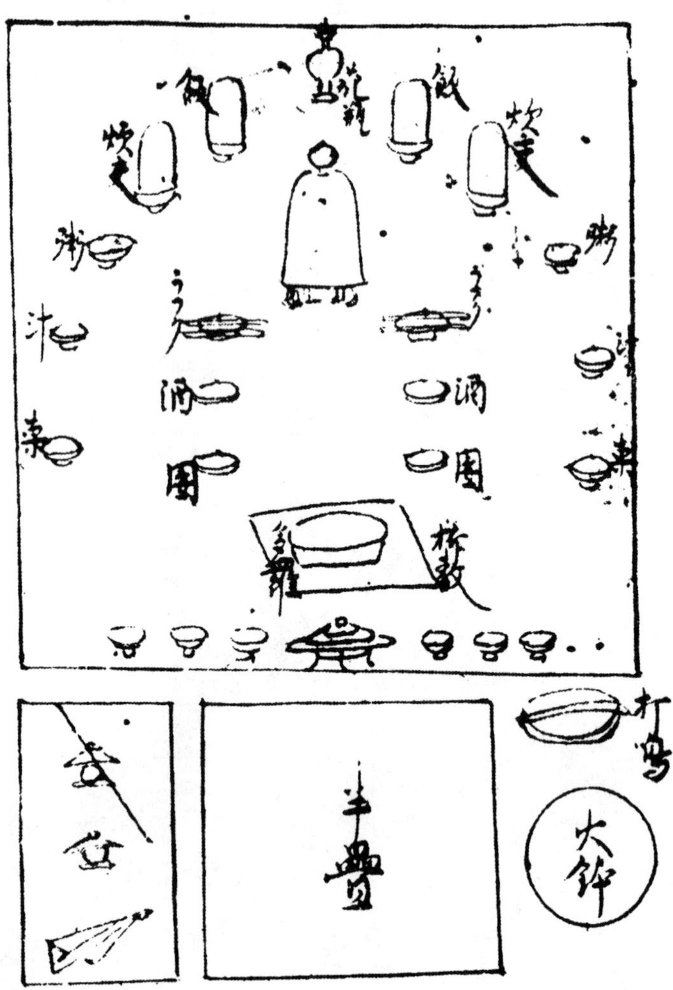

Fig. 4. View of a Gaṇeśa Altar. (Note the *"liṅga-kośa"* covering the dual-bodied central image.)

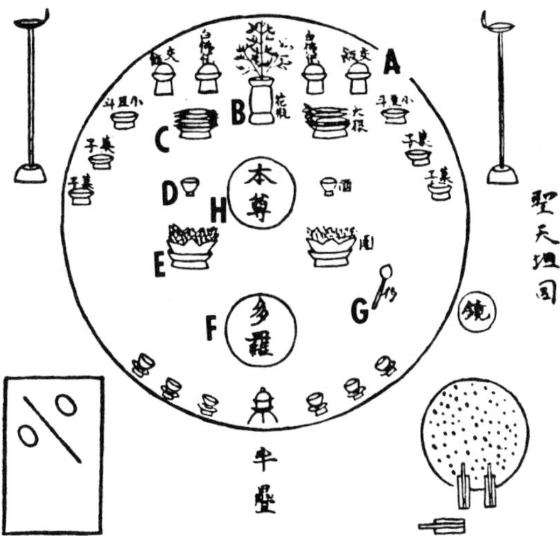

Fig. 5. Diagram of a Gaṇeśa altar.
A. Minor condiments
B. Flower vase
C. Radish offering
D. Wine offering
E. Bliss-buns offering
F. Oil bowl
G. Dipper
H. Central image (Honzon)

Fig. 6. Bliss bun

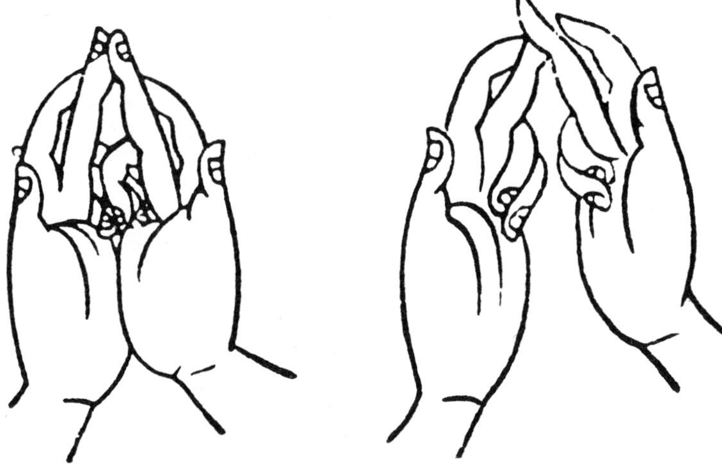

Fig. 7. Calling-in *Mudrā* of Gaṇeśa (two variants).

Fig. 8. Gaṇeśa's heart *mantra,* "Gaḥ," and the nondual Heart of the Hearts *mantra,* "Gaḥ, gaḥ."

Fig. 9. Image of the dual-bodied Vaiśravaṇa.

List of Contributors

Robert L. Brown is Assistant Professor of Art History at the University of California, Los Angeles. He was formerly Curator of Indian and Southeast Asian Art at the Los Angeles County Museum of Art. He is author (with Pratapaditya Pal, et al.) of *Light of Asia: Buddha Sakyamuni in Asian Art* (Los Angeles, 1984) and of the forthcoming *Form, Context, and History: Indianization and Localization in Early Thailand.* He works particularly on topics dealing with cultural relationships between India and Southeast Asia, about which he has published numerous articles.

Amy Catlin is Visiting Assistant Professor in the Department of Ethnomusicology at the University of California, Los Angeles. Her Ph.D. dissertation (Brown University, 1980) dealt with Gaṇeśa and was entitled *Variability and Change in Karṇāṭak Music.* She has written numerous articles on the music and related performance traditions of South and Southeast Asia.

Lawrence Cohen works in the Department of Anthropology at Harvard University. He is in his seventh year of the joint M.D./Ph.D. program of the MacArthur Foundation and Harvard Medical School. His current research in north India examines the construction of senility across class.

M. K. Dhavalikar is Senior Fellow of the Indian Council of Historical Research. He was Professor of Archaeology and Director, Deccan College Post-Graduate Research Institute, Pune. His field of study is Indian archaeology and art history and he has concluded excavations at several sites in India. His works include *Ajanta—A Cultural Study* (Pune, 1973), *Masterpieces of Indian Terracottas* (Bombay, 1977), and *Masterpieces of Rashtrakuta Art* (Bombay, 1983).

Kamal Giri is Reader, Department of History of Art, Banaras Hindu University. She is the author of the book (in Hindi) *Personal Decoration* (Varanasi, 1987) and, with Maruti Nandan Tiwari, of the Hindi textbook *Me-*

diaeval Indian Sculpture and Iconography (Varanasi, 1990). She was Assistant Editor of *CHHAVI-2: Rai Krishnadasa Felicitation Volume* (Banaras, 1981) and, with Prof. Tiwari, is editor of the *Art of Khajurāho* (Bhopal, 1990).

Phyllis Granoff is Professor of Religious Studies at McMaster University. She is Associate Editor of the *Journal of Indian Philosophy* and author of *Philosophy and Argument in Late Vedānta: Śrī Harṣa's Khaṇḍana-Khaṇḍaknādya* (Boston, 1978) and *A Strange Attachment and Other Stories* (Oakville, Ont., 1984). She is editor, with Koichi Shinohara, of *Monks and Magicians: Religious Biography in Asia* (Oakville, Ont., 1988). For the past five years she has been working with Koichi Shinohara on the topic of religious biographies.

Lewis R. Lancaster is Professor in the Department of Oriental Languages at the University of California, Berkeley. He serves as the Chairman for the Group in Buddhist Studies. A specialist in the Buddhist tradition of East Asia, he has published a number of works dealing with the history and development of the tradition in that area. His most recent publication is *The Introduction of Buddhism to Korea: New Cultural Patterns* (Berkeley, 1990) edited in collaboration with Prof. C. S. Yu. Current research focuses on the topic of fixed and portable sanctity within Buddhism and Christianity.

A. K. Narain is Emeritus Professor of History and South Asian Studies at the University of Wisconsin. He was formerly Manindra Chandra Nandi Professor of Ancient Indian History, Culture and Archaeology, Principal, College of Indology, and Dean, Faculty of Arts at the Banaras Hindu University. He is editor or past-editor of numerous journals, including the *Journal of the Numismatic Society of India, Bulletin of the Indian Archaeological Society, Journal of the International Association of Buddhist Studies,* and *The Indian Journal of Asian Studies.* He is the author of several books, including *The Indo-Greeks* (Oxford, 1957). He has been a Fellow at the Institute of Advanced Studies, Princeton University.

Ludo Rocher is W. Norman Brown Professor of South Asian Studies and Chairman, Department of Oriental Studies at the University of Pennsylvania. He has published extensively on various aspects of Indian intellectual history, specializing on studies of texts and topics of classical Hindu law. Among his latest books is *The Purāṇas,* in the new *History of Indian Literature,* ed. J. Gonda (Wiesbaden, 1986).

James H. Sanford is Associate Professor of East Asian Religions at the University of North Carolina at Chapel Hill. He is the author of *Zen-man Ikkyū* (Chico, Cal., 1981) and a variety of scholarly articles on Japanese culture and religion. His most recent scholarly investigations are in the area of Japanese Tantrism, especially the popular and unorthodox aspects of the Shingon school.

Maruti Nandan Tiwari is Reader, Department of History of Art, Banaras Hindu University. He is the author of several books on Jaina art, including *Jaina Iconography* (Varanasi, 1981), *Elements of Jaina Iconography* (Varanasi, 1983), *Jaina Antiquities of Khajurāho* (Khajurāho, 1987), and *Ambikā in Jaina Art and Literature* (New Delhi, 1989). He wrote, with Kamal Giri, a textbook in Hindi entitled *Medieval Indian Sculpture and Iconography* (Varanasi, 1990), and is editor with Prof. Giri of the forthcoming Proceedings of the UGS National Seminar on the *Art of Khajurāho* (Bhopal, 1990).

Christopher Wilkinson is on leave from the Doctoral Program in Buddhist Studies at the University of California, Berkeley. He has completed a volume of translations of early Tibetan Tantric literature entitled *Secret Wisdom: Three Tantras on the Great Perfection* (forthcoming).

Index